50% OFF Online PHR Prep Course!

Dear Customer,

We consider it an honor and a privilege that you chose our PHR Study Guide. As a way of showing our appreciation and to help us better serve you, we have partnered with Mometrix Test Preparation to offer **50% off their online PHR Prep Course**. Many PHR courses are needlessly expensive and don't deliver enough value. With their course, you get access to the best PHR prep material, and you only pay half price.

Mometrix has structured their online course to perfectly complement your printed study guide. The PHR Prep Course contains **in-depth lessons** that cover all the most important topics, **video reviews** that explain difficult concepts, **over 750 practice questions** to ensure you feel prepared, and **over 300 digital flashcards**, so you can study while you're on the go.

Online PHR Prep Course

Topics Include:

- Business Management
  - Mission and Vision Statements
  - Ethical and Professional Standards
- Talent Planning and Acquisition
  - Interviewing and Selection Techniques
  - New Employee Orientation Processes
- Learning and Development
  - Coaching and Mentoring
  - Employee Retention
- Total Rewards
  - Job Analysis
  - Benefits Programs
- Employee and Labor Relations

Course Features:

- PHR Study Guide
- Get content that complements our best-selling study guide.
- 5 Full-Length Practice Tests
  - With over 750 practice questions, you can test yourself again and again.
- Mobile Friendly
  - If you need to study on the go, the course is easily accessible from your mobile device.
- PHR Flashcards
  - Their course includes a flashcard mode consisting of over 300 content cards to help you study.

To receive this discount, visit their website: mometrix.com/university/phr or simply scan this QR code with your smartphone. At the checkout page, enter the discount code: **TPBPHR50**

If you have any questions or concerns, please don't hesitate to contact them at universityhelp@mometrix.com.

FREE Test Taking Tips Video/DVD Offer

To better serve you, we created videos covering test taking tips that we want to give you for FREE. **These videos cover world-class tips that will help you succeed on your test.**

We just ask that you send us feedback about this product. Please let us know what you thought about it—whether good, bad, or indifferent.

To get your **FREE videos**, you can use the QR code below or email freevideos@studyguideteam.com with "Free Videos" in the subject line and the following information in the body of the email:

   a. The title of your product

   b. Your product rating on a scale of 1-5, with 5 being the highest

   c. Your feedback about the product

If you have any questions or concerns, please don't hesitate to contact us at info@studyguideteam.com.

Thank you!

PHR Study Guide 2022-2023
PHR Exam Prep Book and Practice Test Questions [7th Edition]

Joshua Rueda

Interested in buying more than 10 copies of our product? Contact us about bulk discounts:
bulkorders@studyguideteam.com

ISBN 13: 9781637757512
ISBN 10: 1637757514

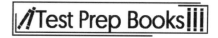

Table of Contents

Quick Overview

As you draw closer to taking your exam, effective preparation becomes more and more important. Thankfully, you have this study guide to help you get ready. Use this guide to help keep your studying on track and refer to it often.

This study guide contains several key sections that will help you be successful on your exam. The guide contains tips for what you should do the night before and the day of the test. Also included are test-taking tips. Knowing the right information is not always enough. Many well-prepared test takers struggle with exams. These tips will help equip you to accurately read, assess, and answer test questions.

A large part of the guide is devoted to showing you what content to expect on the exam and to helping you better understand that content. In this guide are practice test questions so that you can see how well you have grasped the content. Then, answer explanations are provided so that you can understand why you missed certain questions.

Don't try to cram the night before you take your exam. This is not a wise strategy for a few reasons. First, your retention of the information will be low. Your time would be better used by reviewing information you already know rather than trying to learn a lot of new information. Second, you will likely become stressed as you try to gain a large amount of knowledge in a short amount of time. Third, you will be depriving yourself of sleep. So be sure to go to bed at a reasonable time the night before. Being well-rested helps you focus and remain calm.

Be sure to eat a substantial breakfast the morning of the exam. If you are taking the exam in the afternoon, be sure to have a good lunch as well. Being hungry is distracting and can make it difficult to focus. You have hopefully spent lots of time preparing for the exam. Don't let an empty stomach get in the way of success!

When travelling to the testing center, leave earlier than needed. That way, you have a buffer in case you experience any delays. This will help you remain calm and will keep you from missing your appointment time at the testing center.

Be sure to pace yourself during the exam. Don't try to rush through the exam. There is no need to risk performing poorly on the exam just so you can leave the testing center early. Allow yourself to use all of the allotted time if needed.

Remain positive while taking the exam even if you feel like you are performing poorly. Thinking about the content you should have mastered will not help you perform better on the exam.

Once the exam is complete, take some time to relax. Even if you feel that you need to take the exam again, you will be well served by some down time before you begin studying again. It's often easier to convince yourself to study if you know that it will come with a reward!

Test-Taking Strategies

1. Predicting the Answer

When you feel confident in your preparation for a multiple-choice test, try predicting the answer before reading the answer choices. This is especially useful on questions that test objective factual knowledge. By predicting the answer before reading the available choices, you eliminate the possibility that you will be distracted or led astray by an incorrect answer choice. You will feel more confident in your selection if you read the question, predict the answer, and then find your prediction among the answer choices. After using this strategy, be sure to still read all of the answer choices carefully and completely. If you feel unprepared, you should not attempt to predict the answers. This would be a waste of time and an opportunity for your mind to wander in the wrong direction.

2. Reading the Whole Question

Too often, test takers scan a multiple-choice question, recognize a few familiar words, and immediately jump to the answer choices. Test authors are aware of this common impatience, and they will sometimes prey upon it. For instance, a test author might subtly turn the question into a negative, or he or she might redirect the focus of the question right at the end. The only way to avoid falling into these traps is to read the entirety of the question carefully before reading the answer choices.

3. Looking for Wrong Answers

Long and complicated multiple-choice questions can be intimidating. One way to simplify a difficult multiple-choice question is to eliminate all of the answer choices that are clearly wrong. In most sets of answers, there will be at least one selection that can be dismissed right away. If the test is administered on paper, the test taker could draw a line through it to indicate that it may be ignored; otherwise, the test taker will have to perform this operation mentally or on scratch paper. In either case, once the obviously incorrect answers have been eliminated, the remaining choices may be considered. Sometimes identifying the clearly wrong answers will give the test taker some information about the correct answer. For instance, if one of the remaining answer choices is a direct opposite of one of the eliminated answer choices, it may well be the correct answer. The opposite of obviously wrong is obviously right! Of course, this is not always the case. Some answers are obviously incorrect simply because they are irrelevant to the question being asked. Still, identifying and eliminating some incorrect answer choices is a good way to simplify a multiple-choice question.

4. Don't Overanalyze

Anxious test takers often overanalyze questions. When you are nervous, your brain will often run wild, causing you to make associations and discover clues that don't actually exist. If you feel that this may be a problem for you, do whatever you can to slow down during the test. Try taking a deep breath or counting to ten. As you read and consider the question, restrict yourself to the particular words used by the author. Avoid thought tangents about what the author *really* meant, or what he or she was *trying* to say. The only things that matter on a multiple-choice test are the words that are actually in the question. You must avoid reading too much into a multiple-choice question, or supposing that the writer meant something other than what he or she wrote.

2

5. No Need for Panic

It is wise to learn as many strategies as possible before taking a multiple-choice test, but it is likely that you will come across a few questions for which you simply don't know the answer. In this situation, avoid panicking. Because most multiple-choice tests include dozens of questions, the relative value of a single wrong answer is small. As much as possible, you should compartmentalize each question on a multiple-choice test. In other words, you should not allow your feelings about one question to affect your success on the others. When you find a question that you either don't understand or don't know how to answer, just take a deep breath and do your best. Read the entire question slowly and carefully. Try rephrasing the question a couple of different ways. Then, read all of the answer choices carefully. After eliminating obviously wrong answers, make a selection and move on to the next question.

6. Confusing Answer Choices

When working on a difficult multiple-choice question, there may be a tendency to focus on the answer choices that are the easiest to understand. Many people, whether consciously or not, gravitate to the answer choices that require the least concentration, knowledge, and memory. This is a mistake. When you come across an answer choice that is confusing, you should give it extra attention. A question might be confusing because you do not know the subject matter to which it refers. If this is the case, don't eliminate the answer before you have affirmatively settled on another. When you come across an answer choice of this type, set it aside as you look at the remaining choices. If you can confidently assert that one of the other choices is correct, you can leave the confusing answer aside. Otherwise, you will need to take a moment to try to better understand the confusing answer choice. Rephrasing is one way to tease out the sense of a confusing answer choice.

7. Your First Instinct

Many people struggle with multiple-choice tests because they overthink the questions. If you have studied sufficiently for the test, you should be prepared to trust your first instinct once you have carefully and completely read the question and all of the answer choices. There is a great deal of research suggesting that the mind can come to the correct conclusion very quickly once it has obtained all of the relevant information. At times, it may seem to you as if your intuition is working faster even than your reasoning mind. This may in fact be true. The knowledge you obtain while studying may be retrieved from your subconscious before you have a chance to work out the associations that support it. Verify your instinct by working out the reasons that it should be trusted.

8. Key Words

Many test takers struggle with multiple-choice questions because they have poor reading comprehension skills. Quickly reading and understanding a multiple-choice question requires a mixture of skill and experience. To help with this, try jotting down a few key words and phrases on a piece of scrap paper. Doing this concentrates the process of reading and forces the mind to weigh the relative importance of the question's parts. In selecting words and phrases to write down, the test taker thinks about the question more deeply and carefully. This is especially true for multiple-choice questions that are preceded by a long prompt.

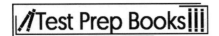

9. Subtle Negatives

One of the oldest tricks in the multiple-choice test writer's book is to subtly reverse the meaning of a question with a word like *not* or *except*. If you are not paying attention to each word in the question, you can easily be led astray by this trick. For instance, a common question format is, "Which of the following is...?" Obviously, if the question instead is, "Which of the following is not...?," then the answer will be quite different. Even worse, the test makers are aware of the potential for this mistake and will include one answer choice that would be correct if the question were not negated or reversed. A test taker who misses the reversal will find what he or she believes to be a correct answer and will be so confident that he or she will fail to reread the question and discover the original error. The only way to avoid this is to practice a wide variety of multiple-choice questions and to pay close attention to each and every word.

10. Reading Every Answer Choice

It may seem obvious, but you should always read every one of the answer choices! Too many test takers fall into the habit of scanning the question and assuming that they understand the question because they recognize a few key words. From there, they pick the first answer choice that answers the question they believe they have read. Test takers who read all of the answer choices might discover that one of the latter answer choices is actually *more* correct. Moreover, reading all of the answer choices can remind you of facts related to the question that can help you arrive at the correct answer. Sometimes, a misstatement or incorrect detail in one of the latter answer choices will trigger your memory of the subject and will enable you to find the right answer. Failing to read all of the answer choices is like not reading all of the items on a restaurant menu: you might miss out on the perfect choice.

11. Spot the Hedges

One of the keys to success on multiple-choice tests is paying close attention to every word. This is never truer than with words like almost, most, some, and sometimes. These words are called "hedges" because they indicate that a statement is not totally true or not true in every place and time. An absolute statement will contain no hedges, but in many subjects, the answers are not always straightforward or absolute. There are always exceptions to the rules in these subjects. For this reason, you should favor those multiple-choice questions that contain hedging language. The presence of qualifying words indicates that the author is taking special care with their words, which is certainly important when composing the right answer. After all, there are many ways to be wrong, but there is only one way to be right! For this reason, it is wise to avoid answers that are absolute when taking a multiple-choice test. An absolute answer is one that says things are either all one way or all another. They often include words like *every, always, best,* and *never*. If you are taking a multiple-choice test in a subject that doesn't lend itself to absolute answers, be on your guard if you see any of these words.

12. Long Answers

In many subject areas, the answers are not simple. As already mentioned, the right answer often requires hedges. Another common feature of the answers to a complex or subjective question are qualifying clauses, which are groups of words that subtly modify the meaning of the sentence. If the question or answer choice describes a rule to which there are exceptions or the subject matter is complicated, ambiguous, or confusing, the correct answer will require many words to be expressed clearly and accurately. In essence, you should not be deterred by answer choices that seem excessively

4

long. Oftentimes, the author of the text will not be able to write the correct answer without offering some qualifications and modifications. Your job is to read the answer choices thoroughly and completely and to select the one that most accurately and precisely answers the question.

13. Restating to Understand

Sometimes, a question on a multiple-choice test is difficult not because of what it asks but because of how it is written. If this is the case, restate the question or answer choice in different words. This process serves a couple of important purposes. First, it forces you to concentrate on the core of the question. to rephrase the question accurately, you have to understand it well. Rephrasing the question will concentrate your mind on the key words and ideas. Second, it will present the information to your mind in a fresh way. This process may trigger your memory and render some useful scrap of information picked up while studying.

14. True Statements

Sometimes an answer choice will be true in itself, but it does not answer the question. This is one of the main reasons why it is essential to read the question carefully and completely before proceeding to the answer choices. Too often, test takers skip ahead to the answer choices and look for true statements. Having found one of these, they are content to select it without reference to the question above. Obviously, this provides an easy way for test makers to play tricks. The savvy test taker will always read the entire question before turning to the answer choices. Then, having settled on a correct answer choice, he or she will refer to the original question and ensure that the selected answer is relevant. The mistake of choosing a correct-but-irrelevant answer choice is especially common on questions related to specific pieces of objective knowledge. A prepared test taker will have a wealth of factual knowledge at their disposal, and should not be careless in its application.

15. No Patterns

One of the more dangerous ideas that circulates about multiple-choice tests is that the correct answers tend to fall into patterns. These erroneous ideas range from a belief that B and C are the most common right answers, to the idea that an unprepared test-taker should answer "A-B-A-C-A-D-A-B-A." It cannot be emphasized enough that pattern-seeking of this type is exactly the WRONG way to approach a multiple-choice test. To begin with, it is highly unlikely that the test maker will plot the correct answers according to some predetermined pattern. The questions are scrambled and delivered in a random order. Furthermore, even if the test maker was following a pattern in the assignation of correct answers, there is no reason why the test taker would know which pattern he or she was using. Any attempt to discern a pattern in the answer choices is a waste of time and a distraction from the real work of taking the test. A test taker would be much better served by extra preparation before the test than by reliance on a pattern in the answers.

FREE Videos/DVD OFFER

Doing well on your exam requires both knowing the test content and understanding how to use that knowledge to do well on the test. We offer completely FREE test taking tip videos. **These videos cover world-class tips that you can use to succeed on your test.**

To get your **FREE videos**, you can use the QR code below or email freevideos@studyguideteam.com with "Free Videos" in the subject line and the following information in the body of the email:

      a. The title of your product

      b. Your product rating on a scale of 1-5, with 5 being the highest

      c. Your feedback about the product

If you have any questions or concerns, please don't hesitate to contact us at info@studyguideteam.com.

Thanks again!

Introduction to the PHR Certification Exam

Function of the Test

The Professional in Human Resources (PHR) Exam is part of the Human Resources Certification Institute's (HRCI's) certification program for human resources employees and managers. The certification process is intended to provide certified individuals with a credential that shows that they are competent and qualified for employment in the field of human resources. The certification process is only open to individuals who meet a certain minimum level of experience in a professional-level HR position, and is intended for those individuals wishing to build upon their experience to further succeed in the HR field. The test is administered and used nationwide. Exact scores on the PHR exam are not reported for passing students, and thus, the scores have no value other than as part of the certification process.

Test Administration

Candidates wishing to take the PHR will incur an application fee as well as an exam fee. Applications for the exam are open throughout the year, although testing takes place only in certain windows at Prometric testing centers. To take the exam, a candidate must meet one of the following combinations of experience and educational requirements:

At least this experience in a professional-level HR position:	At least this educational achievement:
four years	high school diploma
two years	bachelor's degree
one year	master's degree

Candidates may not retake the PHR exam in the same exam period. Instead, they must re-apply for a subsequent period.

HRCI promises to comply with the ADA by making accommodations for test takers who provide documentation of a disability. Documentation should include a description from a licensed or certified professional including the nature of the disability, a description of tests and protocols used in the diagnosis, a description of any accommodations previously provided for the disability, and a description of the specific requested testing accommodations.

Test Format

The test consists of 150 multiple-choice questions and twenty-five pretest questions. Each question has four answer choices and test takers are instructed to pick the best or most correct choice. Questions are written to test knowledge/comprehension, application/problem solving, and synthesis/evaluation. Some questions are presented as hypothetical scenarios that an HR professional might face in the workplace, followed by questions based on those scenarios. Topics covered on the PHR include Business

Management, Talent Planning and Acquisition, Learning and Development, Total Rewards, and Employee and Labor Relations. Test takers have three hours to complete the exam.

Scoring

Each PHR exam receives a scaled score between 100 and 700. The passing score is set at 500. Test takers who surpass 500 are told only that they pass, while those who do not pass are told their exact score.

Typically, around 3,000 to 4,000 people take the PHR exam in a given window, and about half pass the exam. In the November 2015 – January 2016 testing window, 3,698 test takers took the PHR exam for the first time. Of these, 54 percent received a passing score. HRCI does not release data on the success rates of students retaking the PHR exam.

Recent/Future Developments

The newest PHR update went into effect on August 1, 2018. Additionally, the exams are modified and updated for each new testing window to reflect the most current employment laws. PHR exam candidates are strongly encouraged to review and learn the specific HR laws and regulations that were in effect at the time that the exam period in which they are testing began.

Study Prep Plan for the PHR Certification Exam

1   **Schedule -** Use one of our study schedules below or come up with one of your own.

2   **Relax -** Test anxiety can hurt even the best students. There are many ways to reduce stress. Find the one that works best for you.

3   **Execute -** Once you have a good plan in place, be sure to stick to it.

One Week Study Schedule

Day 1	Business Management
Day 2	Learning and Development
Day 3	Employee and Labor Relations
Day 4	PHR Practice Test #1
Day 5	PHR Practice Test #2
Day 6	PHR Practice Test #3
Day 7	Take Your Exam!

Two Week Study Schedule

Day 1	Business Management	Day 8	PHR Practice Test #1
Day 2	Talent Planning and...	Day 9	Answer Explanations #1
Day 3	Learning and Development	Day 10	PHR Practice Test #2
Day 4	Total Rewards	Day 11	Answer Explanations #2
Day 5	Older Workers Benefit Protection Act (1990)	Day 12	PHR Practice Test #3
Day 6	Employee and Labor Relations	Day 13	Answer Explanations #2
Day 7	Knowledge of Employee Relations Activities...	Day 14	Take Your Exam!

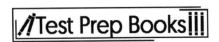
One Month Study Schedule					
Day 1	Business Management	Day 11	Organizational Development (OD) Methods...	Day 21	Diversity and Inclusion
Day 2	Knowledge of Vision, Mission, Values...	Day 12	Practice Questions	Day 22	Data Security and Privacy
Day 3	Effective Data Reporting and Analysis	Day 13	Total Rewards	Day 23	Practice Questions
Day 4	Practice Questions	Day 14	Knowledge of Federal Laws and Regulations...	Day 24	PHR Practice Test #1
Day 5	Talent Planning and Acquisition	Day 15	Older Workers Benefit Protection Act (1990)	Day 25	Answer Explanations for Practice Test #1
Day 6	Knowledge of Federal Laws and...	Day 16	Compensation Policies	Day 26	PHR Practice Test #2
Day 7	Verbal and Written Contracts	Day 17	Practice Questions	Day 27	Answer Explanations for Practice Test #2
Day 8	Practice Questions	Day 18	Employee and Labor Relations	Day 28	PHR Practice Test #3
Day 9	Learning and Development	Day 19	Promote Organizational Policies and Procedures	Day 29	Answer Explanations for Practice Test #2
Day 10	Knowledge of Federal Laws and Regulations...	Day 20	Knowledge of Employee Relations Activities and Analysis	Day 30	Take Your Exam!

Build your own prep plan by visiting:

testprepbooks.com/prep

Business Management

Responsibilities

General Business Environment and Industry Best Practices

General Business and Economic Environment

An organization can engage in **environmental scanning**, the process of finding and interpreting relevant data to identify opportunities and threats in the field. Three important general business and economic environment metrics are the number of competitors, market share, and customer demographics.

To analyze its competition, an organization can look at the number of current **competitors**—how many similar organizations are currently in the same field? —as well as the number of new competitors—how many competitors have entered the market during a particular period? These numbers give an organization a better idea of the industry environment. If the organization faces more competition than expected, it can focus on finding and developing its competitive advantage. For more on competition analysis, read below about Porter's five forces.

An organization can also get a broad view of its field by analyzing **market share.** An organization's market share can be found by taking the total sales of the organization over a fixed period and dividing it by the total sales of all organizations in that industry. In other words, what percentage of industry sales are being made by this organization? If an organization knows its market share as well as the market share of its competitors, it can easily compare its success in the industry and identify its most powerful competitors.

Finally, **customer demographics** provide essential economic information to an organization. This includes information about customers such as age, education, or income. Some organizations also rely on customer credit information, which can be relayed through a consumer reporting agency (CRA), a third party that collects information related to consumer credit. Knowing more about customers helps an organization find its target customer and market to them effectively. Let's look at one example: average income of customers. This metric lets an organization know the purchasing power of its target market and modifies its sales expectations accordingly. For example, a cosmetic company may have a sales presence in two different areas. The average income of customers in one region is $30,000 and $60,000 in another region. In the high-earning region, the company can market more expensive products that would be difficult to sell in the region with a lower average income.

PEST Analysis

This analysis is a macro-environmental analysis that looks at four external factors affecting the organization: Political, Economic, Social, and Technological. **Political factors** include anything related to government influences in the field like laws, taxes, and trade restrictions. These factors combine to create the organization's legal and regulatory environment and help to define the rules under which the organization must operate. **Economic factors** include inflation, economic growth, and the exchange rate. The inflation rate can influence the cost of capital, while the exchange rate would have an impact on international operations. **Social factors** include age distribution and population growth rate, which can be useful in identifying potential markets and targeting customer needs. **Technological factors** include

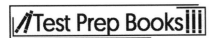

all aspects of new technology like R&D, automation, and new technological regulations. Technological factors can affect the cost and quality of an organization's products or services.

Industry Practices and Developments

To remain competitive with other companies in its industry, an organization must stay up to date on current industry practices and developments. One source of information is publications like magazines, newspapers, and trade journals. Of course, each organization will require different publications that are relevant to its field, but a few big-name publications with general business information are *Forbes*, *The Wall Street Journal*, and *Fortune*. These can provide a broad overview of important business news, while trade journals offer more in-depth coverage of important developments in a specific industry.

By researching industry practices, an organization can identify best practices, actions with proven results, effectiveness, and efficiency compared to other industry practices. Best practices are often identified through the process of benchmarking. To benchmark within an industry, an organization finds the top companies in that field, determines their business processes and results, and compares those practices with its own organization: Which practices are producing the best results? How do those practices differ from our organization's current policies? In this way, the organization can benefit from the success of others by adopting best practices from across the field.

Labor Force

The **labor force** refers to the number of employed and unemployed workers in a given region. The U.S. Bureau of Labor Statistics provides labor force information. In a sense, labor is a business resource and also falls under the rules of supply and demand. By analyzing the current labor force, an organization can get a better picture of the available pool of workers, which is the labor supply. The organization itself provides the demand for labor. Labor supply and demand come together when the organization is in need of new employees and is able to offer competitive wages, working hours, and other job benefits. By analyzing labor force data, HR can determine what level of compensation will attract the necessary workers.

Organizational Core Values Through Modeling, Communication, and Coaching

HR is responsible for formulating and enforcing policies about employee behavior. Of course, HR must first educate employees about the organization's expectations. Let's look at some approaches to developing desired behaviors.

Modeling

Modeling provides a hands-on approach to teaching new behaviors. Some can learn quickly from reading a book or listening to a presentation. For others, the easiest way to learn is by doing—or by watching other people. Employees can learn new behaviors and skills by watching a manager or trainer perform them first. However, while training situations may involve formal modeling, employees also learn from informal modeling as they observe the behavior of other workers. So, it's important to enforce HR policies at all levels of an organization, including upper management. If managers are getting away with unacceptable behaviors like sneaking out of work early or using abusive language in the office, other employees can learn from that modeled undesirable behavior. Both formal and informal modeling should provide positive examples for workers.

Communication

The first step of any business interaction is **communication**. No matter how carefully an idea is researched and planned, it could all fall apart if it isn't properly communicated to those who must carry it out. For this reason, all HR policies must be clearly communicated to employees, particularly when new policies are enacted or when the same HR issues occur often. Communication can occur in a variety of ways, such as through e-mail, individual interviews, or department meetings.

Coaching

HR coaching helps employees achieve their potential and continue to develop their skills, matching them with the needs of the organization. Through evaluations and employee self-assessments, HR can nurture strengths while providing training to overcome weaknesses. Coaching can also help employees progress on their career path by identifying areas for advancement within the organization. This gives employees an incentive to stay with the organization and pursue self-improvement goals.

Cross-Functional Stakeholders

Establishing Relationships: Organization and Individuals

To best serve its organization, HR must have good relationships with other departments and individuals within the organization. The key to any relationship is communication. HR should maintain open dialogue with other departments and help managers with any employee-related issues. While HR must ensure that departments comply with company policies, it's better to coach and educate managers about following policy rather than complaining about every mistake. When HR is a team player and not just a distant authority figure, it's easier for managers to approach HR and solve problems together.

In this way, HR can also demonstrate its usefulness in aiding organization decisions. Any change in the organization will inevitably affect employees, so HR can help balance the needs of the organization with the needs of workers and advise on decisions that will satisfy everyone. HR also acts as a bridge between executive decisions in the organization and how those decisions will be translated into new policies and procedures.

Establishing Relationships: Outside Organizations

As much as organizations must understand and analyze their internal operations, they must also look outward and engage with the industry as a whole. This is equally true of HR relationships, which should be fostered both within and outside of the organization. By building external relationships, HR professionals can stay abreast of industry developments, develop innovative solutions, and be active (or even proactive) members of their field.

Corporate Social Responsibility (CSR)

Corporate Social Responsibility (CSR) refers to an organization's sense of responsibility for its impact on the environment and community. CSR can be evaluated based on the three Ps of the "triple bottom line": people, planet, and profit. **People** refers to fair employment practices as well as the organization's impact on members of the community; **planet** refers to the organization's environmental impact (such as pollution, consumption of natural resources, etc.); and **profit** refers to the organization's overall contribution to economic growth. Having a CSR program encourages an organization to operate within legal, moral, and ethical boundaries. From an HR perspective, an organization's CSR program can also affect employee recruiting because the program demonstrates the organization's commitment to fair working conditions.

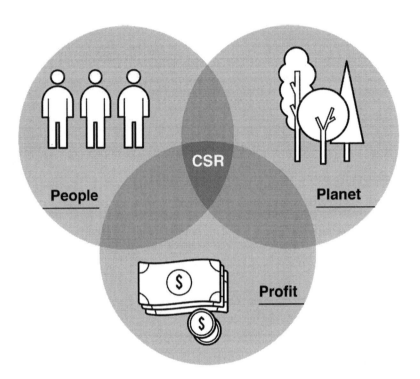

Community Partnership

In addition to financial capital, organizations also rely on **social capital**, the community's relationship with, and attitude toward, the organization. An organization can boost its social capital by engaging community partners from schools to social or volunteer groups to other organizations. These partnerships demonstrate an organization's commitment to the community in which it operates and offer an opportunity for community members to develop a closer relationship with the organization. For example, a computer networking company might partner with the local public school system to offer a free summer camp program for high school students interested in computers.

Mitigating Risk

Protecting employees, minimizing loss, and developing effective safety procedures are central goals for a successful organization. To meet these goals, firms must establish robust and creative policies, procedures, and standards.

Lawsuits

Employers should protect themselves from the risk of lawsuits by complying with all applicable state, federal, and local labor laws. Knowledge of labor laws is not specifically the purview of Human Resources (HR), either; HR leaders should ensure that leaders throughout the organization are familiar with key regulations. This can be achieved through communication initiatives such as training sessions or posting notices about labor regulations as required by law.

There are many laws protecting workers' rights. The **Occupational Safety and Health Administration (OSHA)** oversees and enforces workplace safety regulations. One such regulation is the **Hazard Communication Standard**, which includes standards for safety measures such as the labeling of workplace hazards. Title VIII of the Sarbanes-Oxley Act of 2002 (also known as Sarbox or SOX) provides protections for corporate whistleblowers, people who report illegal or unethical activity, and describes the penalties for interfering with fraud investigations. Title I of the Americans with Disabilities Act (ADA) applies to employers with fifteen or more employees and outlines legal protections for qualified employees with disabilities, including their legal right to reasonable accommodation in the workplace as long as it does not place an undue hardship on the employer.

Workplace Violence Conditions

Workplace violence is any act of physical violence, intimidation, threat, or verbal abuse that occurs in the workplace. This behavior is disruptive both physically and psychologically. Employees may demonstrate violent behavior as a result of a history of violence, a troubled upbringing, issues of substance abuse, and psychological illness. These conditions may foster violent behavior from an employee but do not make violent behavior inevitable. Workplace violence not only interrupts immediate employees, but can cause an organization to lose clients, suppliers, and advertisers. Furthermore, a firm can suffer devastating economic consequences as a result of negative publicity from incidents of workplace violence. Workplace violence attacks the foundation of trust and safety that all workplaces need to operate successfully.

Although an employer cannot completely eliminate the possibility of workplace violence, several steps can be taken to avoid these incidents. One example is a mental health program, such as an **Employee Assistance Program (EAP)**, which provides employees the option to improve their psychological wellbeing. Additionally, offering company parties and functions in alcohol-free locations may reduce the likeliness of workplace violence. Violence may also be introduced in the workplace from the public. In areas with high crime rates, statistics show a higher probability of violence for employers who operate at night. Finally, organizations should establish and enforce a zero-tolerance policy for on-site weapons and acts of violence.

Employer/Employee Rights Related to Substance Abuse

Substance abuse is a dependence on an addictive substance such as illegal drugs. This dependency not only impacts the individual but also may affect families and communities. Programs specifically designed to combat substance abuse can be extraordinarily beneficial. Because substance abuse is not limited to adults, programs may be introduced that focus on children and adolescents as well. In addition to the

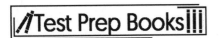
physical dangers of substance abuse, subsequent behavioral patterns compound issues. If treatment is not sought, the likelihood of a life of crime and poverty greatly increases.

Effective substance abuse policies protect both employers and employees in the workplace. Privacy policies generally authorize employers to conduct random drug tests if the employee has given prior consent. The employee should be clearly notified when hired that these tests may be administered by the employer. Employee substance abuse is damaging to the workplace and often results in inappropriate conduct with co-workers, insubordination, and fatal injuries due to improper use of machinery.

Through the Americans with Disabilities Act, federal guidelines exist to protect both employers and employees in regard to substance abuse. Employers do have the right to ensure a drug-free workplace by prohibiting the use of illegal drugs and alcohol. Employers may test for illegal drug use but must meet state requirements to do so. If an employee tests positive for current drug use through proper testing procedures, employers have the right to terminate that employee.

The ADA gives protection to employees who have successfully rehabilitated from past drug use but are no longer engaged in the illegal use of drugs. Employers cannot discriminate against any employee who has either completed a rehabilitation program or is undergoing rehabilitation. Reasonable accommodation efforts should be extended to those individuals who are rehabilitated or are undergoing current treatment.

Ergonomics refers to the ability of a person to fully utilize a product while maintaining maximum safety, efficiency, and comfort. Ergonomic risk factors in the workplace can lead to musculoskeletal disorders such as carpal tunnel, rotator cuff injuries, muscle strains, and lower back injuries. To reduce these risks, employers should evaluate workplace ergonomics and educate employees about potential issues. An ergonomic evaluation tests a product to determine its ease of use and potential safety risks. When employers identify and address ergonomic concerns in the workplace, they protect their workers and likely prevent serious injuries.

Determining Data for Organizational Strategies

To understand its performance, evaluate which strategies are effective, and identify where improvement is needed, an organization must regularly analyze internal business information. Data is analyzed using **metrics** (sometimes known as key performance indicators). A metric is simply a method of measuring a particular set of data. Different metrics can be applied to different areas of an organization.

Worker attrition, or the number of workers who leave due to things like retirement or resignation, affects the workforce supply. The **attrition rate** measures employee turnover over time within an organization. This rate can indicate how well the HR team is retaining their employees. A high attrition rate usually means that employees are leaving often, and a low attrition rate shows that employees are staying longer.

Diversity in hiring involves hiring employees with a variety of backgrounds, personalities, and working styles. Workplaces that are more diverse are associated with better financial gains and higher rates of employee retention, reported satisfaction, and performance. HR professionals can support an organizational culture that values diversity and promotes inclusion by actively recruiting talent with diverse, yet skilled, backgrounds that are otherwise underrepresented in the organization. If this talent

16

pool is not available, HR initiatives can include internship, mentoring, or certification programs for candidates that are interested in careers offered within the organization. Different metrics related to diversity (male to female, employees of color, age ranges) can be evaluated to see if an organization is using diversity in hiring practices.

Time to hire refers to the amount of time between when a potential employee applies for a job and when they are actually hired. Knowing the current time-to-hire helps the company budget for how long it will take to recruit and onboard new employees based on the number of vacancies and available HR staff. Time to hire can be affected by the length of the hiring process, the availability of candidates both internally and externally, the type of role being fulfilled, and other related factors. **Time to fill** is a similar concept to time to hire but represents the time it takes for a job position to be filled. The starting point could be when an opening is advertised or when an open position is approved by HR or a manager. The number of days from the starting point to the point when someone is hired to fill that position is the time to fill.

Another important metric is **return on investment**, or **ROI**. ROI is generally expressed as a ratio or percentage comparing the gains of a particular investment with its initial investment price. In other words, ROI measures the ratio between an investment's profit and its cost. ROI is particularly useful in helping an organization evaluate the overall value of a given investment. For example, one investment may yield a high return, but perhaps the initial investment is costly as well. Another investment with a much lower yield also has a far lower initial cost—so the cheaper investment might actually have a higher ROI than the high-return investment. This metric can help an organization to devote its financial resources to investments with the highest ROI.

If a strategic plan calls for any changes in employee skills and behaviors, it is up to HR management to facilitate these changes by implementing new training and policies. Measuring the **success of training** can be done using a variety of methods. In evaluating the effectiveness of any new training initiatives, HR might compare before-and-after measures of worker productivity or morale. The effectiveness of a high potential development program could be measured using data about retention rates, job satisfaction, or cost comparisons between developing leaders internally and onboarding external hires in leadership roles.

Knowledge of

Vision, Mission, Values, and Structure of the Organization

Mission, vision, and values are all concepts that help define different aspects of an organization. Together, they tell why the organization exists, what it plans to accomplish, and what sort of behaviors it will undertake to reach those goals. All of these concepts are closely related to employee behaviors, so HR can be instrumental in their development and implementation. These essential concepts of the organization's identity become actionable employee policies, and HR helps translate those concepts into action.

Mission and Vision
For any organization to be successful, it must have a clear idea of what it's doing and where it's going. Mission and vision statements are two ways for an organization to verbalize its objectives.

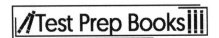

A **mission statement** focuses on the work of the organization on a day-to-day basis and answers the following questions:

- What do we do now?
- Why are we doing it?
- What makes us different from other companies?

A **vision statement** focuses on the organization's future goals and answers the following questions:

- What do we want to accomplish?
- Where do we aim to be in the future?

A successful mission statement should be clear and direct. In short, it states *why* the organization exists, and in turn guides its values, standards, and other organizing principles. For example, an organic restaurant might have the following mission statement: "To serve customers healthy meals made from the freshest, locally sourced organic ingredients." With this mission statement, the restaurant could decide to focus its efforts on building relationships with local farmers or staying up-to-date on health food trends.

A vision statement focuses on specific future goals, and in turn guides the steps that the organization will take to achieve them. The same restaurant might decide on the following vision statement: "To become a top-rated restaurant in the city." The restaurant can then design a plan accordingly, perhaps by focusing on marketing campaigns or inviting influential reviewers to dine at the restaurant.

Values

Just as organizations decide on a mission statement and vision statement, they also must develop a **core values statement**. This tells what the organization stands for and guides standards of expected employee behavior. For example, a value statement could be: "Our organization is committed to diversity. To this end, we are an equal opportunity employer and serve clients without discriminating based on race, gender, ethnicity, or sexuality." By clarifying its values, the organization communicates its character to both employees and customers.

Structure of the Organization

There are many types of organizational structures, each with their own HR needs. One type is a **functional structure**, in which positions are grouped according to similar job roles (defined by skill, expertise, or resources) in a hierarchical chain. This type of structure separates distinct job tasks and creates a clear line of job advancement. An example of this might be a retail store that has separate teams for sales and logistics; the sales team, for instance, is then further divided into sales associate, sales leader, and sales manager positions.

Another type of organization structure is a divisional structure. This often applies to larger companies, and uses a department-based organizational style, where employees who work on similar projects are grouped together. The divisions may be separated by region, product type, or specific customer needs. For example, an electronics company may have different divisions for producing televisions and cellphones, even though both divisions include similar jobs like electronic engineers, product marketers, and sales representatives.

A matrix structure combines elements of both functional and divisional structures. A flat structure seeks to eliminate much of the hierarchy and bureaucracy that exists in traditional companies, while a network structure outsources many key tasks to outside organizations.

Changes in organizational structure can occur during mergers and acquisitions. **Mergers** occur when two companies combine to form a new legal entity. **Acquisitions** occur when one company purchases another without a new legal entity being formed.

Legislative and Regulatory Knowledge and Procedures

How Bills Become Laws

Bills become laws only after gaining the approval of Congress and the President through a multi-step process. First, bills begin as ideas from legislators or citizens. If an idea gains support, it's drafted into a bill. A bill must be sponsored by a Representative or Senator and may have co-sponsors from other members of Congress who support it. Once a bill has a sponsor, it's then introduced to the House of Representatives or the Senate. After being introduced, the bill is assigned to an appropriate committee of experts who will research, debate, review, and revise its contents. For example, a bill about the use of chemicals in farming would be assigned to an agricultural committee. After the committee reviews the bill, one of three things can happen.

- They can decide to simply ignore, or **table**, the bill.
- They can assign it to a subcommittee for further research, after which they (the original committee) will consider the bill again.
- They can move forward by reporting the bill to the House or Senate floor.

When the bill is reported to the floor, it's open to debate, discussion, and amendment. After all of the agreed-upon changes have been made, the bill is finally put to a vote and must get a simple majority (more than 50 percent) of approving votes to pass. A bill that is passed in the House then moves to the Senate, and a bill that is passed in the Senate then moves to the House. If a bill can gain approval from both the House and Senate, it's finally presented to the President, who has ten days to consider the bill.

The President may choose to:

- Sign the bill into law.

- Refuse to sign, or veto, the bill. However, if Congress strongly believes in passing the bill, they can overrule the President's veto if over two-thirds of Senators and Representatives vote to approve it.

- Do nothing. If the President does nothing for ten days and Congress is in session, the bill automatically becomes a law; however, if the President ignores a bill and Congress isn't in session, the bill cannot become a law. This is known as a "pocket veto."

Influencing Legislation

When businesses want a say in legislation, they can write formal letters to elected officials like Senators, Representatives, and local government officials to establish dialogue about new laws. For more in-depth discussion of particular legislative issues, meetings can be scheduled between business representatives and elected officials or authorized members of their staff. Finally, perhaps the most persistent and organized way to influence legislation is through lobbying. Professional lobbyists represent the interests

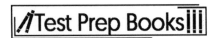

of a particular group or industry (for example, medical association lobbyists may push for anti-tobacco laws). Two businesses in the same field might be in competition and yet could also be united in relying on the same lobbyists to advocate for new laws that serve the best interests of their industry. Lobbying is a highly scrutinized and regulated practice in America, but smart investment in lobbying can also yield high returns for companies.

Corporate Governance Procedures and Compliance

In business, **governance** refers to how senior executives direct and control an organization. Particularly in large organizations where executives cannot be directly involved in every detail of every department, it's important to have a clear process for communicating the most crucial management information to executives so they can continue to make informed decisions. Governance also includes the processes by which executive decisions are communicated to and implemented throughout all levels of the organization.

Compliance refers to following requirements while carrying out business activities. These requirements could be from industry regulations, corporate policies, contract agreements, or local or federal laws. To avoid potential legal problems or fines, organizations should be up-to-date on all relevant laws and regulations and ensure that all departments comply. The **Sarbanes-Oxley Act of 2002** (sometimes known as Sarbox or SOX) is an important business law created in reaction to corporate fraud scandals like Enron in 2001. SOX established new regulations for corporate accounting and created the **Public Company Accounting Oversight Board (PCAOB)**. Some of its other major elements include auditor independence (to prevent conflict of interest) and executive responsibility for corporate financial reports (to increase overall corporate responsibility for accurate accounting). Whenever a new law like SOX is created, the organization's policies must be reviewed and, if necessary, revised to ensure compliance.

Governance and compliance are often grouped together with risk management under the term **GRM** (governance, risk management, compliance). By grouping GRM together, an organization can avoid redundancies in procedures and increase the effectiveness of communication between each area.

Employee Communications

Two-Way Communication

HR professionals can develop effective and satisfactory working relationships with supervisors and HR leaders by engaging in two-way communication about project expectations, deadlines, needs, and goals. These aspects should be discussed and documented when a work assignment is first received and should take priority during the planning aspect of the project. HR professionals should expect superiors to dedicate time to this planning period. In return, HR professionals should utilize this time to ask questions about the project and bring up any questions so as to best respect the time that leadership is providing. Developing a written project proposal with leadership that outlines the timeline, milestones, resources needed, and concrete dates for deliverables can be a useful method to ensure that both HR staff members and leadership have the same expectations. Once expectations are communicated, HR professionals should make every reasonable effort to deliver results autonomously, without the need for constant leadership follow-up.

Communication Among Team Members

As an HR professional, high levels of human interaction are inherent to the nature of the work. Beyond serving employees within an organization, HR professionals can expect to work in a team within and outside of their department. Team members may be assigned by project rather than personally chosen; therefore, it is important to develop wide-ranging engagement skills that promote positive interactions. HR professionals can build their intrapersonal skills by examining their own strengths and weaknesses through analytical personality tests, and actively working to improve areas of weakness. This can be achieved by utilizing pockets of time to practice intrapersonal skills with colleagues, such as over lunch or during a meeting. Developing emotional intelligence (EI) skills also helps one recognize others' feelings and communication styles, and this information can be used to build better relationships. Maintaining a positive attitude, showing appreciation for support and tasks done well, and avoiding negative talk and behaviors also fosters team cohesiveness.

Communication Among Stakeholders and Team Members

A **stakeholder** is someone with an interest in a business. These are not necessarily the same as shareholders, those with ownership in a business who are interested in its financial performance. They can either affect the operations of the corporation or be affected by its actions. Stakeholders in a company are investors, employees, customers, suppliers, as well as communities and municipalities.

It is also important to create teams that have members with similar professional interests and goals, to minimize resistance as the project progresses. However, open communication may be the most crucial component of fostering collaboration among a team. While cultivating open communication lines is a team effort, those who choose to actively model behaviors that lend to open communication are likely to become leaders within the team. Team leaders should promote an encouraging environment that allows all members and stakeholders to voice their opinions and concerns without fearing retribution. This may involve speaking with team members individually, especially if they are quieter or prefer speaking one-on-one. Finally, building relationships outside of the work setting, such as over creative social events, allows team members to get to know one another better. This can allow team members to feel more open and collaborative during the work setting.

Exchanging Organizational Information

Organizational communication must be appropriately delivered by the sender and received by the intended recipient to be effective. Communicating within the HR department may be an easier task for the HR professional than communicating with outside departments, as the HR department is likely to house similar values, interests, goals, and methods of communication. The HR department, however, establishes many crucial programs, practices, and policies that affect the operations and culture of the entire organizations. Entities such as employee benefits, ethical handbooks, and company-wide events often originate in the HR department and must be shared across all departments. Effective communication strategies often employ the influence of top leadership, a reliable mode of dissemination that is favored by the majority of recipients, and evaluation practices that focus on utilizing recipient feedback to analyze the overall efficacy of the communication channel. When communicating, HR professionals should also account for informal avenues, such as break room conversation.

Managers are excellent vectors of communication and leveraging the relationships and influence managers have with their team members can be a method of communicating organizational HR issues. To effectively utilize this resource, HR professionals should network with managers to build rapport and

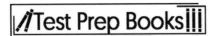
credibility. This also helps HR professionals understand what values are important to the manager; consequently, HR professionals can illustrate how HR issues impact the manager and their team. HR professionals should keep in mind that managers may welcome or resist serving as their team's communication channel for HR topics. It is important to make this process easy for the manager to implement, rather than seem like an additional burdensome responsibility. Finally, once this practice is established, HR professionals should remain an open and reliable liaison for the manager to return to should any HR-related questions or concerns arise.

HR professionals serve as a champion for their department. Their interactions with stakeholders should reflect pride, value, and confidence in the department's work to maintain positive engagement from the stakeholders. Stakeholders are more likely to remain resistant if HR personnel display neutral or negative stances about their own department's initiatives. Additionally, previously engaged stakeholders may begin to lose interest or feel a loss of value. If an instance occurs where the HR professional feels they cannot support an initiative in communications with stakeholders, leadership should be notified to find a resolution. This may involve changing a component of the initiative, altering the communication process between the department and the stakeholder, or shifting job responsibilities to achieve a better fit.

Effective communication with senior HR leaders allows both leadership and subordinate personnel to openly share information related to the organization's HR needs. It allows both groups to communicate in a timely manner. HR personnel should be mindful of leadership's time and commitments. This means limiting unnecessary interaction. Communication should remain concise, professional, and on topic. This can be achieved by specifically addressing why the communication is being made, what is needed from the leader, and if there is a time constraint associated with any of the needs. It can also be beneficial to recognize leadership's preferred method of communication. Finally, HR staff members should take initiative to communicate expected correspondence, such as monthly department reports or deliverables.

Listening
Active listening pushes the listener into an engaged position. Beyond using their sense of hearing, active listeners also use their sense of sight to notice the speaker's body language. Both auditory and visual information are consciously synthesized to perceive what the speaker is trying to communicate. In addition, the listener verbally reflects the information provided by the speaker, and then asks for confirmation that the information was perceived in the way the speaker intended. Only then does the listener formulate a response. Empathetic listening includes placing oneself in the perspective of the speaker and formulating a response based on how the speaker will accept it. HR personnel often face emotionally charged conversations dealing with an employee's job or family. Utilizing active and empathetic listening skills conveys concerns for the employee and helps diffuse tense situations.

Competing points of view, when expressed respectfully, are healthy components of communication that often lead to new perspectives, collaboration, innovation, opportunities, and improvements. HR professionals should always remain open to hearing dissenting opinions and actively seek to understand the reasoning behind them. Rather than perceiving dissenting opinions as a personal attack, competing points of view should be welcomed as part of the inherent business process. They should be treated with logic and objective reasoning to come to a resolution. While it is impossible to satisfy every employee's opinion, HR initiatives and decisions should be made with trying to achieve the highest percentage of employee satisfaction and the best processes for company productivity in mind.

Ambiguity can cause conflict, affect business processes, and cause distress to employees. Unfortunately, ambiguity is not always preventable due to factors that are often outside of the organization's control. In situations that are within the control of the HR professional, active listening practices are an important component of clear communication. The listener may need to directly state that they are confused and ask specific questions that result in a clear "Yes" or "No" answer. The listener may also need to observe the speaker's body language to determine whether the content is purposely being presented with ambiguity. However, speculation is never a good route to take to determine answers. When possible, directly asking the speaker to clarify is most likely to result in a positive result.

Stakeholders are considered as such because they are directly impacted by the actions of the HR department. Therefore, they are highly valuable to the efficacy of HR initiatives. Comments from them should be prioritized. **Stakeholder communications** can take place in person, in meetings as a group, through email, or through social media. There may not always be time to respond to stakeholder questions, especially if they are unanticipated and come up in person. In these instances, it is important for HR professionals to clearly indicate that they will need to source more information and follow up with the stakeholders. Additionally, it is important to always have the best method of contact information for each stakeholder on hand.

When HR professionals **receive communication**, they should be able to accurately identify the reason behind it. While motives for a message may not be directly stated, HR professionals can use contextual understanding. However, HR professionals should form this understanding based on objective logic, without making assumptions that are not rooted in fact. When motives for a message cannot be objectively determined, the HR professional should feel confident responding in a way that asks clarifying questions and dispels any ambiguity. Otherwise, assumptions about intention within a message can cause muddled decision-making that can have widespread ramifications.

Soliciting feedback is a crucial component of program evaluation, guiding and sustaining initiatives, and providing valuable customer service. HR professionals serve all units of an organization. Therefore, they should solicit feedback from leadership in all areas, keeping in mind that different leaders may have various needs and values. Learning organizational needs through the lens of each department can increase employee engagement, provide the value that leadership are asking for, and propel operations. HR professionals can solicit feedback from leadership through online evaluation surveys, in-person meetings, and group meetings. They should ask leadership what initiatives are going well and why, and what areas need more support. HR professionals should always leave open communication channels for leadership to propose new projects and ideas. These endeavors highlight the value of a company's HR department.

Ethical and Professional Standards

Sound business ethics are essential to establishing an organization's trustworthy reputation. If an organization is ethical, its conduct is fair, moral, and socially acceptable. Of course, some unethical practices are expressly prohibited by law. However, in other cases, the difference between ethical and unethical behaviors must be enforced by the organization itself. If the organization has a strong sense of right and wrong, it will be able to maintain positive relationships with customers and vendors. If the organization has questionable ethical practices, it may face legal charges, loss of business, or harm to its reputation.

HR professionals can help organizations have clear and enforceable ethical standards. Three ways to do so are establishing a values statement, establishing a code of conduct, and conducting HR audits. Similar to a values statement (as explained above), a code of conduct also guides employee behavior, but with greater detail. The code of conduct lays out all policies governing employees' actions, defining acceptable and unacceptable behaviors. HR professionals also must carry out HR audits to ensure that all employees are following organization policies. HR managers can also develop and distribute an Employee Handbook that outlines the company's code of conduct and employee expectations.

Other HR policies to consider with respect to ethics include the process of reporting unethical behavior. How will the organization protect employees who report unethical business practices within the organization? Are employees able to make anonymous or confidential reports about unethical behavior? HR professionals should implement training programs to educate managers and other employees about expected standards of ethical behavior. When it comes to controversial business practices, employees may not be sure what behaviors are acceptable or unacceptable. When an organization's code of conduct changes or when new legal regulations are introduced, it's important to provide appropriate training and education for employees. Finally, HR professionals must have organized review systems to evaluate how well the organization is adhering to ethical practices and reporting all business practices appropriately.

Business Elements of an Organization

Competitive Advantage
A **competitive advantage** is anything that gives an organization an edge over its competitors. To determine its competitive advantage, an organization must have a clear understanding of its direct competitors, its products and services, and its target market. For example, a budget clothing company might be successful based on offering lower prices than other stores. Its competitive advantage is its prices. On the other hand, a luxury designer clothing brand could have the opposite competitive advantage—because its product is high quality and expensive, its name-brand reputation makes it successful with customers in a wealthier target market.

Organizational Branding
An organization communicates a unified message about its identity through **organizational branding**. Branding weaves together an organization's purpose, values, and strengths to give employees and customers a clear image of the organization's character. Effective branding is an essential part of marketing because it can build an organization's reputation and help it connect with its target market. When customers come to closely associate an organization with its unique character, organizational branding is succeeding.

Business Case Development
A **business case** is a document that shows the reasoning behind a business change, such as initiating a new project. It makes the case for a change in the business, helping decision-makers inside or outside the organization to justify resources for this activity. To develop a business case, it's important to first understand the needs of the organization—how will this new activity benefit its overall goals? How will it fit into the budget and available resources? What makes this activity a better choice than other options? Next, estimate the cost and benefits of the project. These estimates can come from external quotes and bids as well as from internal data from finance and accounting. However, a business case presents more than just financial information. In many cases, costs, benefits, and risks of a new activity

include non-financial factors. For example, a non-financial risk might be employee resistance to the business change.

Corporate Responsibility

Corporate responsibility extends beyond an organization's responsibility to adhere to all applicable laws and regulations. It also includes concepts like Corporate Social Responsibility (CSR) and ethics, both explained in greater detail in earlier sections. Corporate responsibility shows that an organization cares about conducting business in a fair and ethical way that adds value to its community and industry.

Operations

Business operations are the core of what an organization actually does on a day-to-day basis to transform its assets into profits. This business process is where the organization's products or services are created and delivered to customers. For example, an online printing service's operations might include taking orders, using their equipment to create high-quality prints, and delivering the finished work to customers.

Sales and Marketing

While operations are responsible for actually creating products or services, **sales** and **marketing** help the organization to connect its output with its customers. Even if a company has the highest-quality product on the market, it can't be successful unless it actually reaches customers. Sales and marketing activities include market research, developing leads, and designing and implementing advertisements.

Data Management

We've looked at how organizations evaluate and improve their performance by analyzing data. However, in order for this analysis to occur, an organization needs careful **data management**. This business process encompasses activities like managing database software, protecting data security, and facilitating data access for employees.

Effective Data Reporting and Analysis

Using Human Resources Information Systems (HRIS)

Business technology, of which **HRIS** are a component, manage a great number of operations in organizations today. Business technology can refer to any software, online system, application, or other technological innovation that automates or simplifies jobs within an organization. Based on organization needs, HRIS can perform functions such as the following:

- Creating and managing online employee information systems
- Managing and updating job postings
- Updating candidate profiles over the course of the hiring process
- Managing and storing HR documents and reporting

HRIS can also store data related to the following:

- Employee productivity
- Performance
- Job satisfaction
- Benefit usage
- Historical data

This data can be analyzed through the HRIS to generate reports indicating internal trends, which can pinpoint organizational problems, needs, or successes. Due to the advent of HRIS, it is critical for business professionals to embrace new technologies and continuous learning on the job.

Providing Data

One essential way that HR participates in its organization's budget is by projecting human capital needs. Particularly when a new strategic plan is implemented, HR must understand how human capital requirements will evolve as a result. HR should be proactive rather than reactive when it comes to human capital needs (that is, anticipate workforce needs *before* they occur). To do so, HR professionals must have a clear understanding of the organization's current workforce and its skills and competencies (How many employees do we have? What is their experience level? What tasks are they capable of performing?). Next, they must look at the activities involved in carrying out the strategic plan and determine the activities' workforce requirements (How many employees are needed for this activity? What skills are required to perform this task?). Finally, HR compares the two, identifies any gaps (Do we have enough employees for this task? Do they have the necessary skills?) and works to fill those gaps by providing additional training, reassigning staff, or recruiting new employees.

Of course, training and recruiting cost money, so these human capital projections also aid budgeting for any new plans and projects. In anticipating workforce needs, HR helps managers get a more complete view of a project's budget requirements and avoid any surprise costs later.

Change Management Theory

To remain competitive, adopt industry best practices, and adapt to changing markets, an organization will undergo change at many points. Change might be undertaken to benefit company shareholders and increase the profitability of the company. Change can also occur to reduce costs and increase efficiency. However, especially from an HR perspective, it's important to keep in mind how change affects employees. The truth is that most people don't like change. Also, work force changes in particular (such as outsourcing or downsizing) are certain to be met with employee resistance. Even more minor changes like revised vacation policies may go through an unpopular adjustment period. Change management helps to smooth over these difficulties.

Change Management

Change is inevitable for any organization, especially in fields affected by global markets and technological innovation. **Change management** seeks to aid organizations through significant transitions in resource allocation, operations, business processes, or any other large-scale changes. Careful change management helps the organization to function effectively even while undergoing a major evolution.

Implementing Change

How should an organization implement change? The classic 1961 text *The Planning of Change* tackles this question. The book outlines three strategies for managing change: the empirical-rational strategy, the normative-reductive strategy, and the power-coercive strategy.

The **empirical-rational strategy** assumes that people are rational and will naturally follow any course that's in their self-interest. Therefore, they are likelier to accept change when they think it will directly benefit them. To implement change in line with this strategy, an organization must either 1) demonstrate the benefit of the change or 2) demonstrate the harm of the status quo (or both). One way of accomplishing this is to incentivize change. For example, a growing company is gaining new employees, but it doesn't want to expand its available parking. The company decides to limit the number of parking spots and encourage public transportation use. Employees are reluctant to give up the freedom to drive, so the company holds an educational seminar about how to save money by using public transportation and also offers monthly reimbursement for employees who use public transportation.

The next approach proposed in *The Planning of Change* is the **normative-reductive strategy**. This strategy assumes that people will closely follow social norms and expectations. To implement change, it's necessary to first change people's idea of what is socially acceptable. This is the strategy that harnesses the power of advertising. For example, think of anti-tobacco advertising campaigns over the past few decades. Throughout most of the twentieth century, smoking was socially acceptable just about anywhere. However, especially in the 1990s and 2000s, aggressive anti-smoking advertisements attacked the tobacco industry and started anti-smoking education programs for students. The social norm turned *against* smoking in most public places, and now there are more anti-smoking laws than ever before.

Finally, the **power-coercive strategy** assumes that people are followers who will listen to authority and do as they are told. This approach to change is basically, "My way or the highway!" Where the empirical-rational strategy seeks to demonstrate how change will benefit employees, the power-coercive strategy says that *not* following change will be *harmful* to employees, who might be punished or even fired for failure to comply. For example, a factory undergoes an intense safety inspection and decides to completely renovate its safety standards. Employees now have new dress code requirements. If they don't follow the dress code, they aren't allowed to work that day; after the third dress code violation, they will be fired.

Deciding which strategy to employ depends on the overall character of the organization as well as the importance and sensitivity of the change. For example, an otherwise friendly and collegial office might respond negatively to usage of the power-coercive strategy. The power-coercive strategy would be useful for changes with clear legal or financial liabilities, such as when an organization must follow new government regulations.

Risk Management

An organization engages in **risk management** when it identifies, targets, and strives to minimize unacceptable risks. While a variety of different risks may arise, an organization's principal risks are generally workplace health, safety, security, and privacy. Failure to protect from these risks can result in serious consequences and may lead to negative company publicity, low employee morale, and burdensome expenses. Organizations must prioritize risk management and comply with federal laws and regulations. By doing so, employers will increase productivity and build sustainable relationships between employees and management.

Cost-Benefit Analysis (CBA)
A **cost-benefit analysis (CBA)** is an important factor in many business decisions. A CBA compares the cost of a particular option with the benefits it will bring to the organization. A CBA has two main uses. First, it helps to determine whether a particular option is worthwhile (Do the benefits sufficiently offset the costs?). Secondly, it's a method of comparison when making a decision that has several options.

Of course, any cost-benefit analysis involves a certain level of uncertainty because it's predicting future values under future conditions. For example, a change in the cost of a certain resource or the exchange rate of foreign currency could impact the results of a CBA. For this reason, a CBA usually includes a sensitivity analysis, which determines how much a change in uncertain variables will affect the CBA. This sensitivity analysis takes into account the expected conditions (what will happen if everything proceeds according to the status quo?) as well as worst-case conditions (what will happen if all possible problems arise in this situation?). In this way, a CBA can also reveal the level of risk involved in a decision. An option that appears attractive at first may seem less certain after a sensitivity analysis.

A cost-benefit analysis can also be approached differently depending on the view of the analysis—short-, mid-, or long-term. For many business decisions, the costs are upfront while the benefits may appear immediately or after a longer period of time. For this reason, a short-term and long-term CBA could yield very different results. If an organization needs a quick return on benefits, it might place more emphasis on a short-term CBA. However, if it's willing to wait longer to reap the benefits of a decision, it might compare its options based on long-term CBAs.

Enterprise Risk Management (ERM)
No matter how carefully an organization conducts research, carries out analyses, and develops strategic plans, the organization will always face unknowns. There are risks that activities will fail, outside obstacles will appear, or new threats will emerge. **Enterprise risk management (ERM)** is a method of managing unknowable risks by anticipating potential risks, focusing on those with the greatest likelihood or potential impact, and planning a response strategy for when risks become realities.

An organization could choose four different responses to a particular risk: reduce the effects of the risk, share it, avoid it, or accept it. To reduce the effects of the risk, the organization finds ways to decrease its likelihood or to soften its potential harmful impact. If the organization wants to avoid the risk altogether, it will simply cease all activity associated with that risk. Finally, an organization might decide to go ahead and accept a risk; this might happen when cost-benefit analysis has determined that the benefits greatly outweigh all potential risk to the organization.

Risk management is especially important in human resources, which can account for a significant portion of an organization's financial risk, especially in terms of liability and legal concerns. For example, the organization can be held liable for compliance (or non-compliance) with labor laws, proper management of employee information, and legal concerns of employees like workplace safety and sexual harassment. HR can identify which risks are the most pressing for their organization and plan accordingly, perhaps through an HR audit. Like any audit, an HR audit is an inspection—in this case, of an organization's HR policies and practices. The purpose of an HR audit is to check that policies are in line with all applicable laws and regulations and are properly followed by all employees.

Qualitative and Quantitative Methods and Tools for Analytics

Qualitative Methods
Qualitative methods contrast with quantitative methods. Whereas **qualitative methods** are based on things like observations, interviews, and case study analyses, **quantitative methods** are based on numbers, statistics, and other measurable data. Many companies prefer quantitative methods because their results seem more tangible and objective in comparison to the subjective nature of qualitative studies. However, much can be learned from qualitative methods. For example, a quantitative analysis could answer the question, "What is our employee turnover rate?" but only a qualitative study could

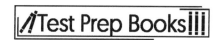

answer, "Why do employees leave?" or "What motivates employees to stay?" Qualitative methods are needed to give context and relevance to statistical data.

Quantitative Job Evaluation Methods

Quantitative job evaluation methods use a scaling system and provide a score that indicates how valuable one job is when compared to another job. The two specific examples are the point factor method and the factor comparison method.

Point Factor Method

The **point factor method** is less complex and most commonly used. This method uses specific, compensable factors, such as skill, responsibility, effort, working conditions, and the supervision of others, to evaluate the relative worth of each job. Each job receives a total point value, and then the relative worth of all jobs within an organization can be compared.

Factor Comparison Method

The **factor comparison method** is more complex and rarely used. This method involves a ranking of each job by each selected compensable factor and then identifies dollar values for each level of each factor to develop a pay rate for an evaluated job. It is best to use this method when wages are not frequently changed, and the organization uses a flat rate of pay for each job. This method can sometimes be used as part of a labor contract.

Reliability and Validity of Selection Tests/Tools/Methods

Selection tests, tools, and methods must be both reliable and valid. They are said to be reliable if they are free from random errors and are able to predict or measure behavior consistently. For example, an intelligence test is said to be reliable if an individual takes the test on two different occasions and receives similar scores, because intelligence tends to be stable over time.

The following is a list of known errors that can create inconsistent results when evaluating the reliability of selection tests, tools, and methods:

- An interviewer who asks irrelevant questions to a candidate during an interview
- An employer who allows candidates different amounts of time when completing a test
- A test that fails to measure an important attribute
- An interviewer who is biased when evaluating candidates

Although selection tests, tools, and methods may be deemed reliable, this does not necessarily mean they are also valid.

To be valid, a screening process should collect information on the candidate relevant to the position. If the process does not test qualifications, or tests irrelevant material, it can be deemed unfair or inaccurate. Information collected should be well defined, relevant, and job related.

A Human Resources professional usually evaluates three elements to determine the validity of a selection tool:

- Content validity
- Construct validity
- Criterion-related validity, which is further categorized into:

- ○ Concurrent validity
- ○ Predictive validity

Content validity measures how well the tool's subject matter covers the knowledge, skills, and abilities required for a specific job. The Uniform Guidelines on Employee Selection Procedures and the Equal Employment Opportunity Commission regulate that any pre-employment test or tool must be related to the job position for which it is intended. For example, if a candidate who is interviewing for a bank teller position is asked to take a test that measures mechanical ability, this can be deemed an invalid test. Again, this is important to ensure there are no legal repercussions against the recruiting organization.

Construct validity determines if a screening tool effectively tests and measures the characteristic it claims to measure, such as intelligence, and that the characteristic in question is indeed important for successful performance of the job.

Evaluations with demonstrated **criterion-related validity** can predict how an individual will behave in the workplace based on their test scores. This is done by comparing test result data to specific metrics or criteria required by the job, or to wider company goals, such as the total number of sales or the overall employee retention rate. After testing is completed, a measurement comparing test scores with job performance is taken and expressed as a correlation coefficient ranging from -1.0 to +1.0. Because testing this validity requires a large sample size, it is often the most difficult type of validity to measure.

Human Resources professionals can measure two types of criterion-related validity: predictive and concurrent.

Predictive validity is a measure of whether an individual will possess the required skills, knowledge, or behavioral traits in the future. To be valid, the test results should correlate and accurately predict job performance in the future; in other words, the test should yield a positive correlation coefficient.

Concurrent validity determines if an individual currently possesses the required skills, knowledge, or behavioral traits. To assess this type of criterion validity, a company administers a test to current employees to determine and compare their results to existing measures of job performance. The test is deemed to be valid if the individuals who receive the highest scores also perform best on the job.

Uncertain, Unclear, or Chaotic Situations

The only certainty in any business is the opportunity for uncertainty. HR professionals are sure to deal with situations that are uncertain, unclear, or even chaotic. However, there are still knowable strategies to deal with unknowable situations.

These situations can be described by the concept of **VUCA**, which stands for volatility, uncertainty, complexity, and ambiguity. Especially in the context of global markets and swiftly developing technologies, everything can change at a moment's notice. A company may have started in a completely different business environment from one that exists just five years later.

Volatility refers to something unstable with frequently unexpected changes, like wild price fluctuations, effects of weather or natural disasters, politically unstable regions). **Uncertainty** refers to a situation in which the organization faces a lack of information. An example would be a competitor working on developing and launching a new, top-secret product. **Complexity** refers to a situation with various interconnecting parts and factors, like a tech upgrade that requires new hardware, software, user support, and training; or a global merger that requires knowledge of local laws, culture, and customs in a new country. Finally, **ambiguity** occurs in situations with "unknown unknowns," when the company has no experience to base predictions on, like moving into emerging industries.

In all of these situations, the organization faces various information gaps and unpredictable outcomes. The key for handling them is to understand what you do and don't have control over. This involves being open about what you can't predict—pretending that you know everything, whether to company executives or to rank-and-file employees, can be disastrous in the long run. For example, if employees are reassured that the company won't take a hit from a recent economic downturn, only to be hit with mass layoffs a few months later, anger and mistrust can easily spread throughout employees. Or, presenting a plan to leadership without explaining the various opportunities for unpredictability and uncertainty prevents them from effectively evaluating and planning for risk.

In fact, the best way to handle VUCA is to balance planning with flexibility. In areas in which the company lacks knowledge, build on the knowledge that you do have and engage in controlled experimentation to gather new data. For example, if an organization plans to launch a new product in a totally new market, it might build on knowledge and experience it has gained from other markets, and test various types of limited product releases before engaging in a full launch. Companies can also work on building a culture of flexibility and innovation to prepare employees to handle change. Engaging and communicating with employees, including knowing when to ask for input and ideas, empowers workers to feel more in control of chaotic business situations.

Glossary

Acquisitions	Occur when one company purchases another without a new legal entity being formed
Active Listening	Pushes the listener into an engaged position; Beyond using their sense of hearing, active listeners also use their sense of sight to notice the speaker's body language.
Ambiguity	Lack of clear communication and can cause conflict, affect business processes, and cause distress to employees
Ambiguity (VUCA)	Occurs in situations with "unknown unknowns," when the company has no experience to base predictions on, like moving into emerging industries
Attrition Rate	Measures employee turnover over time within an organization
Business Operations	Core of what an organization actually does on a day-to-day basis to transform its assets into profits
Change Management	Seeks to aid organizations through significant transitions in resource allocation, operations, business processes, or any other large-scale changes
Communication	Can occur in a variety of ways, such as through e-mail, individual interviews, or department meetings
Competing Points of View	Can be components of communication that often lead to new perspectives, collaboration, innovation, opportunities, and improvements
Competitive Advantage	Anything that gives an organization an edge over its competitors
Competitors	How many similar organizations are currently in the same field?
Complexity (VUCA)	A situation with various interconnecting parts and factors, like a tech upgrade that requires new hardware, software, user support, and training; or a global merger that requires knowledge of local laws, culture, and customs in a new country
Compliance	Following requirements while carrying out business activities
Concurrent Validity	Determines if an individual currently possesses the required skills, knowledge, or behavioral traits
Construct Validity	Determines if a screening tool effectively tests and measures the characteristic it claims to measure
Content Validity	Measures how well the tool's subject matter covers the knowledge, skills, and abilities required for a specific job
Core Values Statement	Tells what the organization stands for and guides standards of expected employee behavior
Corporate Responsibility	Shows that an organization cares about conducting business in a fair and ethical way that adds value to its community and industry
Corporate Social Responsibility (CSR)	An organization's sense of responsibility for its impact on the environment and community
Cost-Benefit Analysis (CBA)	Compares the cost of a particular option with the benefits it will bring to the organization
Criterion-Related Validity	Can predict how an individual will behave in the workplace based on their test scores
Customer Demographics	This includes information about customers such as age, education, or income. This information can provide essential economic information to an organization.
Data Management	This business process encompasses activities like managing database software, protecting data security, and facilitating data access for employees.
Diversity In Hiring	Involves hiring employees with a variety of backgrounds, personalities, and working styles
Economic Factors	Include inflation, economic growth, and the exchange rate
Empirical-Rational Strategy	Assumes that people are rational and will naturally follow any course that's in their self-interest

Employee Assistance Program (EAP)	Provides employees the option to improve their psychological wellbeing
Enterprise Risk Management (ERM)	Method of managing unknowable risks by anticipating potential risks, focusing on those with the greatest likelihood or potential impact, and planning a response strategy for when risks become realities.
Environmental Scanning	Process of finding and interpreting relevant data to identify opportunities and threats in the field
Functional Structure	Positions are grouped according to similar job roles (defined by skill, expertise, or resources) in a hierarchical chain
Governance	How senior executives direct and control an organization
GRM (Governance, Risk Management, Compliance)	Governance and compliance are often grouped together with risk management. By grouping them together, an organization can avoid redundancies in procedures and increase the effectiveness of communication between each area.
Hazard Communication Standard	Includes standards for safety measures such as the labeling of workplace hazards
HR Coaching	Helps employees achieve their potential and continue to develop their skills, matching them with the needs of the organization
Labor Force	Number of employed and unemployed workers in a given region
Market Share	Can be found by taking the total sales of the organization over a fixed period and dividing it by the total sales of all organizations in that industry
Mergers	Occur when two companies combine to form a new legal entity
Metrics	Method of measuring a particular set of data; Different metrics can be applied to different areas of an organization.
Mission Statement	Focuses on the work of the organization on a day-to-day basis; It states why the organization exists, and in turn guides its values, standards, and other organizing principles.
Modeling	Provides a hands-on approach to teaching new behaviors
Normative-Reductive Strategy	In order to implement change, it's necessary to first change people's idea of what is socially acceptable. This is the strategy that harnesses the power of advertising.
Occupational Safety and Health Administration (OSHA)	Oversees and enforces workplace safety regulations
Organizational Branding	Document that shows the reasoning behind a business change
People (CSR)	Fair employment practices as well as the organization's impact on members of the community
Planet (CSR)	Organization's environmental impact (such as pollution, consumption of natural resources, etc.)
Political Factors	Includes anything related to government influences in the field like laws, taxes, and trade restrictions
Power-Coercive Strategy	Assumes that people are followers who will listen to authority and do as they are told; this approach to change is basically, "my way or the highway!"
Predictive Validity	Measure of whether an individual will possess the required skills, knowledge, or behavioral traits in the future
Profit	Organization's overall contribution to economic growth
Public Company Accounting Oversight Board (PCAOB)	Created by SOX to establish auditor independence (to prevent conflict of interest) and executive responsibility for corporate financial reports (to increase overall corporate responsibility for accurate accounting).
Qualitative Methods	Based on things like observations, interviews, and case study analyses

Quantitative Job Evaluation Methods	This method involves a ranking of each job by each selected compensable factor and then identifies dollar values for each level of each factor to develop a pay rate for an evaluated job.
Quantitative Methods	Based on numbers, statistics, and other measurable data
Return On Investment (ROI)	Generally expressed as a ratio or percentage comparing the gains of a particular investment with its initial investment price; in other words, ROI measures the ratio between an investment's profit and its cost.
Risk Management	Identifies, targets, and strives to minimize unacceptable risks
Sales and Marketing	Help the organization to connect its output with its customers; includes market research, developing leads, and designing and implementing advertisements
Sarbanes-Oxley Act Of 2002 (SOX)	Important business law created in reaction to corporate fraud scandals like Enron in 2001; It established new regulations for corporate accounting.
Social Capital	The community's relationship with, and attitude toward, the organization
Social Factors	Include age distribution and population growth rate, which can be useful in identifying potential markets and targeting customer needs
Soliciting Feedback	Crucial component of program evaluation, guiding and sustaining initiatives, and providing valuable customer service
Stakeholder	Someone with an interest in a business; These are not necessarily the same as shareholders, those with ownership in a business who are interested in its financial performance.
Stakeholder Communications	Can take place in person, in meetings as a group, through email, or through social media
Substance Abuse	Dependence on an addictive substance such as illegal drugs
Success Of Training	The effectiveness of a high potential development program could be measured using data about retention rates, job satisfaction, or cost comparisons between developing leaders internally and onboarding external hires in leadership roles.
Technological Factors	Include all aspects of new technology like R&D, automation, and new technological regulations
Time To Fill	Similar concept to time to hire but represents the time it takes for a job position to be filled
Time To Hire	Refers to the amount of time between when a potential employee applies for a job and when they are actually hired
Title I of the Americans with Disabilities Act (ADA)	Applies to employers with fifteen or more employees and outlines legal protections for qualified employees with disabilities
Title VIII of the Sarbanes-Oxley Act Of 2002 (SOX)	Provides protections for corporate whistleblowers, people who report illegal or unethical activity, and describes the penalties for interfering with fraud investigations
Uncertainty (VUCA)	Situation in which the organization faces a lack of information
Vision Statement	Focuses on specific future goals, and in turn guides the steps that the organization will take to achieve them
Volatility (VUCA)	Refers to something unstable with frequently unexpected changes, like wild price fluctuations, effects of weather or natural disasters, politically unstable regions)
VUCA	Stands for volatility, uncertainty, complexity, and ambiguity
Workplace Violence	Any act of physical violence, intimidation, threat, or verbal abuse that occurs in the workplace

Practice Quiz

1. Which best describes corporate social responsibility?
   a. Corporate social responsibility is a policy mandated by the government to coerce corporations to improve their communities.
   b. Corporate social responsibility refers to the responsibility that corporations have toward shareholders.
   c. Corporate social responsibility is an issue of ethics, pursued by corporations that see the health of their business as contingent upon the health of their community.
   d. Corporate social responsibility refers to the social climate of the organization and the policies created to sustain the strength of that climate.

2. CSR can be evaluated on which three P's of the "triple bottom line"?
   a. People, prizes, and proxy
   b. Planet, profit, and projects
   c. People, profit, and prizes
   d. People, planet, and profit

3. What's the purpose of a vision statement?
   a. A vision statement is a memo drafted by management that articulates that if company policy is breached, there will be severe consequences.
   b. A vision statement is a succinct explanation of how an organization plans to deliver quality products/services.
   c. A vision statement is a lengthy and detailed speech given by a CEO to shareholders and other investors.
   d. A vision statement is a short address that low-level employees give to management.

4. What is the main purpose of a cost-benefit analysis?
   a. When evaluating a policy or program, a cost-benefit analysis empirically tests its efficacy to ensure that resources aren't squandered.
   b. Cost-benefit analyses are rarely conducted because they are expensive and unreliable.
   c. When evaluating a policy or program, a cost-benefit analysis is conducted that rationally tests its efficacy to ensure that resources aren't squandered. However, because cost-benefit analyses are antiquated, management typically decides on the policy or program based on its organizational popularity.
   d. A cost-benefit analysis is the empirical testing of a policy or program. However, management is typically disdainful of them because of a belief that the testers are inherently biased.

5. During a project meeting, Mary creates a table that includes a detailed description of every task needed for the project, a deliverable date for each task, and the owner of each task. Each member is able to access and update the table with status updates. What is Mary helping her team do?
   a. Helping each member feel accountable
   b. Micromanaging
   c. Modeling ethical behavior
   d. Collecting data

See answers on next page.

35

Answer Explanations

1. C: Corporate social responsibility is an ethical standard pursued by corporations that see the health of their business as contingent upon the health of their community. This ethical issue emphasizes becoming a part of the community and its social fabric. Corporate social responsibility can engender controversy by suggesting that a business has an obligation greater than merely supplying goods and services at a low cost.

2. D: CSR can be evaluated by people, planet, and profit. *People* refers to the organization's treatment of their employees as well as members of the community. *Planet* refers to the impact the organization has on the environment. *Profit* refers to the organization's overall contribution to economic growth. Choices *A, B,* and *C* are all incorrect.

3. B: A vision statement is a concise statement that reflects organizational confidence and long-term aspirations about how the firm will achieve more than just economic success. Some questions that may be answered in a vision statement include: How does this firm fit into the marketplace? How would it positively change the world? Institutionally, how does the company plan to deliver their product or service cheaper and more efficiently than competitors? Ultimately, vision statements serve the purpose of boosting trust, confidence, and an image that the firm is engaging in a task larger than itself.

4. A: A cost-benefit analysis is an objective empirical study of the precise effects of a specific policy or plan. Cost-benefit analyses are critically important because they indicate if a policy or plan will save resources or squander them. If the costs outweigh the benefits, then an action isn't financially sensible. But if the analysis indicates that benefits will outweigh costs, then the policy can be pursued with confidence.

5. A: Mary is providing clear, visible expectations of project tasks and completion dates. By sharing who is assigned to each task, it provides a sense of transparency and ownership. Together, these help individual members feel accountable for the role they play on the project.

Talent Planning and Acquisition

Responsibilities

Federal Laws and Organizational Policies Regarding Ethical Requirements in Hiring

Title VII of the Civil Rights Act of 1964

Title VII was originally passed as part of the Civil Rights Act of 1964. This portion of the act protects employees from management decisions regarding their employment (i.e., recruiting, hiring, advancement, compensation, work environment, etc.) based on race, color, nationality, or sex. State and local acts may expand this to include sexual orientation. Title VII applies to most employers with fifteen or more employees.

There are a few exceptions to Title VII. Legitimate work-related requirements may prevent an employer from hiring a specific individual, as they may be physically unable to perform the essential job functions associated with a certain position. For example, a work-related requirement for a firefighter may be that they must be able to carry two hundred pounds up eight flights of stairs. Additionally, seniority systems that are already in effect at a workplace are allowed. Finally, Bona Fide Occupational Qualifications (BFOQs) are exceptions to the discrimination rules that allow employers to take into account an individual's age, origin, sex, or religion when considering them for a job (note that race and color are not included). For example, an employer would not want to hire a sixty-five-year-old woman to model children's clothing.

Rehabilitation Act

The **Rehabilitation Act** was passed in 1973 to prohibit employment discrimination based on physical or mental disabilities. This legislation charges employers with taking affirmative action to hire qualified disabled persons. The act further requires that reasonable accommodation(s) be made for the disabled unless the employer can show an undue hardship based on business necessity or financial cost (spending in excess of $1,000 per employee). The Civil Service Commission, Department of Labor, Department of Veterans Affairs, and the Department of Health and Human Services administer this law, which applies to the federal government, federal contractors with contracts over $10,000, and companies who are in receipt of funds in excess of $10,000 by a company that receives federal monies.

Under this law, disability is defined as a physical or mental impairment that substantially limits one or more major life activities. Examples of reasonable accommodations that can be made under the Rehabilitation Act consist of the following:

- A change in job design: eliminating tasks that are not really necessary to perform the job

- Qualifications: getting rid of unnecessary job specs for everyone, such as requiring a medical exam prior to employment (which will allow the disabled to be hired)

- Job accessibility: adding wheelchair ramps, brail in elevators, etc.

- Nondiscriminatory treatment: eliminating hiring decisions based on people's fear of, or uneasiness with, disabilities

37

Equal Opportunity Employment (EEO) Reporting

Annual workforce data reporting is required by the **Equal Employment Opportunity Commission (EEOC)** for all employers with one hundred or more employees and federal contractors with at least fifty employees and contracts of $50,000. The reports are due each year by September 30. In addition, these employers must place EEO posters and notices in prominent locations within their workplaces. EEO reporting aids employers in determining their workforce composition, to ensure they are not discriminating against protected classes.

The various EEO reports collect data by some type of job grouping about race/ethnicity and gender. There are nine EEO job reporting categories:

- Officials and managers
- Professionals
- Technicians
- Sales
- Office and clerical
- Craft workers (skilled)
- Operatives (semiskilled)
- Laborers (unskilled)
- Service workers

As an example, the EEO-1 Report, which is also known as the Employer Information Report, categorizes data by race/ethnicity, gender, and job category. This report applies to employers who are required to file an annual report of employee sex and race/ethnic categories under Title VII of the 1964 Civil Rights Act. Government guidelines for the reporting of race are detailed in the EEO1 report form, which is jointly produced by the EEOC and the Office of Federal Contract Compliance.

Sourcing Methods

Recruiting refers to procedures and strategies designed to encourage and find potential, qualified candidates who seek employment. If the labor pool is unsuitable, then reaching these staffing goals is impossible, and so recruiting is essential for any organization's staffing plan.

An organization usually uses three types of recruiting: external, internal, and alternative. **External recruiting** seeks individuals from outside the organization for employment and usually emphasizes the advantages of employment with the organization, advertising benefits such as pay, insurance, leave, or employee discounts. Internal recruiting encourages individuals from within the organization to seek transfers or promotions to fill vacant positions. Alternative recruiting seeks candidates from internships or temps to perform specific tasks for a limited period of time.

When a company seeks to **recruit from within**, some of the most common strategies to find potential candidates include internal announcements, which are made to employees before the general public; job bidding, which involves an employee expressing an interested in a position, whether or not it is available; and promotion plans, which detail an employee's skills and training and future positions for which they're qualified.

While the majority of companies will recruit in the ways that are mentioned above, some may look elsewhere to find the required number of candidates. Some of these methods include:

- Passing out fliers
- Recruiting in professional organizations
- Finding employees through prison work programs
- Recruiting outgoing employees from a company's clients, vendors, or suppliers
- Offering sign-on bonuses to prospective employees

The labor pool of available candidates can further be classified into three categories: active, semi-active, and passive.

Active candidates are those engaging in a search for new employment, whether they're already employed or unemployed. Most often these individuals are looking for new opportunities, concerned about their current employer's stability due to their employer's outsourcing, bankruptcy, etc. The most common method employers use to reach active candidates is through job postings. Using social media can aid in reaching the highest audience possible but can sometimes also attract a large number of unqualified candidates. Another recruiting method involves active sourcing, which is made easier as these candidates are looking to be noticed. Again, using social media such as LinkedIn is an effective way in finding these jobseekers.

Semi-active candidates are not actively looking for work but are preparing themselves for new opportunities. These individuals most often do not have a resume prepared and businesses looking to recruit them often allow submissions of alternatives, such as an online social media profile.

Passive candidates are employed but not looking for work. These individuals are sometimes still worth pursuing by employers, if candidates are willing to listen to a recruiter about a better career opportunity. Proactive searching is the most effective way of reaching this group, again, through avenues like social media.

Employee Referral

Employee referrals can serve as a great tool when recruiting for positions requiring specialized skills that are difficult to fill via regular recruiting methods. Individuals who interview via employee referrals typically know what to expect regarding the work environment from their interactions with the employees who already work there, so there are fewer surprises. Employees who refer candidates usually benefit from a monetary incentive and can experience increased loyalty because they are having a "say" in the building of the workplace culture. It is important for a company not to rely solely on employee referrals to fill all open positions, so as to avoid creating cliques throughout the workplace. Such groups typically include individuals who are very similar to one another, which limits innovation.

Social Networking/Social Media

Social networking/media is a great tool for locating both passive and active candidates. LinkedIn, Facebook, and Twitter are the three most popular social media sites. However, other social media sites, such as Instagram, are quickly gaining more attention. A company's social media recruiting strategy allows candidates to view job openings and gain a better understanding of the company's personality and culture. It is important for companies to designate an individual who will respond to candidates' questions and concerns in a timely manner. In addition, a company's social media efforts can be easily

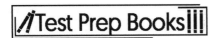

monitored (i.e., page likes, number of followers, etc.) to analyze what is truly working, and then adjust strategy accordingly.

Diversity Groups

Organizations are also working to recruit potential employees via various **diversity groups**, which also help to further promote their inclusion efforts. Examples include groups for African Americans, Asian Americans, Latino Americans, disability awareness, LGBTQIA (lesbian, gay, bisexual, transgender, questioning, intersex, and allies), former members of the military, multicultural, emerging professionals, and women.

Talent Acquisition Lifestyle

Interviewing

An **interview** allows an employer to further evaluate a candidate's skills and knowledge while giving the candidate a chance to demonstrate their abilities.

The four most commonly used styles of interviewing are:

- Structured
- Semi-structured
- Unstructured
- Non-directive

A **structured interview** is controlled by the interviewer, who has a list of specific, job-related questions prepared prior to the start of the interview. The same questions are asked of all applicants in an effort to make comparisons between them easier. This can result in a better selection decision. A structured interview tends to be much more valid and reliable than other interview approaches.

Semi-structured interviews occur when interviewers have guided conversations with applicants that involve both broad questions and new questions that come about from the discussions that take place.

Unstructured interviews occur when interviewers improvise and ask applicants questions that were not prepared prior to the start of the interview. This can give the interviewer a chance to see how well the applicant thinks on their feet, and whether they can handle a lack of formalities or structure within a professional setting.

A **non-directive interview** utilizes open-ended questions that may be developed from an applicant's answers to previous questions. The interviewer must strive to keep the conversations job-related and to obtain comparable data from each applicant interviewing for the same position. This type of interviewing style is best used sparingly because comparing applicants is much more subjective than with the other styles.

Reference and Background Checking

Reference checks are very important for companies during the hiring process. They can verify if an individual has the necessary skills, knowledge, and experience, based on prior job performance, while also validating an individual's application for employment.

Reference checks are also an important way for companies to protect themselves from lawsuits or damage to their reputation. For example, **negligent hiring** takes place when an employer hires an

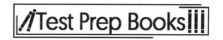

employee, and the employer either knew or should have known that the employee posed a risk to other employees or to customers. An example of negligent hiring is when an employee who is hired as a controller at a financial institution is later charged with embezzlement. The employer (financial institution) can ultimately be found liable for failing to conduct a proper background check on the employee if this employee did have a past history of criminal activity at a previous employer.

Employers can prevent negligent hiring claims by conducting criminal background checks, verifying employment histories and college degrees, checking on past employment gaps, and reaching out to the references of potential employees. In some industries, employers can also perform drug screenings, require physicals, perform credit checks, and check driving records for specific jobs.

A **reference list** is usually provided upon request, meaning the individual provides the references after a prospective employer asks for them. There are two main types of reference checks a company would need to complete: education and employment.

Education references refer to any certifications, degrees, diplomas, licenses, or any professional documents that can validate an applicant's knowledge and education. Sometimes these reference checks provide employers with specific grades or indicators of performance, but they're mostly made to verify that education was completed.

Employment references refer to feedback from past employers, co-workers, customers, or clients who can verify the individual's professional experience. The main information sought from these reference checks are on-the-job performance feedback from previous employers, as well as the individual's position(s), wages, and duration with past companies.

Two less common reference checks are financial and driving history.

Financial reference checks relate to credit history and how an individual handles money. These are usually for positions where this would be important, such as in the banking industry, but also in the public services industry (positions in schools, hospitals, or government).

Driving history checks relate to an individual's driving record and verify that they are able to drive safely. This is necessary for positions where driving is required, including an employee's need to use rental vehicles while conducting company business.

Knowledge of

Federal Laws and Regulations: Talent Planning and Acquisition Activities

There are many federal laws to consider when planning for new hires. One is the Civil Rights Act of 1964—specifically, **Title VII**, which prohibits employers from discriminating against employees on the basis of sex, race, color, national original, and religion. This act led to the creation of the **Equal Employment Opportunity Commission (EEOC)**, which enforces and oversees laws against workplace discrimination. The definition of workplace discrimination has since been expanded to include protection from discrimination based on an employee's disability, children, sexual orientation, gender identity, genetic information, and reporting discriminatory practices. Title VII generally applies to employers with fifteen or more employees.

HR should keep EEOC rules in mind when crafting job descriptions and advertisements. For example, a job posting should not say that the company is only looking for workers in a specific age range (such as, "Only graduates from after 1999 should apply") or gender. These rules also need to be followed during all hiring procedures, including job interviews and background checks. Interviewers should not ask any questions related to the protected identities listed above.

For example, questions like, "Do you have children?" or "Would you prioritize your children above your job duties?" are prohibited discriminatory questions. The interviewer should consider what skills and capabilities are actually important, and rephrase the question accordingly—perhaps something like, "How do you prioritize competing obligations?" or "Are you able to work a flexible schedule?" This is also true when checking references and contacting past employers. For example, the interviewer would not be able to ask questions such as, "Can you describe the employee's medical history?" or "Did the employ take many sick days or have any health problems that made them unable to work?" because these questions would be discriminating based on disability. Better questions might be, "Did the employee have good attendance?" or "Did the employee complete all essential job tasks?"

In 1978, the EEOC along with the Department of Labor, Department of Justice, and U.S. Civil Service Commission adopted the **Uniform Guidelines on Employee Selection Procedures (UGESP)** to provide standards on what constitutes discriminatory hiring practices. UGESP established the four-fifths rule, which states that if the selection rate for any race, sex, or ethnic group is less than four-fifths of the selection rate for the group with the highest selection rate, the hiring practice is generally considered discriminatory. For example, from a pool of applicants, a company hires 8 percent of the men who applied, but only 2 percent of the women who applied. In this case, the selection rate for women is only 25 percent of the selection rate for men—less than four-fifths (or 80 percent). This would be deemed discriminatory hiring.

Another relevant law is the **Fair Labor Standard Act of 1938 (FLSA)**, which establishes standards for a minimum wage, overtime pay, recordkeeping, and child labor standards. There are some exemptions to FLSA (for example, many tip-based professions such as food service), but it generally covers employers with at least $500,000 of business in a year.

There are also other laws related to pay for specific professions. The Walsh-Healey Public Contracts Act of 1936 establishes labor rights for U.S. government contracts, and it applies to any contracts exceeding $10,000 for goods. Like the FLSA, it sets standards for overtime pay and child labor, prohibiting the employment of those under the age of 16. It sets a separate minimum wage using the prevailing wage, as determined by state departments of labor. The prevailing wage is defined as the standard hourly wage, overtime, and benefits paid to the majority of workers in a given area.

Another contract act is the McNamara-O'Hara Service Contract Act of 1965 (SCA), which applies to contractors and subcontractors working on service contracts exceeding $2,500. Those contractors or subcontractors are also required to pay service employees no less than the prevailing wage. The Department of Labor oversees compliance with each of these laws.

Planning Concepts and Terms

Succession Planning
Succession planning is the practice of identifying and evaluating specific employees to fill leadership positions within an organization. Once identified, the employees selected need to be trained to fill these

capacities. Because of the chronically evolving nature of organizations, succession planning is critical. There are many reasons why positions would open, such as promotions, firings, and retirements.

Forecasting

The two main **forecasting** methods used by companies to determine staffing needs are known as qualitative and quantitative forecasting.

Qualitative forecasting is based on the opinions and estimations of industry experts or managers. **Management forecasting** involves determining staffing needs from the managers of each department and making decisions by using their reports. **Expert forecasting** utilizes industry experts who are able to make decisions based on wider changes in the industry.

A specific example of expert forecasting is the **Delphi method**, where questionnaires are sent to a variety of experts, the results are shared, and then choices are updated. The objective of this method is to reach the most correct decision via consensus.

Quantitative forecasting is based on raw mathematical data and previous trends, such as employee productivity and output. Some common quantitative forecasting methods include ratio analyses, trend analyses, turnover analyses, and probability models. **Ratio analyses** compare current with past employment ratios to determine where staffing needs may change, such as the number of employees to the number of products made. **Trend analyses** compare single amounts instead of ratios, such as the number of employees. **Turnover analyses** compare the number of employees who leave the company over a certain period of time with past data. Using this data, a company can utilize a **probability model** to predict future changes.

Companies need to determine whether their needs are short- or long-term when deciding which kind of method to use. Qualitative methods are usually more effective in the short term because they can manage changing staffing needs. Quantitative methods are usually more effective in the long term because staffing needs change at a steadier rate. Companies typically require both of these forecasting methods.

Current Market Situation and Talent Pool Availability

Workforce Reduction (Downsizing)

Workforce reductions are the planned elimination of a number of personnel to make an organization more competitive.

Once a company realizes it has a talent surplus, Human Resources can take the following steps to implement a workforce reduction:

- Reduce employees' hours
- Implement a hiring freeze
- Institute a voluntary separation program, also known as an early retirement buyout program

Although workforce reductions help companies cut costs in the short term, they often hurt productivity. For an organization to successfully implement a workforce reduction, it should communicate with employees throughout the entire process, and provide downsized employees with outplacement services to assist with resume writing, career counseling, and interview preparation. It can also provide referral assistance to exiting employees. Companies should strive to build the trust and commitment of the remaining employees so as to boost employee morale, especially during a downsizing situation.

Employees who are laid off are typically asked to sign a document known as a **separation agreement and general release**. This document, when signed, is a legally binding agreement that states the employee cannot sue or make any claims against the company in exchange for agreed upon severance benefits. Severance pay is not required by law, but most companies will pay employees who are laid off a set number of weeks of salary continuation, based upon their years of service (typically one or two weeks' pay per year of service), to ease their financial burden and to preserve the organization's image. Some companies also include a continuation of healthcare benefits for a set period of time.

An employee is given the agreement during their exit meeting and is allowed to take it home and review it with a lawyer. They have twenty-one days to sign and return the agreement for an individual separation and forty-five days to sign and return the agreement in cases of a group reduction in force. Once the agreement is signed, an employee still has seven days to revoke their signature.

Workforce Expansion

Some companies have a talent shortage. Instead of hiring full-time employees, Human Resources can utilize the following tactics to manage the workforce:

1. Allow existing staff to work overtime hours
2. Outsource work to an external service provider
3. Institute alternate work arrangements (i.e., telecommuting, job sharing, and nontraditional work schedules)
4. Reemploy recent retirees on a temporary or part-time basis
5. Utilize contingent workers to fill available positions and manage the extra workload (i.e., independent contractors)

Turning to alternative sources for workers can help the company save money on the hiring and interviewing process—a significant cost for many companies. Because many of the above candidates have already been screened for the job and proven themselves on the job, they may be a better match for filling short-term and even long-term staffing needs.

Staffing Alternatives

Outsourcing

Outsourcing is the practice of delegating work responsibilities in a business to a separate third-party individual or organization not associated with the company.

There are three different types of outsourcing:

- **Onshore**: The vendor is located within the same country as the business
- **Nearshore**: The vendor is in a country adjacent to the business
- **Offshore**: The vendor is in a country far from the business

Frequently, a company will outsource when:

- The expertise needed for a specific task cannot be found within the business
- Cost-cutting is needed
- A greater focus on in-business operations is needed

Outsourcing work does have a disadvantage in that the company may find it difficult to monitor the third-party business's operations as opposed to its own employees. Additionally, there is a risk in entrusting business confidentiality to a third party not near the business at all—especially with elements such as financial information. It is also worth noting that the idea of outsourcing can decrease morale for onsite employees. They may become worried about their own job security, so it's important for employers to introduce the concept carefully.

Job Sharing

Job sharing involves two or more employees performing the tasks of a role normally performed by one person. Usually, the individuals are employed on a part-time basis. Job sharing has become more prevalent in recent times due to an evolving work culture and the development of alternative work arrangements.

Candidates looking for a work/life balance may see benefits in job sharing, even though the pay is lower, and benefits are fewer, and consequently, overall productivity can increase for the business. However, it is essential for the individuals involved to have excellent communication with each other to succeed in a role normally designated for one person.

Phased Retirement

Phased retirement for older employees involves both the cutting back of working hours (or days of work) and the phasing in of retirement benefits such as Social Security funds. Phased retirement arrangements can take the form of part-time work, temporary or seasonal work, or job sharing.

Most commonly, these are informal agreements between an employer and an employee. A possible reason for the lack of formalized programs is the lack of legislation regarding regulations of benefits and salary coverage for potential retirees.

Phased retirement benefits employers by allowing more senior employees with years of workplace knowledge and experience to train their replacements over time.

Interviewing and Selection Techniques

Behavioral Interviews

The **behavioral interview** technique involves interviewers asking candidates to use specific examples to describe how they have handled a problem or performed a task in a past work situation. The thought behind this method is that past behavior is the best predictor of future job performance. Examples of behavioral-based interview questions are: "Can you tell me about a time when you had to go above and beyond the call of duty to get a job done?" and "Tell me about the last time you tackled a project that demanded a lot of initiative." Candidates can best answer these types of questions by using the STAR method, meaning they describe the past Situation or Task, explain the Action(s) they took, and describe the Results they achieved. It has been found that responses to questions about candidates' actual, past experiences tend to have high validity.

45

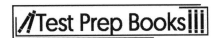

Situational Interviews

Situational interviews relate more to hypothetical situations that may take place in the future. For example, an employer may present a problem that could occur in the position for which the candidate is interviewing and ask the applicant how they might handle it. While this type of interview is useful in determining the candidate's suitability for the position, situational interviews can neglect an applicant's past work experience.

Panel Interviews

Panel interviews are conducted by a group of individuals from the organization that may consist of managers, Human Resources representatives, and other future team members, to better evaluate whether or not a candidate is suitable. Panel interviews can help to reduce personal biases in the selection decision and are especially useful in work environments where teamwork is an important factor. This type of interview also gives candidates the opportunity to meet more people from the company and see how they interact with each other.

Applicant Tracking Systems

An **applicant tracking system** is a method used to make the selection process more effective by utilizing a software application to electronically process a company's recruitment needs. An applicant tracking system allows an organization to do this by sorting through large numbers of resumes that are submitted to find the candidates who are the best possible fit for a specific open position, based on a search for certain keywords. This allows employers to stay better organized, save time, and stay on top of the hiring process.

All institutions that receive federal contracts are required to track what is known as applicant flow data. This is information collected on the gender and race of all applicants who apply for open positions within an organization. The goal of collecting such data is to be able to perform an analysis of differences in selection rates among various groups for a specific position, to ensure a proper demographic pool is being sourced for the role. This data can be collected by the use of an Equal Employment Opportunity (EEO) information form. Employers must make a reasonable effort to obtain this information. It is important to note that any such type of information obtained is not to be used in hiring decisions. It is for Human Resources' eyes only and cannot be kept with an employee's application or personnel file. This is clearly disclosed in the application, so that the applicant is aware that the company is not basing their hiring decision on demographic information the applicant shares.

Total Rewards

Benchmarking

Employers use salary surveys to assist them when working to establish the pay structures for their organizations. These surveys collect information from multiple employers regarding salary and benefits, such as employees' starting salaries, merit increases, bonus amounts, and work hours. To be comparable, salary surveys are conducted by focusing on a specific geographic region or industry.

Employers can make use of free government salary surveys and inexpensive industry-specific salary surveys, such as those for civil engineering and construction. Employer associations, like the **Society for Human Resource Management (SHRM)**, also conduct salary surveys and provide the results to their members at no charge. Additionally, companies can elect to outsource a salary survey to a survey vendor, which can be quite pricey.

It is important to note that salary survey data contains time-sensitive data that can become outdated rather quickly. Salary data may also need to be aged and/or leveled. **Aging** is the process of adjusting salary data to keep pace with market movement. **Leveling** can be used if a job included on the salary survey is similar—but not identical—to a position within the organization. The data for that job can be weighted or leveled to create a better match.

Employee Surveys

Employee surveys are an additional tool that can be used by companies to gather input on needs or preferences regarding compensation and benefits programs, as well as employees' satisfaction with the existing offerings. Some examples of the types of questions that employees may be asked include the following:

- Whether employees feel that they are compensated fairly compared to the local market
- If they feel that the company offers a competitive benefits package that meets their needs
- If they feel they are recognized for their performance when they go above expectations
- If performance incentives are clearly linked to strategic objectives.

To gather the most candid feedback, employees are usually allowed to remain anonymous when responding to these surveys. Management is expected to provide feedback to the participants upon conclusion of the survey and to address any outstanding concerns in a timely manner.

Trend Analysis

In order for a company's compensation and benefits offerings to remain meaningful, it is important for employers to track current and upcoming trends in these areas. In the field of health and welfare, additional employers will promote consumer-directed healthcare by introducing high-deductible health plans. A new cost savings innovation to assist employees will involve a way to visit medical professionals virtually—via video chat on the computer or telemedicine.

Additionally, employers will continue to stress the importance of employees using **health saving accounts (HSAs)** or **health reimbursement arrangements (HRAs)** to assist in funding their out-of-pocket healthcare expenses. Employees will also be encouraged to become informed consumers by researching the necessity of procedures, along with the most affordable facilities in which to have their procedures performed.

In the field of compensation, employers will move away from granting across-the-board increases for the entire employee population. Rather, a move will be made towards gaining a greater return on investment by rewarding top performers through the creation of customized rewards packages. Employers will also continue to provide greater transparency to employees regarding the communication of their companies' pay-philosophies.

Equity Compensation

Equity compensation is another form of non-cash compensation; it is used to attract and retain employees to work for a startup company. Employees who decide to work for a startup company often do so to gain real world experience, make a difference in their line of work, and/or to have increased flexibility and a more laid-back office environment. In return, those employees are typically paid a salary that is less than the market. The balance of that salary is given in equity compensation, which is a way for the employees to have an ownership interest in the company. The company gives the employees stock options, allowing them to purchase shares of the company's stock at preset prices. Employees gain control of the option according to a set-vesting schedule, which encourages them to work for the company for many years.

Candidate/Employee Testing Procedures

Conducting Job Analysis

A **job analysis** is a way of systematically gathering and analyzing information about the context, content, and human requirements of jobs within an organization. Typically, a member of Human Resources, an external consultant, or a manager conducts a job analysis. The following methods can be used to gather data during a job analysis to identify the knowledge, skills, and abilities that are needed to qualify an individual to perform a job effectively:

- Observations
- Interviews
- Highly structured questionnaires
- Open-ended questionnaires
- Work logs or work diaries

A job analysis is used to develop or create the following three items:

- **Job descriptions**: A detailed breakdown of specific tasks, skills, and knowledge required for a position. Job descriptions summarize the most important features of a job, include any duties that support exempt status, and also include the physical requirements of the job for consideration under the Americans with Disabilities Act (ADA).

- **Job competencies**: A detailed list of broad skills or traits needed for a position, such as leadership skills or attention to detail. Core competencies are those competencies that are aligned with key business objectives believed to contribute to organizational success.

- **Job specifications**: A detailed description of specific qualifications (i.e., professional licenses or certifications), experience, or education needed to perform the tasks. Job specifications can be included in a separate document or in a separate section of the job description, and they should reflect what is necessary for satisfactory performance in the role, instead of what specific skills the ideal candidate should possess.

Reviewing Essential Job Functions

While updating job descriptions, an employer must also be able to identify and update the essential functions for all positions.

Essential job functions are those tasks and responsibilities that are fundamental to a specific position. Each position is made up of both essential job functions and marginal job functions (duties that are ancillary or incidental to the nature or purpose of the job). For example, essential job functions for a hairstylist are coloring and cutting hair. A marginal job function for a hairstylist may involve answering the telephone to schedule appointments for clients.

There are three main considerations to take into account when determining if a job function is essential or marginal:

- How frequently the task is performed
- The percentage of time spent working on the task
- The importance of the task being completed

Under the Americans with Disabilities Act, for a disabled individual who is qualified, an employer may be asked to make reasonable accommodations to enable them to perform the essential (or core) job functions. That is why it is so important for organizations to properly identify essential job functions in advance.

Establishing Criteria for Hiring, Retaining, and Promoting

Job descriptions should communicate the type of work involved, the difficulty of the work, any unusual elements that may be required, and the frequency with which various tasks need to be performed. Job descriptions should be up to date and reflect current expectations, not past or future expectations, when used as part of the hiring process.

Criteria for job promotions (which can lead to higher retention) involve a number of different factors, such as:

- **Seniority**: An employee's tenure can be a common element and a prerequisite in determining a promotion. For example, a job description may state that, "An employee must have a minimum of two years' experience with the company to be eligible for a promotion."

- **Performance**: An employee's results from their performance reviews can also be a factor. This can be based on a recent assessment or from a longer period. For example, a job description can state "Must have attained 'Expected Level' in annual review for the past three years."

- **Fit**: This is usually determined before the decision to promote and is based on the company's framework of competencies. "Good fit" is determined by comparing an employee's current abilities with those required to perform in the new position.

- **Workforce planning**: If an employee is promoted without an open position created by a vacancy, then it's a general indicator of job progression with increased responsibilities, competencies, etc. Any promotion that requires the old vacancy to be filled requires a manpower and reorganization plan. This is useful for determining promotion eligibility.

Analyzing Labor Market Trends

The supply pool from which employers attract new hires is called the **labor market**. Employers must identify the labor markets (i.e., geographic, global, industry-specific, educational, and technical) from which they can recruit candidates based on the jobs that need to be filled, especially for key positions.

An analysis of labor markets during workforce planning has a number of benefits, including:

- Gaining an understanding of the unemployment rate
- Identifying where employers are competing for labor
- Researching salaries paid for certain positions
- Identifying employment trends in a particular industry

The main federal institution that measures and collates nationwide employment data is the Bureau of Labor Statistics within the US Department of Labor. This department has separate state departments that also report state-specific data. Among the data collected are market activity, average salaries, basic job duties, and working conditions.

Verbal and Written Contracts

Employment Offers and Negotiations

A company goes through the process of analyzing application forms, prescreening, inviting selected candidates to participate in on-site interviews, and conducting any necessary selection tests and background investigations. Then a contingent job offer is made to the top-rated candidate. This is a conditional job offer and may depend on verification of the individual's identity and right to work (under the Immigration Reform and Control Act) and/or the pending results of a medical exam (if it is proven to be consistent with business necessity and is job related).

The next step in the hiring process is extending an employment offer to the top candidate. This is communicated formally through an offer letter. Because time is of the essence, the offer letter is often sent electronically. A job offer can also be extended over the telephone, which is then followed up with a formal offer letter mailed to the candidate. The following items are typically communicated within the offer letter:

- Basic position information: job title, responsibilities, and reporting structure
- Salary information (including guaranteed or discretionary bonuses and signing bonus, if applicable)
- Information about any deferred compensation (i.e., stock option programs)
- Benefits information (i.e., health insurance, short- and long-term disability insurance, retirement plans, etc.)
- Clauses referencing non-compete agreements
- Acceptance details and deadline

An employment-at-will situation is always presumed if there is no written employment contract.

A candidate will frequently reach out to a prospective employer in an attempt to negotiate some terms of the employment offer, such as salary or vacation time. If the employer does not have room to increase the candidate's base salary, a discussion can take place about other perks that the employer may be willing to offer, such as a set number of work-at-home days per month, additional time off during the Christmas holiday or another typical period of down time, use of a company car, relocation assistance (if applicable), or a signing bonus.

If an employer knows there is room to negotiate a base salary with a candidate, it is important for the employer not to offer the highest possible base salary amount in the offer letter, so there is still room to negotiate. Ultimately, it is imperative that the employer be upfront and honest with a candidate about what is possible in terms of negotiation, to stress the value of the corporate benefits that the candidate would receive, and to openly discuss if there is room for growth in the role itself or in other opportunities within the company over time. These can all be convincing reasons for a candidate who is on the fence to choose to accept the employment offer.

It is also important for an employer to know when it is time to stop negotiations with a candidate. Offering a significantly higher salary than what was initially planned to a candidate risks throwing off the internal pay equity of a team and also reducing morale if the other employees find out.

The offer letter is placed in the candidate's personnel file after they have accepted the position and returned a signed hard copy.

New Hire and Orientation

Orientation
Orientation is part of the administrative, transactional aspect of the overall on-boarding process, focused on having employees complete the following types of tasks within their first couple of days of employment:

- Have their photograph taken to create their corporate ID badge
- Take a tour of the building in which they will be working on a daily basis
- Complete I-9 verification
- Register for health care and other company benefits
- Participate in training on the company's time entry system
- Gain an understanding of the payroll process
- Review the company's history, vision, and mission, along with key policies and procedures
- Receive and sign off on a copy of their formal job description

It is also important to note that the workspace for new hires is often set up in advance with the necessary office supplies and a welcome note or card to ensure as smooth of a transition as possible.

Administering Post-Offer Employment Activities
Once a new employee is hired, a number of activities need to be completed for that individual to have a smooth transition into the organization. Some of the typical post-offer activities include:

- Perform any other necessary background checks
- Make copies of the offer letter
- Work with IT and other internal departments to prepare for the new employee's arrival (establish the workstation, create an email account, etc.)
- Prepare the new hire's packet of paperwork that they will need to complete on the first day
- Work to develop an on-boarding plan that includes a list of important people in the company that the new hire should meet
- Inform any internal applicants who were not selected for the position and provide them with feedback
- Notify any external applicants who were not selected for the role

Executing Employment Agreements
Employment-at-will is always presumed when a written employment agreement does not exist; it is a common-law doctrine that states employers have the right to hire, promote, demote, or fire whomever they choose, provided there is not a law or contract in place to the contrary. Under this doctrine, employees are also free to leave an employer whenever they choose to seek other employment.

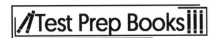

There are two types of employment contracts (agreements): implied and express. **Implied contracts** are inferred from an employer's conduct or actions. An example of an implied contract is when an employer promises an employee job security or hires an employee for an indefinite timeframe. An employee expectation is established, especially when the employer and the employee have enjoyed a long-term business relationship.

An **express contract** is based on an employer's written or oral words and is a formal agreement that outlines the details of the employment arrangement. In the past, these types of contracts were reserved for executive and senior management positions. Now they are also being used for technical and highly specialized employees who possess skills that are harder to come by.

Completing I-9/E-Verify Process

Companies must be vigilant in their verification of new hires' right to work in the United States and their identities via the I-9 process within the first three days of employment. Because timeliness is of the essence, the Department of Homeland Security runs a government program to assist with this process; it is called **E-Verify**. At the current time, use of E-Verify is only mandatory for government contractors and subcontractors. For more information about I-9, please see the content under *Immigration Reform and Control Act (IRCA)* content of the *Federal Laws and Regulations* portion of this section.

Coordinate Relocations

Many companies offer relocation benefits to assist new hires during a very stressful time in their lives. Such benefits can include any or all of the following:

- Paying for temporary living expenses
- Reimbursing for moving fees
- Assisting a "trailing spouse" with their job search
- Allowing for the use of a company car
- Providing financial assistance with selling a home (or buying a new home)

Immigration

Organizations are held responsible for the verification of their new hires' credentials and identities. They must ensure that the documents presented to them (i.e., visas, passports, Social Security cards, etc.) are indeed official and are not fabricated in any way. At any time, the U.S. **Immigration and Customs Enforcement (ICE)** can audit a company's records to guarantee compliance with employment eligibility laws. If a company's Human Resources department is found with fraudulent documents, the company can be held liable. For more information about immigration, please see the *Immigration Reform and Control Act (IRCA)* content of the *Federal Laws and Regulations* portion of this section.

Internal Workforce Assessments

Skills Testing

A **skills audit** is performed for the purpose of identifying the current skills and knowledge within a company and the skills and knowledge the company will need in the future. A successful skills audit ultimately allows management to build a skills matrix that details the skills and competencies that employees need to fulfill each of their roles.

The skills audit begins by putting together a list of all the major roles within the organization, which is not necessarily every single position found on the organizational chart. Then both the technical and behavioral skills for each of these roles are listed. Surveys are created and distributed to the workforce. It is important to tell employees why they are being asked to participate in the surveys and to explain what will be done with the associated survey results. Depending on the size of the workforce, it may not make sense to survey every employee against every skill. The final steps are to compile the results (knowing what skills are required in each role and knowing what skills each employee has) and to analyze the survey data (identifying skill gaps in roles in the company, as well as determining needs for future skills).

Skills Inventory

A **skills inventory** is a listing of a company's current employees' education, skills, and real-world experience, and is typically tracked in an internal database or a commercial software program. There should be a process in place to prompt employees to update their skills inventory so that it remains current, such as prior to annual review time. The skills inventory loses its value if it is not updated in a timely fashion. Managers use the skills inventory to identify gaps between the existing workforce's education, skills, and experience and what they know will be needed to meet present and future business needs. In addition, the skills inventory assists management with making decisions regarding hiring, staffing internal project teams; assigning employees to different areas; and identifying training and development opportunities for staff.

Workforce Demographic Analysis

Workforce demographics are the statistical characteristics, such as gender, income, and age that make up the human population at work. It is important for individuals working in human resource management to study and analyze trends in the labor force because this will help them recruit the specific types of talent that their organization needs. Current trends in workforce demographics include an aging population. In fact, the fastest growing employee population is those individuals in the age group of fifty-five and older. Many of these workers are interested in a phased retirement approach. This will affect organizations as they work to control the rising costs of benefits and health care, focus efforts to re-train older workers, and strive to attract, retain, and train younger employees.

Another current trend in workforce demographics is increased diversity in terms of gender, race, and ethnicity. In today's world, there are more women in the paid labor force than in the past, and employees that fall within the Asian and "other groups" categories are experiencing birthrates and immigration rates above the national average. This will affect organizations as they work to comply with the immigration laws and associated audits and paper trails. In addition, companies must strive to create cultures that value diversity and promote career development and advancement for women and minorities.

A third workforce demographics trend is increased skill deficiencies in the workplace. Many computers now perform routine tasks that employees used to do. Therefore, employers are looking for staff that, more often than not, hold college degrees and possess verbal, mathematical, technical, and interpersonal skills. Companies who are unable to find qualified candidates must agree to train employees on basic skills or partner with a community college or university that will offer basic courses for their staff.

Transition Techniques

Corporate Restructuring

Corporate restructuring involves the act of reorganizing a company to make it more profitable for its present-day situation. Corporate restructuring can take on one of two forms: financial or organizational restructuring.

Financial restructuring may be necessary due to a significant decrease in sales as a result of a poor economy. In this case, a company might make changes to its equity holdings, debt-servicing schedule, and cross-holding pattern based on the recommendations of financial and legal advisors to sustain its profitability.

Organizational restructuring may be necessary as a cost cutting measure, in an attempt by a company to pay off debt and continue with its business operations. In this case, the structure of the organization is changed in some manner, such as through redesigning jobs and changing reporting relationships, reducing the number of hierarchical levels (creating a flatter organization), or a workforce reduction (also known as downsizing).

Mergers and Acquisitions (M&A)

Corporate restructuring that involves **mergers and acquisitions** require complying with certain laws and regulations and also performing due diligence to evaluate a business contract before making any big decisions. **Due diligence** is typically performed when a company is buying another company (acquisition) and helps to uncover any potential liabilities or evaluate business and financial risk.

The due diligence process may involve spending time at the business location, reviewing sales numbers, learning about future plans for expansion, and carefully studying documents with vendors such as purchase order and sales agreements. An attorney may be hired to assist with the due diligence process to check for any discrepancies and verify the validity of certain documents and contracts.

To cut costs, reduce inefficiencies, or recover financially from a recent downturn, a company may decide to dispose of some or all of its business units by selling the company to another company, closing down permanently, declaring bankruptcy, or relocating overseas (offshoring). This is known as divesting a business. Divestitures can help a company better manage its portfolio of assets by closing some units to focus on others, or by selling off one or more business units to recover from a loss.

Metrics to Assess Past and Future Staffing Effectiveness

Cost per Hire

The **cost per hire** is calculated by adding together the external and internal recruiting costs and dividing that amount by the total number of new hires during a specific time period. Examples of external recruiting costs include items such as: advertising the position on job boards, recruitment outsourcing, recruitment technology, background checks and drug testing, and pre-hire assessments. Examples of internal recruiting costs include such items as: in-house recruiting staff, payment of referral rewards, and internal recruiting systems.

Selection Ratios

There are a number of different **selection ratios** used to evaluate recruitment sources. For example, to find the percentage of qualified applicants, the number of qualified applicants is divided by the number of total applicants for a particular position. The percentage of minority applicants is calculated by taking the number of minority applicants divided by the total number of applicants for a position. Additionally, the percentage of offers accepted is the number of offers accepted divided by the number of offers that were extended.

Adverse Impact

There are two types of discrimination: disparate treatment and disparate or adverse impact. **Disparate treatment** occurs when an employer treats protected classes differently than other employees. Examples of disparate treatment include holding genders to different standards, sexual harassment, and blatantly rejecting a member of a protected class due to stereotypes.

A famous disparate treatment case was McDonnell Douglas Corporation vs. Green. Green was a black employee who was laid off during a regular reduction in force. He protested at the company (as part of a group), chained and locked company doors, and blocked an entrance to company property. His activities did not please the company. When the company began hiring again, they advertised, and Green reapplied. He was denied, and the company continued looking for candidates. Green claimed the rejection was due to his race and his involvement in civil rights activities. This was a precedent-setting EEO case that established criteria for disparate treatment and ruled that a *prima facie* (at first glance) case can be shown if an employee:

- Belongs to a protected class
- Applied for a job when the employer sought applicants
- Was qualified and yet rejected
- Was rejected but the employer kept looking

In disparate treatment cases, an individual must prove:

- They are a member of a protected class
- They applied for a job for which they were qualified and for which the employer was seeking applicants
- They were not hired even though they were qualified
- After they did not get the job, the position remained open and the employer continued to receive applications

Adverse impact refers to a form of discrimination where an employer's policy seems neutral but in fact has an adverse impact on a certain group or a certain characteristic such as race, sex, or disability. This was identified by the Supreme Court in 1971 in the case of Griggs v. Duke Power Co., where it was proven that the requirement of a high school diploma for higher-paid positions was unfairly affecting African-American employees in lower-paid labor positions who had a history of receiving inferior education.

As another example, if an employer requires a potential employee for a position to be at least 5'10'', it may exclude an entire group, such as women. Because statistically, men are taller, this requirement is based solely on biological reasons rather than if the candidate can adequately perform the required role.

An employer discriminating based on certain physical elements, however, can be justified if it is in correlation with job requirements. For example, it is necessary for a fire department to discriminate based on height, facial hair, or grooming to ensure the safety of its employees.

Turnover Statistics

Turnover is typically calculated on either a monthly or an annual basis. Analyzing turnover is necessary to accurately forecast the number of new employees that are needed to replace individuals who have recently moved out of job positions. To calculate turnover, the number of separations per year is divided by the average number of individuals employed per month, multiplied by 100. For example, if fifty individuals separated during the year and there is an average of two hundred individuals employed per month, the turnover rate is:

$$\frac{50}{200} \times 100 = 25\%$$

Glossary

Active Candidates	Those engaging in a search for new employment, whether they're already employed or unemployed
Adverse Impact	Form of discrimination where an employer's policy seems neutral but in fact has an adverse impact on a certain group or a certain characteristic
Aging	Process of adjusting salary data to keep pace with market movement
Applicant Tracking System	Method used to make the selection process more effective by utilizing a software application to electronically process a company's recruitment needs
Behavioral Interview	Interviewers asking candidates to use specific examples to describe how they have handled a problem or performed a task in a past work situation
Corporate Restructuring	Act of reorganizing a company in order to make it more profitable for its present-day situation
Cost Per Hire	Calculated by adding together the external and internal recruiting costs and dividing that amount by the total number of new hires during a specific time period
Delphi Method	Questionnaires are sent to a variety of experts, the results are shared, and then choices are updated.
Disparate Treatment	Occurs when an employer treats protected classes differently than other employees
Diversity Groups	Includes groups for African Americans, Asian Americans, Latino Americans, disability awareness, LGBTQIA+, former members of the military, multicultural, emerging professionals, and women
Driving History Checks	Relate to an individual's driving record and verify that they are able to drive safely
Due Diligence	Typically performed when a company is buying another company (acquisition) and helps to uncover any potential liabilities or evaluate business and financial risk
Education References	Any certifications, degrees, diplomas, licenses, or any professional documents that can validate an applicant's knowledge and education
Employee Referrals	Can serve as a great tool when recruiting for positions requiring specialized skills that are difficult to fill via regular recruiting methods
Employee Survey	An additional tool that can be used by companies to gather input on needs or preferences regarding compensation and benefits programs, as well as employees' satisfaction with the existing offerings
Employment References	Feedback from past employers, co-workers, customers, or clients who can verify the individual's professional experience
Employment-At-Will	Common-law doctrine that states employers have the right to hire, promote, demote, or fire whomever they choose
Equal Employment Opportunity (EEO) Reporting	Annual workforce data reporting is required for all employers with one hundred or more employees and federal contractors with at least fifty employees and contracts of $50,000.
Equal Employment Opportunity Commission (EEOC)	Enforces and oversees laws against workplace discrimination
Equity Compensation	Another form of non-cash compensation; it is used to attract and retain employees to work for a startup company.
Essential Job Functions	Tasks and responsibilities that are fundamental to a specific position
E-Verify	Government program run by the Department of Homeland Security to assist with verifying future employees' rights to work in the U.S.
Expert Forecasting	Utilizes industry experts who are able to make decisions based on wider changes in the industry
Express Contract	Based on an employer's written or oral words, this is a formal agreement that outlines the details of the employment arrangement.

External Recruiting	Seeks individuals from outside the organization for employment and usually emphasizes the advantages of employment with the organization, advertising benefits such as pay, insurance, leave, or employee discounts
Fair Labor Standard Act Of 1938 (FLSA)	Establishes standards for a minimum wage, overtime pay, recordkeeping, and child labor standards
Financial Reference Checks	Relates to credit history and how an individual handles money
Financial Restructuring	A company might make changes to its equity holdings, debt-servicing schedule, and cross-holding pattern based on the recommendations of financial and legal advisors to sustain its profitability.
Forecasting	Methods used by companies to determine staffing needs are known as qualitative and quantitative forecasting
Health Saving Accounts (HSAs)	Sometimes called health reimbursement arrangements (HRAs), these assist in funding employees' out-of-pocket healthcare expenses.
Immigration And Customs Enforcement (ICE)	Can audit a company's records to guarantee compliance with employment eligibility laws
Implied Contracts	Inferred from an employer's conduct or actions
Interview	Allows an employer to further evaluate a candidate's skills and knowledge while giving the candidate a chance to demonstrate their abilities
Job Analysis	Way of systematically gathering and analyzing information about the context, content, and human requirements of jobs within an organization
Job Competencies	Detailed list of broad skills or traits needed for a position, such as leadership skills or attention to detail
Job Descriptions	A detailed breakdown of specific tasks, skills, and knowledge required for a position.
Job Sharing	Involves two or more employees performing the tasks of a role normally performed by one person
Job Specifications	Detailed description of specific qualifications (i.e., professional licenses or certifications), experience, or education needed to perform the tasks
Labor Market	Supply pool from which employers attract new hires
Leveling	Can be used if a job included on the salary survey is similar—but not identical—to a position within the organization
Management Forecasting	Involves determining staffing needs from the managers of each department and making decisions by using their reports
McNamara-O'Hara Service Contract Act Of 1965 (SCA)	Applies to contractors and subcontractors working on service contracts exceeding $2,500
Nearshore	Vendor is in a country adjacent to the business
Negligent Hiring	This takes place when an employer hires an employee, and the employer either knew or should have known that the employee posed a risk to other employees or to customers.
Non-Directive Interview	Utilizes open-ended questions that may be developed from an applicant's answers to previous questions
Offshore	Vendor is in a country far from the business
Onshore	Vendor is located within the same country as the business
Organizational Restructuring	The structure of the organization is changed in some manner, such as through redesigning jobs and changing reporting relationships, reducing the number of hierarchical levels (creating a flatter organization), or a workforce reduction (also known as downsizing).
Orientation	Part of the administrative, transactional aspect of the overall on-boarding process, focused on having employees complete tasks within their first couple of days of employment

Outsourcing	Practice of delegating work responsibilities in a business to a separate third-party individual or organization not associated with the company
Passive Candidates	Those who are employed but not looking for work
Phased Retirement	Involves both the cutting back of working hours (or days of work) and the phasing in of retirement benefits such as Social Security funds
Probability Model	Mathematical representation used to predict future changes
Qualitative Forecasting	Based on the opinions and estimations of industry experts or managers
Quantitative Forecasting	Based on raw mathematical data and previous trends, such as employee productivity and output
Ratio Analyses	Compare current with past employment ratios to determine where staffing needs may change, such as the number of employees to the number of products made
Recruit From Within	Some of the most common strategies to find potential candidates include internal announcements, job bidding, and promotion plans.
Recruiting	Procedures and strategies designed to encourage and find potential, qualified candidates who seek employment
Reference Checks	These can verify if an individual has the necessary skills, knowledge, and experience, based on prior job performance, while also validating an individual's application for employment.
Reference List	The individual provides the references after a prospective employer asks for them.
Rehabilitation Act	Passed in 1973 to prohibit employment discrimination based on physical or mental disabilities
Selection Ratios	Used to evaluate recruitment sources
Semi-Active Candidates	Are not actively looking for work but are preparing themselves for new opportunities
Semi-Structured Interviews	Occur when interviewers have guided conversations with applicants that involve both broad questions and new questions that come about from the discussions that take place
Separation Agreement and General Release	Document that employees who are laid off are typically asked to sign
Situational Interviews	Conducted by a group of individuals from the organization, that may consist of managers and other future team members, in order to better evaluate whether or not a candidate is suitable
Skills Audit	Performed for the purpose of identifying the current skills and knowledge within a company and the skills and knowledge the company will need in the future
Skills Inventory	A listing of a company's current employees' education, skills, and real-world experience
Social Networking/Media	A company's social media recruiting strategy allows candidates to view job openings and gain a better understanding of the company's personality and culture. It is important for companies to designate an individual who will respond to candidates' questions and concerns in a timely manner.
Structured Interview	Controlled by the interviewer, who has a list of specific, job-related questions prepared prior to the start of the interview
Succession Planning	Practice of identifying and evaluating specific employees to fill leadership positions within an organization.
Title VII	Originally part of the Civil Rights Act of 1964, this prohibits employers from discriminating against employees on the basis of sex, race, color, national original, and religion.
Trend Analyses	Compare single amounts instead of ratios, such as the number of employees

Turnover Rate	Percentage of employees who leave the workforce during a period of time, typically during a calendar or fiscal year; To calculate turnover rate, simply take the number of employees who exited the company during the year, divide it by the average number of employees during the year, and then multiply that amount by 100.
Turnover Analyses	Compare the number of employees who leave the company over a certain period of time with past data
Uniform Guidelines on Employee Selection Procedures (UGESP)	Provides standards on what constitutes discriminatory hiring practices
Unstructured Interviews	Interviewers improvise and ask applicants questions that were not prepared prior to the start of the interview
Workforce Demographics	The statistical characteristics, such as gender, income, and age that make up the human population at work
Workforce Planning	Any promotion that requires the old vacancy to be filled requires a manpower and reorganization plan.
Workforce Reductions	The planned elimination of a number of personnel in order to make an organization more competitive

Practice Quiz

1. A detailed description of specific qualifications, experience, or education that is needed to perform tasks is known as which of the following?
    a. Job description
    b. Job specification
    c. Job competency
    d. Job analysis

2. Which type of interview occurs when an interviewer has guided conversations with applicants that involve broad questions and new questions that come about from the discussions that take place?
    a. Semi-structured
    b. Structured
    c. Non-directive
    d. Unstructured

3. Which of the following pre-employment activities can assist companies with protecting themselves from lawsuits or damage to their reputation?
    a. Interviewing
    b. Selection tests
    c. Reference and background checks
    d. Employment agreements

4. Which of the following statements is true regarding Title VII of the Civil Rights Act of 1964?
    a. Equal working conditions must be provided to all employees.
    b. Discrimination against sex and race is prohibited.
    c. All employees must be provided with an equal opportunity to participate in training.
    d. Sexual harassment training must be provided to all employees.

5. The Americans with Disabilities Act applies to which of the following?
    a. An employer with fifty or more employees
    b. All employers regardless of their size
    c. Employers who have at least $50,000 in federal contracts
    d. An employer with fifteen or more employees

See answers on next page.

Answer Explanations

1. B: Job specification is a detailed description of specific qualifications, experience, or education that is needed to perform tasks. Choice *A,* job description, is a detailed breakdown of specific tasks, skills, and knowledge required for a position. Job competency, Choice *C,* is a detailed list of broad skills or traits needed for a position. Finally, job analysis, Choice *D,* is a way of gathering and analyzing information systemically about the context, content, and human resource requirements of jobs within an organization.

2. A: A semi-structured interview occurs when an interviewer has guided conversations with applicants that involve broad questions and new questions that come about from the discussions that take place. A structured interview, Choice *B,* is controlled by the interviewer, who has a list of specific, job-related questions prepared prior to the start of the interview. The same questions are asked of all applicants. A non-directive interview, Choice *C,* utilizes questions that are developed from an applicant's answers to previous questions. Finally, Choice *D,* an unstructured interview, takes place when an interviewer improvises and asks applicants questions that were not prepared prior to the start of the interview.

3. C: Reference and background checks are pre-employment activities that can assist companies with protecting themselves from lawsuits or damage to their reputation (for example, in the event of negligent hiring claims). Interviewing candidates, Choice *A,* may not reveal all pertinent information. Choices *B* and *D,* selection tests and employment agreements, do not provide information that would protect the company's interests.

4. B: Title VII of the Civil Rights Act of 1964 prohibits discrimination against sex and race.

5. D: The Americans with Disabilities Act applies to employers with fifteen or more employees. The number of value of federal contracts an employer has is irrelevant.

Learning and Development

Responsibilities

Professional Growth and Development Consultation

HR should connect employees from all levels of the organization with the professional growth and development opportunities that best fit their needs. The first way to do this is to actually understand what their needs are by communicating directly with workers from various job roles. Through structured interviews and informal conversations, HR can assess what challenges employees are facing in their roles, where skill gaps exist, and what core competencies will be needed in the company in the future. This involves aligning individual employee development with the organization's overall needs.

Especially for managers, HR should promote professional development opportunities that will help prepare managers for future leadership roles with increased responsibilities. This is part of succession planning, or preparation for the next generation of leadership while ensuring that essential skills and knowledge are not lost. This consultation might involve participation of current leaders to give insight into what skills and knowledge are necessary to move into the next level of business; benchmarking with other organizations to determine what education, licenses, and other qualifications are valued by their leadership; and conversation with managers to uncover their future professional goals. While professional development for higher-level positions may take place outside of the organization by means of earning a higher degree or license, there may also be opportunities within the organization for a lower-level manager to participate in a mentorship with a higher-level manager.

The same ideas also apply to other employees. HR should assess the company's needs, the employee's needs, and find opportunities that align with both. Although some companies worry that professional development will simply lead to qualified employees who then leave the company for jobs elsewhere, research shows that professional development opportunities are closely tied to employee engagement and retention. If employees see how their professional development can translate into increased opportunities within the company, they are less likely to seek opportunities elsewhere. Find out what career paths and professional challenges employees want to tackle within the organization. Again, there are also low-cost options for development within the organization, such as coaching, mentoring, so-called stretch assignments (assigning employees tasks that are a step above their current skills or responsibilities), job shadowing, and cross-training or job rotation.

Career Development and Training Programs

Career Development
Career development encompasses six primary stages: assessment, investigation, preparation, commitment, retention, and transition. Career development is an important process when attempting to make a person attractive to prospective employers. During the **assessment** stage, a person begins to realize that they are unsure about their values, weaknesses, interests, and strengths. This stage requires a conscious effort on behalf of the person to begin an exploration process. In the **investigation** phase, a person begins to search for opportunities that the world of work has to offer. After the investigation stage, a person has acquired knowledge about what best suits them and begins **preparation**. The **commitment** stage comes after a person recognizes their talents, prompting a commitment to a

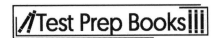

particular job or career. After a person feels most comfortable in their career, they begin to sharpen their skills and become acclimated with the industry—this is the **retention** stage. Lastly, the **transition** stage forces a person to assess their happiness and make connections to a new career.

In addition to career development, there are other ways that enable a person to advance their career. Other methods include support programs, employee counseling, training workshops, and coaching programs. **Support programs**, which attempt to remedy personal and utility problems, create channels for employers to assist employees who are not maximizing their potential with training or counseling. Similarly, to support programs, **employee counseling** is an institutional program used by employers to maximize productivity within the organizational structure. **Training workshops** enable employers and employees to identify particular skills and ensure that they are placed in a position of maximum utility. **Coaching workshops** place workers under the supervision of a counselor to equip them with the tools to solve problems that may be inhibiting their work capacities.

To create an environment that allows all workers to maximize their potential in an organizational structure, employers offer programs that are designed to benefit the career development of employees. A few of these methods are evaluating, mentoring, counseling, and coaching. A proper **evaluation** of the deficiencies, skills, and psychological health of employees is important to identify their strengths and weaknesses, while determining their most efficient roles in the organization. **Mentoring** programs for employees are a critical component to making sure that they are under guardianship at a professional and emotional level. Counseling in the workplace permits employees to be given additional personal and professional support. Under the supervision of professional counselors, workshops that offer coaching to employees can bolster both organizational and personal health.

Over the course of their careers, individuals often use various methods to enrich their careers. Some of these methods include networking, pursuing supplementary formal education, and attending training workshops. Networking permits individuals to build beneficial connections with people who may be able to help them obtain employment. At networking events, an individual will attempt to speak to as many people as possible to establish relationships. When job searching, individuals may discover that many opportunities require more skills than they possess. To remedy this problem, many people pursue additional education to make them more marketable and attractive to prospective employers. Training workshops are events designated to let individuals discover their skills, allowing them to pursue careers that correspond to them.

Succession Planning Discussion

Succession planning involves preparing current employees for future advancements or promotions by developing their knowledge, skills, and abilities. Ongoing training for any potential open position in the company ensures no loss of productivity or operational efficiency, should key employees leave.

Some common succession planning techniques employers use include special assignments, creating team leadership roles, and sending staff to internal and external training for their continued development. This can also be used as a retention tactic, as employees may recognize the benefit of staying with a company when they can see a clear path toward promotion.

Knowledge of

Federal Laws and Regulations Related to Learning and Development Activities

Copyright Act of 1976

The **Copyright Act of 1976** is the foundational law in the United States regarding property ownership of film, radio, musical and dramatic works, literary and pictorial works, and architectural structures. Superseding local and state copyright laws, the statute establishes a standardized and universally applied measure to the country's major social and technological transformations in media. Hitherto the act, there were deficient authorship protections that had the capacity to safeguard creative works and lawfully secure remunerative rewards. Written with a broad intent, the landmark legislation is applicable to "original works of authorship fixed in any tangible medium of expression."

To lawfully reproduce, disseminate, modify, publicly display, or perform copyrighted material, one must hold a copyright over such material, published or unpublished. Stipulated by the Copyright Act of 1976, a copyright lasts for the duration of the author's life, plus an additional seventy years after their death. However, the law incorporates a policy of "fair use." **Fair use** enumerates some instances in which a person may use copyrighted material.

Fair Use

The Copyright Act of 1976 specifies instances in which protected material can be used without threat of infringement. These selective requirements fall into the jurisdiction of "fair use." The first qualification is the intended purpose of the work. Is it intended for commercial gain or for non-profit education? Secondly, fair use is determined by the nature or type of work in question. Thirdly, the amount or proportion of the copyrighted work is evaluated. Lastly, the potential variation in market value of copyrighted material is determined. Educational purposes, research, criticism, scholarship, comment, teaching, or news reporting are the categories specifically noted that would determine the applicability of fair use.

Public Domain

When any of the works delineated have no copyright, they enter into the **public domain**. In the public domain, any person can use these works freely. In order for a work to not be protected by federal copyright law, it needs to meet one of two conditions. If the federal government publishes the work, it is regarded as public, and therefore is exempt from copyright infringement. Expiration is the only other way an article would lose copyright protection. Works created on or after January 1, 1978, are protected for the life of the author and seventy years after their death; anonymous works, works-made-for-hire, and articles are protected for ninety-five years from the date of creation or 120 years after being published. Works-made-for-hire include works made by employees or works that are specially ordered or commissioned.

Title 17

Title 17 is a United States copyright law enacted in 1947. It applies to authorship of any tangible medium of expression. Specific works that fall under Title 17 are literary works, architectural works, musical recordings, pictures and graphics, choreographic works, musical works, motion pictures, and audio works.

U.S. Patent Act

The **U.S. Patent Act** expressly prohibits the unauthorized use, sale, reproduction, or distribution of the product without the consent of the patent holder. The legislation's broad composition is designed to preserve and protect the property of inventors. Furthermore, one of two conditions must be met in order for protections to be granted by the act to apply: the invention in question must be created in the United States or the invention must be imported into the country. Although the law explains several prohibitions regarding the unsanctioned use, sale, reproduction, or distribution of an invention, it does not specify any legal recourse in the event of infringement of a particular patent.

Patent Types

There are three types of patents in the United States: utility, design, and plant. The most common type of patent is a utility patent. A **utility patent** involves anything technological, mechanical, chemical, pharmaceutical, or software-related. Utility patents are valid for twenty years after the date the patent is filed. To obtain a utility patent, one must provide a written and meticulously detailed description of the product. The second type of patent is a design patent. **Design patents** are valid for fourteen years after the date they are filed. Unique to the United States, this patent comprises ornamental design—specifically, the way a product looks (aesthetics) and how it actually works. For instance, when applying for a design patent for a bookcase, the inventor must exhibit how it is assembled, how much weight it can withstand, and the size screws that must be used to give it requisite support. A **plant patent** can be filed for an asexually reproducible plant discovered in a cultivated area. These patents last for twenty years after the date they are filed. Plant patents are the least common type of patent.

Trademark Act

The **Trademark Act** was created to provide for the protection and registration of trademarks and service marks.

Title VII

Title VII is a federal law within the Civil Rights Act of 1964. It stipulates that no person shall be discriminated against on the basis of sex, race, color, national origin, and religion. Although Title VII is a federal law, it applies to state and local governments as well. Moreover, the law applies to private and public colleges and universities, private sector employment, and labor unions. Under this law, all employees are guaranteed equal access to career development and training.

Americans with Disabilities Act

The **Americans with Disabilities Act (ADA)** is a federal law that outlaws discrimination based on disability. The ADA precludes discrimination based on race, sex, national origin, and religion. Moreover, the law requires that employers provide reasonable accommodations to employees who have a disability. For instance, this could require employers to build a wheelchair accessible ramp for disabled employers to enter and leave the building. Also, the ADA stipulates that public spaces be accessible for disabled persons. Under this law, all employees are guaranteed equal access to career development and training.

Additionally, all employees are also guaranteed equal access to career development and training under the **Age Discrimination in Employment Act (ADEA)** and the **Uniformed Services Employment and Reemployment Rights Act (USERRA)**.

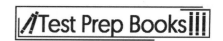

Learning and Development Theories

ADDIE Model

The most commonly used framework that organizations and training developers use to enhance human resource development programs is the **ADDIE model**. Each step in the multi-dimensional and adaptable ADDIE model is intended to bolster programs that bolster systems of personal development and training. As an acronym, each step characterizes a different phase: *A* denotes the Analysis phase, *D* denotes Design, *D* denotes Development, *I* denotes Implementation, and *E* denotes Evaluation. The ADDIE model is not limited to strictly training programs and is widely accepted by educators, instructional designers, industry leaders, and the U.S. Armed Forces. ADDIE is noted for being highly applicable to any project and for its flexibility in practice.

The initial phase of ADDIE is **analysis** wherein the course and primary learning objectives are evaluated and determined. The trainees' potential and aptitude for the subject are assessed and determined, along with any significant learning limitations. The timeline for project completion is also determined during this initial phase.

The second phase in the ADDIE model is the **design** phase where the principal architecture of the training course is constructed. Aside from just learning objectives, relevant subject matter is gathered and determined while exercises are planned. After these are considered, a lesson plan must be carefully fashioned that synthesizes the objectives of the course and the specific abilities or constraints of the subject.

The third phase in the ADDIE model is the **development** phase. After the design of the course is constructed, its methodological efficacy needs to be tested. Creating the content that is drafted in the previous phase performs this test. Development encompasses creating and distributing tangible tools or courseware for successfully engaging the program. For instance, graphics, handouts, or any other learning technologies would be circulated.

The fourth phase in the ADDIE model is the **implementation** phase. The implementation phase consists of establishing a procedure for training both facilitators and learners. Facilitators should continuously amend the course to maximize efficiency. After extensive analysis, the course should be amended and redesigned accordingly. For learners, this phase embodies preparation and gaining increasing familiarity with the course and content. In addition, learners should also develop an acute knowledge of the course materials and tools.

The fifth phase of the ADDIE model is the **evaluation** phase. Although the course is constantly being evaluated, this is a designated phase that empirically studies the efficiency and productivity of the course and material. Some of the questions that may be asked include: Were the course's primary objectives met? Were the learners' specified goals achieved? What (if any) were the most arduous aspects of the course or its materials, and how could any problems be appropriately addressed?

Training Program Facilitation, Techniques, and Delivery

Learning Techniques

Organizations often employ several methods when attempting to teach new knowledge, capacities, or skills. A few of the principal methods instructors use to train subjects are lectures, group discussions, case studies, and demonstrations. A **lecture** is the act of an educator verbally articulating how to

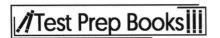
perform a task or a branch of knowledge. Educators plan a **group discussion** when they want students to work cooperatively. These permit students to engage collectively, verbalize key concepts, and improve aptitudes for listening and comprehension. **Case studies** give students the opportunity to situate themselves into real world, tangible scenarios. This brand of training allows students to think critically about how they would approach problem solving. A **demonstration** is a type of training that presents students with the opportunity to observe an educator in the act of performing a task.

Learning Styles

When considering a particular avenue of training, it is important to determine which will create an experience that will be conducive to learning. It is important to create in-class activities that will appeal to the various learning styles: visual, auditory, and kinesthetic. **Visual learners** prefer to associate information with images (e.g., watching videos or looking at PowerPoint slides) while **auditory learners** depend on hearing and speaking to learn (e.g., listening to lectures and participating in group discussions). **Kinesthetic learners** benefit most from participating in physical, hands-on activities (e.g., looking at the inside of an automobile or taking apart some type of model).

The most crucial objective for the educator is not to strictly possess understanding and expertise of the particular subject matter, but to also be able to articulate and impart those skills in an effective manner to others. A useful barometer for evaluating the efficacy of an instructor is to conduct a thorough evaluation of their students. If students demonstrate an aptitude for the particular knowledge, ability, or skill being taught, then one can safely assume that the faculties and techniques of the instructor can be considered proficient. Discussion, demonstration, and communication are all equally integral components of training.

Seating Arrangements

Seating arrangements are an important configuration that can severely impact the flow of ideas within a training program.

Theater-style seating reflects a movie theater setting; all seats are facing the same direction. However, there is no room for taking notes or consuming food or beverages. In addition, without adequate space, leaving while a meeting is in progress can be distracting and cumbersome.

Classroom-style seating remedies the problem of the lack of ability to take notes and consume food and drink, but such a close seating arrangement leaves room for distractions.

Herringbone-style seating may be a more effective solution to prevent chatter during a meeting, but the problem of navigating the boardroom is still present.

U-shape-seating style is frequently used when presentations are being given, allowing presenters to more easily interact and engage audience members. However, since a majority of audience members are not facing the presenter, keeping the focus on the presenter can be difficult.

Horseshoe-seating style resembles the U-shape-seating style, but without desks. This allows the audience to focus on the presenters more easily, but without desks, there is inadequate space for audience members to take notes.

Hollow square-seating style is similar to the U-shaped-seating style, but it is fully enclosed on all four sides. This permits all audience members to face each other and for a presenter to fully engage them, but it fails to provide a focal point for a presenter.

Similar to the hollow square seating style, the **boardroom-seating** style features long tables for audience members to lean on, permitting audience members to face each other encourages interactions and exchanges. Unfortunately, this arrangement does not allow presenters to engage with and approach the audience.

Banquet-seating style provides circular tables for audience members to lean on and is designed to encourage discussion and dialogue. However, this style places audience members at different tables, which precludes a unified discourse.

Cabaret-seating style is slightly more attractive than banquet-seating style because it leaves an open space at each table as a focal point for a presenter. However, it does not sufficiently address the issue of separate tables.

Cocktail-seating style allows for audience members to move freely and roam as they wish. However, in the absence of desks or tables, there is no room to take notes or consume food or drink.

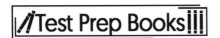

Pilot Programs

In order for an organization to develop a large-scale project, it must launch a pilot program to test the feasibility of the intended project. Also called a feasibility study or an experimental trial, **pilot programs** are small-scale and should not be of significant cost. Before investing substantial time, financial, or human resources into a project, organizations need to determine its revenue-wielding potential, logistical considerations, and possible planning or structural deficiencies. Pilot programs are tests or trials that sample a small group of people and use empirical analyses to improve strategies.

Types of Training Programs

Harassment Prevention

To for an organization to successfully meet its goals, it must preclude any form of harassment from occurring. Aside from moral incentives, there are also major financial incentives for employers preventing harassment of all forms. From burdensome legal costs to potential loss of clients, harassment suits can incur significant costs for an organization. To abate the possibility of situations of harassment, employers should design programs in which employees must participate and establish a policy of zero tolerance.

Leadership Skills

Quality leadership skills are essential to any organization, and thus, leadership training is typically provided to mid and upper management. Signs of effective leadership skills are strategic thinking, solving problems as they come, and managing time in the most financially responsible manner. While these skills are essential, there are also more human characteristics that must be mentioned. A successful leader must have the ability to: build confidence within their organization, obtain the trust of others, inspire others, and engender a sense of pride and purpose within their company.

Computer Skills

In a world of increasing competition where technology has become integral, it is imperative that employers invest in research and technology to constantly find cheaper and more efficient ways to increase productivity. In addition, employees should be well trained in the latest technological machinery. The task to remain competitive must lay with employers and employees. While employers must provide the tools, employees need to be proficient in the proper use of those tools to be productive.

Adult Learning Processes

Although many education principles remain consistent across various age groups, there are specific concerns to consider in the **adult learning process**, and particularly in job-related learning. Notable adult educator Malcolm Knowles adopted the theory of **andragogy**, or adult education—as distinct from **pedagogy**, or children's education—to describe some of the differences. In particular, in education contexts structured for children, instructors are responsible for guiding, motivating, and evaluating learners, and learners follow the topic, structure, and pace set by the instructor. However, according to the theory of andragogy, adult learners tend to be more self-motivated and have a higher capacity for self-evaluation.

One way to incorporate this into the workplace is to offer more opportunities for employees to self-evaluate their strengths and weaknesses, and to identify and select areas in which they would like to improve themselves. The higher level of involvement in choosing and directing their own learning process also makes adult learners more engaged in what they are learning. Unlike children, who learn things because they are told to, adult learners need to be involved in deciding what is important to them—if they can see how an education program will benefit their career or help them gain desired skills, they will perform better. To assist in this, HR must understand employees' career goals and provide information about the success rate of its recommended continuing education programs, such as showing how completing a specific certification increases the chances of getting a promotion.

Another difference—and strong advantage—for adult learners is their wealth of experience. During training sessions, allow experienced employees to share any relevant insights. They can apply what they know from firsthand experience to new concepts and strategies. In group learning situations, this can also help bridge the gap between newer and more seasoned workers. Real-life application of what they are learning is key for adult learners.

Adult learning programs are often structured on the experiential learning process developed by David Kolb. His description of the adult learning process involves four steps: experiencing, reflecting, thinking, and applying. This process accounts for the fact that adult learners approach their education with real-world experience, an ability to self-evaluate and think critically about workplace problems, and a desire to see real benefits from applying what they learn.

First, learners begin by **experiencing** something directly, thereby gaining a concrete experience in the target topic. Then they are asked to **reflect** on that experience by comparing it with what they already know or have experienced. Next, after making those reflective observations, students enter the **thinking** stage; based on their observations, they come up with abstract ideas about how things work. Finally, they **apply** these ideas through active experimentation, which is a chance to try out the results of their critical thinking and see what works.

This learning cycle is a highly recursive process, as application of knowledge often leads to new observations and new ideas. An example of this process in action might involve showing an employee a demonstration of a new piece of project management software (experiencing), allowing them to compare it with their existing project management methods (reflecting), letting them think of ways this new software could better perform key tasks (thinking), and then asking them to model a project with those new ideas (applying).

Instructional Design Principles and Processes

Needs Analysis

A **needs analysis** is the process in which an organization gathers information about the principal needs and requests of its members. This analysis studies the expectations and requirements of subjects who are affected by workplace programs or regulations. Such individuals may include employers, teachers, administrators, donors, and family members of students. Needs analysis results may be used to clarify the objectives of an organization, or as a teaching tool in a classroom.

A needs analysis typically starts by gathering data. This process can be accomplished through a multitude of channels such as surveys, interviews, questionnaires, or polls. In a needs analysis, problems and inefficiencies are clearly identified. These issues are ultimately addressed by the organization through the implementation of improvements to maximize results. A needs analysis may serve as an efficient means of examining organizational procedures and techniques of training at minimal cost.

Additionally, a needs analysis can be a helpful tool to develop occupational injury prevention programs within an organization.

If the needs analysis is conducted properly, the organization's next step is to implement the suggested changes in a way that promotes success. This endeavor requires the allocation of resources and personnel to the proposed plan. The proposed changes should meet the organization's productivity targets and fulfill the requirements of governmental agencies.

Process Flow Mapping

Instructional design requires analysis of the overall learning process. One way to visualize this is through process flow mapping (sometimes also called a process flowchart). **Process flow mapping** creates a visualization of the steps in a process, as well as how those steps are connected to each other, allowing planners to see the key decision areas.

In instructional design, one of the most common process models is the **ADDIE model**: analysis, design, development, implementation, and evaluation. By mapping out these steps during the planning process, HR can ensure that educational programs are as effective and efficient as possible. The first step, analysis, involves identifying areas where employees would most benefit from additional training. Design involves the ideas behind the program, while development involves turning the ideas into an actionable program. In the implementation step, the program is actually utilized in the workplace. Finally, evaluation allows HR to review the effectiveness of the program and gather data for improving future initiatives. In translating this model into a process flowchart, any individual step can be further broken into more detailed processes as needed (for example, the design stage might identify steps in research and consulting).

Assessing Training Program Effectiveness

A **training needs assessment** is conducted to determine whether a training program will be an adequate solution to correct a performance issue. A training program might be an appropriate solution when poor performance is due to an employee's lack of knowledge or skills, legislation requiring new knowledge or skills, higher performance standards, new technology, or placement in new jobs. On the flip side, the creation and implementation of a training program will not be effective in resolving poor performance that results from a recruiting, selection, or compensation issue, failure to provide proper coaching and feedback to an employee, problems with an employee's physical work environment, or a lack of employee motivation. These particular issues are best addressed through a non-training intervention, such as job redesign, improved communication and employee feedback, and goal-setting.

A thorough training needs assessment involves an organizational analysis, a task analysis, and a learner analysis. The **organizational analysis** is conducted to ensure that the company is on board with the training initiative and will be supportive. The goal is to ensure that the training is aligned with the overall business strategy, supported by the necessary stakeholders, and that available resources are committed to the training program. Data is gathered for this analysis from holding focus groups of mid-level and senior-level managers, since they are the individuals who make decisions regarding training budget allocations and strategic planning. The organizational analysis is performed first, as there is no reason to move forward with the task and learner analyses if low interest or support for the training is found.

It is important to note that the task analysis and learner analysis can be completed simultaneously. The **task analysis** focuses on specific tasks employees must complete to successfully perform their jobs. Data is gathered through interviews with or surveys of individuals, such as managers, top-performing employees, or subject matter experts (SMEs), who have direct knowledge of the work tasks and the associated, expected level of performance. The overall goal of a task analysis is to define what good performance looks like in the jobs that are chosen to be analyzed. A list of tasks that are performed in each of the jobs that are being analyzed is created. The individuals being interviewed/surveyed are asked to rate the frequency with which the tasks are completed, the importance each task has to the overall work, and the difficulty of each task. The results from this analysis are used to identify performance gaps in either desired or actual employee performance and to then decide if training can be used to address those gaps. If the decision is to move forward with a training program intervention, then the information from this analysis can also be used in the training design process.

The **learner analysis** identifies if the employees' performance issues are occurring due to a lack of knowledge, skills, and abilities, or due to some other issue, such as a lack of motivation or insufficient tools. During this analysis, it is important to determine if the learners are cognitively and physically able to complete their assigned tasks. Moreover, it is crucial to ascertain if the learners understand the level of performance that is expected of them and to determine if they are indeed receiving accurate and timely feedback regarding their performance. Additionally, the learner analysis identifies which employees are in need of the training and determine their readiness for training. Data is gathered from managers, learners, and document reviews, such as personnel records and previous training records.

Data gathering methods that are used during a training needs assessment include: observation, questionnaires (surveys), interviews, focus groups, and document reviews. Each method has its pros and cons, and some methods may be more realistic to use than others considering time and resources constraints. It can also be helpful to collect data using multiple methods, such as using a questionnaire (survey) format that is followed by a one-on-one interview to clarify and expand upon responses.

Management personnel in some organizations do not want to take the time to conduct a formal training needs assessment. However, the information gathered during the training needs assessment will ultimately influence how a training program is designed, developed, implemented, and evaluated. Therefore, although there can be challenges associated with performing a training needs assessment, such as time constraints and lack of management support, when the proper information is not gathered, a training program may not be properly designed to address the true performance issue at hand.

Organizational Development (OD) Methods, Motivation Methods, and Problem-Solving Techniques

Kurt Lewin's Change Process Theory
Kurt Lewin's change process theory is a three-step organizational program that seeks to explain how entities change, the catalysts that precipitate change, and how change can be successfully accomplished. Fundamental to the theory is the notion that an entity will respond to the need for change when there is an external stimulus that compels it.

The first phase of the theory is unfreezing. **Unfreezing** means that there is immense importance for an organization to understand the need for change and to brace for the anticipated impact of change. The second phase is transition. **Transition** stipulates that for any entity to change, there must be a transitory period in which inner motivating factors come to terms with the need for change. The final phase is freezing, in which the new adjustments are solidified and cemented into the functions of an entity. **Freezing** is the reestablishment of new compositions, norms, rules, and procedures.

73

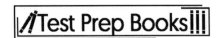

Implementation Theory

Implementation theory is the study of the goals that can be achieved in the change phase when rational agents work cooperatively. When agents work cooperatively, the ability and degree of modification, adaptability, identification, and improvement of malfunctions of an organization is augmented. The implementation of these changes is designed to benefit the entire organization. This theory is imperative to Kurt Lewin's process change theory, since it identifies and targets areas of unfreezing, transition, and freezing to maintain the intended function of an organization.

Change Management and Organization Development

Change management refers to an organization's ability to implement changes in a diligent and comprehensive manner. This concept of change is holistic and encompasses sweeping change of an organization. Equally important is how the changes made will affect pre-existing institutions (regulations, hierarchies). Similarly, **organization development** is a strategy of systematically planned interventions that are employed by an organization. The primary purpose of organization development is to raise the infrastructural efficiency of bureaucracies by devising more operative processes. Change management and organization development are two concepts that focus on evaluation, implementation, and development strategies that are complementary and, in many ways, similar to one another.

Organization Development Intervention

An **organization development intervention** outlines various strategies that an organization employs to effect a desired change. After identifying a problem, organizations target it by employing systematic and designated institutional processes that endeavor to maximize productive potential. An organization development intervention is instrumental in analyzing, directing, and restructuring any underperforming phases in an organizational process. Within this process, there are three primary types of interventions: human process interventions, sociotechnical interventions, and techno-structural interventions.

Human process interventions are specific types of interruptions in an organization model through human interactions. Specific techniques used in human process interventions are coaching, large-group interventions, and training and development. **Coaching** typically involves working interpersonally (with a supervisor) to enhance techniques for self-management, strategy development, customizing strategies that are proximate to client needs, and meeting core objectives. **Third-party interventions** occur when an agent located outside of the organization mediates or manages disputing parties in problem solving. To sharpen educational capacities and skills, organizations develop **key training and development** programs. An example is a program that will instruct employees on how to use a specific piece of machinery that is integral to performance.

A **sociotechnical intervention** is a process undertaken by organizations to maximize productivity by integrating machinery and technology into a pre-existing organizational structure. Since organizations are immensely affected by technological performance and change, it is imperative that strategies are designed to assimilate it, rather than cause institutional shock. Job rotation is one method organizations use to cope with technological change by ensuring that employees are equipped with the physical and cognitive capacities to perform a variety of disparate tasks. By delegating new tasks to meet expanding needs, job enrichment is a strategy that increases responsibilities and authority. Lastly, process improvement is an approach that investigates and alters the way a group performs specific tasks.

Techno-structural interventions represent a type of organization development intervention that focuses on how to most efficiently incorporate and use a piece of technology to maintain maximum productivity. These interventions describe a technique in which an organization redesigns and restructures by implementing more efficient methods. One of the most well-known examples of a techno-structural intervention is total quality management (TQM). **Total quality management** evaluates and changes an organization's dominant attitudes and culture if they are incongruent with the needs of customers. More precisely, styles of communication, leadership, ethical considerations, trust, training, and teamwork are examples of what total quality management reconsiders, if needed.

Task Process Analysis

To design effective learning and development programs, HR must understand what knowledge, skills, and abilities it needs to foster, and for which essential job functions. This involves careful analysis of the task process associated with a particular position. This **task process analysis** is usually used to create detailed job descriptions, but it should be updated and audited regularly to ensure that it maintains accuracy and relevancy.

The first step is to involve current employees by having them complete a job analysis form and conducting a face-to-face interview in which they describe their essential duties and responsibilities. If they do not do so already, employees can then also fill out a log in which they account for the time spent on each task, as well as more detailed information about those tasks. Collect that information for at least one week. In addition to gathering information directly from employees, directly observe employees throughout the day to see what tasks they are engaging in, and for how long. Interview supervisors, managers, and others who interact with the employee, included subordinates, team members, and customers and clients.

Based on the results of the analysis, a clearer picture of what an employee actually does in a day, what specific competencies are required, and how those tasks interact with other tasks within the organization can be formed. It is also possible to create a more detailed breakdown of individual tasks.

For example, an employee may be tasked with processing customer invoices. This involves receiving information from the sales team, calculating and recording sales information using accounting software, utilizing an invoice template to prepare documentation, sending the invoice to the customer, and filing appropriately. A task flowchart would show each individual step and decision point as well as indicate where input from others is needed. It can be used to evaluate the complexity of tasks (for example, this task involves knowledge of accounting, computer software, and customer communications) and therefore the overall complexity of a job position. It can also highlight the core competencies for a job and ensure that employees receive the training they need (for example, if the company were to adopt new accounting software, this task analysis flowchart would indicate that this employee is a high priority employee to receive new software training).

Coaching and Mentoring Techniques

To improve their leadership abilities and the performance of their companies, managers and executives may enlist a group of coaches. Different than trainers, **coaches** provide a level of self-improvement and teach leaders how to identify and solve problems. In addition, executive coaching also gives business leaders the occasion to receive crucial feedback that only outside coaches could provide. Having the opportunity to receive expert and unbiased analysis from trained professionals is advantageous to develop long-term strategies and thinking that will allow greater prosperity within a firm.

75

Mentoring is a specific process that involves influencing the way managers approach and think about solving problems. Specifically, it does not involve a rigid structure; it is long-term commitment on behalf of mentors and management. Mentoring is also vague and does not deal with specific accomplishments. Different kinds of problems that mentors deal with are preparing for a prospective promotion, personal growth, life transitions and adjustments, and developing an individual personally or professionally.

Facilitation Techniques, Instructional Methods, and Program Delivery Systems
William Edwards Deming

William Edwards Deming is one of the most discussed and influential proponents of quality control management. Deming developed fourteen core principles for improving efficiency and productivity of an organization. Among his principles, Deming emphasized a stringent dedication to constant improvement, firm and active leadership, establishing long-term relationships with suppliers and financial institutions, high levels of job security for employees to raise morale, and diminishing costs while increasing productive value. In addition, Deming prescribed for barriers between departments to be minimal. For example, sales, production, and design must communicate without obstruction. Lastly, Deming felt it was important to encourage self-improvement, eliminate quotas, cultivate a unifying sense of pride throughout the organization, and ensure that all employees familiarize themselves with the fourteen core principles.

Joseph Moses Juran

Joseph Moses Juran was an engineer and a pioneer of quality control management. Similar to William Edwards Deming, Juran has been heralded for resuscitating Japanese industry after World War II. Juran is also responsible for applying the Pareto principle or Pareto analysis system, which is a statistical model used for decision-making in an organization, to quality management. It identifies the disproportionality between input and output. Also known as the 80-20 rule, the principle observes that 80 percent of output can be generated by 20 percent of the population.

For instance, if an employee managed their time effectively, 80 percent of their output could be produced by 20 percent of time spent actually working. In effect, 80 percent of the consequences are brought to fruition by 20 percent of the causes. The **Pareto analysis system** is a methodological process employed by business leaders to effectively determine their most revenue-raising technologies, workforce, and resources. After this evaluation, targeted and sustained investments will be made into the most valuable 20 percent. To satisfactorily identify factors that least and most heavily influence revenue, the Pareto analysis system is typically accompanied by a bar chart. Used for quality control issues, the bar chart is a thorough analysis of a company's net input and net output, used to find more efficient ways of employing scarce resources.

Juran Trilogy

According to Juran, there are three areas of quality management: quality planning, quality improvement, and quality control. These three principles are known as the **Juran Trilogy**. **Quality planning** is focused on the needs of customers—determining the customers, the principal needs of the customers, and figuring out how to develop a product that is congruent to the needs of the customers. **Quality improvement** is a process that revolves around designing a strategy that allows an organization to meet the needs of the customers. It involves creating an organizational infrastructure that serves the demands of customers. **Quality control** is the phase where the process is tested, ensuring that it can suit customer needs with minimal inspection. It is the phase that tests organizational efficiency. Intrinsic to

Juran's philosophy is apt leadership, once stating, "It is most important that top management be quality-minded. In the absence of sincere manifestation of interest at the top, little will happen below."

Philip B. Crosby

In the field of quality management, **Philip B. Crosby** introduced several important ideas that remain highly consequential in organizations attempting to solve quality control issues. One of his principal ideas is "Zero Defects." **Zero Defects** is not just a program that is directed by an organization, but a philosophy of business and pedagogy. It requires one to assess the high cost of quality failures and then realize the relation to deflated revenues. If one is chronically wary of these damaging costs, they are more likely to advocate a Zero Defects philosophy, where errors are scrutinized as much as proficiencies. In conjunction with Zero Defects, Crosby advanced "doing it right the first time," or DRIFT.

DRIFT consists of four basic tenets:

- The need to conform to requirements
- The management system is responsible for preventing errors
- The standard of performance is zero defects
- The quality costs are the standard of measurement.

An enduring emphasis throughout Crosby's thoughts focuses on powerful managerial operations. The four principles of DRIFT are contingent upon firm and authoritative management that establishes rules and standards. Throughout the production process, management is responsible for preventing costly glitches and backing a zero defects philosophy. Additionally, management bears responsibility for making the barometer of all decision-making subordinate to quality costs and the organizational conformation to firm requirements.

DRIFT is a system of managerial accounting that works closely with just-in-time production. **Just-in-time (JIT)** is a management technique where a business will only receive goods according to effective demand, rather than maintaining a stockpile inventory of unused supplies. In order for JIT to be a cost-saving program, DRIFT ensures that demand, inventory, and supply chains are congruent to business accounting expectations. If there is any error in JIT, it no longer becomes a cost-saving proposition, but rather it increases the costs of production. The stringent philosophy of DRIFT enables businesses to increase revenues, keep production costs low, and manufacture low-cost commodities.

Dr. Kaoru Ishikawa

Dr. Kaoru Ishikawa is a central figure in the rebuilding of the Japanese industrial base after the Second World War. He introduced several invaluable ideas, one of the most prominent is that production does not end after the commodity is purchased, but rather it continues to ensure maximum customer satisfaction. If a customer is not satisfied with the product, the organization must mobilize itself to resolve the problem and create a better product. A forerunner in quality assessment, Ishikawa introduced numerous statistical analyses to improve productive processes, ranging from charts, graphs, diagrams, and algorithmic equations. Throughout his career, Ishikawa was a proponent of standardization in quality control. Standardization, according to Ishikawa, did not mean a set of rigid and unchangeable rules, but rather rules that are mutable and constantly subject to improvement.

Another one of Ishikawa's innovations is the **Fishbone**, or **Ishikawa Diagram**. The fundamental objective of the Ishikawa Diagram is to identify the principal causes of an effect of a particular problem to give an assessment of quality. Once there is a consensus on a problem (cause), a focus group can mobilize to

77

identify all of its potential causes. These causes could range from employee performance, underperforming machinery, unsatisfactory calculations or methods, or responses to external stimuli. The Ishikawa Diagram is an efficient way of problem solving by isolating specific components and deconstructing positive or negative consequences through an investigatory lens. When a group employs an Ishikawa Diagram, it can be easily thought of as a brainstorming session, where each member offers contributions to amend and resolve current organizational processes.

Also used in quality assessment are histograms and stratification charts. Resembling a bar chart, a **histogram** incorporates bars and groups numbers into ranges. A histogram includes a horizontal distribution of data and is designed to give a visual representation of a certain distribution. For instance, if one were to calculate a histogram of the federal budget of the United States, the y-axis would measure the amount of money spent and the x-axis would parcel the different areas of spending (military, education, social programs, infrastructure, etc.). As histograms, stratification charts also use bars. However, the purpose of a stratification chart is to separate concentrated data to make identifiable patterns.

Six Sigma

Six Sigma is a methodological strategy that is used by organizations to devise more productive ways to organize processes. The principal reason for employing Six Sigma is to eliminate defects in organizational protocol that impede the ability to maximize profitability. In many instances, those people involved in the method must be highly trained in project management and statistics. The goal of organizations that incorporate Six Sigma into production is to maintain a rationally driven, scientific approach to output. As a preventive strategy, a key concept is to preclude wasteful, defective, and time-consuming policies by improving techniques.

DMAIC is the primary process that incorporates Six Sigma. An acronym, DMAIC stands for define, measure, analyze, improve, and control. The first step is to **define** problems, deficiencies, or areas of improvement. Second, **measure** means to simply measure the process performance. The third step instructs the group to **analyze** the process to ensure that it is the most effective strategy in solving the root cause of the problem. Fourth, the organization needs to **improve** process performance and gauge how successfully it targets and eliminates the root causes of defects. Finally, **control** requires that the most resourceful process be improved and salvaged for future use.

Employee Retention Concepts

After taking the necessary time to recruit the right employees, it is important for companies to work to retain them. Employee turnover has high costs associated with it—lost time and lost productivity. There are many different ways that companies attempt to retain staff, and not one method works for all employees. For example, some employers feel that offering a competitive benefits package that includes health care, a retirement program, and life insurance is the best way to retain employees. However, sometimes low or no cost options that improve employees' work/life balance, such as flextime, telecommuting, and allowing employees to wear jeans to work every day (unless they are attending customer-facing meetings) are the best way to go. In addition, staff can be grateful for, and tend to stay longer at, workplaces that provide perks that are meaningful to them, such as on-site childcare, tuition reimbursement, dry cleaning pickup, and free doughnuts on Fridays.

Employers can stay in touch with how their employees are feeling about the work environment by conducting what is known as **stay interviews**. During these interviews, topics including why employees

78

came to work for the employer, why the employees have stayed at the employer, what would make the employees consider leaving, and what the employees would want to see changed are discussed. This allows management to make necessary improvements before they find themselves conducting exit interviews.

Finally, in a workplace that is serious about retention, open communication between management and employees about the company's mission and future goals is key. It is also important for management to show concern for employees' continued development and to promote from within when possible.

Negligent Retention

Negligent retention occurs when an employer either knew or should have known that an employee is unqualified to remain in their position at the company but was allowed to stay in the role, and the employee caused a violation of rights or an injury to another party during or after work hours.

An example of negligent retention is a supervisor who chooses to "look the other way" when one of their employees is found drinking on the job. Perhaps later that employee offers to drive a co-worker to an offsite meeting, and they are involved in a motor vehicle accident with injury sustained by the innocent co-worker due to the employee's elevated blood alcohol level. Employers can prevent claims of negligent retention by making a point to acknowledge problems with employees in a timely manner, reference company policies, and document issues in employees' evaluations. In some cases, employers may also need to provide employees with additional training. If the problems are repeated, it is important for employers to initiate a progressive discipline process, documenting the disciplinary actions as they occur.

Techniques to Encourage Creativity and Innovation

Companies invest in learning and development programs not just to help employees better themselves, but to help employees better the company. HR can help maximize the investment it makes in corporate learning by ensuring that employees translate those newly developed skills into tangible improvements to the workplace. There are many ways HR can encourage creative and innovation.

The first thing is to create an overall culture of innovation that extends beyond just HR—from the highest levels of company leadership, employees should clearly understand that creative thinking is valued in the workplace. In order for concrete programs to flourish, attitudes and values at the company need to reflect the emphasis on creativity and innovation. This involves creating a culture where employees feel that their perspectives are valued, that they are involved in essential processes and decision making, that risks and mistakes are tolerated (and sometimes even encouraged), and that their suggestions can lead to real change.

Another preliminary step is to define what innovation and creativity mean to a company. Innovation is more than just the latest high-tech gadgetry; even companies outside of technological sectors can benefit from innovation. Essentially, it involves the ability to identify problems, approach the issue from new perspectives, come up with solutions, recognize and develop good ideas, and develop new ways of doing things. Creativity and innovation may translate into new products and services that the company can provide to customers and clients; however, creativity and innovation can also be internal, leading to new processes, policies, organizational structures, and more productivity in the workplace. Employees should be encouraged to identify and tackle problems both inside and outside the company.

Along with establishing clear ideas about what creativity and innovation mean to a company and its employees, HR can also keep those concepts in mind when recruiting and onboarding new employees. Hiring managers who recruit from undergraduate or graduate sources can follow student accomplishments in innovation to make sure they are bringing on the type of talent that will further those goals. HR can also ascertain they are offering competitive compensation to attract a high level of talent. Also, HR should create job descriptions that are challenging but also flexible, empowering employees to deepen or adjust their responsibilities if they feel there is a better way to make their position valuable to the company. Complex and challenging jobs can push workers to greater heights of creativity.

There are various programs that can keep creativity and innovation alive in the workplace. One way is through team development. Foster opportunities for employees to communicate with one another and share ideas. This might be through mentoring, job rotation, or regular brainstorming sessions. Companies can also utilize communications technology and workplace social networking to allow employees to quickly and easily share ideas with each other.

Another program involves performance-based rewards. This allows the company to put its money where its mouth is, so to speak, when it comes to demonstrating value for creativity and innovation. It also shows that employee contributions are recognized and rewarded. For example, if an employee comes up with a successful idea that increases the company's value, the employee could receive a portion of that as a bonus. Or there could be competitions to solve a particular problem, and winners would see their ideas put into action. That is another key factor of supporting a culture of innovation: actually using and applying ideas employees originate. If employees feel that they are contributing to, and being included in, the development process, they will be more invested in coming up with new ideas.

A third program involves education-based approaches. Particularly when a company is first trying to establish a culture of creativity and innovation, employees may need some help developing the skills necessary to think creatively.

Finally, employees need the space to be creative. That includes giving them the time and room to think abstractly, instead of focusing only on routine or limited tasks. It also includes giving employees the freedom to try new ideas—not all of which will be successful—without fear of failure. It might take several wrong tries before getting to the right one, and employees should feel that they can contribute new ideas without being judged by others.

Glossary

ADDIE Model	Most commonly used framework that organizations and training developers use to enhance human resource development programs
Adult Learning Process	Four steps: experiencing, reflecting, thinking, and applying
Age Discrimination in Employment Act (ADEA)	Federal law that outlaws discrimination based on age
Americans with Disabilities Act (ADA)	Federal law that outlaws discrimination based on disability
Analysis (ADDIE)	Initial phase of ADDIE wherein the course and primary learning objectives are evaluated and determined
Analyze (DMAIC)	Third step of DMAIC and instructs the group to analyze the process to ensure that it is the most effective strategy in solving the root cause of the problem
Assessment Stage	A person begins to realize that they are unsure about their values, weaknesses, interests, and strengths.
Auditory Learners	Depends on hearing and speaking to learn (e.g., listening to lectures and participating in group discussions)
Banquet-Seating	Provides circular tables for audience members to lean on and is designed to encourage discussion and dialogue
Boardroom-Seating	Features long tables for audience members to lean on, permitting audience members to face each other encourages interactions and exchanges
Cabaret-Seating	Slightly more attractive than banquet-seating style because it leaves an open space at each table as a focal point for a presenter
Career Development	Six primary stages: assessment, investigation, preparation, commitment, retention, and transition
Case Studies	Give students the opportunity to situate themselves into real world, tangible scenarios
Change Management	An organization's ability to implement changes in a diligent and comprehensive manner
Classroom-Style	Remedies the problem of the lack of ability to take notes and consume food and drink
Coaches	Provide a level of self-improvement and teach leaders how to identify and solve problems
Coaching	Typically involves working interpersonally to enhance techniques for self-management, strategy development, customizing strategies, and meeting core objectives
Coaching Workshops	Places workers under the supervision of a counselor in order to equip them with the tools to solve problems that may be inhibiting their work capacities
Cocktail-Seating	Allows for audience members to move freely and roam as they wish
Commitment Stage	Comes after a person recognizes their talents, prompting a commitment to a particular job or career
Control (DMAIC)	Fifth step of DMAIC, requiring that the most resourceful process be improved and salvaged for future use
Copyright Act of 1976	Foundational law in the United States regarding property ownership of film, radio, musical and dramatic works, literary and pictorial works, and architectural structures
Define (DMAIC)	First step of DMAIC, which means to define problems, deficiencies, or areas of improvement
Demonstration	Type of training that presents students with the opportunity to observe an educator in the act of performing a task
Design (ADDIE)	Second phase in the ADDIE model where the principal architecture of the training course is constructed

Design Patents	This patent comprises ornamental design—specifically, the way a product looks (aesthetics) and how it actually works. They are valid for fourteen years after the date they are filed.
Development (ADDIE)	Third phase in the ADDIE model and encompasses creating and distributing tangible tools or courseware for successfully engaging the program
DMAIC	Primary process that incorporates Six Sigma; stands for define, measure, analyze, improve, and control
Dr. Kaoru Ishikawa	Central figure in the rebuilding of the Japanese industrial base after the Second World War
Employee Counseling	Institutional program used by employers to maximize productivity within the organizational structure.
Evaluation (ADDIE)	Fifth phase of the ADDIE model that empirically studies the efficiency and productivity of the course and material
Fair Use	Enumerates some instances in which a person may use copyrighted material
Fishbone (Ishikawa) Diagram	For identifying the principal causes of an effect of a particular problem to give an assessment of quality
Freezing	Reestablishment of new compositions, norms, rules, and procedures
Group Discussion	These permit students to engage collectively, verbalize key concepts, and improve aptitudes for listening and comprehension.
Herringbone-Style	May be a more effective solution to prevent chatter during a meeting
Histogram	Incorporates bars and groups numbers into ranges
Hollow Square-Seating	Similar to the U-shaped-seating style, but it is fully enclosed on all four sides, and permits all audience members to face each other and for a presenter to fully engage them
Horseshoe-Seating	Resembles the U-shape-seating style, but without desks, and allows the audience to focus on the presenters more easily
Human Process Interventions	Specific types of interruptions in an organization model through human interactions
Implementation (ADDIE)	Fourth phase in the ADDIE model and consists of establishing a procedure for training both facilitators and learners
Implementation Theory	Study of the goals that can be achieved in the change phase when rational agents work cooperatively
Improve (DMAIC)	Fourth step of DMAIC, which means the organization needs to improve process performance and gauge how successfully it targets and eliminates the root causes of defects
Instructional Design	Requires analysis of the overall learning process
Investigation Stage	A person begins to search for opportunities that the world of work has to offer.
Joseph Moses Juran	An engineer and a pioneer of quality control management
Juran Trilogy	Three areas of quality management: quality planning, quality improvement, and quality control
Just-In-Time (JIT)	Management technique where a business will only receive goods according to effective demand, rather than maintaining a stockpile inventory of unused supplies
Key Training and Development	An example is a program that will instruct employees on how to use a specific piece of machinery that is integral to performance.
Kinesthetic Learners	Learners who benefit from participating in physical, hands-on activities (e.g., looking at the inside of an automobile or taking apart some type of model)
Kurt Lewin's Change Process Theory	Three-step organizational program that seeks to explain how entities change, the catalysts that precipitate change, and how change can be successfully accomplished

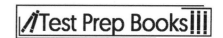

Learner Analysis	Identifies if the employees' performance issues are occurring due to a lack of knowledge, skills, and abilities, or due to some other issue, such as a lack of motivation or insufficient tools
Lecture	Act of an educator verbally articulating how to perform a task or a branch of knowledge
Measure (DMAIC)	Second step of DMAIC, which means to simply measure the process performance
Mentoring	Specific process that involves influencing the way managers approach and think about solving problems
Mentoring Programs	Critical component to making sure that they are under guardianship at a professional and emotional level
Needs Analysis	Process in which an organization gathers information about the principal needs and requests of its members
Negligent Retention	This occurs when an employer either knew or should have known that an employee is unqualified to remain in their position at the company but was allowed to stay in the role, and the employee caused a violation of rights or an injury to another party during or after work hours.
Organization Development	Strategy of systematically planned interventions that are employed by an organization
Organization Development Intervention	Outlines various strategies that an organization employs to effect a desired change
Organizational Analysis	Conducted to ensure that the company is on board with the training initiative and will be supportive
Pareto Analysis System	Methodological process employed by business leaders to effectively determine their most revenue-raising technologies, workforce, and resources
Pedagogy	Children's education
Philip B. Crosby	Introduced several important ideas that remain highly consequential in organizations attempting to solve quality control issues
Pilot Programs	Small-scale and should not be of significant cost
Plant Patent	Can be filed for an asexually reproducible plant discovered in a cultivated area
Preparation Stage	Person has acquired knowledge about what best suits them and begins preparing
Process Flow Mapping	Creates a visualization of the steps in a process, as well as how those steps are connected to each other, allowing planners to see the key decision areas
Public Domain	When any of the works delineated have no copyright; Any person can use these works freely.
Quality Control	Phase where the process is tested, ensuring that it can suit customer needs with minimal inspection
Quality Improvement	Process that revolves around designing a strategy that allows an organization to meet the needs of the customers
Quality Planning	Focused on the needs of customers—determining the customers, the principal needs of the customers, and figuring out how to develop a product that is congruent to the needs of the customers
Retention Stage	After a person feels most comfortable in their career, they begin to sharpen their skills and become acclimated with the industry.
Seating Arrangements	Important configuration that can severely impact the flow of ideas within a training program
Six Sigma	A methodological strategy that is used by organizations to devise more productive ways to organize processes.
Sociotechnical Intervention	Represent a type of organization development intervention that focuses on how to most efficiently incorporate and use a piece of technology to maintain maximum productivity

Stay Interviews	During these interviews, employers can stay in touch with how their employees are feeling about the work environment.
Support Programs	Attempt to remedy personal and utility problems, create channels for employers to assist employees who are not maximizing their potential with training or counseling
Task Analysis	Focuses on the specific tasks employees must complete to successfully perform their jobs
Task Process Analysis	Is usually used to create detailed job descriptions, but it should be updated and audited regularly to ensure that it maintains accuracy and relevancy
Theater-Style	Seating reflects a movie theater setting; All seats are facing the same direction.
Theory of Andragogy	Adult learners tend to be more self-motivated and have a higher capacity for self-evaluation.
Third-Party Interventions	Occur when an agent located outside of the organization mediates or manages disputing parties in problem solving
Title 17	United States copyright law enacted in 1947; It applies to authorship of any tangible medium of expression.
Total Quality Management	Evaluates and changes an organization's dominant attitudes and culture if they are incongruent with the needs of customers
Trademark Act	Created to provide for the protection and registration of trademarks and service marks
Training Needs Assessment	Conducted to determine whether a training program will be an adequate solution to correct a performance issue
Training Workshops	Enables employers and employees to identify particular skills and ensure that they are placed in a position of maximum utility
Transition	Stipulates that for any entity to change, there must be a transitory period in which inner motivating factors come to terms with the need for change
Transition Stage	Forces a person to assess their happiness and make connections to a new career
U.S. Patent Act	Expressly prohibits the unauthorized use, sale, reproduction, or distribution of the product without the consent of the patent holder
Unfreezing	Means that there is immense importance for an organization to understand the need for change and to brace for the anticipated impact of change
Uniformed Services Employment and Reemployment Rights Act (USERRA)	Federal law that outlaws discrimination based military service
U-Shape-Seating	Frequently used when presentations are being given, allowing presenters to more easily interact and engage audience members
Utility Patents	Anything technological, mechanical, chemical, pharmaceutical, or software-related
Visual Learners	These learners prefer to associate information with images.
William Edwards Deming	One of the most discussed and influential proponents of quality control management
Zero Defects	Philosophy of business and pedagogy developed by Philip B. Crosby; It requires one to assess the high cost of quality failures and then realize the relation to deflated revenues.

Practice Quiz

1. What is the purpose of a pilot program?

    a. The purpose of a pilot program is to assign leadership and decision-making roles to a program, designating leaders as "pilots."

    b. The purpose of a pilot program is to function as a test program, in which leadership conducts analyses to assess the program's feasibility and revenue-wielding potential.

    c. The purpose of a pilot program is to rescue a pre-existing project from certain failure.

    d. The purpose of a pilot program is to validate the success of a project by awarding higher salaries and bonuses to leadership.

2. One of the six stages of career development is assessment. What occurs during this stage?

    a. The assessment stage demands that people assess their new occupation and begin working on assignments.

    b. The assessment stage requires that people begin looking for opportunities that reflect their interests and skills.

    c. The assessment stage occurs when people begin to feel a comfort and familiarity with their careers and become acclimated.

    d. Assessment is an introspective stage that requires that one be aware of their values, interests, and skills to discover a career that is most suitable.

3. Kinesthetic learning is accomplished most efficiently through which of the following?

    a. Kinesthetic learning is learning that is done by listening to lectures or group discussions.

    b. Also called spatial learning, kinesthetic learning is learning that is best done by watching videos, looking at maps, or copying notes from a blackboard.

    c. Kinesthetic learning is learning that takes place through physical touching or moving. Examples of kinesthetic learning are using building blocks or drawing.

    d. Kinesthetic learning is learning that is best done by reading text and writing down an alternate interpretation of that text.

4. Which is a primary principle of DRIFT?

    a. One primary purpose of DRIFT is to distribute high profits to employees so that they will be more loyal.

    b. One primary purpose of DRIFT states that as long as they are dealt with immediately, errors can be tolerated.

    c. One primary purpose of DRIFT is that stockpiling commodities can be profitable because supplies are easily accessible.

    d. One primary purpose of DRIFT is that supply and demand must be congruent with management expectations.

5. Which of the following pieces of legislation guarantee that all employees have equal access to career development and training?

    a. Title VII of the Civil Rights Act of 1964

    b. Fair Labor Standards Act (FLSA)

    c. Older Workers Benefit Protection Act (OWBPA)

    d. Davis Beacon Act

See answers on next page.

Answer Explanations

1. B: Also known as an experimental trial or feasibility study, a pilot program is designed to be small-scale. A pilot program's purpose is to enable an organization to test new methods, new products, or engineer new methods or techniques without incurring significant cost. Tremendously important to research, pilot programs can be considered laboratories of innovation and experimentation because they allow logistical considerations, structural efficiencies and deficiencies, and profitability to be evaluated and determined. Pilot programs are widely used in application by many companies, notably Microsoft Corporation, Pfizer Inc., The Dow Chemical Company, and Xerox Corporation.

2. D: Assessment is the first stage of career development. This stage asks that an individual do soul-searching. It demands that a person discover their values, interests, skills, and passions to find a career that is most suitable. It can be seen as a stage of self-affirmation that precedes the journey of job searching. During this stage, a person may ask: "What inspires me?" and "What is my purpose?" Assessment is unique to the other stages of career development because it is independent and exists outside of the workplace.

3. C: Kinesthetic learning can most easily be described as learning by doing. Whereas auditory learning occurs by listening, visual learning occurs through sight, and reading/writing learning occurs through interacting with text, kinesthetic learning occurs distinctly through touch and movement. Kinesthetic learners may grasp concepts more easily by physical activity – playing sports, laboratory exercises, drawing, charades, building, or role-play. To properly accommodate kinesthetic learners, one may use field trips, memory games, or flash cards. Studying while loud music is playing, poor penmanship and spelling, inability to sit still for long periods of time, and emphasis on breaks while studying are a few of the signs of a kinesthetic learner.

4. D: DRIFT is a technique that organizations adopt to harmonize supply and demand. In practice, DRIFT can only be successful if the costs of production are in accordance with expectations. Just-in-time is a concept that is accompanied with DRIFT. To control the costs of stockpiling unused wares, long-term and close-knit relationships with suppliers and creditors are imperative. If an organization did not have easy access to supplier and financial institutions, then its ability to respond to the vacillations of the market would not be as swift.

5. A: Title VII of the Civil Rights Act of 1964 guarantees that all employees have equal access to career development and training. The Fair Labor Standards Act (FLSA) was put into effect to establish employee classification (exempt/non-exempt) and regulate minimum wage, overtime pay, on-call pay, associated recordkeeping, and child labor. Under the Older Workers Benefit Protection Act (OWBPA) it is illegal for employers to discriminate based on an employee's age in the provision of benefits, such as pension programs, retirement plans, life insurance, etc. Finally, the Davis Beacon Act requires contractors and subcontractors working on federally funded contracts in excess of $2,000 to pay all laborers at construction sites associated with such contracts at least the prevailing wage and fringe benefits that individuals working in similar projects in the area are receiving.

Total Rewards

Responsibilities

Compensation and Payroll Issue Resolution

Payroll Vendors
Some of the reasons that companies may elect to outsource their payroll function include the following:

- Freeing up staff time to allow resources to be more strategic in nature
- To reduce costs
- To improve compliance
- Possibly to avoid fines associated with incorrect/late payments or IRS filings
- To have the ability to offer direct deposit of payroll checks to employees

An employer can choose to outsource its entire payroll function or only one or more areas of its payroll function, such as W-2 form printing services. When outsourcing payroll, an employer should select a vendor with an excellent reputation for paying employees on time and providing a high level of customer service.

In an effort not to create additional work, it is important to determine if the vendor's systems are able to effectively integrate with the employer's systems—e.g., time tracking and self-service technologies used to update employees' personal data and payroll-related information. An employer should ensure that the vendor chosen will be able to provide the level of service that the company requires at an affordable cost.

COBRA Administration
When administering COBRA, the length of time that an employee is eligible for coverage is determined by the type of qualifying event. For example, eighteen months is the period of eligibility for an employee's reduction in hours or an employee's termination, while twenty-nine months is the period of eligibility for the disablement of an employee. Additionally, thirty-six months is the period of eligibility for a divorce/legal separation or death of an employed spouse, as well as for a dependent child who loses eligibility status under the plan rules. Employees and their family members have sixty days to elect COBRA coverage from the time that a qualifying event has taken place.

Covered employers are required to provide an initial COBRA notice within ninety days of the date an employee/spouse is covered under the plan. Employers are also required to provide a notice of unavailability of continuation of coverage within fourteen days of the date of the qualifying event, if the employee/spouse is not covered. Employees must be notified of their coverage ending before the maximum continuous period allowed.

Employee Recognition Vendors
Due to a lack of staff resources, time, or in-house expertise, companies may choose to outsource their employee rewards program to a trusted recognition vendor. Since a vendor can, ultimately, determine the success or failure of a company's rewards program, there are a number of items that an employer should evaluate when entering into this type of relationship.

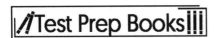

An exceptional recognition vendor will take the time to learn about a company's culture, business goals, employee reward needs, and program budget. The recognition vendor should have an offering of high-quality awards and be able to accommodate rush orders and unique awards, if needed.

Additionally, world-class customer service is the key to employees receiving timely reward fulfillment and recognition for their efforts and achievements. An employer should be assured that the company will receive correct invoices and accurate reporting from the vendor. The ultimate goal for both the employer and the recognition vendor is to ensure that employees feel valued and remain loyal.

Non-Cash Rewards

Managers are frequently being asked to do more with less, including stretching their compensation budgets. This is where non-cash rewards can be factored in with cash compensation to motivate the workforce effectively. **Non-cash rewards** include such items as personalized thank-you notes for a job well done, company merchandise, and gift cards. Some organizations have factored non-cash rewards into their formal recognition programs, making them more meaningful.

For example, there are peer-to-peer recognition programs in place, where one employee can send a personalized thank-you eCard to another employee for a job well done. In that same system, managers can acknowledge an employee for their extra effort on a project by assigning a number of recognition points, along with sending an eCard. Once an employee accumulates a bank of recognition points, they can cash in the points to receive either a gift card or an item from the company store.

Benefit Programs

Employee benefits fall into two categories: discretionary and non-discretionary.

Non-Discretionary Benefits
Non-discretionary benefits are those benefits that employers are mandated to provide based on certain statutes. These benefits include social security, Medicare, workers' compensation, unemployment insurance, unpaid family medical leave (based on FMLA), and continuation of healthcare coverage (based on COBRA).

Discretionary Benefits
Discretionary benefits are not mandated by law. Employers choose to provide these benefits to attract, motivate, and retain their workforce. Discretionary benefits fall into three main categories: health and wellness, deferred compensation, and work-life equity.

- **Health and wellness benefits** include all aspects of healthcare coverage that employers offer, such as major medical plans, dental and vision plans, prescription drug coverage, addiction and substance abuse programs, employee assistance programs (EAPs), wellness programs, and disability/life insurance.

- **Deferred compensation** includes the various types of retirement plans those employers offer, where income is realized at a later date as compensation for work that is performed at the present time.

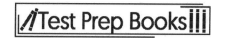
- **Discretionary benefits** that fall under the category of work-life equity help employees to manage their work schedules with their personal commitments, paid time off for holidays, short-term illness, vacation, jury duty, and bereavement, along with flexible work schedules and telecommuting options. Some employers provide additional discretionary benefits that fall into this category, such as on-site childcare, tuition reimbursement, and relocation assistance.

Health and Welfare

Employers are moving towards consumer-directed healthcare in an effort to keep costs manageable. This simply means making employees responsible for how they spend their healthcare dollars, with the goal of smarter choices.

A direct outcome of this has been the evolution of high-deductible health plans. These plans do not pay for medical services until employees have first paid a very steep out-of-pocket amount, which can be close to a $2,500 deductible for an individual plan and a $5,000 deductible for a family plan. In an effort to help employees offset their costs, high-deductible health plans are often coupled with either a health savings account (HSA) or a health reimbursement arrangement.

- A **health savings account (HSA)** allows employees to pay for approved healthcare expenses pre-tax up to the contribution limits that are set by the IRS. Employers may also make contributions to these accounts, and any remaining balances roll over to the next calendar year, are portable, and can be used into retirement.

- A **health reimbursement arrangement (HRA)** is an employer-funded medical plan that reimburses employees only for eligible healthcare expenses. Each employee receives an employer-paid contribution that is treated as a benefit, not as compensation. Employees can roll over any unpaid funds into the next calendar year, but the funds are not portable.

Managed Care Plans

Managed care plans are healthcare plans that seek to ensure that the treatments an individual receives are medically necessary and performed in a cost-effective manner. There are several different types of managed care plans:

Health Maintenance Organization

A **health maintenance organization (HMO)** is structured to emphasize preventative care and cost containment. Under this plan, physicians are paid on a per-head basis, rather than for actual treatment. Employees covered under an HMO must seek treatment by physicians who are under the HMO contract.

Preferred Provider Organization

A **preferred provider organization (PPO)** is formed by an employer who negotiates discounted fees with networks of healthcare providers. In return, the employer guarantees a certain volume of patients. Individuals enrolled in a PPO can elect to receive treatment outside of the network, but they will pay higher copayments or deductibles for doing so.

Point-of-Service Organization

A **point-of-service organization (POS)** is a combination of a PPO & HMO that provides direct access to specialists.

Exclusive Provider Organization

An **exclusive provider organization (EPO)** is a plan in which the participants must use the providers who are in the network of coverage or no payment will be made.

Flexible Benefit Plans

Flexible benefit plans—under section 125 of the Internal Revenue Code—allow employers and employees to save taxes on the money they pay toward their group-sponsored health and dental plans, as well as on out-of-pocket medical expenses.

Flexible Spending Accounts

Flexible spending accounts (FSAs) allow employees to use pretax dollars to pay for approved, out-of-pocket healthcare expenses that are not covered by insurance and dependent-care expenses. This increases employees' take-home pay while decreasing employer payroll taxes, since Social Security (FICA) payroll taxes are lowered.

Each employee determines the amount of pay to have deposited into their FSA account each month during the year. Unpaid funds cannot be rolled over into the next calendar year, so the money is commonly referred to as "use it or lose it." However, if the employee decides to leave their company prior to the end of the year before contributing the full dollar amount of a claim that was previously paid by the company, they cannot be held responsible for the remaining balance of the claim.

Full Cafeteria Plans

Full cafeteria plans—under section 125—allow employees to choose from a menu of eligible, qualified healthcare benefits and typically pay for them with pre-allocated benefit credits. Some plans permit employees to cash out any unused benefit credits or to buy additional benefits through pretax salary reductions. Full cafeteria plans allow employees to choose the benefits that are most important to them and their families.

Dental and Vision Insurance

Dental and vision insurance are additional health and wellness benefits frequently provided by employers. Dental and vision plans often stress preventive care, and it is common practice to have employees share in paying a portion of plan premiums.

Life Insurance

Life insurance is another health and wellness benefit typically provided by employers. In the event of an employee's death, the surviving family members will normally receive anywhere from one to two times the employee's annual salary as payment. Some companies allow their employees to purchase life insurance in addition to what they provide.

Disability Insurance

Disability insurance is provided by employers as a health and wellness benefit.

- **Short-term disability insurance** pays an employee a percentage of their salary—typically 50 percent to 70 percent—after a brief waiting period. This is in the event that they are unable to work for a short period of time—normally between ten and twenty-six weeks—following a non-work-related injury or illness.

- **Long-term disability insurance** takes over when an employee is still unable to return to work after being out on short-term disability. Long-term disability insurance pays an employee a percentage of their salary—typically 50 to 60 percent—until he or she can return to work or for the number of years listed in the company's policy.

Wellness

Corporate wellness programs are gaining in popularity and are used to maintain and improve employees' health before serious problems arise, in an effort to offset the rising costs of healthcare. Often companies kick off these programs by having their employees participate in voluntary health risk assessments and biometric screenings, testing for such things as blood pressure, body mass index, and cholesterol/blood glucose levels.

Based on employees' individual scores, they can be referred to participate in various wellness workshops—e.g., cardiovascular disease prevention, diabetes prevention, healthy aging, nutritional counseling, or understanding back pain—and/or personalized coaching to bring about healthy changes. Employee participation in a wellness program is often tied to an incentive, such as a specific dollar amount taken off of their healthcare premiums, to create a change in behavior. Employers directly benefit from employee participation in wellness programs through decreased absenteeism, improved productivity, and decreased spending on healthcare and workers' compensation.

Retirement

In **defined benefit plans**, employers agree to provide employees with a retirement benefit amount based on a formula. There are different approaches to this formula:

Flat-Dollar Approach

Plans using a **flat-dollar approach** pay a set dollar amount for each year of service under the plan. This is usually seen in plans covering hourly employees under a collective bargaining agreement.

Career Average

Plans utilizing a **career average** have two methods of computing their formula. In the first method, an employee earns a percentage of pay for each year they are a plan participant. In the second method, an employee's yearly earnings are totaled and then averaged over the number of years they are in the plan. At retirement, the benefit equals a percentage of the career average pay multiplied by the employee's years of service.

Final Pay Approach

Plans using a **final pay approach** base their benefits on the average earnings during a specified number of years—usually towards the end of an individual's employment.

Cash Balance Plans

Cash balance plans are a specific type of defined benefit plan. These plans express the promised benefit in terms of a hypothetical account balance. They are easily communicated to plan participants, and the accrued benefit is portable. Each year, a participant's account is credited with two types of credits:

- **Pay credit**: equates to a percentage of their compensation
- **Interest credit**: a fixed or variable rate linked to an index, such as U.S. Treasury bills

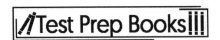

Defined Benefit Plans

Some advantages of **defined benefit plans** are that the benefit is known to the employee, and the employer bears the burden of the financial risk. However, the cost is unknown. These plans tend to create higher rewards for longer-tenured employees.

Defined Contribution Plans

In **defined contribution plans**, employees and/or employers pay a specific amount into the plans for each participant. Employer contributions are often based upon a percentage of salary or a percentage of profits. Performance of the funds in these plans ultimately determines employees' benefits.

Examples of defined contribution plans are 401(k) plans, where the yearly amount employees can put into the plan is set by the IRS and adjusted annually for inflation. 403(b) plans are similar in nature and set aside for employees of certain tax-exempt organizations, such as K–12 public schools, colleges and universities, hospitals, libraries, churches, and philanthropic organizations. Additionally, profit-sharing plans are yet another example of this type of plan.

Some advantages of defined contribution plans are that they can provide valuable benefits to employees with less service and the cost is known. However, the benefit is unknown, and the employee bears the burden of the financial risk.

Here's a breakdown:

Characteristics Of Defined Benefit And Defined Contribution Plans Advantages		
	Defined Benefit Plan	**Defined Contribution Plan**
Employer Contributions and/or Matching Contributions	Employer funded. Federal rules set amounts that employers must contribute to plans in an effort to ensure that plans have enough money to pay benefits when due. There are penalties for failing to meet these requirements.	There is no requirement that the employer contribute, except in SIMPLE and safe harbor 401(k)s, money purchase plans, SIMPLE IRAs, and SEPs. The employer may have to contribute in certain automatic enrollment 401(k) plans. The employer may choose to match a portion of the employee's contributions or to contribute without employee contributions. In some plans, employer contributions may be in the form of employer stock.
Employee Contributions	Generally, employees do not contribute to these plans.	Many plans require the employee to contribute in order for an account to be established.
Managing the Investment	Plan officials manage the investment and the employer is responsible for ensuring that the amount it has put in the plan plus investment earnings will be enough to pay the promised benefit.	The employee often is responsible for managing the investment of his or her account, choosing from investment options offered by the plan. In some plans, plan officials are responsible for investing all the plan's assets.
Amount of Benefits Paid Upon Retirement	A promised benefit is based on a formula in the plan, often using a combination of the employee's age, years worked for the employer, and/or salary.	The benefit depends on contributions made by the employee and/or the employer, performance of the account's investments, and fees charged to the account.
Type of Retirement Benefit Payments	Traditionally, these plans pay the retiree monthly annuity payments that continue for life. Plans may offer other payment options.	The retiree may transfer the account balance into an individual retirement account (IRA) from which the retiree withdraws money, or may receive it as a lump sum payment. Some plans also offer monthly payments through an annuity.
Guarantee of Benefits	The Federal Government, through the Pension Benefit Guaranty Corporation (PBGC), guarantees some amount of benefits.	No Federal guarantee of benefits.
Leaving the Company Before Retirement Age	If an employee leaves after vesting in a benefit but before the plan's retirement age, the benefit generally stays with the plan until the employee files a claim for it at retirement. Some defined benefit plans offer early retirement options.	The employee may transfer the account balance to an individual retirement account (IRA) or, in some cases, another employer plan, where it can continue to grow based on investment earnings. The employee also may take the balance out of the plan, but will owe taxes and possibly penalties, thus reducing retirement income. Plans may cash out small accounts.

Stock Purchase

Employee stock plans are another tool that companies can use to incentivize employees by making them think and behave as owners in the company. A stock option plan affords employees the opportunity to purchase a fixed number of shares of the company's stock at a fixed, or exercise price, during a certain period of time. Employees hope to buy the shares of the company's stock when those shares are trading at a price higher than the exercise price, which will lead to a profit.

An **employee stock ownership plan (ESOP)** is an example of a qualified defined contribution retirement plan that is a stock bonus program. ESOPs give employees significant stock ownership in their companies and allow them to benefit from any associated profitability and growth, which can motivate them to be more focused on the performance of their organizations. Although ESOPs can provide valuable benefits, the employees bear the burden of the financial risk.

Employee Assistance Programs (EAPs)

Employee Assistance Programs (EAPs) are employer-sponsored benefit programs that are used to provide help for employees who are experiencing difficulties in the areas of anxiety, depression, marital or family relationship problems, legal issues, and financial concerns. These programs assist employees with identifying their problems with short-term interventions. For example, employees may be referred to an expert for assistance with complex matters. Employees' use of EAPs is voluntary and confidential, and employers typically provide this service by contracting with a counseling agency.

Knowledge of

Federal Laws and Regulations Related to Total Rewards

A company's **total rewards strategy** is used to attract, motivate, engage, and retain employees through compensation packages made up of pay, incentives, and benefits. This rewards system should be aligned with the company's mission, strategy, and corporate culture, and it must comply with all applicable laws and regulations.

Davis Bacon Act (1931)

The **Davis Bacon Act** applies to contractors and subcontractors working on federally funded contracts in excess of $2,000. The act requires employers to pay all laborers at construction sites—associated with such contracts—at least the prevailing wage and fringe benefits those individuals working in similar projects in the area are receiving. Employers who fail to comply with this act risk losing their federal contracts and the ability to receive new federal contracts for a period of up to three years.

Walsh-Healey Public Contracts Act (1936)

The Walsh-Healy Public Contracts Act applies to contractors working on federally funded supply contracts in excess of $10,000. Under this act, employers associated with such contracts must pay employees at least the federal **minimum wage**—currently set at $7.25 per hour—and overtime pay. **Overtime pay** is calculated as one and one-half times an individual's regular rate of pay for any hours worked in excess of eight hours in a single workday or any hours worked in excess of forty hours in a single workweek.

The employment of youth under the age of sixteen and convicts is also prohibited under this legislation. Additionally, the act calls for job safety and sanitation protocols. Failure to comply with this law may result in the withholding of contract payments to reimburse any underpayment of wages or overtime pay due to employees. There is also a penalty of $10 per person per day for any employer who is found to be employing youth or convicts, along with possible additional legal action. Employers may ultimately

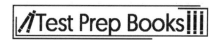
face losing their federal contracts and the ability to receive new federal contracts for a period of up to three years for non-compliance.

Fair Labor Standards Act (1938)

The **Fair Labor Standards Act (FLSA)** is also known as the **Wage and Hour Law**, and it covers most governmental agencies and private-sector employers. This includes companies with employees involved in interstate commerce, employers with $500,000 or more in annual sales or business completed, and organizations caring for the physically and mentally ill, the aging population, and educational institutions. The act does not apply to employers working in industries who are covered under other labor standards that are specific to those industries. The law was put into effect to establish employee classification and to regulate minimum wage, overtime pay, on-call pay, associated record keeping, and child labor, as discussed in detail below.

Employee Classification

The FLSA requires employers to classify all employee positions into two categories, exempt and non-exempt, depending on the type of work the employees do, the amount of money the employees are paid, and how the employees are paid.

- **Non-exempt** positions fall directly under the FLSA regulations. These employees earn a salary of less than $23,600 per year or $455 per week. Non-exempt positions do not involve the supervision of others or the use of independent judgment; they also do not require specialized education.

- **Exempt** positions do not fall under the FLSA regulations. These employees are paid on a salary basis and spend more than 50 percent of their work time performing exempt duties. Exempt level duties fall into three main categories: executive, professional, and administrative.

  - **Executive employees** are responsible for directing the work of two or more full-time employees. Management is a key focus of their role, and they have direct input into the job status of other employees, such as hiring and firing.

  - **Professional employees** can fall into the category of learned professionals, meaning their positions require knowledge in a specific field of science or learning, such as doctors, lawyers, engineers, and accountants. Professional employees can also fall into the category of creative professionals, meaning their positions involve the invention, imagination, originality, or talent in a recognized field of artistic or creative endeavor—e.g., writing, acting, and graphic arts.

  - **Administrative employees** are responsible for exercising discretion and judgment with respect to matters of significance, which can be directly related to management of the general business or in dealings with the customers of the business.

Minimum Wage

Under the **Minimum Wage Act**, employers must pay nonexempt employees at least the federal minimum wage. However, if the state in which an employee works pays a higher minimum wage than the current federal minimum wage, the employee will receive the higher state minimum wage. Additionally, employers must pay $2.13 per hour in direct wages to employees who receive tips as their form of salary. The total of the employer's wage and the employee's tips should then equal the minimum wage.

Overtime

Under the **Overtime** law, employers must pay nonexempt employees overtime pay at the rate of one and one-half times an individual's regular rate of pay for any hours worked in excess of forty hours of work in a single workweek. The act does not require that overtime be paid to employees for work performed on Saturdays, Sundays, or paid time-off days, such as sick days, vacation days, or holidays. Overtime pay that is earned in a specific workweek must be paid out in the pay period during which it was earned, instead of averaging overtime hours across multiple workweeks.

On-Call

Under this act, employers must pay nonexempt employees their regular rate of pay for **on-call time**— the time that they are required to remain at the employer's place of business while waiting to engage in work as required by their employer. An example of this would be medical employees who are asked by their employer to wait to engage in work in an on-call room at a hospital. Since they are not free to leave the hospital and are expected to work if called upon, they must be compensated for their time spent on-call.

Record Keeping

Under **Record Keeping** legislation, employers are required to keep specific records as defined by the Department of Labor. In regard to nonexempt employees, employers must specifically keep track of the following personal information for an employee:

- Name, address, occupation, gender, and date of birth, if employee is under the age of nineteen
- Day and time of the start of the workweek
- Total hours an employee worked during each workday and for the workweek as a whole
- Employee's daily and weekly straight-time earnings
- Employee's regular hourly rate of pay for weeks when any overtime is worked
- Total overtime pay for the workweek
- Any additions or deductions to an employee's wages
- Total wages paid to an employee during each pay period
- Date the employee received payment for work performed and the pay period that payment covered

Child Labor

This legislation also put provisions in place—commonly referred to as **child labor laws**—to ensure that working youth were guaranteed a safe workplace environment that did not pose a risk to their overall health and well-being or prevent them from pursuing additional educational opportunities.

Youth under the age of fourteen are only allowed to perform such functions as newspaper delivery, babysitting, acting, and assisting in their parents' business, as long as that business is non-hazardous in nature. They may also perform non-hazardous agricultural work on a farm that employs one of their parents. Youth ages fourteen and fifteen are allowed to perform non-hazardous work, such as positions in retail, some yard work, and some kitchen and food service work. Youth in this age group are not allowed to work more than three hours a day or eighteen hours a week when school is in session.

However, when school is not in session, these youths can work up to eight hours a day and up to forty hours a week.

Youth in this age group do have restricted work hours of 7:00 am to 7:00 pm during the school year. The evening time is extended to 9:00 pm during the period of June 1 through Labor Day. Youth ages sixteen and seventeen can work unlimited hours. However, youth in this age group are still prohibited from working on hazardous jobs, such as operating trash binders, shredders, or material-handling equipment.

Age	Legal Requirements
Under 14	Children under fourteen years of age may not be employed in non-agricultural occupations covered by the FLSA, including food service establishments. Permissible employment for such children is limited to work that is exempt from the FLSA (such as delivering newspapers to the consumer and acting). Children may also perform work not covered by the FLSA such as completing minor chores around private homes or casual baby-sitting.
14 & 15	Fourteen and fifteen-year-olds may be employed in restaurants and quick-service establishments outside school hours in a variety of jobs for limited periods of time and under specified conditions. Child Labor Regulations No. 3, 29 C.F.R. 570, Subpart C, limits both the time of day and number of hours this age group may be employed as well as the types of jobs they may perform. **Hours and times of day standards for the employment of 14- and 15-year-olds:** 1. outside school hours; school hours are determined by the local public school in the area the minor is residing while employed; 2. no more than three hours on a school day, including Fridays; 3. no more than eight hours on a non-school day; 4. no more than eighteen hours during a week when school is in session; 5. no more than forty hours during a week when school is not in session; 6. between 7 a.m. and 7 p.m., except between June 1 and Labor Day when the evening hour is extended to 9 p.m. **Occupation standards for the employment of 14- and 15-year-olds:** 7. They may perform cashiering, shelf stocking, and the bagging and carrying out of customer orders. 8. They may perform cleanup work, including the use of vacuum cleaners and floor waxes. 9. They may perform limited cooking duties involving electric or gas grills that do not entail cooking over an open flame. They may also cook with deep fat fryers that are equipped with and utilize devices that automatically raise and lower the "baskets" into and out of the hot grease of oil. They may not operate NEXCO broilers, rotisseries, pressure cookers, fryolaters, high-speed ovens, or rapid toasters. 10. They may not perform any baking activities. 11. They may not work in warehousing or load or unload goods to or from trucks or conveyors. 12. They may not operate, clean, set up, adjust, repair, or oil power driven machines including food slicers, grinders, processors, or mixers.

Age	Legal Requirements
	13. They may clean kitchen surfaces and non-power-driven equipment, and filter, transport, and dispose of cooking oil, but only when the temperature of the surface and oils do not exceed 100 degrees Fahrenheit. 14. They may not operate power-driven lawn mowers or cutters, or load or unload goods to or from trucks or conveyors. 15. They may not work in freezers or meet coolers, but they may occasionally enter a freezer momentarily to retrieve items. 16. They are prohibited from working in any of the Hazardous Orders.
16 & 17	Sixteen and seventeen-year-olds may be employed for unlimited hours in any occupation other than those declared hazardous by the Secretary of Labor. Examples of equipment declared hazardous in food service establishments include: **Power-driven meat and poultry processing machines** (meat slicers, meat saws, patty forming machines, meat grinders, and meat choppers), commercial mixers and certain power-driven bakery machines. Employees under eighteen years of age are not permitted to operate, feed, set-up, adjust, repair, or clean any of these machines or their disassembled parts. **Balers and Compactors.** Minors under eighteen years of age may not load, operate, or unload balers or compactors. Sixteen and seventeen-year-olds may load, but not operate or unload, certain scrap paper balers and paper box compactors under certain specific circumstances. **Motor Vehicles.** Generally, no employee under eighteen years of age may drive on the job or serve as an outside helper on a motor vehicle on a public road, but seventeen-year-olds who meet certain specific requirements may drive automobiles and trucks that do not exceed 6,000 pounds gross vehicle weight for limited amounts of time as part of their job. Such minors are, however, prohibited from making time sensitive deliveries (such as pizza deliveries or other trips where time is of the essence) and from driving at night.
18	Once a youth reaches eighteen years of age, he or she is no longer subject to the federal child labor provisions.

Employers who fail to comply with the FLSA may face lawsuits from both the Secretary of Labor and wronged employees for the repayment of backpay of proper minimum wages and/or overtime pay. If it is found that an employer willfully violated this law, the Department of Labor can also impose a $1,100 penalty per violation for repeated offenses.

Employees and Independent Contractors

It is important for employers to be able to discern between employees and independent contractors who are performing work for them for the purpose of withholding taxes, paying overtime and on-call pay with regard to the Fair Labor Standards Act (FLSA), providing benefits, and granting legal protection to the appropriate individuals, all of which apply only to employees.

Employers are able to use independent contractors as a way to grow and reduce their workforce as needed while reducing their legal liability. There can also be a significant cost savings associated with having independent contractors complete work as they can typically be paid less than regular, full-time staff, and they do not receive healthcare benefits.

The Internal Revenue Service has developed a list of twenty factors that fall under three categories for employers to use to determine if an individual working for them is an employee or an independent contractor:

IRS 20-Factor Test
Behavioral Control
1. Instruction: A company-employee relationship could exist if the company dictates where, when, and how the employee works.
2. Training: A training relationship indicates the company has control over the type of work done by the employee.
3. Business Integration: Workers are likely to be considered employees if the success of the business depends on the work they do.
4. Personal Services: Independent contractors are free to assign work to anyone. Likewise, a company-employee relationship may dictate a particular person to carry out a specific task.
5. Assistants: An independent contractor may hire, supervise, and pay their own assistants, while a company-employee relationship may indicate that the company has control over the hiring, supervising, and paying of the worker's assistants.
Financial Control
6. Payment Method: Usually, hourly, weekly, or monthly payments indicate a company-employee relationship. Independent contractors are usually paid by commission or upon project completion.
7. Business or Travel Expenses: Employers who pay business or travel expenses for their employees are usually part of a company-employee relationship.
8. Tools and Materials: A company-employee relationship usually exists if the company provides the worker with tools and materials.
9. Investment in Facilities: Independent contractors usually invest in their own facilities, while employees for companies are usually provided facilities.
10. Profit or Loss: Workers who realize profits or losses are usually independent contractors.
Type of Relationship
11. Continuing of Relationships: An ongoing relationship between a company and a worker could indicate an employment relationship.
12. Set Hours: The implementation of a set schedule indicates that a company-employee relationship exists.
13. Full-Time: While independent contractors choose to work when and for whom they choose, employees sometimes must devote their schedules to full-time work for employees.
14. On-Site Services: If the work must be done on company property, a company-employee relationship probably exists.
15. Sequence of Work: A company-employee relationship is indicated if the worker must perform work in order of company preference and is not able to choose the sequence themselves.
16. Reports: If a worker is required to give oral or written reports to a company, this may indicate a level of control the company has over an employee.
17. Multiple Companies: Workers who provide services for multiple companies at one time are usually considered independent contractors.
18. Availability to Public: Workers who make their work available to the general public are often considered to be independent contractors.
19. Right to Discharge: Employers who have the right to discharge employees indicate a company-employee relationship.
20. Right to Terminate: Independent contractors are usually under contract to work, so they cannot terminate their employment as easily as employees.

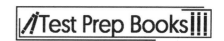
Portal-to-Portal Act (1947)

This amendment to the Fair Labor Standards Act (FLSA) deals with the **preliminary tasks**—activities prior to the start of principal workday activities—and **postliminary tasks**—activities following the completion of principal workday activities.

- Examples of postliminary tasks include on-call or standby time, meals and breaks, travel time, and training time. The act requires employers to pay employees who are covered under the Fair Labor Standards Act for time spent traveling to perform job-related tasks, if that travel is outside of the employees' regular work commute.

- Employers must also pay employees for any time they spend waiting to start work when requested to do so by their employer. Additionally, employees are to be paid for hours spent in job-related training that is outside of their normal workday.

Employers who fail to comply with this law may face consequences similar to those detailed above in the FLSA section.

Equal Pay Act (1963)

This law requires employers to pay equal wages to both men and women who perform equal jobs in the same establishment. The job titles need not be identical, but rather, the content of the jobs that must be equal in nature. Equivalent jobs are required to have equal skill, working conditions, effort, and responsibility defined as follows:

- Skill: The educational and professional background of the employee performing the job, combined with their ability and training

- Working conditions: The physical surroundings in which the work is performed, along with any associated hazards

- Effort: A measurement of the physical or mental exertion that an employee needs to have to perform their job

- Responsibility: The employee's degree of accountability in performing their job

The act does allow for pay differentials when based on other factors other than gender, such as seniority, merit, production quantities or quality, and geographic work differentials. If brought into question, the employer is faced with the burden to prove that these types of **affirmative defenses** do indeed apply.

If there is a need to correct a difference in pay, an employee cannot be penalized by having their pay reduced. Rather, the lower-paid employee's pay rate must be increased. Employers who fail to comply with this act may face up to $10,000 in fines and/or imprisonment up to six months.

Employee Retirement Income Security Act (1974)

The **Employment Retirement Income Security Act (ERISA)** establishes the minimum standards for benefit plans of private, for-profit employers. It states that to receive tax advantages, these plans must conform to the Internal Revenue Code's requirements.

This law also established the federal agency known as the **Pension Benefit Guaranty Corporation (PBGC)**. In return for the plans or their sponsors paying premiums to the PBGC, it guarantees payment of vested benefits up to a maximum limit to employees covered by pension plans.

Vested benefits are simply benefits from a retirement account or from a pension plan belonging to an employee that they get to keep regardless of whether they remain employed at the company. Companies have different rules regarding the number of years at which benefits vest; many are five years. Therefore, if an employee resigns after the vesting period of five years, then they can retain the benefits.

Minimum eligibility requirements were also established by ERISA. To participate in a plan, an employee must be at least twenty-one years of age and have completed one year of service with the company. However, company plans may be more generous concerning these minimum eligibility requirements.

ERISA established minimum vesting schedules for graded and cliff vesting. **Graded vesting** is a set schedule where employees are vested at a percentage amount less than 100 percent each year, until they accrue enough years of service to be considered 100 percent vested. **Cliff vesting** refers to employees becoming 100 percent vested after a specific number of years of service. ERISA established that employees are always 100 percent vested in their own contributions towards their retirement plans. The vesting schedules differ based on the type of retirement plan an employer is offering.

Minimum reporting standards for benefit plans were set up by ERISA. The act requires benefit plan sponsors to prepare and distribute summary plan descriptions (SPDs) to participants at least once every five years. Participants must also receive a summary annual report (SAR) that contains financial information about the plan.

Employers who fail to comply with this act may face both civil and criminal penalties. Some criminal penalties can cost companies as much as $500,000 and up to ten years in prison.

Older Workers Benefit Protection Act (1990)

The **Older Workers Benefit Protection Act (OWBPA)** was passed as an amendment to the Age Discrimination in Employment Act (ADEA) of 1967. Under this act, it is illegal for employers to discriminate based on an employee's age in the provision of benefits, such as pension programs, retirement plans, or life insurance. The goal is for companies to offer equal benefits to all employees, regardless of age. However, when it can be justified by substantial cost considerations, an employer can reduce benefits to older workers.

The OWBPA also prevents older workers from waiving rights when it comes to the topic of severance agreements. An older worker is to be given twenty-one days for the purpose of consulting with an attorney and considering a severance agreement, which turns into forty-five days for group terminations. An older worker then has seven days after signing such an agreement in which they can revoke the agreement if they change their mind.

The releases associated with these agreements must reference ADEA age discrimination claims. This limits an employer's lawsuit exposure should an employee decide to challenge the criteria that was used to make decisions about which employees were retained and which employees were let go. Employers who fail to comply with this act may face both civil and criminal penalties.

Retirement Equity Act (1984)

This amendment to the **Employee Retirement Income Security Act (ERISA)** was passed to address concerns around the needs of divorced spouses, surviving spouses, and employees who left the workforce for some period of time to raise a family. Automatic survivor benefits were now required of qualified pension plans in the event of a plan participant's death, and the waiver of these benefits could only occur with the consent of both the plan participant and the participant's spouse.

Additionally, pension plans are now required to make benefit payments in accordance with a domestic relations court order to the former spouse of a plan participant. Under this act, plans were no longer allowed to consider maternity or paternity leave as a break in service for the purposes of plan participation or vesting. Employers who fail to comply with this act may face both civil and criminal penalties.

Pension Protection Act (2006)

This amendment to the Employee Retirement Income Security Act (ERISA) was passed to strengthen the pension system by increasing the minimum funding requirements for pension plans, thereby eliminating existing loopholes that previously allowed missed payments for underfunded plans.

Additionally, the **Pension Protection Act** allows employees to be automatically enrolled in their employer's retirement plan at a default contribution rate after receiving notification. Employees are initially enrolled in default investments, typically according to the age group that the fall within, and there are provisions in place for their contributions to increase on a periodic basis.

If employees choose, they can elect to save at a different contribution rate, select different investments, or opt out of the retirement plan altogether. The automatic enrollment of employees into retirement plans allows employers to increase participation in their plans and employees to take advantage of pre-tax contributions. Employers who fail to comply with this act may face both civil and criminal penalties.

Consolidated Omnibus Budget Reconciliation Act (1986)

The **Consolidated Omnibus Budget Reconciliation Act (COBRA)** is an amendment to ERISA that allows for the continuation of healthcare coverage in the event that such coverage would end due to certain situations, such as the termination of employment, a divorce, or the death of an employee. The act covers employers with twenty or more employees.

Under this law, employees can pay to continue group medical insurance coverage for a period of up to eighteen to thirty-six months, if they elect to do so in a timely manner and pay the full costs of coverage. They can also be charged a 2 percent administrative fee. Employers who fail to comply with this act may face both civil and criminal penalties.

Health Insurance Portability and Accountability Act (1996)

The **Health Insurance Portability and Accountability Act (HIPAA)** is an amendment (ERISA). It was passed to improve the continuity and portability of healthcare coverage. This act addresses pre-existing medical conditions or those for which an employee or a member of their immediate family received medical advice or treatment during the six-month period prior to their enrollment date into the employer's healthcare plan, such as a serious illness, injury, or pregnancy.

If an employee had creditable healthcare coverage—a group health plan, Medicare, or a military-sponsored healthcare plan—for a period of twelve months, with no lapse in coverage of sixty-three days

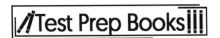

or more, then an employer cannot refuse them coverage in a new group health plan due to a pre-existing medical condition and cannot charge them a higher rate for coverage. However, if an employee did not previously have creditable healthcare coverage, then an employer can exclude coverage for the treatment of a preexisting medical condition for a period of twelve months—with the exception of pregnancy—or for a period of up to eighteen months for late enrollees in the plan.

Additionally, this act only permits covered entities to use or disclose protected health information for treatment, payment, and healthcare operations. If protected health information is to be released for any other reason, written authorization is required from the patient.

Medical records related to the request for work-related accommodations under the Americans with Disabilities Act (ADA) and leaves of absences under the Family Medical Leave Act (FMLA) are not covered under this law. Employers must have a designated privacy officer who will oversee the organization's privacy policy, along with conducting all necessary training for employees. Employers who fail to comply with this act may face both civil and criminal penalties. Some criminal penalties can cost companies as much as $250,000 and up to ten years in prison.

Patient Protection and Affordable Care Act (2010)

This act—also known as **Obamacare**, after President Barack Obama—was phased in over a four-year period, making access to healthcare available to several million more Americans. If individuals do not have access to employer-sponsored healthcare coverage, Medicare, or Medicaid, they are now able to purchase healthcare from an insurance exchange and possibly receive a subsidy.

One of the goals of this act is to keep the overall cost of healthcare coverage down by having individuals take advantage of preventative care, such as blood pressure and cholesterol screenings, well-woman visits, and vision screening for all children. Additionally, under this act, children are now permitted to stay under the coverage of their parents' healthcare until the age of twenty-six, and individuals with preexisting medical conditions cannot be denied coverage.

Every American citizen was required to have health insurance each year or face paying an income tax surcharge, until the Trump Administration removed the individual mandate in 2017. An employer mandate is still being enforced, which is a requirement that all companies employing fifty or more full-time employees provide at least 95 percent of those employees and their dependents with affordable health insurance or be subject to a per-employee fee, based on several factors.

Mental Health Parity Act (1996)

The **Mental Health Parity Act (MHPA)** was put into place to ensure that large group health plans provide coverage for mental health care in the same manner that they provide coverage for physical health care, such as surgical and medical benefits. For example, this act prevents an employer's group health plan from placing a lower lifetime limit on mental health benefits than the plan's lifetime limit on surgical and medical benefits.

This act applies to employers with more than fifty employees, as long as compliance with the act will not increase the employer's cost by at least one percent. It is important to note that this act does not require large group health plans to include mental health coverage in the benefits that they offer. The law only applies to large group health plans that already include mental health benefits in their packages.

104

Family Medical Leave Act (1993)

The **Family Medical Leave Act (FMLA)** was passed to allow eligible employees to take up to twelve weeks of job-protected, unpaid leave during a twelve-month period for specific family and medical reasons. Employees are covered under this act if their employer has at least fifty employees—full or part-time—working within seventy-five miles of a given workplace and if they have worked for their employer for at least twelve months and for a total of 1,250 hours over the past year.

FMLA covers leave for the following reasons:

- The birth of a child, adoption, or foster-care placement

- The serious health condition of a spouse, child, or parent

- The serious health condition of the employee, one requiring inpatient care or continuing treatment by a healthcare provider

- Qualifying exigency leave, or leave to address the most common issues that arise when an employee's spouse, child, or parent is on active duty or call to active duty status—e.g., making financial and legal arrangements or arranging for alternative childcare

- Military caregiver leave or leave to care for a covered service member, such as the employee's spouse, child, parent, or their next of kin, with a serious injury or illness. Employees are to be granted up to twenty-six weeks of job-protected, unpaid leave during a twelve-month period to care for a covered service member.

Instead of taking all of their leave at once, employees can choose to take FMLA leave intermittently or in blocks of time for specific, qualifying reasons as approved by their employer. One reason for doing so would be for an employee to attend medical appointments for their ongoing treatment and testing for a serious health condition.

Spouses who work for the same employer must share the amount of FMLA time they take for the birth of a child, adoption, or foster care placement or for the serious health condition of a child or parent. The total amount of leave taken by both spouses must add up to twelve weeks for the reasons stated above or twenty-six weeks for the care of a covered service member.

Employers also have the right to require employees to take unpaid FMLA leave concurrent with and relevant paid leave, such as sick time or vacation time, to which the employees are entitled under their current policies. In addition, a week containing a holiday still counts as a full week of FMLA, whether or not the holiday is considered to be paid time.

Employers are required to maintain an employee's group health care coverage while they are out on FMLA leave when the employee was covered under such a plan prior to leave. Once an employee's FMLA leave has ended, they are to be reinstated to their original job or to an equivalent job with equivalent conditions of employment, pay, and benefits.

Employers who fail to comply with the FMLA act may face both civil and criminal penalties. Also, if the Department of Labor finds that an employer did not post FMLA rights and responsibilities notices in the workplace, then a penalty of $110 can be assessed for willful failure to post.

Uniform Services Employment and Reemployment Rights Act (1994)

The **Uniform Services Employment and Reemployment Rights Act** was passed to protect the employment, reemployment, and retention rights of civilian employees who serve in uniformed services, veterans, and members of the Reserve. The act requires covered employees to provide their employers with at least thirty days' notice of their need for leave, if possible, and covers them for up to five years of unpaid leave.

Under the Fair Labor Standards Act, exempt employees must be paid their full salary while out on leave (see 29 C.F.R. §541.602), less any compensation that they receive for serving in the military (§541.603). Employees who are out on military leave are also expected to receive the same seniority-based benefits that they would have received had they not been out of work on leave, such as vacation time and 401(k) contributions.

Additionally, if an employee's military leave will be less than one month, an employer must continue healthcare coverage under the same terms as if the employee is still actively employed. After the first month of military leave, employers are not required to continue group healthcare coverage at their expense. Instead, employers can make healthcare coverage available at the employee's expense for a period of twenty-four months or the duration of their military service, whichever is less. Employers are also not allowed to count an employee's military leave as a break in service for pension plan purposes.

The act requires covered employees returning from leave to apply for reemployment within a specific timeframe following completion of their military service:

- If an employee has been out on leave less than thirty-one days, they must return to work on the first workday following completion of military service.

- If an employee has been out on leave between thirty-one and 180 days, they must apply for reemployment within fourteen days of completing military service.

- If an employee's leave has been in excess of 180 days, they must apply for reemployment within ninety days of completing military service.

When an employee returns from military leave, they are to be reinstated to a position that they would find themselves in if they had not been out of work on leave, which may require some retraining efforts on the part of the employer. If after some period of time and retraining efforts, the employee is found not to be qualified for the new position, the employee can return to the position that they held prior to military leave.

Under this act, employers are also encouraged to make reasonable efforts to accommodate disabled veterans returning from military leave. Such individuals have up to two years after completing their military service to apply for reemployment.

Employers who fail to comply with USERRA may face both civil and criminal penalties, ultimately repaying any wronged employees for backpay and lost benefits.

Old Age, Survivor, and Disability Insurance (OASDI) Program

The Social Security Act (SSA) of 1935 designed the **Old Age, Survivor, and Disability Insurance (OASDI) Program** to ensure a continuation of income for individuals who are retired, spouses and dependent

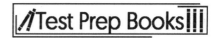
children of employees who are deceased, and individuals who qualify for social security disability. This OASDI program is funded by contributions made by both employees and employers.

At a minimum, employees must work at least forty quarters or ten years to qualify for this program. A surviving spouse or dependent child's eligibility is determined by the length of time the spouse or parent has worked. The number of benefits paid out to individuals who qualify is dependent upon the length of time the employee worked and the amount they paid into the program.

The majority of payments under this program are made in the category of Old-Age benefits. Individuals who qualify must be at least sixty-two years of age to receive partial benefits and between sixty-five and sixty-seven years of age to receive full benefits, depending on the year they were born. In most cases, a non-working spouse can expect to receive half of the number of benefits of the working spouse.

Individuals who qualify for Social Security disability and receive benefits under this program must prove that they are unable to perform profitable work because they are totally disabled.

Federal-State Unemployment Insurance Program

Unemployment Insurance was created under the Social Security Act (SSA) of 1935 as a way to provide partial income replacement for a period of time to individuals who find themselves unemployed involuntarily. This benefit is funded primarily by employers—via a state unemployment tax—and administered by the individual states under national guidelines.

The number of weeks for which an employee can receive unemployment benefits can range from one to thirty-nine weeks, with twenty-six weeks being the most common duration. During some periods of high unemployment, the period of twenty-six weeks can be extended up to an additional thirteen weeks.

Eligibility in most states is contingent upon an employee having worked a minimum number of weeks, not being terminated for misconduct, not having left their job voluntarily, not finding themselves unemployed due to a labor dispute, being available and actively seeking work, and not refusing suitable employment.

Medicare (1965)

Medicare is an amendment to the Social Security Act (SSA) of 1935 with the purpose of providing healthcare for individuals age sixty-five and older, which is not dependent on their income or ability to pay. Some individuals under the age of sixty-five who are disabled, as well as those individuals suffering from end-stage renal disease, are also eligible for coverage under Medicare. The program is funded by employees and employers paying a percentage of salaries.

Medicare has four distinct parts:

- **Medicare Part A** is hospital insurance, which is considered mandatory, and most individuals do not have to pay for this coverage.

- **Medicare Part B** is medical insurance and covers such healthcare expenses as physicians' services and outpatient care. Medicare Part B is optional, and most individuals pay a monthly fee to have this coverage.

- **Medicare Part C** is referred to as Medicare Advantage Plans, such as HMOs or PPOs that are offered by private companies and approved by Medicare. The Medicare Advantage Plans are available to individuals who are entitled to Medicare Part A and enrolled in Medicare Part B. These plans provide participants with hospital and medical coverage, as well as with additional coverage, such as dental, vision, and hearing, and, in some cases, prescription drug coverage. Medicare Advantage Plans can provide substantial cost savings for individuals who are eligible to enroll in them once a year, during an open enrollment period.

- **Medicare Part D** is prescription drug coverage and is considered optional. Individuals who choose Part D pay a monthly fee to have this coverage. Part D is available to individuals who are entitled to Medicare Part A and enrolled in Medicare Part B.

Compensation Policies

Broadbanding
Broadbanding occurs when employers decide to combine multiple pay levels into one, which results in only a handful of salary grades with much wider ranges. This type of pay structure is easier to administer and eliminates the green-circle and red-circle rates as described in the section above. Broadbanding also leads to a flatter organizational structure, which encourages employees' horizontal movement through skill acquisition versus the traditional vertical movement through promotions to new pay grades. Therefore, employees may feel that there are fewer promotion opportunities in a broadbanding pay structure.

Wage Compression
Wage Compression takes place when a new employee is paid at a higher wage than an individual who is currently employed in a similar position and with similar skills in an organization. Wage compression creates a pay inequity and should be avoided, if possible, as it can lead to existing employees becoming unmotivated.

Compa-ratio
A **compa-ratio** is computed by dividing the pay level of an employee by the midpoint of the salary range.

For example, in Company A, salaries in a certain position range from $12-$16 an hour, and an entry-level employee's salary is $12 an hour. The midpoint of the salary range is $14. The pay level of the employee ($12) is then divided by the midpoint of the salary range ($14), resulting in a compa-ratio of .86 or 86 percent.

Compa-ratios are used as indicators as to how wages match, lead, or lag the market. If a compa-ratio is below 100 percent, as with the example above, the employee is paid less than the midpoint of the salary range. This can be attributed to the fact that an employee is new to a job and/or an organization, is a low performer, or is working for a company that has adopted a lag behind the market pay strategy.

If a compa-ratio is above 100 percent, the employee is paid more than the midpoint of the salary range. This can be attributed to the fact that an employee is long-tenured, a high performer, or is working for a company that has adopted a lead ahead of the market pay strategy.

Base Pay
Base pay is fixed compensation that an employee receives in return for work that they have performed. An employee's base salary does not include any additional compensation, such as bonuses, and can be paid out in the form of an hourly wage or a salary, based on the nature of the job. Hourly wages are paid

out per pay period, based on the number of hours an employee works; a salary is paid out the same amount of money each pay period, no matter how many hours an employee works.

Base pay is determined by a number of factors, such as the value of the job to the organization, an individual's knowledge, skills, and abilities, and the supply/demand of talent. An employee is often paid at a higher base pay if their job is perceived to have greater value as it has a greater impact and contribution towards an organization's strategic goals and objectives.

Additionally, an employee's base pay is often reflective of the essential duties and responsibilities associated with their position, along with the required knowledge, skills, educational background, and professional experience to perform in the role.

Finally, supply and demand of talent refers to the availability of individuals who are able to perform a specific role within the employer's geographic location. This determines how quickly the employer is able to fill an open position. For example, if an electric company is located within close proximity to a college with a reputable engineering program, then engineer talent will be readily available and will not need to be recruited at a premium base pay.

Differential and Performance-Based Pay (Merit Pay)

Even though it is not required by law under the **Fair Labor Standards Act (FLSA)**, many employers elect to reward their employees in certain situations with compensation that is in addition to their base pay. Pay practices regarding these types of situations vary greatly among employers.

Differential pay programs are used to reward employees for performing work that is viewed as less than desirable. There are time-based and geographic differential pay programs.

- **Time-based differential pay** is allotted to employees based on when they work. For example, some employees receive additional pay, called **shift pay**, for working second or third shift or for being called in to work during an emergency, also known as **emergency shift pay**.

- **Premium pay** is sometimes paid to employees as a higher rate of overtime pay for working holidays or vacation days.

- Employees who work in a risky environment can be paid **hazard pay**.

- **Reporting pay** can be paid to employees who arrive at their place of employment and find that there is no available work for them to perform.

- **Geographic differential pay** is allotted to employees based on where they work. For example, sometimes employers have different pay structures for different locations and pay extra to attract workers to certain locales, such as remote, offshore oil rigs, and institute pay differentials for work in foreign countries.

Performance-based pay plans are used to motivate employees to perform their work at a higher level. Performance-based pay plans can be instituted at the individual, group, and organization-wide levels.

- Examples of **individual performance-based pay plans** are piece rates, commissions, and cash bonuses. These promote productivity (by 30 percent) but do not promote teamwork and may be difficult to measure.

109

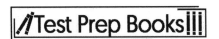

- In **group performance-based pay plans**, an entire group is rewarded for exceeding performance standards and each person in the group receives the same amount of incentive as a percentage of their pay. An example of a group performance-based pay plan is a gainsharing plan, where a portion of the gains an organization realizes from group effort is shared with the group. These promote teamwork but have a moderate impact on productivity (13 percent).

- **Organization-wide performance-based pay plans** are profit-sharing plans, performance-sharing plans, and stock ownership plans. These increase shareholder returns and company profits but generate only a 6 percent increase in productivity.

Internal/External Equity

A company's total rewards system should be appropriate for its workforce and be both internally and externally equitable. **Internal equity** exists if employees are compensated fairly according to their performance on the job, as well as for the knowledge, skills, and abilities that are required for their positions and the responsibilities that are expected of them. A lack of internal equity can lead to employees' perceptions of unfairness, poor attitudes, and lack of commitment.

External equity exists if a company's rewards are equitable when compared to other organizations in similar industries, occupations, and geographic locations. Employers can measure external equity by referring to salary surveys and benchmarking competitors' compensation policies. A lack of external equity can make it difficult to recruit individuals who are truly qualified and in high-demand, and it can result in higher turnover.

Budgeting, Payroll, and Accounting Practices

Since the costs of providing employee benefits continues to rise, employers should take part in strategic planning to ensure they are providing affordable benefits that are desired by employees. This, in turn, will result in the creation of controlled budgets.

Based on the withholdings that an employee has selected on their W-4 form, federal income tax is withheld from an employee's gross wage income. State income tax is then deducted from an employee's gross pay. Employers are also responsible for withholding FICA—Federal Insurance Contributions Act— or Social Security taxes from an employee's pay. FICA is broken down into two taxes: Medicare and OASDI—Old Age, Survivor, and Disability Insurance.

Then, employee deductions for participation in a company-sponsored healthcare program are computed. Other potential deductions from an employee's pay could include city and county taxes, pretax employee contributions, and contributions to a 401(k), 403(b), HSA account, or FSA account. Employers can make payments on behalf of their employees, which may include matching 401(k) or 403(b) contributions, workers' compensation premiums, Federal Unemployment Tax (FUTA), State Unemployment Tax (SUTA), and the employer portion of Social Security taxes.

When considering accounting practices as they relate to employee benefits, dollars spent by employers on company-sponsored healthcare programs are excluded from their employees' gross income. Therefore, wellness program incentives, such as reductions in employee healthcare premiums and employer contributions to employees' health savings accounts (HSAs) and health reimbursement accounts (HRAs), are non-taxable, as these types of incentives and accounts are being used for medical care and treatment.

A gift card used to incentivize an employee is considered taxable income. However, a tangible achievement award given to an employee in a meaningful presentation to recognize their years of service is non-taxable. Additionally, an employee's business use of a company vehicle, as well as employee discounts on employer goods and services, are also considered non-taxable income.

Job Analysis and Evaluation

After a job analysis is performed, which results in job descriptions and job specifications, a job evaluation is conducted to determine the relative worth of each job position by creating a hierarchy. This ultimately leads to the establishment of a pay structure.

- **Job analysis**: the process used to determine the requirements and importance of duties for a particular job.

- **Job descriptions**: a list of general duties and responsibilities for a particular job.

- **Job specifications**: a statement of the essential parts of a particular class of jobs. This includes a summary of the duties to be performed, and responsibilities and qualifications necessary to do the job.

- **Job evaluation**: the ways to determine the value or worth of a job in relation to other jobs in a company.

There are two main job evaluation methods: non-quantitative and quantitative.

Non-Quantitative Job Evaluation Methods
Non-quantitative job evaluation methods are also known as **whole-job methods**. The three specific examples are job ranking, paired comparison, and job classification.

Job Ranking
Job ranking involves a job-to-job comparison by developing a hierarchy of jobs from the lowest to the highest, based on each job's overall importance to the organization. This is a quick, inexpensive way for small organizations to compare one job to another.

Paired Comparison
Paired comparison is a process of comparing each job to every other job for the purpose of ranking all jobs on a scale from high to low. This is also an effective, low-cost job evaluation method for small companies.

Job Classification
Job classification involves grouping jobs into a predetermined number of grades, each of which has a class description to use for job comparisons. Benchmark jobs that fall into each class can be defined as reference points. An example of job classification put into practice is the Federal Government's use of the General Schedule classification system.

Quantitative Job Evaluation Methods
Quantitative job evaluation methods use a scaling system and provide a score that indicates how valuable one job is when compared to another job. The two specific examples are the point factor method and the factor comparison method.

Point Factor Method

The **point factor method** is less complex and most commonly used. This method uses specific, compensable factors, such as skill, responsibility, effort, working conditions, and the supervision of others, to evaluate the relative worth of each job. Each job receives a total point value, and then, the relative worth of all jobs within an organization can be compared.

Factor Comparison Method

The **factor comparison method** is more complex and rarely used. This method involves a ranking of each job by each selected compensable factor and then identifies dollar values for each level of each factor to develop a pay rate for an evaluated job. It is best to use this method when wages are not frequently changing, and the organization uses a flat rate of pay for each job. This method can sometimes be used as part of a labor contract.

Job Pricing and Pay Structures

Following the completion of job evaluations and the collection of data from salary surveys, a company works to establish an overall pay structure. A **pay structure** provides the overall framework for an organization to use to deliver its total rewards strategy. When creating a pay structure, companies establish pay grades by grouping jobs together that are found to have the same relative internal worth. Jobs within the same pay grade will pay the same rate or within the same pay range. When employers are setting pay ranges, they determine the minimum, midpoint, and maximum compensation for a pay grade and set some overlap between pay ranges.

Not every employee fits perfectly within the set pay ranges. For example, an employee who is paid a **red-circle rate** is paid at a rate above the range maximum. If this tends to be a common occurrence, it may mean that the organization's pay ranges lag the market and need to be re-examined. In contrast, an employee who is paid a **green-circle rate** is paid at a rate below the range minimum.

Non-Cash Compensation

Non-monetary compensation is the category of employee benefits that do not carry tangible value. This includes flexible working schedules, company parties, a nice office, rewarding work, and a supportive work environment.

Align and Benchmark Compensation and Benefits

Compensation and benefits can be an essential element in retaining employees and attracting new candidates. Retaining current employees avoids the additional time and costs associated with training a new candidate altogether, as well as the risk of losing any clients or customers the individual may take along when they exit the organization.

Competitive salary and wages can be important in recruiting and retaining staff. However, unless the difference in salary is significant, it is usually not a factor—especially if the overall compensation package value is comparable. A lower take-home pay paired with a wider selection of healthcare and retirement plans may allow a company to offer a better long-term financial plan to its workers. Bonuses are yet another technique for employers to compensate and reward worthy employees.

Benefits can also assist in retention while saving the company money. Voluntary benefits help employees save money by utilizing group discounts with no added cost to the business. Retention of employees is possible with benefits such as health insurance because many employees would not be able to afford having medical insurance if they exited their companies.

Benefits Programs Policies

Communication and training on a company's compensation and benefits programs, policies, and processes is essential to ensure that employees have realistic expectations about benefits and pay decisions, understand the link between performance and rewards, and are informed about potential career paths. Companies should also share information with employees when a competitive market analysis is performed and how the study was completed.

In addition to more formal, organization-wide communications that may take place only a few times a year, ongoing, informal communications should be encouraged between managers and employees. In an effort to make these communications more personal, companies are distributing total reward statements to their employees to demonstrate that their pay is just one piece of the picture.

A **total reward statement** breaks down the rest of an employee's comprehensive benefits package to show them everything that goes into their total compensation, along with the company's contributions toward each of the items. The goal is to show employees an overall picture of the value and associated cost of their total compensation package.

Another component of the overall strategy is to communicate a **rewards program** that will drive employee behaviors that are needed to accomplish the business strategy. For example, creative problem solving may be the employee behavior directly related to customer loyalty—a strategic business goal—which may result in the creation of an employee training and development program in that area.

Self-Service Technologies
Self-service technologies allow employees, via an online system, to complete personal data updates—e.g., contact information, direct deposit information, federal and state withholding information—as well as their annual benefits selections, during an open enrollment period. Throughout the year, employees are also able to make any necessary, allowable benefits changes and check their benefits balances, as well as submit questions they may have regarding their benefits to human resources and, possibly, to benefits providers. Additionally, some self-service applications allow employees and managers to complete the performance management process and access their pay statements and end-of-the-year tax documentation.

Employee self-service programs are user-friendly, available twenty-four hours a day, seven days a week, and are accessible either from the office or from employees' homes. These programs greatly reduce the number of inquiries made to the human resources department, since employees can typically answer a vast majority of their own questions. Additionally, there is a significant reduction in paper printing and postage as well as in transaction processing costs. Transactions are also posted faster in these systems and with a higher degree of accuracy.

Glossary

Administrative Employees	Responsible for exercising discretion and judgment with respect to matters of significance
Base Pay	Fixed compensation that an employee receives in return for work that they have performed
Broadbanding	Occurs when employers decide to combine multiple pay levels into one, which results in only a handful of salary grades with much wider ranges
Career Average	In the first method, an employee earns a percentage of pay for each year they are a plan participant. In the second method, an employee's yearly earnings are totaled and then averaged over the number of years they are in the plan.
Cash Balance Plans	Specific type of defined benefit plan
Child Labor Laws	These ensures that working youth are guaranteed a safe workplace environment that did not pose a risk to their overall health and well-being or prevent them from pursuing additional educational opportunities.
Cliff Vesting	Refers to employees becoming 100 percent vested after a specific number of years of service
Compa-Ratio	Computed by dividing the pay level of an employee by the midpoint of the salary range.
Consolidated Omnibus Budget Reconciliation Act (COBRA)	An amendment to ERISA that allows for the continuation of healthcare coverage in the event that such coverage would end due to certain situations
Corporate Wellness Programs	Used to maintain and improve employees' health before serious problems arise, in an effort to offset the rising costs of healthcare
Davis Bacon Act	Applies to contractors and subcontractors working on federally funded contracts in excess of $2,000
Deferred Compensation	Includes the various types of retirement plans that employers offer, where income is realized at a later date as compensation for work that is performed at the present time
Defined Benefit Plans	Employers agree to provide employees with a retirement benefit amount based on a formula.
Defined Benefit Plans	The benefit is known to the employee, and the employer bears the burden of the financial risk.
Defined Contribution Plans	Employees and/or employers pay a specific amount into the plans for each participant.
Dental and Vision Insurance	Additional health and wellness benefits that often stress preventive care, and it is common practice to have employees share in paying a portion of plan premiums
Differential Pay Programs	Used to reward employees for performing work that is viewed as less than desirable
Disability Insurance	Provided by employers as a health and wellness benefit
Discretionary Benefits	Not mandated by law; Employers choose to provide these benefits in order to attract, motivate, and retain their workforce.
Discretionary Benefits	Fall under the category of work-life equity help employees to manage their work schedules with their personal commitments, paid time off for holidays, short-term illness, vacation, jury duty, and bereavement, along with flexible work schedules and telecommuting options
Emergency Shift Pay	Some employees receive additional pay for being called in to work during an emergency.
Employee Assistance Programs (EAPs)	Employer-sponsored benefit programs that are used to provide help for employees who are experiencing difficulties in certain areas
Employee Stock Ownership Plan (ESOP)	Example of a qualified defined contribution retirement plan that is a stock bonus program; ESOPs give employees significant stock ownership in their companies and allow them to benefit from any associated profitability and growth, which can motivate them to be more focused on the performance of their organizations.

Employee Stock Plans	Another tool that companies can use to incentivize employees by making them think and behave as owners in the company
Employment Retirement Income Security Act (ERISA)	Establishes the minimum standards for benefit plans of private, for-profit employers
Equal Pay Act (1963)	Requires employers to pay equal wages to both men and women who perform equal jobs in the same establishment
Exclusive Provider Organization (EPO)	Plan in which the participants must use the providers who are in the network of coverage or no payment will be made
Executive Employees	Responsible for directing the work of two or more full-time employees
Exempt	These employees are paid on a salary basis and spend more than 50 percent of their work time performing exempt duties. Exempt level duties fall into three main categories: executive, professional, and administrative.
External Equity	Exists if a company's rewards are equitable when compared to other organizations in similar industries, occupations, and geographic locations
Factor Comparison Method	More complex and rarely used, this method involves a ranking of each job by each selected compensable factor and then identifies dollar values for each level of each factor to develop a pay rate for an evaluated job.
Fair Labor Standards Act (FLSA)	Also known as the Wage and Hour Law, it covers most governmental agencies and private-sector employers.
Family Medical Leave Act (FMLA)	Passed to allow eligible employees to take up to twelve weeks of job-protected, unpaid leave during a twelve-month period for specific family and medical reasons
Final Pay Approach	Base their benefits on the average earnings during a specified number of years—usually towards the end of an individual's employment
Flat-Dollar Approach	Pay a set dollar amount for each year of service under the plan
Flexible Benefit Plans	Allow employers and employees to save taxes on the money they pay toward their group-sponsored health and dental plans, as well as on out-of-pocket medical expenses
Flexible Spending Accounts (FSAs)	Allow employees to use pretax dollars to pay for approved, out-of-pocket healthcare expenses that are not covered by insurance and dependent-care expenses
Full Cafeteria Plans	Allow employees to choose from a menu of eligible, qualified healthcare benefits and typically pay for them with pre-allocated benefit credits
Geographic Differential Pay	Allotted to employees based on where they work
Graded Vesting	A set schedule where employees are vested at a percentage amount less than 100 percent each year, until they accrue enough years of service to be considered 100 percent vested
Green-Circle Rate	Paid at a rate below the range minimum
Group Performance-Based Pay Plans	An entire group is rewarded for exceeding performance standards and each person in the group receives the same amount of incentive as a percentage of their pay
Hazard Pay	Paid to employees who work in a risky environment
Health And Wellness Benefits	Include all aspects of healthcare coverage that employers offer, such as major medical plans, dental and vision plans, prescription drug coverage, addiction and substance abuse programs, employee assistance programs (EAPs), wellness programs, and disability/life insurance
Health Insurance Portability and Accountability Act (HIPAA)	An amendment to ERISA that was passed to improve the continuity and portability of healthcare coverage
Health Maintenance Organization (HMO)	Structured to emphasize preventative care and cost containment
Individual Performance-Based Pay Plans	Piece rates, commissions, and cash bonuses; These promote productivity (by 30 percent) but do not promote teamwork and may be difficult to measure.
Interest Credit	Fixed or variable rate linked to an index, such as U.S. Treasury bills

Internal Equity	Exists if employees are compensated fairly according to their performance on the job, as well as for the knowledge, skills, and abilities that are required for their positions and the responsibilities that are expected of them
Job Analysis	Process used to determine the requirements and importance of duties for a particular job
Job Classification	Involves grouping jobs into a predetermined number of grades, each of which has a class description to use for job comparisons
Job Descriptions	A list of general duties and responsibilities for a particular job
Job Evaluation	The ways to determine the value or worth of a job in relation to other jobs in a company
Job Ranking	Involves a job-to-job comparison by developing a hierarchy of jobs from the lowest to the highest, based on each job's overall importance to the organization
Job Specifications	A statement of the essential parts of a particular class of jobs; This includes a summary of the duties to be performed, and responsibilities and qualifications necessary to do the job.
Life Insurance	Health and wellness benefit typically provided by employers; In the event of an employee's death, the surviving family members will normally receive anywhere from one to two times the employee's annual salary as payment.
Long-Term Disability Insurance	Takes over when an employee is still unable to return to work after being out on short-term disability
Managed Care Plans	Healthcare plans that seek to ensure that the treatments an individual receives are medically necessary and performed in a cost-effective manner
Medicare	An amendment to the Social Security Act (SSA) of 1935 with the purpose of providing healthcare for individuals age sixty-five and older, which is not dependent on their income or ability to pay
Medicare Part A	Hospital insurance, which is considered mandatory; Most individuals do not have to pay for this coverage.
Medicare Part B	Covers such healthcare expenses as physicians' services and outpatient care
Medicare Part C	These plans provide participants with hospital and medical coverage, as well as with additional coverage, such as dental, vision, and hearing, and, in some cases, prescription drug coverage.
Medicare Part D	Prescription drug coverage and is considered optional
Mental Health Parity Act (MHPA)	Put into place to ensure that large group health plans provide coverage for mental health care in the same manner that they provide coverage for physical health care, such as surgical and medical benefits
Minimum Reporting Standards	ERISA requires benefit plan sponsors to prepare and distribute summary plan descriptions (SPDs) to participants at least once every five years.
Minimum Wage	Currently set at $7.25 per under the Walsh-Healy Public Contracts Act
Minimum Wage Act	Employers must pay nonexempt employees at least the federal minimum wage
Non-Cash Rewards	Include such items as personalized thank-you notes for a job well done, company merchandise, and gift cards
Non-Discretionary Benefits	Benefits that employers are mandated to provide based on certain statutes
Non-Exempt	These employees earn a salary of less than $23,600 per year or $455 per week. Non-exempt positions do not involve the supervision of others or the use of independent judgment; they also do not require specialized education.
Non-Monetary Compensation	Category of employee benefits that does not carry tangible value
Non-Quantitative Job Evaluation (Whole-Job) Methods	The three specific examples are job ranking, paired comparison, and job classification.

Old Age, Survivor, and Disability Insurance (OASDI) Program	Designed by the Social Security Act (SSA) of 1935 to ensure a continuation of income for individuals who are retired, spouses and dependent children of employees who are deceased, and individuals who qualify for social security disability
Older Workers Benefit Protection Act (OWBPA)	Under this act, it is illegal for employers to discriminate based on an employee's age in the provision of benefits, such as pension programs, retirement plans, or life insurance.
On-Call Time	Employers must pay nonexempt employees their regular rate of pay.
Organization-Wide Performance-Based Pay Plans	Profit-sharing plans, performance-sharing plans, and stock ownership plans; These increase shareholder returns and company profits but generate only a 6 percent increase in productivity.
Overtime Law	Employers must pay nonexempt employees overtime pay at the rate of one and one-half times an individual's regular rate of pay for any hours worked in excess of forty hours of work in a single workweek.
Overtime Pay	Calculated as one and one-half times an individual's regular rate of pay for any hours worked in excess of eight hours in a single workday or any hours worked in excess of forty hours in a single workweek
Paired Comparison	Process of comparing each job to every other job for the purpose of ranking all jobs on a scale from high to low
Patient Protection and Affordable Care Act (2010)	Also known as Obamacare; If individuals do not have access to employer-sponsored healthcare coverage, Medicare, or Medicaid, they are now able to purchase healthcare from an insurance exchange and possibly receive a subsidy.
Pay Credit	Equates to a percentage of their compensation
Pay Structure	Provides the overall framework for an organization to use to deliver its total rewards strategy
Pension Benefit Guaranty Corporation (PBGC)	In return for the plans or their sponsors paying premiums to the PBGC, it guarantees payment of vested benefits up to a maximum limit to employees covered by pension plans.
Pension Protection Act (2006)	Allows employees to be automatically enrolled in their employer's retirement plan at a default contribution rate after receiving notification
Performance-Based Pay Plans	Used to motivate employees to perform their work at a higher level
Point Factor Method	Less complex and most commonly used; This method uses specific, compensable factors, such as skill, responsibility, effort, working conditions, and the supervision of others, in order to evaluate the relative worth of each job.
Point-Of-Service Organization (POS)	Combination of a PPO & HMO that provides direct access to specialists
Postliminary Tasks	Activities following the completion of principal workday activities
Preferred Provider Organization (PPO)	Formed by an employer who negotiates discounted fees with networks of healthcare providers
Preliminary Tasks	Activities prior to the start of principal workday activities
Premium Pay	Sometimes paid to employees as a higher rate of overtime pay for working holidays or vacation days
Professional Employees	Can fall into the category of learned professionals, meaning their positions require knowledge in a specific field of science or learning
Quantitative Job Evaluation Methods	Use a scaling system and provide a score that indicates how valuable one job is when compared to another job
Record Keeping Legislation	Employers are required to keep specific records as defined by the Department of Labor.
Red-Circle Rate	Paid at a rate above the range maximum
Reporting Pay	Can be paid to employees who arrive at their place of employment and find that there is no available work for them to perform

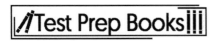

Retirement Equity Act (1984)	Passed to address concerns around the needs of divorced spouses, surviving spouses, and employees who left the workforce for some period of time to raise a family
Rewards Program	Drive employee behaviors that are needed to accomplish the business strategy
Self-Service Technologies	Allow employees, via an online system, to complete personal data updates
Shift Pay	Some employees receive additional pay for working second or third shift.
Short-Term Disability Insurance	Pays an employee a percentage of their salary—typically 50 percent to 70 percent—after a brief waiting period.
Time-Based Differential Pay	Is allotted to employees based on when they work.
Total Reward Statement	Breaks down the rest of an employee's comprehensive benefits package to show them everything that goes into their total compensation, along with the company's contributions toward each of the items
Total Rewards Strategy	Used to attract, motivate, engage, and retain employees through compensation packages made up of pay, incentives, and benefits
Unemployment Insurance	Created under the Social Security Act (SSA) of 1935 as a way to provide partial income replacement for a period of time to individuals who find themselves unemployed involuntarily
Uniform Services Employment and Reemployment Rights Act	Passed to protect the employment, reemployment, and retention rights of civilian employees who serve in uniformed services, veterans, and members of the Reserve
Vested Benefits	Benefits from a retirement account or from a pension plan belonging to an employee that they get to keep regardless of whether they remain employed at the company
Wage Compression	Takes place when a new employee is paid at a higher wage than an individual who is currently employed in a similar position and with similar skills in an organization

Practice Quiz

1. Which of the following individuals would qualify for non-exempt status under the Fair Labor Standards Act (FLSA)?
    a. An employee whose position does not require specialized education
    b. An individual who supervises the work of two or more staff members
    c. An employee who must use independent judgment in their daily work
    d. An employee who earns more than $455 per week

2. Which of the following is NOT one of the three categories that the IRS's twenty factors fall under for determining if an individual working at a company is an employee or an independent contractor?
    a. Financial control
    b. Reporting accountability
    c. Behavioral control
    d. Type of relationship

3. Which of the following items is NOT a covered provision under the Fair Labor Standards Act (FLSA)?
    a. Overtime pay
    b. Employee classification
    c. Child labor
    d. Hazard pay

4. A pension plan that meets the minimum standards set by the Employee Retirement Income Security Act (ERISA) must do which one of the following?
    a. Allow new hires to participate beginning in their first month of employment
    b. Provide plan participants with a copy of the summary plan description once every ten years
    c. Include schedules for graded and cliff vesting
    d. Allow the employer to keep pension plan assets together with other company assets

5. Which of the following is an example of a defined benefit plan?
    a. Cash balance plan
    b. 401(k) plan
    c. 403(b) plan
    d. Section 125 plan

See answers on next page.

Answer Explanations

1. A: Employees who qualify for non-exempt status under the Fair Labor Standards Act (FLSA) are those who earn a salary of less than $23,600 per year or $455 per week, do not supervise others, and whose positions do not require specialized education or the use of independent judgment.

2. B: The three categories that the IRS's twenty factors fall under for determining if an individual working at a company is an employee or an independent contractor are Choice *A,* financial control, Choice *C,* behavioral control, and Choice *D,* type of relationship. Reporting ability is not one of the categories.

3. D: Hazard pay is not a covered provision. The Fair Labor Standards Act (FLSA) establishes guidelines around Choice *A,* overtime pay, Choice *B,* employee classification (exempt and non-exempt status), minimum wage, on-call pay, record keeping, and Choice *C,* child labor.

4. C: The plan must include minimum vesting schedules for graded and cliff vesting. In order for a pension plan to meet the minimum standards set by ERISA, employees must be at least twenty-one years of age and have completed one year of service with the company to participate in the plan. Plan participants must be provided with a copy of the summary plan description at least once every five years. Additionally, the pension plan assets must be kept separate from other company assets.

5. A: In defined benefit plans, employers agree to provide employees with a retirement benefit amount based on a formula. Cash balance plans are a specific type of defined benefit plan. Advantages of defined benefit plans are that the benefit is known to the employee, and the employer bears the burden of the financial risk. However, the cost is unknown. These plans tend to create higher rewards for longer tenured employees.

Employee and Labor Relations

Responsibilities

Analyze Functional Effectiveness Throughout the Employee Lifecycle

On-Boarding

On-boarding, also known as **organizational socialization**, is the process by which new hires obtain the knowledge, skills, and behaviors they need to become valued, productive contributors to the company. The success of on-boarding programs is crucial because new employees decide whether or not to stay with an organization during their first six months of work. Therefore, it is important for companies to make an effort to ensure that new employees feel supported and get adjusted to the social and performance aspects of their new roles quickly.

On-boarding can begin by having an employee's new managers and teammates reach out to them via email to welcome them even prior to their formal start date with the company. On the first day at work, the manager can introduce the new hire to the team member who will serve as their "buddy," to whom they can feel free to go to with any questions or concerns. Taking the new hire out of the office for a welcome lunch on the first day with a couple of staff members is always a nice gesture, as well as ensuring they have lunch partners for the first couple of weeks on the job.

Other aspects of successful on-boarding programs involve the new hire's manager scheduling meet-and-greet appointments to learn more about the roles that each teammate in the department plays and how the new hire will interact with them. These types of meetings can also be scheduled with individuals throughout the company who have key relationships with the department, such as members of IT, Marketing, Human Resources, etc. Additionally, providing the new hire with an on-boarding schedule that involves various team members who will train on various processes and applications can be helpful. It is also important for the manager to meet with the new hire to discuss their performance and development plans for the first three months, to provide clear expectations. Finally, to help a new hire build contacts throughout the company, it is imperative to get them involved in a cross-functional project.

There is no set time limit for on-boarding programs, but at some companies, these programs can last throughout an employee's first year.

Retention

After taking the necessary time to recruit the right employees, it is important for companies to work to retain them. Employee turnover has high costs associated with it—lost time and lost productivity. There are many different ways that companies attempt to retain staff, and not one method works for all employees. For example, some employers feel that offering a competitive benefits package that includes health care, a retirement program, and life insurance is the best way to retain employees. However, sometimes low or no cost options that improve employees' work/life balance, such as flextime, telecommuting, and allowing employees to wear jeans to work every day (unless they are attending customer-facing meetings) are the best way to go. In addition, staff can be grateful for, and tend to stay longer at, workplaces that provide perks that are meaningful to them, such as on-site childcare, tuition reimbursement, dry cleaning pickup, and free doughnuts on Fridays.

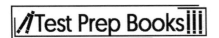
Employers can stay in touch with how their employees are feeling about the work environment by conducting what is known as **stay interviews**. During these interviews, topics including why employees came to work for the employer, why the employees have stayed at the employer, what would make the employees consider leaving, and what the employees would want to see changed are discussed. This allows management to make necessary improvements before they find themselves conducting exit interviews.

Finally, in a workplace that is serious about retention, open communication between management and employees about the company's mission and future goals is key. It is also important for management to show concern for employees' continued development and to promote from within when possible.

Exit Interviews

Individuals who are leaving a company are given an exit interview to uncover their reasons for parting ways with the organization. **Exit interviews** are typically conducted by a neutral party, such as an HR professional, rather than by the departing employee's direct supervisor. HR will typically summarize and analyze the data from exit interviews at regular intervals to share information with management regarding possible improvement opportunities.

Alumni Program

Employee engagement can continue even after employees have left the organization. One way is through an **alumni program** that allows HR to communicate with and keep up with former employees. There are several reasons to maintain an alumni program. First, former employees can be a valuable source of referrals and rehires because they are already familiar with the structure, culture, and skills involved with the company. Former employees may also later become clients, customers, or consultants for the company.

One way to ensure the effectiveness of such a program is to have a positive and professional process when employees leave the company. This ensures that former employees leave with a great impression of their former company, allowing them to act as ambassadors and relationship builders for the company even as they continue their careers elsewhere. Learning about an employee's future goals and securing their contact information before they leave sets the stage for future ongoing communication, which is also imperative. Personalized outreach messages—for example, information about entry-level positions for former interns versus consultancy opportunities for former specialists—ensure that communications are relevant and effective. Ways to evaluate the effectiveness of the company's alumni program include analyzing the number of rehires and how long they stay with the company upon rehire; analyzing the number and value of business connections made through former employees; and tracking the number of hiring referrals from former employees.

Employee Engagement Data

Although HR can gain valuable insights into employee engagement by hearing from individual employees, conducting organization-wide studies on employee engagement allows HR to build a larger dataset that can give an overall picture of how employees in the aggregate are engaging with the company, identify patterns and problems, and highlight areas in need of improvement.

Generally, organizations collect data through employee engagement surveys. Some companies choose to work with third-party vendors that provide surveys and data analysis services. Some advantages of contracting out data analysis are the ease of implementation (no need for a company to design its own questions and response software) and the availability of benchmarking (third-party vendors work with many companies and have access to other datasets to provide comparisons of where other companies stand with engagement). Some companies choose to create surveys themselves, perhaps to save costs or have more control over the survey format.

Either way, even when working with a vendor that provides a survey template, review and select the types of questions. In fact, most surveys are structured as statements, and respondents are then asked to rank their level of agreement or disagreement (this discrete ranking response is called a *Likert scale*). Statements fall into common categories such as **leadership** (how leaders communicate with and motivate employees), **alignment** (how well employees' knowledge, skills, and abilities match their tasks), **development** (whether employees have opportunities for professional growth), **facilitation** (whether employees have access to the tools and resources they need to perform their jobs), and **company culture** (the personality of a company). The scores that employees assign to each statement can then be translated into quantitative data on engagement. Surveys generally also include a few open-ended response questions that allow employees to share comments or concerns that may not be covered by other parts of the survey.

After gathering data, HR then must analyze it. To make the data meaningful, there needs to be a point of comparison. For example, having similar or identical survey items every year allows HR to track if certain aspects of engagement are changing or remaining stable. However, HR also must judge whether any change is statistically meaningful. After pulling meaningful results from the data, the next step is to see what story they tell. This involves relating the survey results to other organizational metrics. For example, HR might notice that this year, there was a 10 percent increase in respondents who agreed with the statement, "I have many opportunities to challenge myself." HR finds that the highest positive responses came from the newest employees; last year, HR implemented a new cross-training program for new hires. HR might then conclude that the program led to increased employee engagement in the realm of development.

In communicating the results of the survey, HR must look at the bigger picture of what the organization is trying to achieve and how employee engagement supports that role. In the above example, HR might demonstrate how the cross-training program leads to more highly qualified employees who stay with the company longer, decreasing hiring costs and increasing customer retention. Employee engagement metrics should be considered in the context of overall business metrics.

Organizational Culture

Organizational Climate and Culture
How employees think and feel about a company is critical to an employer. If members of an organization have negative associations with it, it can be difficult to motivate them. The overall "mood" of an organization is known as its **climate**, and organizational climate cannot be directly controlled. However, climate is closely affected by work environment, company standards, interactions, and a general sense of "how things are done around here." All these factors add up to what is called organizational culture. So, if an employer wants to improve the company's climate, they need to make changes to the company culture.

Encouraging Communication and Involvement
Encouraging communication and involvement is often a step in the right direction toward changing company culture. And much like climate and culture, communication and involvement are closely

related, but not necessarily identical. For example, if John's boss gives him increased responsibility over an aspect of his work, then John has become more involved. However, if John still has no input from his boss on the decision process or has no formal way to share his ideas with management, then the boss has not encouraged communication. Conversely, if John's boss starts sending regular memos detailing company activities and the strategies behind them, this is an increase in communication. However, if John and other employees have no way to act or contribute to this knowledge, then the boss has not encouraged involvement. To make meaningful changes to company culture, both communication and involvement should be addressed.

Involvement Strategies

There are numerous involvement strategies that companies can use. For example, the act of delegating authority allows an employee to make more decisions. By granting people more responsibility, an employer can encourage them to take a greater sense of ownership over a company's successes. An **employee survey** can be used to ask employees how they feel about the company. Surveys can be formal (written or online) or informal (simply asking around), and can address topics such as concerns, suggestions for improvement, and priorities. It should be noted that, even in an anonymous survey, employees may feel hesitant to share their true feelings if the workplace culture is viewed as unfriendly.

In addition to surveys, a **suggestion program**, via an idea box or an online submission form, allows employees to recommend ways to address company problems. Unlike a survey, a suggestion program is an ongoing part of company involvement. Employees can also work together in a formal capacity as part of a committee to address company concerns. Committees may be temporary or ongoing, and employees' service on a committee may also be for a specific term or a permanent appointment.

Moreover, an **employee-management committee** is a specific kind of committee where employees work alongside management to address company concerns. Sometimes known as employee participation groups, these committees also can be temporary or ongoing, depending on the needs of the organization.

Finally, employees can also serve on a **task force**, which is similar to a committee but focused on a specific problem and is usually temporary in nature. Employees on a task force work to determine the cause of a problem and work to develop a solution.

Communication and Strategies

There are also numerous communication strategies that companies can implement. For instance, a **brown bag lunch program** is an informal meeting including employees and management that is used to discuss company problems. The company-provided meal can help create a relaxed setting for exchanging ideas. Additionally, department meetings allow everyone involved to share solutions to company challenges.

Town hall meetings are formal gatherings for the entire company that are commonly referred to as "all-hands meetings." They tend to focus on sharing information "from the top down" concerning the overall organization. Thus, town hall meetings are not usually designed to allow feedback from employees about smaller detail issues. An **open-door policy** is used to establish a relationship where employees feel comfortable speaking directly with management about problems and suggestions. In essence, an open-door policy enables a supervisor to be a "human suggestion box." There are several potential roadblocks to a successful open-door policy. In certain situations, it can be difficult to create an environment where employees feel comfortable discussing problems in person. In addition, depending

124

on the problem reported, it may not be possible to maintain confidentiality. However, in the right situation, an open-door policy can help companies identify problems quickly without having to wait for a formal meeting.

Management by Walking Around (MBWA), as the name suggests, involves having managers and supervisors physically get out of their offices and interact with employees in person. MBWA allows management to check on employee progress, inquire about potential issues, and gain other feedback without relying on employees to "make the first move" through an open-door policy or online suggestion form. This strategy prevents management from becoming isolated behind a desk and disinterested in employee's problems.

Communication Types

There are multiple means that a company can use to communicate with its employees. Each method has its own potential advantages and drawbacks. **Email** makes it easy to get information to a lot of people very quickly. However, this communication method can result in employees suffering from "information overload" from too many emails, making it more likely that important information is overlooked. Also, there is a danger that confidential information may be accidentally communicated to the wrong people.

The **intranet** (internal website and computer network) has the benefit of no risk of important information being accessed by someone outside the organization. Intranets can be very effective at communicating important ongoing information about the company, such as policies and procedures. In addition, companies often store necessary workplace documentation, such as HR-related forms, on an intranet, allowing employees to access that information when they need it. However, if outside parties need information on the intranet, they cannot access it. In addition, intranet communication is often "top-down" and does not allow for feedback from employees. It is also important to note that some intranet systems are not user-friendly, and employees can be discouraged from using them.

Newsletters can provide a variety of information and have the potential to do so in an engaging, welcoming manner. However, newsletters can be labor-intensive. Since they are relatively infrequent (compared to the ease of sending an email), newsletters are not always useful for communicating urgent or immediate information. In addition, newsletters do not allow for formal two-way communication from employees (although this can be remedied by involving employees in the creation of the newsletter).

Finally, **word-of-mouth** communication can quickly spread information throughout a group of people. However, as in the children's game "Telephone," information can become muddled, misinterpreted, and downright unrecognizable as it is passed from person to person. A manager or supervisor has no control over misinterpretations and misunderstandings that can result from word-of-mouth communication.

Federal Laws to Promote Outreach, Diversity, and Inclusion

Implementing an Affirmative Action Plan (AAP) as Required

Affirmative action aids employers with identifying imbalances in the workforce and assists them with placing a focus on hiring, training, and promoting groups of workers who are underrepresented. The following employers are required to have affirmative action plans (AAPs) in place (otherwise, having an AAP is voluntary):

- Employers with fifty or more employees and $50,000 in federal contracts

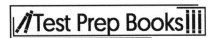
- Employers who are a member of the federal banking system
- Employers who issue, sell, or redeem U.S. Savings Bonds

The following is a listing of the major elements that make up an AAP:

Introductory Statement

An **introductory statement** is essentially a company overview that includes information concerning headcount, along with any significant employment changes that have taken place in the past calendar year. In addition, the company's policy on affirmative action and equal opportunity employment is also mentioned.

Organizational Profile

An **organizational profile** depicts the organization's staffing patterns, to determine if any barriers exist to equal opportunity employment. The organizational structure is presented in some format (i.e., graphical chart, spreadsheet, etc.) to show the following information:

- Unit names
- Employees job titles, gender, and minority status
- Total number of males and females
- Total number of males and females who are also minorities

Job Group Analysis

A **job group analysis** is a list of all titles that comprise each job group. Jobs are grouped according to whether they have similar content, responsibilities, salaries, and opportunities for advancement. This analysis represents jobs by functional alignment versus departmental alignment.

Job Group Analysis

Title	Salary	Total	Male Female	White	Black	Hispanic	Asian	Native Hawaiian	Indian	Two or More	Minority
Vice President Operations	28	1	1	1	0	0	0	0	0	0	0
			0	0	0	0	0	0	0	0	
Vice President Sales	28	1	1	0	0	1	0	0	0	0	1
			0	0	0	0	0	0	0	0	
Chief Financial Officer	29	1	0	0	0	0	0	0	0	0	1
			1	0	1	0	0	0	0	0	
Chief Operating Officer	30	1	1	1	0	0	0	0	0	0	0
			0	0	0	0	0	0	0	0	
Chairman	32	1	1	1	0	0	0	0	0	0	0
			0	0	0	0	0	0	0	0	
Summary of 1A – Executive		5	4	3	0	1	0	0	0	0	2
			1	0	1	0	0	0	0	0	

Availability Analysis

Organizations examine the internal (employees who are trainable, promotable, and transferable) and external (candidates in the reasonable geographical recruitment area) availability of women and minorities to determine their theoretical availability. External availability statistics can be obtained

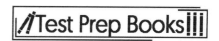

through state and local governments, which provide statistical data and may even publish it on their websites.

Utilization Analysis

The availability of women and minorities is compared with their current representation in each job group at the company. Companies typically define underutilization as the "80 percent rule." This rule is used to determine adverse impact in the employee selection process by comparing the rates at which different groups of people are hired for a job. Eighty percent was arbitrarily selected as an indication of underutilization. Then, for job groups where underutilization is found, reasonable placement goals are set (expressed as placement rates). It is also important to note that a company can have underutilization without experiencing adverse impact.

Other Required Elements

- Identify the individual who is ultimately accountable for the affirmative action plan
- List all of the problem areas
- Detail the action-oriented affirmative action programs that will aid in reaching set goals
- Discuss how the affirmative action program will be monitored and reported on to management
- Provide executive approval and signature on the affirmative action plan
- Create separate affirmative action plans for qualified, covered veterans and individuals with disabilities
- Ensure proper notices are posted on company bulletin boards about affirmative action and equal opportunity employment

Promote Outreach, Diversity, and Inclusion

A commitment to diversity and inclusion improves a company's relationship with its employees, customers and clients, and the community. Both a business case and a legal case can be made for engaging in diversity and inclusion initiatives. As previously discussed, the EEOC prohibits discriminatory hiring practices. Companies may also be subject to affirmative action laws in their states, and companies that have contracts with the federal government must comply with several federal laws. Section 503 of the Rehabilitation Act of 1973, which applies to contractors with contracts over $10,000, requires those employers to take affirmative action for qualified individuals with disabilities. The Vietnam Era Veterans' Readjustment Assistance Act of 1974 (VEVRAA), later amended by the Jobs for Veterans Act, requires companies to have an affirmative action for veterans with service-connected disabilities and applies to contractors with 50 or more employees and contracts of $100,000 or over. Executive Order 11246 requires contractors with 50 or more employees and contracts of $50,000 or more to maintain an affirmative action program regarding women and minorities.

One common way for companies to improve community outreach and develop a new generation of diverse employees is through an internship program. Having interns can be a win-win for the company and the community. People who are new to their field have a chance to develop their skills and learn more about the business. The company gets to evaluate new talent and build a pool of prospective employees; many companies hire full-time employees from previous interns, and these employees already have a great deal of loyalty to and knowledge about the organization. However, federal law should still be considered when designing an internship program. The FLSA establishes clear guidelines regarding wages and overtime pay for employees; for-profit companies planning unpaid internship programs must ensure that their interns are not in fact employees, using a seven-point test created by the Department of Labor. Generally, the test evaluates whether unpaid interns are primarily gaining educational benefit, understand they will not be compensated, and are not displacing paid employees.

Organizations may also have employee resource groups (ERGs), which are formed by groups of employees who belong to similar demographic groups (for example, an ERG for female employees at a company, or one for veterans). ERGs help employees feel represented within the organization, allow them to build relationships and share experiences with others who can understand their background, and give employers valuable insights into the unique needs and perspectives of a specific employee group.

Workplace Programs Related to Health, Safety, Security, and Privacy

Workplace policies should strictly follow federal laws to legally secure a workplace that satisfies minimum health, safety, security, and privacy standards. Failure to meet federal standards can result in fines or the loss of a license. Federal laws and regulations function as minimum standards that all workplace policies must meet. Employers are allowed to pursue policies that go beyond what is legally required if they believe such policies will benefit the organization. Many employers strive to understand the delicate balance between meeting federal guidelines and maintaining high profit margins. Therefore, organizations often find innovative ways to meet federal standards while using efficient business strategies.

Five federal agencies and laws regarding workplace issues are the Occupational Safety and Health Administration (OSHA), the Drug-Free Work Place Act, the Americans with Disabilities Act, the Health Insurance Portability and Accountability Act, and the Sarbanes-Oxley Act.

The **Occupational Safety and Health Act**, passed in 1970, established the Occupational Safety and Health Administration (OSHA) of the federal government in 1971. This agency creates and enforces workplace safety standards. Employers who are engaged in commerce and have one or more employees must observe the regulations established by OSHA. Not only does OSHA set minimum standards, the agency ensures job training for workers in a language they can understand. Additionally, OSHA protects employees who work in substandard conditions and informs them of their rights. A critical provision of OSHA is the protection of employees who reach out to OSHA in an attempt to open an investigation of their working conditions. These employees are protected by OSHA from employer retaliation. OSHA regulations empower employees to help accomplish safety and security.

OSHA regulations focus on employer and employee rights and responsibilities. Employers must provide a safe workplace for employees. Employers are required to meet all OSHA safety standards and correct any violations. Employers are required to attempt to reduce hazards to workers and must supply free protective equipment to workers. OSHA guidelines require employers to provide safety training and to prominently display OSHA posters that detail employee rights. Employers must keep accurate records of any injuries or illnesses that occur in the workplace and notify OSHA promptly of any injuries. Furthermore, employers may not retaliate if an employee uses their right to report an OSHA violation.

OSHA regulations provide specific rights to employees. Employees have the right to demand safety on the job and obtain information concerning work hazards. Every employee has the right to file a complaint with OSHA and request a workplace inspection without fear of employer retaliation. Employees have the right to meet privately with a licensed OSHA inspector. Additionally, OSHA regulations allow employees to refuse work that may be abnormally dangerous or life-threatening.

128

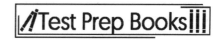
The **Drug-Free Workplace Act of 1988** requires organizations to establish a drug-free workplace, provide a copy of this policy to their employees, and institute a drug awareness program. This law applies to federal contractors with contracts of $100,000 or more and all organizations that are federal grantees. These different penalties exist for employers who do not comply with the act, including contract suspension or contract termination. Although an employer may discuss alcohol and tobacco use in its policies, the Drug-Free Workplace Act does not address the use of these substances.

The **Americans with Disabilities Act (ADA)** is a federal law that prevents discrimination based on disability. This law requires employers to provide reasonable accommodations to employees with a disability. For example, an employer may accommodate a disabled employee by building a wheelchair accessible ramp to enter and exit the building. Additionally, the ADA stipulates that public entities be accessible for disabled persons. The ADA does include both mental and physical medical conditions, and temporary conditions may qualify as a disability. ADA protections apply to every aspect of job application procedures, employment, and promotions.

The **Health Insurance Portability and Accountability Act of 1996 (HIPAA)** addresses issues of healthcare access and portability as well as aspects of healthcare administration. HIPAA provisions allow workers that change jobs or become unemployed to transfer and continue their healthcare coverage. Additionally, HIPAA regulations establish standards for healthcare administration to reduce waste, fraud, and abuse. HIPAA laws strengthen privacy standards and provide benchmarks for medical records in areas such as electronic billing.

HIPAA is applicable to health insurance plans issued by companies, HMOs, Medicare, and Medicaid. Moreover, these regulations apply to healthcare providers who conduct transactions electronically and healthcare clearing houses that process certain information. HIPAA's Privacy Rule gives rights to the insured regarding the disclosure of medical information. Individuals may view health records and request an edit of inaccurate information. Additionally, individuals may file a complaint if rights are being denied or health information is not protected. Patient information with heightened protection is placed in the insurer's database and may include conversations about patients between medical professionals and billing information. Lastly, HIPAA creates strict rules regarding how healthcare information is disseminated and specifies who is given access.

The **Sarbanes-Oxley Act of 2002**, or **SOX**, is federal legislation that is designed to establish higher levels of accountability and standards for U.S. public institution boards and senior management. The act was passed in reaction to major global corporate and accounting scandals such as WorldCom and Enron, companies caught engaging in dubious financial practices. Sarbanes-Oxley specifically targets senior executives responsible for accounting misconduct and record manipulation. The law protects shareholders from any activity that conceals or misleads investors about the firm's finances. The firm has a mandate to transparently and accurately report financial information either to shareholders or the Securities and Exchange Commission (SEC). Moreover, SOX imposes more stringent penalties for white-collar crime and requires detailed reporting to the SEC if a company's finances significantly alter.

Promote Organizational Policies and Procedures

Employee Handbooks

Employee handbooks are important tools to communicate information to staff concerning the company's culture, work hours, safety, harassment, attendance, benefits, pay, electronic communication policies, and discipline policies. It is important for companies to keep employee

129

handbooks current, simple to read, and to make accommodations for any multilingual requests. Additionally, it is important to include a disclaimer that the employee handbook is not intended to be any type of contractual agreement between the company and the employee. By making the employee handbook accessible on the company's intranet site, this eliminates outdated paper copies from floating around the office, and employees can access important policies at any time. Companies typically also require employees to sign off on a form stating that they have received and read the latest version of the employee handbook.

SOP, Time and Attendance, and Expenses

There are many reasons to promote formalized policies and procedures in the workplace. They can guide and clarify standards of employee behavior, ensure fairness and consistency in employee treatment, promote compliance with federal law, and reduce risk of lawsuits. Although HR generally gives employees an overview of these policies and procedures during onboarding, employees may need reminders throughout their period of employment, or policies may change, and HR needs to communicate those changes.

The first step is to clarify the policies and procedures in HR before promoting them throughout the organization. Policies must be written in clear, plain language that includes a purpose statement (why the policy is needed), specific details (what the policy entails), implementation section (who is responsible for carrying out which aspects of the policy), effective date (when the policy will go into effect), and glossary (what specific terms mean within the context of the policy).

HR can then begin promoting the new policy throughout the organization. Depending on the organization's size and structure, several approaches are available, and HR may choose to use several of them. Particularly for large and decentralized organizations, HR should hold face-to-face meetings with managers and supervisors to communicate the specifics of the policy, state the business case for the policy, describe relevant changes from previous policy, emphasize the legal implications (if any) of violating the policy, and answer any questions. Because managers may interact more directly with employees on a daily basis, their buy-in is key. HR may then have other meetings with employees or send a policy notice by email. Either way, employees should be required to sign off on the new policy and acknowledge their understanding. HR should keep a file of employee acknowledgement forms.

Time and attendance policies guide things like when employees arrive at and leave the office, how they record their time, overtime procedures, and requests for time off. A **standard operating procedure**, or **SOP**, is a written description of the steps involved in completing a specific task. It may conform to industry standards, legal regulations, or company-specific rules. **Expense policies** describe how employees can charge business expenses for items like travel and accommodation, food, and other covered costs incurred in carrying out their job function.

Managing Complaints

Settling Discrimination Charges

Unfortunately, discrimination exists in some organizations, and sometimes official charges are brought forth. In these cases (and even in cases where the organization is confident that no wrongdoing has taken place), an organization has a decision to make. It can follow the process through the Equal Employment Opportunity Commission (EEOC) and be investigated by a Fair Employment Practices Agency (FEPA) at the local or state level. Or, the organization may choose to settle the charges rather than face an investigation. Employee charges of discrimination must be filed with the EEOC within 180 days of the alleged incident. If probable cause is found, then the EEOC will attempt conciliation, and the employer is required to settle.

The complaint charge is either settled, or the process may move to litigation with either the EEOC or a private court. If the EEOC is not able to determine probable cause, the employee can request a right-to-sue letter after the end of the 180-day period and must file suit in court within ninety days. Finally, if the EEOC does not find probable cause, the employer and employee are both notified. The employee can request a right-to-sue letter, and the EEOC's involvement with the case ends. The employee can then sue the employer in court.

There are a number of factors that can influence a company's decision to settle discrimination charges. One is the financial cost of an investigation. Lawyers and court fees can be a financial strain on a company's finances, not to mention additional obligations if the court rules against the company. There are also the challenges of the investigation itself to consider. If charges are brought to the EEOC or FEPA, a company may be required to devote considerable time and resources to cooperating with the investigation. Thus, an organization may decide that a one-time financial penalty is preferable to an extended period of disruption. A company also faces damage to its reputation.

A long, drawn-out trial and investigation, potentially widely covered on social and traditional media, can do irreparable harm to the company's image. Even in cases where the company is found to be blame-free in the case, the general public may still associate the organization with the charges of discrimination. Therefore, a company may find it is better to accept the financial expense to avoid the potential long-term damage to its reputation. Finally, there are systemic problems to think about. If the company is aware of deeper issues of discrimination among its employees, it may choose to settle charges to avoid having the investigation uncover an ongoing pattern that may be hard to address.

Front Pay

If a company is found guilty of workplace discrimination, it is usually required to allow the individual in question to return to their position within the organization. However, in some instances, the court may rule that the company should require front pay. **Front pay** is money awarded to an individual in a workplace discrimination case and is generally equal to lost earnings. Front pay is usually required when the position is not available, the employer has not made any effort to address an ongoing issue of discrimination throughout the company, or the employee would be forced to endure a hostile work environment if they were to return to the original position.

Mediation Process

Mediation often serves as a precursor to the more official step of arbitration. In general terms, arbitration is sometimes thought of as a form of mediation, but legally there are important differences. Most notably, a mediator doesn't serve as a final "judge" of the dispute, but rather attempts to work with both parties to help them reach a resolution without having to take additional legal steps.

The mediation process usually begins with both parties agreeing to use a mutually acceptable mediator. The mediator sets the ground rules for the process and defines details such as what the dispute is about, who is involved, when and where the negotiations will take place, and the negotiation procedure. When the actual meeting takes place, the mediator reiterates the ground rules for the process. Both sides present their case. The mediator attempts to help both parties reach a compromise or find other solutions. If both sides agree to a compromise, a written document will be signed to ensure that both sides will follow through on the agreed-upon actions. If both sides do not agree, they may choose to pursue arbitration or litigation (court action).

Constructive Confrontation

Constructive confrontation is a type of mediation used in some extremely complicated or contentious disputes, particularly ones where neither party is able to agree to a compromise. Constructive confrontation can sometimes break these stalemates by temporarily skipping the main issue in dispute, and instead, focusing first on secondary issues. Sometimes, by first resolving these smaller details, a mediator can affect parties' willingness to compromise on bigger issues.

Arbitration

Arbitration is a way to settle disputes without taking the issue to court. In a general sense, arbitration is a form of mediation. However, arbitration typically refers to a more formal process that takes place after an initial mediation attempt has failed. In arbitration, a neutral third party (known as an arbitrator) makes a decision based on the facts presented. There are different kinds of arbitration, decisions, and arbitrators.

In **compulsory arbitration**, the disputing parties are required by law to go through the arbitration process. This could be the result of a court order, but it could also arise from a contract that dictates that arbitration take place in certain situations.

In **voluntary arbitration**, the disputing parties choose to undergo the arbitration process, usually because they cannot come to an agreement, but do not want to go through a potentially expensive and time-consuming lawsuit.

In a **binding decision**, the disputing parties are required by law to follow the decision reached as a result of the arbitration process. This means that the losing party must follow the actions laid out by the decision (such as payments or reinstatement to a disputed position). In addition, a binding decision marks the end of the legal process. No party may pursue further legal action after the decision has been reached.

As the name suggests, **non-binding decisions** carry no legal weight. Either party may choose to follow or not follow the terms of the decision. In addition, a dissatisfied party may choose to follow additional legal action after the decision of the arbiter is reached.

A **permanent arbitrator** is someone who routinely judges arbitration cases for a company or other organization. An arbitrator may be trained and certified by a professional organization, but they also may simply be a person who the disputing parties trust to provide an unbiased opinion on the dispute.

An **ad-hoc arbitrator** may also be a certified professional or a mutually trusted third party. But unlike permanent arbitrators, ad-hoc arbitrators do not have a regular arbitration relationship with either party. Instead, they are chosen as a one-time solution to address only the unique dispute in question.

An **arbitrator panel** functions just like an ad-hoc arbitrator, but it is comprised of multiple arbitrators (usually three). They are sometimes called arbitral tribunals or tripartite arbitration panels.

Positive Employee and Labor Relations

Americans with Disabilities Act (ADA)

The Americans with Disabilities Act (ADA) was passed in 1990 to protect individuals with disabilities against discrimination in relation to aspects such as employment, pay, and benefits. The EEOC defines such disabled individuals as having a physical or mental impairment that limits one or more major life activities.

The ADA applies to companies and organizations with fifteen or more employees. The act specifically dictates that as long as a company or organization does not undergo "undue hardship," they are required to make reasonable accommodations for any disabled employees, such as modifying existing facilities to make them more accessible or adjusting the circumstances under which a job is performed. It is important to know that disabled employees must still be able to perform the essential functions of their job positions, with or without accommodations, when hired.

Identifying reasonable accommodations is an interactive four-step process. First, barriers to the performance of the essential job functions must be identified for a disabled employee. Then possible accommodations that may be helpful in overcoming the barriers are discussed. The feasibility of each of the accommodations is assessed, including whether or not the accommodations are the employer's responsibility and if they will impose an undue hardship to the employer. Finally, the appropriate accommodations are chosen for the disabled employee. An employer is allowed to ask for proof of a disability if it is not obvious, along with information about the accommodation before deciding to make it. An employer cannot ask if an individual has a disability during a job interview. If an interview candidate comes to an interview in a wheelchair, the employer can ask the individual what type(s) of accommodations would be needed. Examples of reasonable accommodations include the following:

- Modifying work sites
- Accessible facilities
- Flexi-time
- Flexi-place
- Providing readers and interpreters
- Modifying work schedules
- Assistive devices
- Reassignment (only available as a last resort)

Pregnancy Discrimination Act

The **Pregnancy Discrimination Act**, passed in 1978, was an amendment to Title VII of 1964. The act applies to all employers with fifteen or more employees and states that while pregnant women are working, they are to be treated in the same way as other employees who are performing their jobs. Therefore, pregnancy must be treated in the same manner as any other type of temporary disability.

Under this legislation, an employer:

- Cannot refuse to hire a pregnant woman
- Cannot force a woman to take leave or terminate her employment because she is pregnant
- Must give a woman a comparable position to the one that she held prior to her maternity leave (if the company already does so with employees taking short-term disability) upon her return to work

- Must provide a pregnant woman with reasonable accommodation(s) if she is unable to do her job and approaches her manager to that effect
- Cannot discriminate against a woman who has undergone an abortion

When a pregnant woman is interviewing for a job position, she is not required by law to disclose the fact that she is pregnant. If it is obvious that a female interview candidate is pregnant, a prospective employer can only state the job requirements for the position (ignoring the pregnancy) and ask the candidate when she is available to start work.

Uniform Guidelines on Employee Selection Procedures

The **Uniform Guidelines on Employee Selection Procedures**, passed in 1978, were designed to prohibit selection procedures that have an adverse impact on protected groups. Adverse impact occurs when the rate for a protected group is less than 80 percent of the rate for the group with the highest selection rate. This is also known as the 80 percent rule, or the four-fifths rule. Below are two examples:

Example 1

Four hundred white candidates applied and two hundred were hired – 50 percent
One hundred Hispanic candidates applied and forty-five were hired – 45 percent
80% of 50 = 40
There is no adverse impact here. If the number was lower than forty, there would be.

Example 2

Sixty male candidates interviewed and thirty were hired – 50 percent
Forty female candidates applied and ten were hired – 25 percent
80% of 50 = 40
Yes, there is adverse impact here, since there were only 25 percent females hired. Females must be hired at a selection rate of 40 percent.

Under these guidelines, procedures that have an adverse impact on women and minorities must be proven to be valid in predicting and/or measuring performance, so as not to be viewed as discriminatory. The **bottom line concept** was an outcome of these guidelines, and it means that an employer is not required to evaluate each component of the selection process individually if the end result is shown to be predictive of future job performance.

If adverse impact is found (which is not always intentional), the employer has alternatives:

- Abandon the procedure
- Modify the procedure to eliminate adverse impact
- Demonstrate job relatedness
- Conduct validation studies
- Keep detailed records
- Investigate alternatives with less adverse impact
- Show the business necessity associated with the need to keep the procedure (which is difficult to do)

Immigration Reform and Control Act (IRCA)

The **Immigration Reform and Control Act (IRCA)** was passed in 1986 and amended in 1990. This act was created to prevent discrimination against individuals based on national origin or citizenship on elements

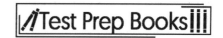

such as employment, pay, or benefits, so long as they are legally able to work in the United States. Employers are also required to verify new employees by making them complete an employment eligibility verification form (I-9) and receiving proof of lawful status within their first three working days. The back of the I-9 form lists all of the documents that are used to show legality to work in the United States, verifying an individual's right to work and identity. Employers must retain I-9 forms for three years, or for one year after an employee's termination, whichever comes later. In addition, this act established civil and criminal penalties for hiring illegal immigrants.

Furthermore, this act instituted categories for visas. Immigrant visas are known as green cards. They are permanent or indefinite visas and are obtained through family relationships or employment. Nonimmigrant visas are temporary. An example is the H1-B visa, for which there is a yearly cap. This type of visa is set aside for certain kinds of working professionals who travel to the United States for a specified period of time.

Sexual Harassment in the Workplace

There are two types of sexual harassment that occur in the workplace: quid pro quo and hostile work environment. The translation of quid pro quo is "this for that." **Quid pro quo sexual harassment** takes place when a superior conditions employment (i.e., promotional opportunity, raise, etc.) on sexual favors.

The type of sexual harassment known as **hostile work environment** takes place when sexual or discriminatory conduct creates a work environment that a "reasonable person" would find threatening or abusive (i.e., unwelcome advances, offensive gender-related language, and sexual innuendos). It is important to remember that male employees can also be victims of sexual harassment.

There are four well-known court cases that dealt with sexual harassment in the workplace:

- **Meritor Savings Bank vs. Vinson**: The court held that sexual harassment violates Title VII. This case dealt with an employee who was plagued with unwanted sexual innuendos. The court said that the plaintiff need not prove concrete psychological harm, just an abusive or intimidating environment.

- **Harris vs. Forklift Systems, Inc.**: This case established the "reasonable person" standard for hostile environment sexual harassment.

- **Oncale vs. Sundowner Offshore Service, Inc.**: The court ruled that same-gender sexual harassment is actionable. This case dealt with all males working on an offshore oilrig, where a heterosexual male was threatened with rape.

- **Faragher vs. City of Boca Raton**: The court stated that employers can be held liable for supervisory harassment that results in an adverse employment action. This case dealt with female lifeguards who were sexually harassed. The city was held liable because the lifeguards' supervisors were not informed of the policy (it was not communicated effectively).

The following items are key elements to put in place to prevent sexual harassment from occurring in the workplace:

- Provide staff with a written, zero tolerance policy on sexual harassment that contains clear definitions and examples
- Provide a complaint procedure for staff to utilize
- Hold training sessions for employees and document attendees
- Investigate all sexual harassment complaints
- Follow through with corrective action (up through and including termination), if necessary
- Communicate the policy on sexual harassment using multiple methods to everyone in the company

Performance Management Processes

Recognition Programs

These programs are used to promote a positive organizational culture by recognizing individual employees for the work they have completed. **Recognition programs** include personalized thank you notes for a job well done, company merchandise, and gift cards. For example, there are peer-to-peer recognition programs in place, where one employee can send a personalized thank you eCard to another employee for a job well done. In that same system, managers can acknowledge an employee for extra effort on a project by assigning a number of recognition points along with sending an eCard. Once an employee accumulates a certain number of recognition points, they can cash in the points to receive either a gift card or an item from the company store.

Management and Leadership Development

Management and leadership development is a critical component for organizations to invest in. For this practice to be effective, managers must exercise their capacities to establish objectives and means of attainment. Concurrently, management and leadership development is designed to equip the workforce with the requisite tools and skills to compete in a functional organization. The primary purpose of management and leadership development is to provide a holistic approach for individuals, managers, and leadership. Individuals are able to increase their skills and knowledge working within an organizational apparatus. Managers find more efficient ways to execute predetermined objectives. Leaders improve their ability in a decision-making process that incorporates creative input from the organization's members and accomplishes mutually shared goals.

Dual Career Ladders

A **dual career ladder** is a specific type of program employed by organizations that allow room for advancement without promoting an individual into a supervisory or managerial role. Dual career ladders can be useful for an employee who may not be interested in a managerial position, and they give employers the latitude to offer valuable employees alternative choices of advancement. Within this paradigm, employees do not need to become supervisors to receive a pay increase.

Managing the Placement of High-Potential Employees

High-potential employees, also known as high-pos, are individuals who fall in the top 10 percent of talent. Many companies struggle to keep high-pos engaged and satisfied in the workplace. Several key practices that organizations can use to manage high-pos include:

- Recognizing the talents these individuals possess

136

- Including these individuals in more of an ongoing development process
- Providing these employees with qualified mentors
- Making flexible and substantial opportunities available to these individuals, which will allow them to obtain more visibility and responsibility in the company.

Support Performance and Employment Activities

Supporting performance activities and employment activities are a key HR function that comes with corresponding legal risk. Ideally, HR professionals hope to recruit and hire employees who seamlessly integrate into their job roles and flourish with the company. In reality, though, some employees require coaching, counseling, and sometimes termination. HR needs to manage every step of the way both to ensure that employees are given ample opportunities to remedy their performance and to ensure compliance with labor laws.

Rather than waiting to fend off any wrongful termination suits, HR should establish clear steps and guidelines for addressing employee performance. One early step is coaching, which targets areas in which an employee is underperforming and gives them tools for improvement. This can be in the form of guidance and assistance from more experienced coworkers, such as a manager, as well as additional classes and training sessions. Particularly for new employees, HR should provide plenty of resources for skill development.

However, if an employee is still struggling with key duties and responsibilities even after coaching, HR may choose to implement a **performance improvement plan (PIP)**. A performance improvement plan is a formal written document concluded between the employee and the company (generally a manager, supervisor, or HR). It should detail specific behaviors or performance issues that need improvement, including specific examples of each; clearly state performance expectations; provide guidance on achieving those expectations, including how management will support performance development; clarify how performance is evaluated; and set clear dates and processes for giving feedback and evaluation over the duration of the PIP and at its conclusion. A PIP serves several purposes. First, it is a formalized expression of performance feedback that gives clarity and guidance to the employee. It defines ways for the employee and the company to work together to achieve common goals. In cases where an employee is judged to have not met the goals of the PIP, it is also an important way to document unsatisfactory performance and, if necessary, justifying the employee's dismissal.

There are many legal risks to consider in involuntary terminations. A **reduction in force (RIF)** is often caused by things outside of HR's control, like economic recession and office closures. However, HR can still control the legal risks. First, for large companies with 100 employees or more, the Worker Adjustment and Retraining Notification (WARN) Act requires at least 60 days' notice before any mass layoff or location closing. When faced with making large numbers of layoffs, HR must also consider applicable laws about discrimination.

For example, a company may decide to cut costs by laying off high-salary employees. However, employees who make more money tend to be older employees who have been with the company for a long time; HR may inadvertently be violating the Age Discrimination in Employment Act. Also, under the Family and Medical Leave Act, Americans with Disabilities Act, and Uniform Services Employment and Reemployment Rights Act, HR cannot terminate an employee based on absences for covered medical leave. The Consolidated Omnibus Budget Reconciliation Act (COBRA) is another federal law with implications for layoffs. Under COBRA, companies with at least 20 employees that sponsor group health plans must continue to cover employees (and covered dependents) for 18 months after a qualifying event—including a layoff—that would otherwise result in a loss of coverage.

Knowledge of

Employee Relations Activities and Analysis

Investigation Procedures of Workplace Safety

Strict enforcement of workplace safety and security is contingent on investigative agencies. If an employer is reported, OSHA will conduct an investigation into the workplace. Throughout an investigation, OSHA works in conjunction with employers and employees to ensure greater safety and security policies are implemented. OSHA agents look beyond the immediate causes of an incident and attempt to uncover the systemic causes. OSHA investigators attempt to discover why a particular problem exists if it is determined that the issue is not a result of individual carelessness.

Following an investigation, an OSHA compliance officer can issue citations depending on the severity of the violation. If an OSHA inspector observes a violation of **imminent danger**, the inspector will require the employer to correct the issue immediately, as the violation will lead to serious harm or death. Other violations may be labeled **serious**, which means that the violation will likely cause death or physical harm. **Other-than-serious** is the next level of violation. This means that the condition could impact employees' safety or health but probably would not cause death or serious harm. **De minimis violations** are not directly and immediately related to employees' safety or health and do not require fines or citations. **Willful and repeated citations** are issued to employers who are repeat offenders of hazardous workplace violations. Penalties for unaddressed or intentional safety violations are very costly.

Grievance Procedures

A **grievance** is a complaint made by an employee that is formally stated in writing. A formal grievance procedure allows management to respond to employee dissatisfaction appropriately through formal communication. Additionally, if a unionized employee is being questioned by management in a situation where a disciplinary action may result, they have the right to union representation during that conversation, which is also known as Weingarten rights (after a famous court case). If that right is violated and the unionized employee is let go, they can be reinstated with back pay.

Every contract will lay out a slightly different process to address potential contract grievances. However, many will follow a similar pattern. The goal is always to remedy the situation before it escalates to the need for arbitration. Typically, employees first discuss the grievance with the union steward and the supervisor. Next, the union steward discusses the grievance with the supervisor's manager and/or the HR manager. The next step is for a committee of union officers to discuss the grievance with the appropriate managers in the company. Then, the national union representative discusses the grievance with designated company executives. If, after this process, the grievance is still not settled, it then goes to arbitration. Grievance arbitration is a process in which a third party is used to settle disputes that arise from conflicting interpretations of a labor contract. Decisions that are reached through this process are enforceable and cannot go to court to be changed.

Federal Laws Related to Employment, Labor Relations, Safety, and Security

Sherman Antitrust Act

The **Sherman Antitrust Act** (1890) is a piece of legislation intended to protect free trade. In simple terms, under the act, individuals or organizations cannot enter into any contract that unreasonably prevents others from engaging in similar commerce. Likewise, individuals and organizations cannot form monopolies. In other words, an organization cannot be the only company offering a service or product. There must be *some* competition possible. If a monopoly is suspected, the act gives district courts and/or government attorneys the authority to begin an investigation. It is important to note that the Sherman Antitrust Act does not apply if there is an existing law stating that an organization cannot be defined as a monopoly.

Clayton Act

The **Clayton Act** (1914) provides additional detail clarifying the Sherman Antitrust Act. The Clayton Act provides examples of potentially illegal or monopoly-forming activities, including mergers, exclusive dealings, and price discrimination. In addition, the act states that labor unions and agricultural organizations do not fall under the authority of the Sherman Antitrust Act. Finally, this legislation states that labor disputes are not subject to a court injunction, except in cases involving a threat of property damage.

Railway Labor Act

The **Railway Labor Act** (1926) puts limits on strikes by railroad and airline unions, if those strikes are found to cause major problems to the nation's transportation system and its ability to engage in trade. According to the act, railroad and airline employees can strike over a major contract dispute ("major" disputes are considered those involving pay, working conditions, or changes to the collective bargaining agreement), but only after engaging in a detailed process. All parties must first attempt mediation, arbitration, or another method of dispute negotiation through a National Mediation Board (NMB).

If arbitration fails, and the NMB believes that a work stoppage may cause significant trade or transportation problems for the nation, they must alert the president. At this point, strikes are prohibited for a thirty-day cooling-off period. If, after that time, the president does not create a Presidential Emergency Board (PEB) to investigate the situation, employees may legally strike. If the president does choose to create a PEB, employees must observe another thirty-day cooling-off period while the board investigates and produces the report. After the report is completed, strikes continue to be prohibited for a third thirty-day period. The PEB report is non-binding. Therefore, if there has been no agreement, employees may legally strike after the third thirty-day cooling-off period.

Norris-LaGuardia Act

The **Norris-LaGuardia Act** (1932) is designed to protect workers' rights to form and join a union, as well as their right to strike. The act also protects all non-violent union activities from court injunctions. Lastly, the act protects employees from having to sign what are known as "yellow-dog" contracts, which are contracts that prevent employees from joining unions.

National Labor Relations Act (Wagner Act)

Passed in 1935, the **National Labor Relations Act** (NLRA) grants specific rights to workers who already belong to, or wish to join, a union. In addition to reinforcing the rights covered by the Norris-LaGuardia Act, this piece of legislation also grants employees the right to participate in collective bargaining activities, even if they are not a member of the union in question. There are some restrictions, however, such as the NLRA does not affect the special restrictions of the Railway Labor Act. In addition, the NLRA does not affect certain individuals who may make decisions on behalf of an employer, such as managers, supervisors, independent contractors, and immediate family.

The NLRA also defines what constitutes a legal and an illegal strike. A strike is considered legal when employees are seeking a better work environment, benefits, or compensation, or when an employer is using an unfair labor practice. A strike is considered illegal when employees have signed a contract with a no-strike clause, employees are striking to defend a union's unfair labor practice, or there is a significant concern that the striking employees are expected to cause property damage or bodily harm.

The NLRA also dictates what can be considered unfair labor practices, such as an employer doing one or more of the following: stopping workers from joining or participating in a union, taking control of a union or showing favoritism to any particular union, discriminating against union participants, discriminating against a worker who has filed charges with the National Labor Relations Board (NLRB), and refusing to bargain with the union representing its employees.

In addition, the NLRA created the National Labor Relations Board (NLRB) to encourage union growth. This board is primarily responsible for investigating potential unfair labor practices. The NLRB focuses on protecting employees from unfair treatment by employers or unions. The NLRB has the authority to take various actions to combat unfair labor practices, including the following: forcing employers to rehire employees, forcing employers to negotiate with a union, disbanding employer-controlled unions, forcing unions to refund excessive membership fees, forcing unions to negotiate with an employer, and forcing unions to reinstate members.

Labor Management Relations Act (Taft-Hartley Act)

Passed in 1947, the **Labor Management Relations Act** (LMRA) focuses on union activities that qualify as unfair labor practices. For example, unions cannot force employees to join. Employees also have the right to choose their union representative. Unions must bargain with the employer or its representative. Unions also cannot interfere with the negotiation and enforcement of an employer's contract. Unions cannot discriminate against non-union participants, or those who publicly oppose the union. Unions cannot encourage a secondary boycott (an attempt to encourage non-union members to cease business with an organization) or a hot cargo agreement (an attempt to force an employer to stop doing business with another company or individual). Unions also cannot charge unreasonable membership fees.

The LMRA also established the **Federal Mediation and Conciliation Service**. This piece of legislation granted power to the United States president to obtain an injunction ending a strike or lockout for an eighty-day "cooling off" period if the continuation of the strike could "imperil the health or safety of the nation."

Labor Management Reporting and Disclosure Act (Landrum-Griffith Act)

Passed in 1959, the goal of the **Labor Management Reporting and Disclosure Act (LMRDA)** was to protect employees from corrupt unions. This piece of legislation allowed for a closed shop exception for construction trades. The LMRDA also provided for a Bill of Rights for union members, which gave members the right to secret ballot elections for union offices, protection from excessive dues, freedom of speech in union matters, and the right to sue the union.

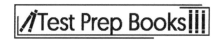
WARN Act

The **Worker Adjustment and Retraining Notification (WARN)** Act of 1988 requires that a minimum of sixty days' notice be given in advance of plant closings and mass layoffs. The notice must be given to local government, state dislocated worker units, and workers or their representatives. This piece of legislation applies to employers with one hundred or more full-time employees, or employers who have a total of full-time and part-time employees working 4,000 hours per week (not counting overtime) at all of their employment sites combined.

A plant closing is the temporary or permanent shutdown of an entire site or one or more facilities or operating units within a single site that results in an employment loss during any thirty-day period of fifty or more full-time employees. A mass layoff is a reduction in force (not a plant closing) during any thirty-day period that results in an employment loss at a single site for either fifty or more full-time employees, if they make up at least 33 percent of the workforce at the employment site, or five hundred or more full-time employees. Employment loss is the involuntary termination of employment (other than for cause), layoff for more than six months, or at least a 50 percent reduction in hours for each month of a six-month period.

The WARN Act provides for three situations in which the sixty-day notice is not required, but the burden is on the employer to show that the reasons are legitimate and not an attempt to thwart the intent of the act. First, the "faltering company" exception applies only to plant closures in situations where the company is actively seeking additional funding and has a reasonable expectation that it will be forthcoming in an amount sufficient to preclude the layoff or closure, and that giving the notice would negatively impact the ability of the company to obtain the funding. The "unforeseeable business circumstance" exception applies to plant closings and mass layoffs and occurs when circumstances take a sudden and unexpected negative change that could not have reasonably been predicted. Finally, the "natural disaster" exception applies to both plant closings and mass layoffs occurring as the result of a natural disaster such as a tornado, earthquake, or hurricane.

Glass Ceiling Act

The **Civil Rights Act of 1991** was enacted to address workplace discrimination, specifically, the practice of preventing employees from reaching higher-level positions of management based solely on race, color, religion, sex, or national origin. The **Glass Ceiling Act** is part of Title II of this Act and established a commission to study how businesses filled management positions, and whether there were significant barriers to protected groups (such as women and minorities) that were preventing them from reaching those positions.

The commission did indeed find significant barriers in a number of organizations and divided the barriers into three categories. Governmental barriers occur when companies do not enforce existing equal opportunity regulations, thus preventing protected individuals from advancing to management positions. Internal structure barriers occur when company cultures (through official policies or unofficial but normal practices) prevent protected individuals from advancing to management positions. Societal barriers occur when protected individuals cannot receive the necessary education for management positions, or when pre-existing prejudice toward the protected group prevents expected advancements. (Note: societal barriers can refer to the larger society beyond that of the company in question).

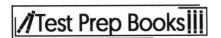
Applications of Human Relations, Culture, and Values Concepts

Human resources as a professional discipline in the workplace grew out of the human relations movement of the 1930s. It was based on the research of Elton Mayo, a psychologist from Australia who studied organizations and industries. At the turn of the century, most workplaces—particularly those with factory and industrial jobs—were organized according to classical management theory. The most prominent of these theories was **scientific management**, or **Taylorism**, after the man who developed it, Frederick W. Taylor. Scientific management emphasized efficiency, maximizing worker production, and minimizing costs. It facilitated the mass production of goods in a factory setting and streamlined processes, eliminating waste and redundancy. However, one of the main drawbacks of scientific management theory was that its machinelike approach to automation also tended to treat human workers as simply another kind of replaceable, interchangeable cog in the machine. Mayo, though, researched how human psychology affected people in the workplace.

Mayo based his observations on research about how improving worker conditions and responding to employee needs could lead to increased productivity. He observed that people naturally form groups, and natural social structures in the workplace could be more powerful than artificial organizational structures. He also believed that multilateral communication was essential, so employees had a way to share their ideas and concerns for improving working conditions. Another tenant of human relations theory is the need to develop company leadership with not just job-specific skills, but also with so-called soft skills—such as being sensitive to the moods and needs of others, communicating well, and mitigating conflict and arriving at fair solutions.

In today's business world, this has evolved into the **total person approach**, where organizations recognize that they are not just hiring a resume or a list of skills—they are hiring a whole person, with their own opinions, emotions, working styles, biases, and personal lives. Human relations theory guides worker motivation and satisfaction. An employee with a family, for instance, might be more satisfied with a flexible work schedule or telework options. This theory is also closely related to **employee morale**, which refers to the emotions, attitudes, and outlook employees have at their workplace.

Higher morale is correlated with higher productivity, so there is a strong business case supporting it. Morale can also be closely tied to a company's culture and values, which are part of its overall identity. This gives workers a sense of *why* they are doing what they do. Particularly for younger workers, close alignment with a company's values—guiding principles like customer satisfaction, community development, or ethical and honest behavior—improves morale, productivity, and employee retention. Values are contained within company **culture**, which refers to the beliefs, behaviors, and values that guide the actions of a company and thereby its employees. If company values align with employee values, employees feel more connected to the workplace and more motivated and engaged in their work.

Assessing Employee Attitudes

Special Events
Companies can use special events as a way to engage employees and promote a positive organizational culture. These events can involve managers serving lunch to employees during customer service appreciation week, organizing monthly employee events such as an ice cream social on a random Friday afternoon or an after-work happy hour, or planning an annual holiday party or company picnic for employees to enjoy with their co-workers and their families at a local amusement park. Additionally,

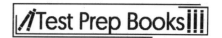

these events can incorporate an element of community service, such as employees getting together to assist a local organization (an animal shelter or a food bank) during a "day of caring" event. Employee wellness can also be factored into these special events by scheduling yoga classes onsite for employees to participate in, or by providing monthly chair massages in a conference room at a reduced price for staff.

Employee Surveys

Employee surveys are a tool that management can use to determine how HR programs are being received by staff, to uncover problem areas in the organization, and to reveal employee preferences or needs. These surveys can be distributed as attitude surveys with the goal of measuring employees' job satisfaction or as opinion surveys with the goal of gathering data on specific issues. It is important that employees know they will be guaranteed anonymity in return for their participation in the survey so they will, in turn, be as honest as possible on how they view their jobs, supervisors, coworkers, organizational policies, etc. This type of employee input provides management with data on the "retention climate" in the company. Collecting this data is extremely important to an organization's retention measurement efforts. It is important for management to share the results of the survey with employees, even if the feedback is negative. By continuing to administer employee surveys annually or at set intervals, management is able to measure improvements in responses over time.

Turnover Rates

Turnover rate is the percentage of employees who leave the workforce during a period of time, typically during a calendar or fiscal year. To calculate turnover rate, you simply take the number of employees who exited the company during the year, divide it by the average number of employees during the year, and then multiply that amount by 100. A high turnover rate can be a costly problem for a company and can have a negative effect on many aspects of organizational performance, such as productivity, safety, and financial performance.

Diversity and Inclusion

Companies are making more of a conscious effort to value the talents of employees through their career development efforts. To promote a positive organizational culture, it is important to embrace employees' unique qualities. Therefore, it is imperative for management to cultivate a workplace that encourages staff to share their suggestions. Staff must work to identify biases and be aware of how these biases affect their decision-making processes. Employees must make an effort to reach out to team members with whom they have not previously connected, and to find opportunities for diversity and inclusion in their daily work activities.

Organizations are also working to increase the level of employee engagement by connecting colleagues through the formation of employee business resource groups. These also further promote diversity and inclusion efforts. Examples include groups for African-Americans, Asian-Americans, Latino-Americans, individuals with disabilities, LGBT (lesbian, gay, bisexual, and transgender) individuals and allies, former members of the military, multicultural groups, emerging professionals, and women.

Recordkeeping

Implementing a Record Retention Process

Internet Applicants

The **Office of Federal Contract Compliance Programs (OFCCP)** created a recordkeeping rule, known as the **Internet Applicant Rule**, to determine what records need to be kept by federal contractors who have Internet applicants applying for their open positions. Under this rule, a job seeker is classified as an Internet applicant by a contractor if they meet four criteria:

- They have expressed an interest in employment over the Internet or through another related electronic data technology

- The employer considers the individual for employment in a particular position

- The individual's expression of interest indicates that they possess the basic qualifications for the open position

- The individual does not remove themselves from consideration at any point during the contractor's selection process

The following record retention requirements are based on federal guidelines. However, individual states may also have record retention requirements that need to be followed.

Pre-Employment Files

Selection, hiring, and employment records are to be kept for either one year after their creation or following the hire/no hire decision (whichever date is later). Federal contractors must keep these same types of records for three years. The following items are examples of what are included in these types of records:

- Employment applications
- Resumes
- Interview notes
- Records related to promotions, transfers, and terminations
- Requests for reasonable accommodations
- AAP records related to hiring benchmarks

I-9 forms are to be kept for three years after the date of hire or one year after the date of termination (whichever date is later).

Credit reports have no record retention requirement. However, the law requires an employer to shred all documents containing information from such a report.

Drug test records are to be kept for one year from the date the test was administered, or up to five years for any job positions related to the Department of Transportation.

Medical Files

Records associated with family medical leave (for a company with fifty or more employees) are to be kept for three years. The following items are examples of what is included in these types of records:

- Basic employee data
- Dates of leave taken
- Hours of leave taken for intermittent Family and Medical Leave Act of 1993 (FMLA) leave
- Copies of employee notices
- Records of premium payments of employee benefits
- Records of any disputes regarding designation of leave

Benefits Files

Records associated with employment benefits are to be kept for six years. The following items are examples of what are included in these types of records:

- Summary plan descriptions
- Annual reports
- Plan amendments
- Plan terminations

There are no record retention requirements for documentation associated with employees and their dependents who wish to continue group healthcare coverage under the Consolidated Omnibus Budget Reconciliation Act (COBRA) after a qualifying event. However, it is recommended that companies maintain these records for six years to be consistent with the requirements of the Employment Retirement Income Security Act (ERISA).

Injury and Illness Prevention

Occupational Injury and Illness Prevention and Compensation Programs

Injuries and illnesses are a burden for both employers and employees. The loss of productivity due to workplace injuries and illnesses can be significant, and the loss of income for employees can affect an individual and economy as a whole. Therefore, organizations must establish programs that minimize or prevent these incidents. If a workplace injury or illness does occur, **workers' compensation** may provide fixed payments to the employee. Workers' compensation also covers dependents of those who are killed as a result of workplace accidents. Limits do exist for these compensation benefits, such as caps on what can be collected from employers.

OSHA, a federal agency that is designed to ensure safe working conditions for employees, established process safety management standards that deal with hazardous chemicals in the workplace. If an employee could potentially come into contact with the hazardous substance during the normal course of their jobs, these substances must be properly evaluated, classified, and labeled. This information is recorded in **material safety data sheets** (MSDS), which must be easily accessible to individuals who work with any hazardous materials. The MSDS should state what should be done if someone has inappropriate contact with the chemicals, such as an employee who splashes a dangerous chemical in their eye.

OSHA has developed standards for employee **personal protective equipment** (PPE) in hazardous working environments. These items may include safety glasses, hard hats, and safety shoes. Employees are provided these items at no cost and must be paid their rate of pay for the time required to put on and take off protective equipment.

OSHA has established guidelines to assist employers in the event of a pandemic disease outbreak by utilizing proper safety equipment and procedures. The guidelines are also meant to assist the company to continue operations with a reduced workforce.

Ergonomics, or the study and design of the work environment to address physical demands placed on employees, is yet another area addressed by OSHA. In the workplace, ergonomics deals with elements such as lighting, placement of controls, equipment layout, and fatigue. OSHA examines work-related injuries that result from repetitive stress and repetitive motion, such as carpal tunnel. These are also known as cumulative trauma disorders. These workplace injuries may be reduced by redesigning workstations and improving workplace environments.

Workplace Safety and Security Risks

Security Plans

Obtaining a safe and secure working environment is not accomplished by simply strategizing. The staff of an organization must have adequate training to appropriately respond to diverse situations. Workplace security plans and policies address a variety of issues from a sudden crisis to an act of intentional harm. A clear understanding of security plans and policies can minimize unpredictability and panic and teach employees how to respond to a crisis.

Employees should understand security plans and how they address the physical security needs of the work environment. **Workplace security plans** may include security measures such as control badges, keycard access systems, backup communication systems, locks on various rooms and closets, and concealed alarms. When developing workplace security plans, a team approach is vital to ensuring its success. Representatives are needed from human resources, legal counsel, security, and facilities to provide a comprehensive perspective of security needs. Once the security plans and policies are established, employees should be trained annually to review the plans and their importance.

Theft is the act of taking property without the consent of the owner. Theft can occur by deception or force, with or without the knowledge of the owner. Theft can be very costly to an organization, and management should take steps to prevent any opportunity for theft. Such measures may include hidden video cameras, a private security force, and incentives for employees who disrupt incidents of theft. Theft can be accomplished by employees, management, and customers. Therefore, prevention policies should apply to all levels of the organization.

Corporate espionage is a form of spying that occurs between competitive companies. The principal purpose of corporate espionage is to obtain industrial secrets and learn about a competitor's plans, future products, business strategies, or total profits. Knowing these secrets can give a competitor an unfair advantage when trying to increase market share. A company must hire trustworthy employees, particularly employees privy to classified information. A firm should employ strategies to test employee loyalty and offer incentives that encourage employees to report suspicious activity.

Sabotage is the act of purposely weakening or corrupting a country or a company. In the workplace, sabotage is the intentional thwarting of successful planning models to create dysfunctional conditions at odds with the organization's best interests. Those who commit sabotage are known as saboteurs, and

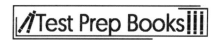

they generally conceal their identity and intentions. Sabotage is debilitating to a company and can cultivate an environment of distrust and hostility. Therefore, management must conduct frequent tests to ensure that all members and employees act in good faith.

Workplace Safety Risks

Minimizing injuries in the workplace is a primary concern for employers. Accidents and injuries triggered by safety risks diminish productivity and reduce savings because of costly workers' compensation payments. Furthermore, failure to adequately protect workers can result in employer penalties and fines. Two common workplace safety risks are tripping hazards and blood-borne pathogens.

Trip hazards cause a person's foot to hit an object that does not budge, plunging the person forward involuntarily. Tripping can occur in the workplace for many reasons such as obstructed views, poor lighting, excessive clutter, uneven walking surfaces, wrinkled carpeting, or unsecure wires. Tripping may result in injuries such as sprains, broken bones, or torn ligaments. Employers should maintain an orderly workplace and arrange for bright lighting to reduce the likelihood of tripping. Accordingly, employees should pay attention when walking, make wide turns when walking, and walk with feet pointed outward.

Bloodborne pathogens are infectious microorganisms in human blood that can cause disease in humans. Specifically, some of these pathogens are hepatitis B virus (HBV), hepatitis C virus (HCV), and human immunodeficiency virus (HIV). One potential cause of spreading bloodborne pathogens is through improper usage and/or disposal of needles. Occupations such as nursing, healthcare professionals, medical first responders, and housekeepers who work in medical environments are the most likely to encounter a needle with bloodborne pathogens. Due to growing concerns within the medical field, The Needlestick Safety and Prevention Act of 2000 revised OSHA's Bloodborne Pathogens Standard. This law provides requirements in selecting medical devices and establishes oversight through a sharps injury log, which details all sharps-related workplace injuries.

Additional workplace safety risks with OSHA regulations are occupational noise exposure, emergency exit procedures, control of hazardous materials, lockout/tagout procedures, machine guarding, and confined space environments.

Workers' compensation laws are designed to protect employees who are injured in the workplace. The primary purpose of workers' compensation is to provide injured employees with fixed monetary sums. Worker's compensation benefits cover medical expenses due to workplace injuries. Furthermore, workers' compensation benefits are extended to dependents of employees killed by an injury or illness that occurs in the workplace. In addition to employee protection, some worker's compensation laws protect employers by limiting the amount of money that can be distributed to employees. The program also has provisions that restrict co-worker liability in most workplace accidents. Most workers' compensation programs are structured at the state level by legislative bodies and agencies. However, worker's compensation exists at the federal level, where it is limited to federal employment and industries that considerably affect interstate commerce.

Emergency Response, Business Continuity, and Disaster Recovery Process

Emergency Response

All organizations must have procedures that secure an orderly response in the event of an emergency. **Emergency response plans** incorporate several elements of maintaining safety and order. These elements may include practiced evacuations, reserved resources to preserve organizational function, and a plan that seeks to minimize property damage. An organization with no emergency response plan is vulnerable to instability, disorder, and distrust. An effective emergency response plan not only protects lives and property but provides security that management has control over the situation. This knowledge provides an element of calm in an otherwise stressful emergency situation, which can be as important as the response protocol.

An emergency response is planned and practiced protocol used during an emergency. These strategies should be planned rationally and practiced frequently to mitigate the impact of a disaster. Workplace emergency responses should plan for a wide range of scenarios, such as machinery malfunctions or workplace violence. Once created, emergency response plans should be communicated to all staff, frequently tested by the organization, and kept up to date.

An **evacuation** is a coordinated and planned exit from a place that is considered to be dangerous. It is a principal component of general health and safety policies. Conditions that may prompt evacuation are fire, flood, or violence. The most effective way to orchestrate an orderly and calm evacuation is through practice of an evacuation plan. This routine practice familiarizes staff with expedient exit routes and ensures that exits remain visible and unobstructed.

Hazard communication is the notification of employees concerning the noxious health effects and physical dangers of hazardous chemicals in the workplace. Workers should be clearly notified of any physical hazards (corrosion or flammability) or health hazards (skin irritation and carcinogenicity) that they will come into contact with in the workplace. OSHA created the Hazard Communication Standard (HCS) to ensure that chemical information is accessible to all individuals who may interact with the substance. In addition to the HCS, all employers are required to implement a hazard communication program that encompasses training, access to material safety data sheets (MSDS), and labeling of hazardous chemical containers.

Developing Business Continuity and Disaster Recovery Plans

In the event of a crisis, an organization may face multiple challenges such as mitigating casualties, protecting property, and testing disciplinary protocol. Aside from protecting human life, the most challenging priority during a crisis is maintaining business continuity. Business continuity maintains productivity during and after a potential disruption.

Business continuity plans identify potential threats and their associated impacts to maintain organizational productivity during an operational interruption. These plans establish procedures to handle disruptions and/or loss of business functions. There are four components to a business continuity plan: business impact analysis, recovery strategies, plan development, and testing and exercises. A business impact analysis (BIA) assesses the potential consequences of a disruption and collects information to develop recovery strategies. A BIA is a risk assessment tool, and information can be gathered by means of a questionnaire. The second step is to identify, document, and implement the most comprehensive of the proposed strategies. Recovery strategies frequently identify gaps in necessary resources. The third step, plan development, builds a business continuity team and crafts the business continuity plan. Finally, extensive training and testing are conducted to test strategies, personnel, and the business continuity plan.

Business continuity plans respond to a variety of crisis scenarios, such as a loss of administrative capacities, a hack into the operating system, and threat of workplace violence. These plans must be observed by all staff to ensure the plan's effectiveness. If an employee does not comply, disciplinary measures should be enforced by the organization.

A **disaster recovery plan (DRP)** is a set of procedures that prepares for a disaster so that destructive effects are reduced, and essential data can be recovered. A DRP increases a firm's ability to recover from an unexpected, devastating incident. A DRP assists the organization in resuming normal business functions as quickly as possible. As information technology systems become more sophisticated and complex, solving critical organizational technology questions becomes more difficult. The ability of hackers and viruses to infiltrate these systems makes an effective organizational DRP more important than ever.

Technological increases have created viable scenarios for employers to offer alternative work locations. If a corporation offers alternative work locations, these employees are allowed to work from home or another off-site location rather than a traditional office space. Communication between organizations and its remote employees generally takes place through the Internet and phone calls. Alternative work locations can be helpful in disaster recovery because organizational data is decentralized and more difficult to corrupt entirely.

A procedure is a recognized and established way of accomplishing a desired goal. Procedures provide a plan of action for organizations in a time of vulnerability or crisis. The business continuity plan, disaster recovery plan, and any additional organizational policies should be studied and practiced frequently by employees.

Business Continuity and Disaster Recovery Plan Training

A business continuity plan or disaster recovery plan is only as good as the organization's ability to implement the plan. If all levels of employees and management are not familiar with the plan, they will not be able to execute it when the need arises. Employees and management must possess unwavering familiarity with the DRP. The best defense against disruption is training that allows the workforce to react according to the DRP, maximizing the allocation of resources and reducing panic.

The organization should devote sufficient time and resources to ensure proper training for its employees. This training should begin with an awareness of the plan and its components. Employees should understand the plan's framework and their role in the plan. If a staff member has a specific role in the plan, this staff member may require additional time and training.

Scenario training is the next essential step in ensuring a successful business continuity and/or disaster recovery plan. Employees and management respond to mock scenarios that provide them opportunities to utilize their training. These scenarios may also be used as an opportunity to test critical backup systems, applications, and facilities. During scenario training, all areas of response should be documented for further evaluation and review.

After scenario training is complete, the organization can review what aspects of the plan were successful and unsuccessful. This evaluation assists in determining potential changes to the plan and updating the plan as necessary. All areas of management should review the scenario training to determine the best possible course of action.

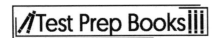

Internal Investigation, Monitoring, and Surveillance Techniques

Companies should maintain maximum security while possessing the personal information of customers and employees. Each organization should utilize an apparatus that monitors and reports security breaches, notifying employees, customers, and various authorities. In addition, internal privacy policies must comply with current laws and regulations. These laws are intended to deter security breaches.

A company's **internal privacy policy** should address sensitive information such as addresses, telephone numbers, credit reports, medical reports, employee records, company technology, and data systems that collect personal information. An effective privacy policy explains the purposes of investigations and monitors the conduct of employees. Episodic privacy tests can be useful, particularly if management has reason to believe that employee misconduct has occurred. A company should communicate regularly with its employees about security issues and technology. Additionally, written policies must exist to protect employers from employee claims of privacy invasion. Employees should be notified of these policies and agree to all conditions. An effective privacy policy will identify and monitor employees suspected of violating protocol and procure the necessary information to review the employee's practices.

Identity theft occurs when a person wrongfully obtains and uses another individual's personal information, typically for financial gain. This form of fraud can be very damaging and is difficult to prevent. To commit identity theft, a perpetrator does not need a person's fingerprint. The criminal simply needs a Social Security number, credit card number, bank statements, or any piece of information that will allow access to personal documents. The expense of identity theft to the victim can be shocking, and in some cases may be in excess of $100,000. Identity theft primarily occurs in public places through methods such as "shoulder surfing." This technique involves watching over somebody's shoulder when they are using an ATM machine or rummaging through someone's garbage in search of confidential material that was not disposed of properly.

Data protection is the process of securing personal information from identity theft or other corruptive activities. Data protection involves storing important materials and can be done through a variety of means, such as file locking, disk mirroring, and database shadowing. The principal purpose of data protection is to maintain the integrity and proper storage of information. Two effective means of achieving maximum data protection while ensuring availability is to pursue data lifecycle management (DLM) and information lifecycle management (ILM), which may provide better data protection in the event of a virus or hack. A feasible data protection plan is also applicable to disaster recovery and business continuity.

Workplace monitoring is a policy that employers use to monitor a suspicious person and gather information. Employers may use a workplace monitoring program to discover activities that threaten the integrity and interests of the firm. Particular monitoring techniques involve wiretapping, reviewing Internet content usage, GPS tracking, checking employees' social media accounts, and interviewing other employees about suspicious activity. Management surveillance programs are easier to execute if employees are required to use company phones and computers. However, before such actions are taken by an employer, all employees should be given ample documentation of rules and regulations. This will ensure that any breach of protocol is intentional and deliberate on the part of the employee.

Data Security and Privacy

Secure data storage is a difficult but necessary policy to prevent corruption from malware and hackers. Data corruption is a widespread concern for firms of all sizes and locations. Organizations with sensitive and confidential data, such as government agencies, continue to take steps to strengthen their data security. Data backup requires copying and archiving current information to separate drives to restore information in the event of data corruption. Data storage and backup are essential to protect organizational plans, policies, and secrets in the event of a data breach.

The Collective Bargaining Process

Collective bargaining is the act of negotiation between an employer and its employees, where a union represents the employees' interests. The NLRA addresses the collective bargaining process and lays out legal definitions for negotiating in good faith, both on the part of the employer and the union. Some examples of negotiating in bad faith include employers making contract proposals directly to employees without working through the union that represents them, employers urging employees to engage in activities that would weaken the union's negotiating power (for example, encouraging employees to decertify the union), and employers making unfavorable changes to workplace terms and conditions (such as pay, hours, and special pay) during the process of collective bargaining. Additional examples of negotiating in bad faith include unions refusing to disclose critical information during the collective bargaining process, unions refusing to reasonably cooperate in the logistics of the negotiation process (for example, time and location), and unions engaging in an unfair labor practice, as defined by the Labor Management Relations Act.

The NLRB helps define and limit the subjects that can be discussed during a collective bargaining negotiation. Illegal subjects cannot be discussed during negotiations and generally involve actions that fall outside the realm of contract negotiations. Examples include hot cargo agreements, security clauses, or any illegal activity on the part of the employer or union. Mandatory subjects must be discussed during negotiations. Mandatory subjects typically involve the basics of employees' working conditions and terms, covering areas such as hours, benefits, pay, and worker safety concerns. Voluntary subjects are topics that parties are permitted to discuss but may choose not to. Voluntary subjects include all issues not covered under the categories of illegal or mandatory subjects.

The goal of collective bargaining is to develop a mutually agreed-upon collective bargaining agreement (CBA). The CBA should address basic terms and conditions including the following:

- Hours, benefits, pay, and workplace safety

- The contract grievance process, which is a clear statement of the procedures to be followed in case of a dispute as well as the actions the organization can take if employees do not follow the terms of the contract

- A zipper clause stating that the CBA has been agreed to and is final. The zipper clause also dictates that any issues not covered in the current contract cannot be discussed until it expires.

There are several strategies that are commonly employed by unions during a collective bargaining negotiation. **Single-unit bargaining** occurs when union representatives meet with one employer at a time and don't attempt to use the process as a springboard in separate negotiations. **Coordinated**

bargaining takes place when unions within an organization meet with the employer to negotiate beneficial results for the groups they represent (also called multi-unit bargaining). **Multi-employer bargaining** occurs when a union with employees in multiple companies meets with all of those companies as a single negotiation. Finally, **parallel bargaining** occurs when a union successfully negotiates an agreement with a company, then uses the result of that negotiation as an example while dealing with a different company (also called leapfrogging or whipsawing).

Organization or union representatives typically use one of two approaches when engaging in a collective bargaining process. **Distributive bargaining** takes place when a group negotiates with the goal of achieving specific objectives (also called positional bargaining). **Principled bargaining** occurs when a group negotiates while remaining mindful of the key issues to each side of the process. The negotiation then becomes a process of searching for solutions from both sides in hopes that an agreement can be reached.

Collective Bargaining Activities
Unions
In its broadest sense, a **union** (also known as a labor union) is simply a formally organized group of employees who work together to accomplish goals. These goals usually involve working conditions, pay, and other aspects of a common trade, but can vary widely depending on the union and the particular situation.

Types
A **local union** refers to either a union for a small organization or a union for a smaller geographic area. In many cases, the local union serves as a branch of the larger national union for a particular trade. A **national union** is often comprised of smaller, local unions. These groups represent a wide geographic area. A national union could represent employees of a single organization or employees of multiple organizations that happen to be working in the same trade. A **federation** is made up of different national unions representing different industries that nevertheless share some commonalities and have common goals. Finally, an international union represents workers in multiple countries.

Organizing Process
Unions must go through a specific process to be officially organized and recognized as a legitimate representative for a group of workers. Employees must demonstrate an interest in participating in the union and must sign authorization cards indicating their interest in the union. At least 30 percent of eligible employees are required to sign authorization cards by the NLRB before they can order an election. The union must inform the employer of the employees' desire to unionize. If at this point the employer refuses, the union may take action through the NLRB. The NLRB then holds an election where employees vote on whether to be represented by the union. Employees are eligible to vote in the election if they were on the company's payroll during the pay period directly prior to the calling of the election and during the pay period immediately preceding the election date. Any employees who were striking and then were permanently replaced are allowed to vote in an election that is conducted within twelve months following the end of the strike.

Picketing
Picketing is an act of protest where a group of people (picketers) gather in front of a business to raise awareness of an issue or to discourage people from entering a building to work or do business. The NLRB outlines what kinds of picketing activities unions may legally participate in. Employees may engage

in informational picketing, where they picket to announce to the public that they are not represented by any one authority and thus plan to organize. Employees may also engage in organizational picketing, where they picket to convince employees to join or support their union. Finally, employees may engage in recognitional picketing, where they picket to encourage the employer to recognize their union as the employees' representative.

While in disputes with an employer, unions may engage in common situs picketing. This is where employees picket at a location used by the targeted employer as well as other organizations. This is legal as long as the picketers make clear which employer is being protested, so that other organizations are not adversely affected by the picketing. Unions may also use consumer picketing, where employees picket to discourage the public from doing business with the employer in question. Finally, unions can take advantage of double breasting picketing, where employees picket at a location where the employer's workers are not unionized. This is only legal in certain situations.

Decertification

If a company's employees feel that their union is not doing a good enough job to represent them, they can go through the process of **decertification**, which strips the union of its official status as the employees' representatives. To decertify the union, 30 percent of employees must first sign a petition. Then, the employees can file the petition with the NLRB. The petition cannot be filed less than twelve months after the union was officially certified. If the NLRB approves the petition, then it holds a decertification election among the company employees. The union is decertified if a majority of the voting employees vote in favor of the decertification (a tie vote also means the union is decertified).

Deauthorization

Deauthorization is a process of removing a union's security clause and its authority to negotiate. A security clause is basically a condition in a contract that requires employees to join a union. The deauthorization process is identical to that of decertification. First, 30 percent of employees must sign a petition in favor of deauthorization. Then, the employees file the petition with the NLRB. If the NLRB approves the petition, then it holds a decertification election among the company employees. Deauthorization is approved if a majority of the employees, who are eligible to vote, vote in favor of deauthorization. In this instance, a situation where employees who are eligible and do not exercise their right to vote equates to a vote against deauthorization.

Performance Management

Performance Appraisal

Performance appraisal is a process that is integral to maintaining standards that are essential to consistent productivity in an organization. An intricate process, performance appraisal measures and evaluates the quality of work that is performed by employees. It is a barometer by which employees must exceed pre-established benchmarks and simultaneously uphold organizational protocol. Moreover, managers and administrators compare performance appraisal results with other employees and expectations while making rational decisions regarding efficacy and value. From the process, management crafts a compilation of results and data with the intention of performing a cost-benefit analysis. After these analytical methodologies are conducted, management and administrators will enact appropriate changes for improvement.

After a performance appraisal, management will affect these improvements through incentivizing programs. Increasing salaries or rewarding promotions are typically two strategies that are used to

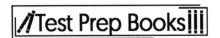

reinforce desired behavior. For employees who are found to be less efficient or productive, training or counseling programs are a means of providing underperforming individuals with the tools to improve. In some instances, management will pursue punitive responses to underperformance: demotions, reductions in pay, or termination of employment. Essential to performance appraisal is the establishment of firm standards and procedures for an organization in which underperformance will be quickly rectified. An inflexible organizational infrastructure forces employees to conform to the institution, rather than institutional codes being disregarded and ignored.

Communicational development is a crucial advantage of performance appraisal. A channel of communication is clearly delineated through two principal means: organizational rules and regulations, and explicit managerial examinations. Organizational policies offer nonverbal guidance to employees by consistently challenging them to assimilate to protocol while sustaining maximal productive capacities. After performance appraisals are conducted, managerial expectations can be developed, and solutions to remedy underperformance can be pursued. Any disputes between labor and management can quickly be softened by maintaining stringent channels of communication, where both sides have assigned responsibilities and coordinate to meet shared goals.

Instruments

Some types of performance appraisals are the 360-degree feedback, general appraisal, employee self-assessment appraisal, and the technological/administrative performance appraisal. The 360-degree feedback method is a way for employees to receive feedback about their performance in an anonymous manner from individuals they frequently work in close contact with, such as their managers, peers, direct reports, customers, and suppliers. The employee self-assessment appraisal forces employees to examine their own work, while management conducts a concurrent appraisal. After these are completed, the two are jointly compared. The technological/administrative performance appraisal concentrates on employees who perform technical jobs. The type of work they do, productivity levels, output, and other important tasks are barometers by which employers measure.

Ranking/Rating Scales

Another system for rating employees is the behaviorally anchored rating scales, or (BARS). **BARS** is a unique system because it specifically focuses on behaviors that are necessary for performing a task successfully, rather than evaluating more analytical employee habits. Instead of appraising general behaviors that are required to be present in all employees, BARS examines precise behaviors that are unique to a certain job or task. After an investigation has taken place, management will employ a designated rating scale that appropriately locates an employee based on performance. On the rating scale, a "1" designates unsatisfactory performance, a "2" designates marginal performance (troublesome employees), a "3" designates fully competent performance, a "4" designates excellent performance, and a "5" designates exceptional performance.

The 1–5 rating scale method demonstrated above is just one of the numerous varieties. In addition to the 1–5 rating scale, they can also express a 1–3 model, 1–4 model, 1–5 model, or 1–10 model. These models are known as **rating scale methods**. Moreover, another prominent method of appraisal is the checklist method. The checklist method features a series of questions that determine a specific level of performance, with the participant placing a check next to applicable statements.

Goal Setting

A robust system of planning can be incorporated into an organization's agenda to set expectations and devise strategies to meet them. Monitoring performance levels enables organizations to ensure that

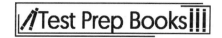

operations harmonize with expectations. If specific goals are not met, this indicates an error in planning or execution. Identifying any unmet goals makes organizations more likely to become more productive by constantly improving.

Relationship to Compensation

Rating is a tactic that employers use to incentivize employees to efficiently fulfill tasks in a timely manner. In addition, rating is a way that employers can measure and identify their productive, talented, and best workers. After employees are rated, the highest-performing individuals will be rewarded. Similarly to rating, rewarding is a mechanism used to incentivize and reinforce positive behavior. In all successful organizations, employers have discovered the most efficient means of regulating, monitoring, and sculpting maximal performance strategies.

Training for Evaluators

One key reason why performance appraisals tend to be ineffective is that most individuals who evaluate employee performance have received little or no training on how to do so, and they are not adequately supported throughout the performance appraisal process.

Therefore, many types of performance appraisal errors may result. Evaluators make the **similar-to-me error** when they rate employees more favorably who are like themselves. **Contrast errors** come into play when an evaluator focuses on a particular stereotype, such as age or race, instead of on performance when rating employees, or when an evaluator compares two employees who have similar performance records and rates one of the employees higher than the other due to their likeability. **Excessive leniency** or **excessive strictness** occurs when performance appraisals are written to be too accommodating or too harsh and tend to be more about the evaluator's temperament than about the employee's job performance. The **halo effect** takes place when an employee receives a glowing performance appraisal (is rated highly in all areas regardless of actual job performance), after the evaluator notices that he or she is really very good at performing one aspect of their job (perhaps something that the evaluator values personally).

The opposite of halo effect is what is known as the horn effect. The **horn effect** takes place when an employee receives a negative performance appraisal (is rated poorly in all areas regardless of actual job performance), after the evaluator notices that he or she is poor at performing one aspect of their job (perhaps something that the evaluator values personally). In addition, central tendency error takes place when the evaluator gives all employees a middle of the range performance appraisal score (i.e., a 6 out of 10), so he or she cannot be perceived as "the bad guy" if the truth about employees' job performance is told. The recency effect takes place when an evaluator bases an employee's performance appraisal solely on a recent event (good or bad) instead of on the employee's entire performance history during the established rating period. The opposite of this is what is known as the primacy error. This error takes place when an evaluator bases an employee's performance appraisal solely on their initial impression of the employee (good or bad) instead of on the employee's performance history during the established rating period.

Evaluators should receive the necessary training to ensure that employees' performance appraisals are free from all bias and discrimination. This involves training on how to use the performance tool, training on the various types of performance appraisal errors listed above and how to avoid them, along with how to manage difficult conversations with employees. Performance appraisals should be based on formal evaluation criteria that has been previously set and on evaluators' personal interactions with the employees. Evaluators should accurately describe employees' behavior by citing specific examples using objective criteria and to document situations as they occur. Additionally, equitable treatment should be provided to all employees during the performance appraisal process.

Outcomes of Performance Management Programs
There are several outcomes of the performance management process, including:

- Disciplinary actions that can be taken for underperforming employees
- Pay increases and incentive rewards
- Opportunities for employee advancement and promotions
- Employee development plans
- Career/succession planning

Performance management gives organizations the opportunity to identify the most suitable jobs for the most qualified people. After analyzing the results of goal setting, if certain individuals possess skill sets that indicate that they would be more productive in other areas of the business, this phase allows those transitions, or transfer assignments, to occur. Furthermore, promotions can be used to reinforce positive behavior. Another strategic use of promotions is to maximize each individual's utility by encouraging them to take positions that they may not have otherwise been interested in. These types of employment moves should be properly documented through the employees' performance appraisals to ensure that the organization is protected should any legal concerns arise.

Termination Concepts

Termination
Termination is the final step in the progressive discipline process and when an employee is removed from their job. Terminations occur for behavioral issues, poor job performance, and policy violations. It is imperative that employees receive sufficient warning regarding the seriousness of their offenses prior to their termination.

Once the decision is made to end a staff member's employment, the actual termination takes place in a swift manner, typically during a face-to-face meeting. During the termination meeting, with the employee's manager and sometimes with a member of HR, the employee's building and systems access is deactivated, while the employee's co-workers are gathered together in a conference room. This allows the terminated employee a few minutes of privacy to gather personal belongings under the supervision of building security, HR, or the employee's manager. Then the terminated employee is escorted out of the building.

In some situations, terminated employees are given formal contracts known as separation agreements. The agreements state that the terminated employees agree not to sue the employer in exchange for some previously agreed-upon severance pay and/or other conditions.

Reductions in Force (RIFs)
RIFs are the planned elimination of a number of personnel to make an organization more competitive through reducing costs, using technology to replace labor, leveraging mergers and acquisitions, or by moving a company to a more economical location. Although RIFs do help companies to cut costs in the short-term, they often hurt productivity. For an organization to successfully implement a RIF, it should communicate with employees throughout the entire process; provide any downsized employee with outplacement services to assist them with resume writing, career counseling, interview preparation, and

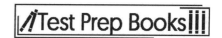
referral assistance; and strive to build the trust and commitment of the remaining employees to boost their morale.

Employees who are laid off are typically asked to sign a document known as a separation agreement and general release. This document, when signed, is a legally binding agreement that states the employee cannot sue or make any claims against the company in exchange for agreed-upon severance benefits. Severance pay is not required by law, but most companies will pay employees who are laid off a set number of weeks of salary continuation based on their years of service (typically one or two weeks' pay per year of service) to ease their financial burden and to preserve the organization's image. Some companies also include a continuation of health care benefits for a set period of time. An employee is given the agreement during their exit meeting and is allowed to take it home and review it with a lawyer. They have twenty-one days to sign and return the agreement for an individual separation and forty-five days to sign and return the agreement in cases of a group RIF. Once the agreement is signed, an employee still has seven days to revoke their signature.

Wrongful Discharge

A **wrongful discharge** occurs when an employee is terminated after they refuse to do something unsafe, unethical, or illegal, such as a pharmacist refusing to sign off on a prescription to be dispensed that does not have a date. This type of termination is wrongful because it violates public policy. Additionally, a charge of wrongful discharge can also occur when an employee is terminated after an employer promised them job security, thus violating an implied employment agreement.

Glossary

Ad-Hoc Arbitrator	May also be a certified professional or a mutually trusted third party, but do not have a regular arbitration relationship with either party; Instead, they are chosen as a one-time solution to address only the unique dispute in question.
Affirmative Action Plan	Aids employers with identifying imbalances in the workforce and assists them with placing a focus on hiring, training, and promoting groups of workers who are underrepresented
Alignment (Likert Scale)	How well employees' knowledge, skills, and abilities match their tasks
Alumni Program	Allows HR to communicate with and keep up with former employees
Arbitration	Way to settle disputes without taking the issue to court; In a general sense, arbitration is a form of mediation.
Arbitrator Panel	Functions just like an ad-hoc arbitrator, but it is comprised of multiple arbitrators (usually three)
Behaviorally Anchored Rating Scales (BARS)	Unique system because it specifically focuses on behaviors that are necessary for performing a task successfully, rather than evaluating more analytical employee habits
Binding Decision	Disputing parties are required by law to follow the decision reached as a result of the arbitration process.
Bloodborne Pathogens	Infectious microorganisms in human blood that can cause disease in humans
Bottom Line Concept	An employer is not required to evaluate each component of the selection process individually if the end result is shown to be predictive of future job performance.
Brown Bag Lunch Program	Informal meeting including employees and management that is used to discuss company problems
Business Continuity Plans	Identify potential threats and their associated impacts in order to maintain organizational productivity during an operational interruption
Clayton Act	Provides additional detail clarifying the Sherman Antitrust Act; It provides examples of potentially illegal or monopoly-forming activities, including mergers, exclusive dealings, and price discrimination.
Collective Bargaining	Act of negotiation between an employer and its employees, where a union represents the employees' interests
Company Culture	Refers to the beliefs, behaviors, and values that guide the actions of a company and thereby its employees
Company Culture (Likert Scale)	Personality of a company
Compulsory Arbitration	The disputing parties are required by law to go through the arbitration process.
Constructive Confrontation	Type of mediation used in some extremely complicated or contentious disputes, particularly ones where neither party is able to agree to a compromise
Contrast Errors	Come into play when an evaluator focuses on a particular stereotype or an employee's likeability
Coordinated Bargaining	Takes place when unions within an organization meet with the employer to negotiate beneficial results for the groups they represent (also called multi-unit bargaining)
Corporate Espionage	Form of spying that occurs between competitive companies
Data Protection	Process of securing personal information from identity theft or other corruptive activities
De Minimis Violations (OSHA)	Not directly and immediately related to employees' safety or health and do not require fines or citations
Deauthorization	Process of removing a union's security clause and its authority to negotiate

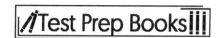

Decertification	Strips the union of its official status as the employees' representatives
Development (Likert Scale)	Whether employees have opportunities for professional growth
Disaster Recovery Plan (DRP)	Set of procedures that prepares for a disaster so that destructive effects are reduced, and essential data can be recovered
Distributive Bargaining	Takes place when a group negotiates with the goal of achieving specific objectives (also called positional bargaining)
Drug-Free Workplace Act of 1988	Requires organizations to establish a drug-free workplace, provide a copy of this policy to their employees, and institute a drug awareness program
Dual Career Ladder	Specific type of program employed by organizations that allow room for advancement without promoting an individual into a supervisory or managerial role
Emergency Response Plans	Incorporate several elements of maintaining safety and order
Employee Handbooks	Important tools to communicate information to staff concerning the company's culture, work hours, safety, harassment, attendance, benefits, pay, electronic communication policies, and discipline policies
Employee Morale	Refers to the emotions, attitudes, and outlook employees have at their workplace
Employee Survey	Can be used to ask employees how they feel about the company
Employee Survey	A tool that management can use to determine how HR programs are being received by staff, to uncover problem areas in the organization, and to reveal employee preferences or needs
Employee-Management Committee	Specific kind of committee where employees work alongside management to address company concerns
Ergonomics	Study and design of the work environment to address physical demands placed on employees
Evacuation	Coordinated and planned exit from a place that is considered to be dangerous
Excessive Leniency or Strictness	Occurs when performance appraisals are written to be too accommodating or too harsh and tend to be more about the evaluator's temperament than about the employee's job performance
Exit Interviews	Typically conducted by a neutral party, such as an HR professional, rather than by the departing employee's direct supervisor
Expense Policies	Describe how employees can charge business expenses for items like travel and accommodation, food, and other covered costs incurred in carrying out their job function
Facilitation (Likert Scale)	Whether employees have access to the tools and resources they need to perform their jobs
Faragher Vs. City of Boca Raton	The court stated that employers can be held liable for supervisory harassment that results in an adverse employment action.
Federal Mediation and Conciliation Service	Granted power to the United States president to obtain an injunction ending a strike or lockout for an eighty-day "cooling off" period if the continuation of the strike could "imperil the health or safety of the nation"
Glass Ceiling Act	Established a commission to study how businesses filled management positions, and whether there were significant barriers to protected groups that were preventing them from reaching those positions
Grievance	Complaint made by an employee that is formally stated in writing
Halo Effect	Takes place when an employee receives a glowing performance appraisal after the evaluator notices that they are really very good at performing one aspect of their job
Harris Vs. Forklift Systems, Inc.	This case established the "reasonable person" standard for hostile environment sexual harassment.
Hazard Communication	Notification of employees concerning the noxious health effects and physical dangers of hazardous chemicals in the workplace

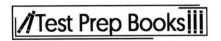

High-Potential Employees	Also known as high-pos, these are individuals who fall in the top 10 percent of talent.
Horn Effect	Takes place when an employee receives a negative performance appraisal after the evaluator notices that they are poor at performing one aspect of their job
Hostile Work Environment	Takes place when sexual or discriminatory conduct creates a work environment that a "reasonable person" would find threatening or abusive (i.e., unwelcome advances, offensive gender-related language, and sexual innuendos)
Identity Theft	Occurs when a person wrongfully obtains and uses another individual's personal information, typically for financial gain
Immigration Reform and Control Act (IRCA)	Created to prevent discrimination against individuals based on national origin or citizenship on elements such as employment, pay, or benefits, so long as they are legally able to work in the United States
Imminent Danger (OSHA)	Violation against OSHA standards that will lead to serious harm or death
Internal Privacy Policy	Address sensitive information such as addresses, telephone numbers, credit reports, medical reports, employee records, company technology, and data systems that collect personal information
Internet Applicant Rule	A job seeker is classified as an Internet applicant by a contractor if they meet four criteria.
Intranet	Internal website and computer network. It has the benefit of no risk of important information being accessed by someone outside the organization
Introductory Statement	A company overview that includes information concerning headcount, along with any significant employment changes that have taken place in the past calendar year
Job Group Analysis	A list of all titles that comprise each job group
Labor Management Relations Act (LMRA)	Focuses on union activities that qualify as unfair labor practices
Labor Management Reporting and Disclosure Act (LMRDA)	Intended to protect employees from corrupt unions
Labor Union	A formally organized group of employees who work together to accomplish goals. Unions can be local, national, or federal
Leadership (Likert Scale)	How leaders communicate with and motivate employees
Management and Leadership Development	Critical component for organizations to invest in
Management by Walking Around (MBWA)	Involves having managers and supervisors physically get out of their offices and interact with employees in person
Material Safety Data Sheets (MSDS)	This is documentation which informs if an employee could potentially come into contact with the hazardous substance during the normal course of their jobs, these substances must be properly evaluated, classified, and labeled.
Mediation	Often serves as a precursor to the more official step of arbitration
Meritor Savings Bank Vs. Vinson	This case dealt with an employee who was plagued with unwanted sexual innuendos. The court said that the plaintiff need not prove concrete psychological harm, just an abusive or intimidating environment.
Multi-Employer Bargaining	Occurs when a union with employees in multiple companies meets with all of those companies as a single negotiation
National Labor Relations Act (NLRA)	Grants specific rights to workers who already belong to, or wish to join, a union
Non-Binding Decisions	Carry no legal weight; Either party may choose to follow or not follow the terms of the decision.
Norris-LaGuardia Act	Designed to protect workers' rights to form and join a union, as well as their right to strike
Occupational Safety and Health Act	Passed in 1970, established the Occupational Safety and Health Administration (OSHA) of the federal government in 1971

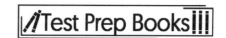

Office Of Federal Contract Compliance Programs (OFCCP)	Created a recordkeeping rule to determine what records need to be kept by federal contractors who have Internet applicants applying for their open positions
On-Boarding (Organizational Socialization)	Process by which new hires obtain the knowledge, skills, and behaviors they need in order to become valued, productive contributors to the company
Oncale Vs. Sundowner Offshore Service, Inc.	The court ruled that same-gender sexual harassment is actionable.
Open-Door Policy	Used to establish a relationship where employees feel comfortable speaking directly with management about problems and suggestions
Organization Climate	The overall "mood" of an organization
Organizational Profile	Depicts the organization's staffing patterns, to determine if any barriers exist to equal opportunity employment
Other-Than-Serious (OSHA)	Means that the condition could impact employees' safety or health but probably would not cause death or serious harm
Parallel Bargaining	Occurs when a union successfully negotiates an agreement with a company, then uses the result of that negotiation as an example while dealing with a different company (also called leapfrogging or whipsawing)
Performance Appraisal	Process that is integral to maintaining standards that are essential to consistent productivity in an organization
Performance Improvement Plan (PIP)	Formal written document concluded between the employee and the company (generally a manager, supervisor, or HR)
Permanent Arbitrator	Someone who routinely judges arbitration cases for a company or other organization
Personal Protective Equipment (PPE)	Items used for hazardous working environments, which include safety glasses, hard hats, and safety shoes
Picketing	Act of protest where a group of people (picketers) gather in front of a business to raise awareness of an issue or to discourage people from entering a building to work or do business
Pregnancy Discrimination Act	Applies to all employers with fifteen or more employees and states that while pregnant women are working, they are to be treated in the same way as other employees who are performing their jobs
Principled Bargaining	Occurs when a group negotiates while remaining mindful of the key issues to each side of the process
Quid Pro Quo Sexual Harassment	Takes place when a superior conditions employment (i.e., promotional opportunity, raise, etc.) on sexual favors
Railway Labor Act	Puts limits on strikes by railroad and airline unions, if those strikes are found to cause major problems to the nation's transportation system and its ability to engage in trade
Rating Scale Methods	In addition to the 1–5 rating scale, scales can be expressed as a 1–3 model, 1–4 model, 1–5 model, or 1–10 model.
Recognition Programs	Include personalized thank you notes for a job well done, company merchandise, and gift cards
Reductions in Force (RIF)	Planned elimination of a number of personnel to make an organization more competitive
Sabotage	Act of purposely weakening or corrupting a country or a company
Scientific Management (Taylorism)	Emphasized efficiency, maximizing worker production, and minimizing costs; It facilitated the mass production of goods in a factory setting and streamlined processes, eliminating waste and redundancy.
Secure Data Storage	Difficult but necessary policy to prevent corruption from malware and hackers
Serious (OSHA)	Means that the violation will likely cause death or physical harm
Sherman Antitrust Act	Piece of legislation intended to protect free trade

Similar-To-Me Error	When evaluators rate employees more favorably who are like themselves
Single-Unit Bargaining	Occurs when union representatives meet with one employer at a time and don't attempt to use the process as a springboard in separate negotiations
Standard Operating Procedure (SOP)	Written description of the steps involved in completing a specific task
Suggestion Program	Allows employees to recommend ways to address company problems
Supporting Performance and Employment Activities	Key HR function that comes with corresponding legal risk
Task Force	Similar to a committee but focused on a specific problem and is usually temporary in nature
Termination	Final step in the progressive discipline process and when an employee is removed from their job
Total Person Approach	Organizations recognize that they are not just hiring a resume or a list of skills—they are hiring a whole person, with their own opinions, emotions, working styles, biases, and personal lives.
Town Hall Meetings	Formal gatherings for the entire company that are commonly referred to as "all-hands meetings"
Trip Hazards	Cause a person's foot to hit an object that does not budge, plunging the person forward involuntarily
Turnover Rate	Percentage of employees who leave the workforce during a period of time, typically during a calendar or fiscal year
Voluntary Arbitration	The disputing parties choose to undergo the arbitration process, usually because they cannot come to an agreement, but do not want to go through a potentially expensive and time-consuming lawsuit.
Willful and Repeated Citations (OSHA)	Issued to employers who are repeat offenders of hazardous workplace violations
Worker Adjustment and Retraining Notification (WARN) Act of 1988	Requires that a minimum of sixty days' notice be given in advance of plant closings and mass layoffs
Workers' Compensation	May provide fixed payments to the employee if a workplace injury or illness occurs
Workplace Monitoring	Policy that employers use in order to monitor a suspicious person and gather information
Workplace Security Plans	Include security measures such as control badges, keycard access systems, backup communication systems, locks on various rooms and closets, and concealed alarms
Wrongful Discharge	Occurs when an employee is terminated after they refuse to do something unsafe, unethical, or illegal

Practice Quiz

1. Which of the following statements is true about the Landrum-Griffith Act?
   a. This act outlawed yellow-dog contracts.
   b. This act established the Federal Mediation and Conciliation Service.
   c. This act created the NLRB to encourage union growth.
   d. This act created a Bill of Rights for union members.

2. Which of the following pieces of legislation established a commission to study how women and minorities face significant barriers and are prevented from reaching management positions?
   a. Title II
   b. The Civil Rights Act of 1991
   c. Equal Pay Act
   d. The Glass Ceiling Act

3. Which of the following communication strategies is used to allow management to check on employee progress, inquire about potential issues, and gain other feedback without relying on employees to "make the first move"?
   a. Open-door policy
   b. Brown bag lunch program
   c. Town hall meetings
   d. Management by Walking Around (MBWA)

4. Which of the following types of picketing is done by employees for the purpose of convincing other employees to join their union?
   a. Informational picketing
   b. Recognitional picketing
   c. Organizational picketing
   d. Common situs picketing

5. Does OSHA offer any rights to employees, and if so, what do these rights entail?
   a. OSHA does not offer rights to employees, only safety protections.
   b. OSHA does grant rights to employees, such as the right to a pay increase if hazardous substances are introduced to the workplace.
   c. OSHA does grant rights to employees, such as the right to register complaints against their employer without fear of retaliation and the right to meet privately with an OSHA inspector.
   d. OSHA does grant rights to employees, but only after one year of employment.

See answers on next page.

Answer Explanations

1. D: The Landrum-Griffith Act created a Bill of Rights for union members. The Norris-LaGuardia Act outlawed yellow-dog contracts, Choice *A*. The Taft-Hartley Act established the Federal Mediation and Conciliation Service, Choice *B*. Finally, the Wagner Act created the NLRB to encourage union growth, Choice *C*.

2. D: The Glass Ceiling Act established a commission to study how women and minorities face significant barriers and are prevented from reaching management positions. This act was part of Title II of the Civil Rights Act of 1991, Choices *A* and *B*. Choice *C*, Equal Pay Act, is a law that seeks to abolish the wage disparity based on sex.

3. D: Management by Walking Around (MBWA), as the name suggests, involves having managers and supervisors physically get out of their offices and interact with employees in person. MBWA allows management to check on employee progress, inquire about potential issues, and gain other feedback without relying on employees to "make the first move." An open-door policy, Choice *A*, is used to establish a relationship where employees feel comfortable speaking directly with management about problems and suggestions. A brown bag lunch program, Choice *B*, is an informal meeting (usually including employees and management) that is used to discuss company problems over a "brown bag" lunch. The lunch setting and company-provided meal can help create a relaxed setting for exchanging ideas. Finally, town hall meetings, Choice *C*, tend to focus on sharing information "from the top down" concerning the overall organization. These meetings are not usually designed to allow feedback from employees about smaller detail issues.

4. C: Organizational picketing is done by employees for the purpose of convincing other employees to join their union. Informational picketing, Choice *A*, is done by employees for the purpose of letting the public know that they are not represented by any one authority and thus plan to organize. Recognitional picketing, Choice *B*, is done by employees for the purpose of encouraging their employer to recognize their union as their representative. Finally, when in disputes with an employer, unions may engage in common situs picketing, Choice *D*. This is where employees picket at a location used by the targeted employer as well as other organizations.

5. C: OSHA provides specific rights to workers. These rights include the right to register complaints against their employer without fear of retaliation and the right to meet privately with an OSHA inspector. Lastly, OSHA guidelines give workers the right to receive any information pertaining to health risks and hazards on the job.

PHR Practice Test #1

1. Which of the following is NOT an acceptable standard when ensuring an organization has clear and enforceable ethical standards?
   a. Establishing a code of conduct
   b. Conducting HR audits
   c. Establishing a values statement
   d. Requesting that employees promise they will behave appropriately

2. What factors does a PEST analysis take into consideration?
   a. People, projects, and payments within an organization
   b. Political, economic, social, and technological trends that influence the organization
   c. People, engagement, sustainability, time, limitations, and expectations in relation to a specific project
   d. The most proximal direct competitor

3. In addition to developing strong relationships with external stakeholders, what can an organization's diversity and inclusion programs accomplish as its primary focus?
   a. Provide thorough investigations of complaints.
   b. Ensure a strong training and development program.
   c. Ensure compliance with federal and state statutes.
   d. Build employee relations and satisfaction.

4. HR wants to organize a training program on cultural difference in the workplace. Whom should this training target?
   a. Managers and other employees in leadership positions, so they can communicate key practices to their subordinates
   b. Employees who have had problems with cultural misunderstandings in the past
   c. New employees because they are more likely to come from diverse backgrounds
   d. Employees from all levels of the organization

5. Which of the following is an example of a short-term strategy to develop workforce competencies?
   a. Increase the academic and professional qualifications in job postings
   b. Enroll targeted employees in a high-potential development program
   c. Reassign underperforming employees to positions that better fit their skills
   d. Organize a week-long training class focused on desired skill development

6. Lori has recently worked with her HR team and the organization to recruit and hire many new employees. With production increases and the customer needs changing, the organization set a strategic goal to increase the workforce by 50 percent. With such a dramatic increase in newly hired employees, the workforce culture has changed substantially. Lori wants to ensure that the newly hired employees, as well as the tenured employees, are engaged, involved, and have a positive and inclusive work environment. What should Lori establish to make sure all employees are provided with these opportunities?

    a. Employee satisfaction survey
    b. Employee business resource groups
    c. Department and organization meetings
    d. Performance evaluation meetings

7. After conducting an engagement survey, you review the data and find that your marketing department is disengaged compared to the rest of the company. The information is not precise enough to see why. What would you recommend as a next step?

    a. Wait until a few employees resign and conduct exit interviews.
    b. Make the first Tuesday of every month Marketing Appreciation Day.
    c. Increase the pay for the marketing staff.
    d. Conduct stay Interviews with your current staff to find out more information.

8. What can accurate data tell an HR professional about the internal organization, specifically the employees?

    a. Consumer trends
    b. Customer preferences
    c. Productivity trends
    d. Client engagement

Read the following scenario and answer questions 9-10.

> Margaret has recently hired several new employees in various positions across the organization. She has conducted individual new-hire orientations for each employee to address the specific personal needs of each employee as well as a group orientation to facilitate a speedier entrance into the workplace. Margaret has trained the new employees in the payroll system, provided each with a copy of the employee handbook, and communicated the organization's vision, mission, and values.

9. Margaret wants to stay in frequent contact with the new employees to ensure they are acclimating well to the new organization and position. How should Margaret engage with each new employee?

    a. 360 feedback
    b. Stay interviews
    c. Exit interviews
    d. Satisfaction survey

10. Margaret receives the resignation from one of her recent hires. The employee indicates they are leaving the organization due to receiving an offer for a position of the same level but at a higher salary. Margaret reviews the offer and sees that the amount would equate to a 10 percent increase. What should Margaret do?

    a. Nothing. If the employee wants to leave the organization, Margaret should accept the resignation letter and move forward with a new recruitment.

    b. Attempt to negotiate with the employee directly and provide an immediate counteroffer to work to keep the employee with the organization.

    c. Conduct an exit interview when the resignation letter is received to gather the information needed as to what could have retained the employee.

    d. Communicate with the department manager and determine if there is flexibility in the current process and budget to provide a counteroffer.

11. There is a loud and increasingly aggressive disagreement between two co-workers that is overheard by many people. Human Resources de-escalates the situation and now is going to find out what happened by bringing both employees in individually. What type of documentation should be kept?

    a. There is no documentation needed since so many people overheard.

    b. Ask each employee questions, take notes, and have the employee sign next to the notes saying they agree with the stated version of events.

    c. There is no need to meet with them; just have them write an email stating what happened.

    d. HR should meet with them and take notes, but there isn't a need to have the employees sign the notes.

12. Which of the following is a crucial factor in the new generation of employees selecting their job field?

    a. Compensation and benefits

    b. Retirement programs

    c. Flexible staffing schedules

    d. Social impact and engagement

13. What is the strongest advantage of external recruiting?

    a. Encouraging connections with job seekers

    b. Cost-effective, as the costs are generally low

    c. Candidate familiarity with the organization and culture

    d. Support of building diversity and bringing fresh perspectives

14. Which of the following is not a method of internal recruiting?

    a. Employee referrals

    b. Promotions and transfers

    c. Walk-in applicants

    d. Recruiter-sourced hires

15. Layla is responsible for increasing her company's diversity among all positions and within all departments of the organization. This objective aligns with the organization's corporate social responsibility plan to reflect the social demographics of the metropolitan area. She has been diligently working toward this goal with every recruitment, and the HR director has requested a report to determine the status of this initiative. Which of the following should Layla focus her attention on in this report?
    a. Key performance indicators for all HR metrics
    b. Employee demographics compared to other organizations in the area
    c. Recruitment concerns from the previous five recruitments
    d. Campus recruitment initiative program status

16. Amelia is responsible for sending out Consolidated Omnibus Budget Reconciliation Act (COBRA) notifications when an employee exits the organization. Regardless of the reason for separation, she must adhere to the notification requirements to ensure compliance. When is Amelia required to send out the initial COBRA notice regarding continuation of coverage options?
    a. On the day the separation notice is received
    b. Within ninety days of separation
    c. Within two weeks of separation
    d. On the day of separation

17. Jacobi is a human resources manager who wants to invest in more employee retention initiatives. He is looking to outsource the employee rewards program to an experienced vendor. What should Jacobi look for when evaluating vendors?
    a. The vendor offers the least expensive rewards
    b. The vendor learns about the organization's business goals
    c. The vendor accommodates advance orders
    d. The vendor has a strong company culture

18. What are non-discretionary benefits?
    a. Benefits that utilize group discounts to save the company money
    b. Benefits that employers choose to provide to retain their workforce
    c. Benefits that employers must provide based on legal statutes
    d. Benefits that are offered to employees on a pre-tax basis

19. Which of the following is NOT a type of leave covered by the FMLA?
    a. Qualifying exigency
    b. Professional sabbatical
    c. Foster-care placement
    d. Military caregiver

20. What is a benefit of long-term disability insurance?

a. Long-term disability insurance pays a portion of an employee's salary for five years after a work-related injury.

b. Long-term disability insurance pays a portion of an employee's salary until they can return to work after being out on short-term disability.

c. Long-term disability insurance pays a portion of an employee's salary for up to 26 weeks after a non-work-related injury.

d. Long-term disability insurance pays a portion of an employee's salary for an indefinite number of years after a non-work-related injury.

21. Which of the following is money awarded to an individual in a workplace discrimination case, generally equal to lost earnings?

a. Retroactive pay

b. Front pay

c. Back pay

d. Specialty pay

22. Which of the following agencies ensures safe working conditions for employees by establishing process safety management standards?

a. ADA

b. OSHA

c. HIPAA

d. SOX

23. If OSHA cites an organization with a violation that a condition is not directly or immediately related to employees' safety or health and does not require fines or citations, the organization has been served with which type of violation?

a. Other-than-serious

b. Near miss

c. De minimus

d. Willful and repeated

24. If OSHA cites an organization with a violation that indicates the condition raised could impact employees' safety or health but probably not cause death or serious harm, the organization has been served with which type of violation?

a. Other-than-serious

b. Near miss

c. De minimus

d. Willful and repeated

25. Which of the following is not a standard function of the Occupational Safety and Health Act?

a. Develop standards for employee personal protective equipment.

b. Provide fixed payments to injured employees and their dependents.

c. Establish guidelines to assist employees in the event of a pandemic disease outbreak.

d. Ensure safe working conditions for employees and establish safety management standards.

26. What are the two most common workplace safety risks?
a. Bloodborne pathogens and tripping hazards
b. Lockout/tagout and confined space hazards
c. Noise exposure and bloodborne pathogens
d. Lockout/tagout and tripping hazards

Read the following scenario and answer questions 27–28.

A successful American cosmetics retailer has decided to expand its business to overseas operations in a different country. Rather than building new stores in this location, they have decided to buy out a smaller, local cosmetics retailer and operate out of those stores. The company CEO wants to keep the same business space with some interior updates and would also like to retain as many of the existing employees as possible.

27. What would be the most productive way to manage the relationships in this new workforce scenario?
a. Suggest that the CEO significantly decrease the number of carryover employees and instead assign more of the company's American workers overseas so they can take over operations themselves.
b. Meet with local supervisors and managers to establish areas of shared goals and practices and focus on converging operations.
c. While interior renovations are underway, require all local employees to undergo a multi-week retraining process.
d. Identify high-performing local employees and assign them to newly created leadership positions.

28. HR wants to assist with formalizing work processes between stores in both countries. What is the best way to accomplish this goal?
a. Organize leadership teams in both countries.
b. Set up an online messaging portal to handle all communications.
c. Add the new stores to the American headquarters' meeting schedule.
d. Arrange regular check-in meetings and agree on reporting times and methods.

29. Which of the following laws applies to employers with fifteen or more employees and prohibits discrimination based on race, color, religion, sex, or national origin?
a. Age Discrimination in Employment Act of 1967
b. Fair Labor Standard Act
c. Title VII of the Civil Rights Act of 1964
d. Equal Employment Opportunity Commission

30. What term is defined as a qualification that is determined to be justified by a business purpose?
a. Bona fide occupational qualification
b. Minimum required qualification
c. Preferred qualification
d. Essential job functions

Read the following scenario and answer questions 31–34.

Liz is working on hiring a large group of individuals under the age of eighteen for a youth employment pilot program. Several departments are interested in participating to bring in a group of young individuals to assist with certain jobs that will support the full-time staff. The departments have all identified a specific need and job that will be assigned to the new employees. After the first six months, Liz will evaluate the program to determine if it should continue, be expanded, be altered, or conclude.

31. Liz has received many applications for the youth employment program. She wants to sort the applications into groups by age. What are the age groups she should use?
    a. Ages 14 and under, age 15, age 16, ages 17 and 18
    b. Under 14, age 14, age 15, age 16, age 17, age 18 and over
    c. Under 14, ages 14 and 15, ages 16 and 17, age 18 and over
    d. Ages 14 and under, ages 15 and 16, ages 17 and 18

32. Liz required departments to submit a requisition for the number of youth employees required along with the specific work that would be performed and the hours scheduled to work. If the work and hours aligned with the FLSA standards, Liz approved the request; however, if the work and hours were outside of the scope of the FLSA requirements, the requisition was denied and returned to the department to update for reconsideration. Once approved, Liz determined which age group would be most appropriate for the request to match up the candidates with a position. Which of the following positions would not be suitable for an employee who is fifteen years of age?
    a. Cashier representative—tallying sales and collecting payments via cash or credit
    b. Waitress—taking and delivering food orders to customers as well as collecting payments
    c. Maintenance crew—cleaning office space, including vacuuming, dusting, or other cleaning
    d. Warehouse dock worker—loading and unloading products to or from the conveyor line

33. Liz received several applications from individuals who are eighteen years of age. How do the FLSA child labor laws apply to this group of candidates in the youth employment program?
    a. Youths who are eighteen years of age may not drive on the job or operate a company vehicle.
    b. The FLSA child labor laws do not apply to youths once they reach eighteen years of age.
    c. The FLSA child labor law of specific hours and times of day standards apply.
    d. Youths who are eighteen years of age may perform cashiering, shelf stocking, and bagging.

34. When evaluating the youth employment program, Liz realized there were numerous candidates aged eighteen and over. What should she consider adding to the program details to deter this and ensure that only candidates under the age of seventeen apply?
    a. Nothing, as Liz can use the pool of candidates over the age of eighteen for other full-time positions with the company.
    b. Hire those over the age of eighteen to ensure that the organization has increased flexibility regarding scheduling.
    c. Only accept applications from internal employees' children to ensure the candidates are under the age of eighteen.
    d. Update the applicant requirements to indicate that only individuals under the age of eighteen will be considered.

171

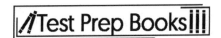

Read the following scenario and answer questions 35-38.

To free up more time for assisting with strategic objectives, the HR department of a large communications company has decided to implement new automation processes. They are currently evaluating specific functions for automating. One function under consideration is performance evaluations. Currently, the company conducts traditional annual performance reviews in which department leaders and other supervisors give feedback to subordinates. However, HR is considering adopting an employee engagement app that allows real-time, anonymous feedback between employees at all levels.

35. From an employee engagement standpoint, what would be the most important advantage of adopting the new app?

a. It lends a game-like appeal to evaluations by allowing employees to use smartphones during work.

b. It gives more timely and dynamic feedback to employees and helps solve performance problems as soon as they arise.

c. It increases the appeal of working for the company by advancing its brand as a leader in modern business technology.

d. It allows supervisors to put less effort into managing subordinates by creating a self-managed feedback system.

36. Which of the following is LEAST likely to be a drawback of using this new technology?

a. It could create a channel for bullying and harassment.

b. Some employees might feel overwhelmed by constant feedback.

c. Some employees might have difficulty learning how to use the system.

d. The app will prove to be expensive and cost prohibitive compared to traditional performance evaluations.

37. In preliminary discussions regarding plans for automation, HR has gotten pushback from some stakeholders who instead prefer augmentation. In terms of workplace technology, what is the difference between automation and augmentation?

a. Automation requires the purchase of new software, while augmentation explores ways to optimize existing software.

b. Automation allows technology to take over manual tasks, while augmentation refers to ways that technology assists employees in their job functions.

c. Automation refers to upgrades in corporate software, while augmentation refers to upgrades in corporate hardware.

d. Automation involves purchasing new software and hardware, while augmentation requires recruiting new employees.

38. How can HR encourage employee buy-in of the new performance management method?

a. Hold a demonstration of how the technology works in different situations, including information about user resources.

b. Require supervisors to phase out all traditional performance evaluation activities within the next six months.

c. Buy new smartphones for employees whose devices are not up-to-date enough to run the new app.

d. Post user testimonial videos on the company intranet.

39. Which of the following is a reason HR might outsource the payroll function?
    a. To eliminate human resources costs
    b. To do away with payroll direct deposit
    c. To avoid taxes associated with improper IRS filings
    d. To free up human resources for other strategic goals

40. Who is the employer required to cover under the Consolidated Omnibus Budget Reconciliation Act (COBRA)?
    a. An employee who left a week before they reached their eligibility date for insurance
    b. A former employee AND that employee's spouse who were on the company's insurance
    c. An employee who declined benefits at work, but now wants COBRA coverage
    d. A current employee is who eligible for benefits

41. What does "benchmarking" refer to in an HR context?
    a. Putting an employee "on the bench" or on the sidelines due to past performance
    b. Linking salary increases to performance metrics
    c. Identifying and setting goals relative to other organizations' performance
    d. Adhering to government regulations and other industry guidance

42. Two employees who perform well individually have been placed on a project team together. However, in a team setting, they have very different work styles and attitudes and often clash angrily. How can an HR staff member help resolve this issue?
    a. Separate the two team members and put them on different projects.
    b. Put them on a probationary warning.
    c. Provide coaching to the employees to find common ground.
    d. Allow them to resolve it autonomously, as this is more empowering.

43. Which of the following is an accurate statement regarding corporate social responsibility?
    a. CSR is championed by local community representatives and leaders.
    b. CSR is a mandatory requirement and governed by federal statute.
    c. CSR identifies the environmental needs and prioritizes them over profitability.
    d. CSR has a positive impact on employee recruiting, retention, and overall satisfaction.

44. What is one way that HR can play a leadership role in an organization's corporate social responsibility (CSR) plan?
    a. Identify a pool of high-performing employees to participate in CSR activities.
    b. Collect, compile, and analyze data to demonstrate the quantitative and qualitative impacts of various CSR initiatives.
    c. Establish separate planning meetings to assign and develop CSR objectives within different business units.
    d. Devise an evaluation component to cite employees for noncompliance with stated CSR objectives.

45. Corporate social responsibility (CSR) refers to an organization's sense of responsibility for its impact on the environment and community. Which of the following are the evaluation factors for CSR?
    a. People, purpose, proceeds
    b. Public, process, profit
    c. People, planet, profit
    d. Public, purpose, proceeds

173

46. The three evaluation factors identified in question 45 that show how effective an organization's CSR is are known as which of the following?
    a. The hat trick
    b. The triple bottom line
    c. The triple play
    d. The social responsibility scale

47. What should Evelyn immediately do to engage the management and supervisory staff in the performance management process?
    a. Provide training, forms, required timeline, (including due dates), and coaching on delivering employee evaluations.
    b. Implement a new policy that requires evaluations be conducted by the annual due date or disciplinary actions will be taken.
    c. Discuss the situation with the HR director and CEO and request their immediate attention to the issue.
    d. Continue to send out emails and communications requesting the documents within the time frame needed.

48. Susan is preparing her team's department objectives that will be used to create individual goals and accomplishments for her employees' performance reviews. What should Susan ensure that each of these objectives includes?
    a. Well-written, clear, concise, and specific language to ensure understanding
    b. Specific, measurable, achievable, relevant, and time-bound aspects
    c. Professional growth, development, training, and learning opportunities
    d. Recognition and appreciation for previous performance and accomplishments

49. Which of the following tools would NOT be used to determine why goals were not achieved or why there was a discrepancy between expected outcomes and actual outcomes?
    a. Six Sigma
    b. Gap analysis
    c. Root cause analysis
    d. Cause-and-effect diagram

50. During the group meetings to train employees on the emergency response plan, HR also emphasizes the evacuation plan for the facility. Visual aids are provided with exit routes mapped out for the entire facility along with meeting places and procedures. In addition to providing this information to employees, what else can HR do to ensure employees effectively evacuate the facility in the case of an emergency?
    a. Require employees to sign an acknowledgment statement at the end of the training.
    b. Post special posters throughout the facility that showcase the exit routes.
    c. Request that supervisors frequently quiz employees on the exit routes.
    d. Coordinate a scheduled and unscheduled practice evacuation.

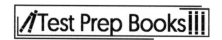

51. Rosie is preparing a training class for all employees to attend to adequately prepare the organization in the case of a security issue. In addition to corporate espionage and theft, Rosie is also focusing on training employees on important security details that include security measures. Which of the following items would not be addressed regarding security measures?
    a. Emergency communication systems
    b. First aid and AED locations and procedures
    c. Alarms locations, secure rooms, and security guard location
    d. Employee badges and facility security protocols

52. How often should Rosie train employees on the security plans and policies?
    a. Annually
    b. During new-hire orientation
    c. Every other year
    d. Every six months

Read the scenario and answer questions 53-54.

After several high-profile cases of other large companies dealing with issues of harassment and misconduct, HR professionals at one company have decided to prioritize training to address these issues with their organization's employees.

53. Which of the following would be the most effective way to present information about workplace misconduct to employees?
    a. Give employees a checklist of workplace DON'Ts based on EEOC guidance.
    b. Show news stories of the recent high-profile cases along with commentary from legal experts about corporate liability and other worst-case scenarios concerning violations of workplace conduct policies.
    c. Set up a self-paced, remote training session to allow for greater flexibility so the information can reach as many employees as possible.
    d. Schedule mandatory in-person training with employee involvement, such as skits, role plays, and mock juries, to encourage engagement and focus on real-world implications.

54. Who would be the best featured speaker(s) for a training on workplace misconduct?
    a. A panel of employees who have made workplace misconduct complaints in the past
    b. Someone from the C-suite
    c. A Department of Justice representative
    d. The HR professionals who organized the training

55. Heather is an HR director who holds biweekly one-on-one meetings, monthly team meetings, and biannual recognition lunches with all her employees. During these meetings, she provides organizational updates, industry news, issues and concerns, and project statuses. She also goes around the room to ensure that all employees have an opportunity to discuss any issues, ask questions, or offer feedback. What is Heather displaying to her team during these sessions?
    a. Transparency and innovation
    b. Leadership and team-oriented culture
    c. Leadership and innovation
    d. Transparency and team-oriented culture

175

56. Kyle has recently been investigated by the organization based on an anonymous complaint received by the HR tip line. After conducting an investigation, the HR director concluded that Kyle had taken multiple pieces of hardware from the IT department. The recommended action is to terminate Kyle immediately with which of the following rationale?
    a. Kyle has committed a felony act against the organization.
    b. Kyle has violated the theft policy of the organization.
    c. Kyle has committed sabotage against the organization.
    d. Kyle has violated the workplace security program.

57. One of the primary responsibilities of HR is to coach employees at every level of the organization on how to avoid illegal and noncompliant behaviors. Ensuring that employees are aware of and understand what is appropriate and inappropriate is vital to ensure that the organization and individual employees are protected. What is a best practice that should be implemented to keep employees up-to-date and informed?
    a. Send an introductory email of all applicable laws and regulations when employees are hired.
    b. Provide employees all policies and procedures during the new-hire orientation.
    c. Direct employees to the internal website where all policies and procedures are located.
    d. Display posters related to applicable laws and regulations in common areas.

58. Which of the following terms is described as the process of removing a union's security clause and authority to negotiate?
    a. Deauthorization
    b. Arbitration
    c. Mediation
    d. Confrontation

59. Which of the following terms refers to the formal process used to settle a dispute?
    a. Deauthorization
    b. Arbitration
    c. Mediation
    d. Confrontation

60. Which of the following federal laws established employee classification and regulated minimum wage, overtime pay, on-call pay, recordkeeping, and child labor?
    a. Family Medical Leave Act
    b. Fair Labor Standards Act
    c. Davis Bacon Act
    d. Walsh-Healy Act

61. Which of the following positions falls under the Fair Labor Standards Act (FLSA) regulations?
    a. Non-exempt positions
    b. Exempt positions
    c. Professional positions
    d. Administrative positions

62. In what circumstance can an employer NOT pay overtime to an employee who works over forty hours a week?

    a. The employee works two different jobs for the same employer. In each job, they only work thirty hours a week.

    b. The employee works sixty hours one work week, but only twenty hours the next work week.

    c. The employee waives the right to overtime by signing a form.

    d. The employee is considered exempt.

63. Which of the following employees could qualify to be exempt under the Fair Labor Standards Act (FSLA)?

    a. An employee earns over $80,000 a year, but makes routine decisions.

    b. The employee earns less than $23,000 a year, but makes non-routine decisions.

    c. The employee is regularly supervising two or more employees and has management as their main job duty.

    d. The FLSA lets employers decide who is and isn't exempt.

64. During a job interview, asking an applicant about their childcare arrangements might be construed as discriminatory against working parents, especially working mothers. Which of the following would be a more appropriate question to ask?

    a. Which is a higher priority for you: workplace or family obligations?

    b. Do you have any commitments that will conflict with your work?

    c. Are you married or single?

    d. How old are your children?

Read the following scenario and answer questions 65–67.

    HR at a rapidly growing tech company is in the process of selecting a new applicant tracking system (ATS) to help handle the projected increase in new hires in the next few years. There are also several hard-to-fill positions in the company that require highly specialized engineering qualifications.

65. When choosing an ATS, which of the following should HR consider a top priority?

    a. HR should evaluate the functionality of the new system from the perspective of stakeholders outside HR.

    b. As a department in an up-and-coming tech company, HR should take the lead on adopting state-of-the-art systems to hold a competitive edge over the other companies.

    c. Because this is still a transition period, HR should select some functions that will remain paper-based.

    d. HR should forgo dealing with a vendor and simply have employees develop the ATS themselves, since they have a high level of technical knowledge.

66. In discussions with ATS software vendors, which of the following is the LEAST important for HR professionals to focus on?

    a. Integration

    b. User experience

    c. Reporting metrics

    d. Industry usage rates

67. How can HR use the new ATS to fill the specialized job positions?

a. Compare the qualifications of applicants with those of current employees to determine whether it is better to retrain or replace current workers.

b. Determine essential qualifications for the job positions to categorize applications and help recruiters focus on a smaller pool of candidates.

c. Use the software to design an integrated application, pre-screening test, and interview selection process that applicants complete in one session.

d. Allow leaders throughout the organization to submit recommendations for internal hires rather than wasting resources on job posting sites.

68. Rita is establishing an orientation session for several employees who will be transferred to a new international location. Which of the following topics would be most critical to these employees?

a. Learning the language, cultural norms, and translation services

b. Scenic and tourist locations, including historical sites and establishments

c. The organization's vision, mission, and values that will be applicable to the new location

d. Specific local labor laws, workplace etiquette, and cultural differences

69. Which of the following laws is designed to establish accountability and standards regarding accounting misconduct, record manipulation, and inappropriate financial practices?

a. Employee Retirement Income Security Act (ERISA)

b. Generally Accepted Accounting Principles (GAAP)

c. US Government Accountability Office (GAO)

d. Sarbanes-Oxley (SOX) Act

70. Which of the following statements is NOT accurate regarding the Americans with Disabilities Act?

a. The ADA only protects employees who have physical medical conditions.

b. The ADA protections apply to every aspect of job application procedures.

c. The ADA requires employers to provide reasonable accommodations to employees.

d. The ADA is a federal law that prevents discrimination based on disability.

71. Veronica is assessing Janine's workstation to ensure that the workspace is efficient and comfortable and makes the best use of space. Additionally, Veronica asks Janine specific questions regarding her physical comfort in the space, including her comfort levels with the keyboard, monitor height, and lighting, to determine if there are any special needs that must be accommodated. What practice is Veronica engaging in?

a. Safety and risk appraisal

b. Ergonomic evaluation test

c. Physical risk assessment

d. Illness and injury report

72. In accordance with the guidance of the National Labor Relations Board (NLRB), which of the following is true of labor relations?

a. The NLRB can facilitate settlements of labor disputes between employers and employees.

b. Employees can achieve lawful recognition only by working through established labor unions.

c. Employers may choose to set up a works council for their employees as a form of lawful representation.

d. Employees must select one form of representation (for example, union, nonunion, legal, or governmental).

73. Bill filed a complaint with the Equal Employment Opportunity Commission (EEOC) alleging that the company he works for has engaged in unfair, unethical, and discriminatory practices related to internal promotions. He has been passed over for a promotion multiple times and believes he is being unfairly targeted due to his age. He submits his paperwork to the EEOC to be investigated. The EEOC investigates and finds there is no probable cause and dismisses the case. What can Bill do next?

a. Nothing; Bill has exhausted his rights and has no further recourse.

b. Bill can file a grievance with his union representative for a new investigation.

c. Bill can request a right-to-sue letter and sue the employer in the court of law.

d. Bill should quit because he will not be able to return to his position now that the employer is aware of his claims.

74. What does an at-will employee mean?

a. The employer can terminate anyone at any time for any reason, and the employee can leave at any time.

b. The employer can terminate an employee for no cause, or for a legal reason, and the employee can leave at any time.

c. The employer must provide a reason for termination, but the employee can resign at any time.

d. The employer and the employee must agree to a mutual separation to end employment.

75. Which of the following benefits is associated with a diverse workplace?

a. Higher employee retention

b. Higher employee complaints

c. Increased training needs

d. Higher employee turnover

76. Rachel is responsible for the campus recruiting program in her organization. She routinely attends hiring fairs and events at the university campuses in the surrounding area. These events always provide a more than adequate number of applicants for the open positions. What should Rachel consider adding to this campus recruiting program for even stronger results?

a. Submit a request to the career centers for candidates to be sent directly to the organization to minimize expenses related to attending the hiring fairs.

b. Expand the list of campuses she visits to outside of the area to include candidates from different backgrounds and locations, ensuring a more diverse candidate pool.

c. Request candidate referrals from current employees while offering a candidate referral bonus program.

d. Continue attending these specific hiring fairs and events because the candidate pool is adequate for the organization's hiring needs.

77. David is conducting a salary survey for the engineering department. Several engineers have left the organization for a competitor, and management wants to determine if the salary is a reason for the departures. Although several engineers have indicated in their exit interview that compensation was a factor, David has reviewed the data and it does not support this reason. He has looked at base salary, overtime opportunities, car allowances, and bonus opportunities. What information is he missing?

a. Benefits costs, vacation time, and retirement costs

b. Promotional opportunities for future growth and salary increases

c. Salary bands for starting pay and maximum pay

d. Number of recognized holidays and time-off opportunities

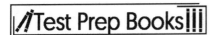

78. To promote an organization's benefits program, which of the following details should be included in a job posting?
    a. Salary range, including when increases will be considered during the calendar year
    b. Alternate work schedules, flexible spending accounts, and wellness programs
    c. Specific daily responsibilities and tasks of the position
    d. Supervisory responsibilities as well as who this position reports to

79. Ling is presenting to the leadership team on a value-based wellness program that will engage employees and require them to take a more active role in their wellness. The program has been shown to decrease insurance rates, and Ling believes this program could also help with future costs as well as promote employee wellness, decrease sick leave usage, and create a more productive workforce. During the presentation, the marketing director asks about the materials provided by the vendor to advertise this initiative to employees or if the organization will have to develop and fund the advertisements. Ling is not prepared for this question and does not have the answer. How should she respond?
    a. Indicate that she does not have this information but will reach out to the vendor to get the information and send it to the team.
    b. Indicate that the vendor will provide all marketing materials and then reach out to the vendor to ask them to do so.
    c. Indicate that she does not have this information and then move on to the next section in her presentation.
    d. Indicate that the vendor will not provide the materials and then reach out to the vendor to see if they can.

80. Melissa is an HR specialist at Acme Corporation. A manager in the accounting department recently approached her with some concerns about a high-performing employee who seems more disengaged and pessimistic than usual. The accounting manager says the employee's change in attitude has started to negatively affect the quality of their work. Which type of benefit program might Melissa suggest as a support for the employee?
    a. Defined contribution plan
    b. Employee assistance program
    c. Managed care plan
    d. Corporate wellness program

81. Two HR staff members who are planning a worksite wellness initiative state that one of their initiative goals is to have healthier employees in their workforce. What is wrong with this goal?
    a. The goal is placing pressure on employees who are already busy
    b. The goal is pushing personal agendas on other employees
    c. The goal is too detailed
    d. The goal is ambiguous

82. David has been an HR manager for six months with his new organization. When setting up his professional goals and milestones for the next year, he used the exact list from his previous position at another organization. He received an outstanding performance rating from his work and believed that by doing the same work at his new organization, he was setting himself up for success. His supervisor, however, did not agree and asked him to redo his goals and milestones. Why would David's supervisor ask him to do this, and what should David do?

    a. The supervisor was simply exerting control over his subordinate. David should go to the next-level supervisor for support.

    b. The supervisor clearly did not read the list of goals and milestones that was submitted, and David should request another meeting to review the original list.

    c. The list of goals and milestones was not specific and applicable to the new organization's goals and achievements.

    d. The list of goals and milestones was not on the proper form, and David should just copy and paste the list to the new form and resubmit the original list.

83. Karen is an employee in an organization's finance department who has been feeling burned out at work. She sets up a meeting with Rita, an HR employee, to discuss this issue. When Karen arrives, Rita notices that Karen looks tired and defeated. As Rita shares her issues, Karen shows empathy and observes Rita's body language. When Rita is finished speaking, Karen shares her perception of Rita's concerns and asks if she is understanding correctly. What is Karen practicing in her conversation with Rita?

    a. Active listening

    b. Conscious listening

    c. Friendly listening

    d. Passive listening

84. Which one of the following is a crucial component of program evaluation, guiding and sustaining initiatives, and providing valuable customer service?

    a. Soliciting feedback

    b. Interpreting the context of received communications

    c. Seeking further information

    d. Responding to communications

85. Davina is conducting an analysis to determine the organization's next product launch. The launch must be successful to ensure the well-being of the organization, employees, customers, and community. What analysis should Davina conduct to make sure she takes into account all of the information that could influence this product launch?

    a. SWOT

    b. PEST

    c. Cost-benefit

    d. Risk assessment

86. Which of the following is an example of a performance-based pay plan?

    a. Commission pay

    b. Base pay

    c. Shift pay

    d. Reporting pay

87. Which of the following is a characteristic of an ineffective salary and benefits survey?
    a. Includes multiple positions
    b. Reflects comparable industries
    c. Avoids controversial topics
    d. Ignores inaccurate information

88. What is the purpose of a W-4 form?
    a. To tell an employer how much an employee paid in federal income taxes
    b. To tell an employee how much of their paycheck is designated for state income taxes
    c. To tell an employer how much to take out of an employee's paycheck for federal income taxes
    d. To tell an employee how much they earned during the previous calendar year

89. What types of taxes comprise the Federal Insurance Contributions Act (FICA)?
    a. Federal, Social Security, and Medicare
    b. Federal, Social Security, Medicare, and Additional Medicare
    c. Federal, State, Local, Social Security, and Medicare
    d. Social Security, Medicare, and Additional Medicare

90. How can HR determine ROI on total rewards package design?
    a. Consult market data on total rewards best practices
    b. Analyze relevant performance metrics (such as sales per quarter)
    c. Conduct a total remuneration survey
    d. Defer to business executives in determining employee value to the organization

91. What type of programs are used to promote organizational culture by identifying and rewarding individual employees for the work done?
    a. Special event programs
    b. Recognition programs
    c. Inclusion programs
    d. Incentive programs

92. Which of the following policies encourages openness and transparency with employees?
    a. Communications policy
    b. Social media policy
    c. Open-door policy
    d. Code of conduct policy

93. Which organizations are more likely to have a decentralized structure?
    a. New small businesses that have not yet centralized their HR function
    b. Large organizations that operate in several locations
    c. Innovative organizations that rely on technology
    d. Family-run organizations

94. What is an employee resource group (ERG)?
    a. An independent review group within HR where employees can anonymously submit their complaints or concerns about workplace behavior
    b. A coaching and mentoring group where new employees can meet more experienced workers from each department
    c. A group created and led by employees who share common backgrounds or demographic factors
    d. An extracurricular group that helps relocated employees orient themselves to their new environment

95. Which of the following statements is inaccurate regarding employee newsletters?
    a. Newsletters are not always useful for communicating urgent or immediate information.
    b. Newsletters are labor-intensive and infrequent.
    c. Newsletters have the potential of providing information in a welcoming manner.
    d. Newsletters allow for formal two-way communications between the employer and employees.

96. Amber receives an email from a department leader in her organization that outlines a new program that will be implemented as a pilot program. As a member of the team that will be creating the implementation plan, she is confused about the intent and reasoning for the program. Multiple pieces of information are missing, and there are various conflicting messages throughout the memo. What should Amber do?
    a. Proceed forward with her specific duties and tasks related to the program and allow the leader and her manager to address the issues.
    b. Forward the email to the department leader's direct supervisor to ensure they are aware of the discrepancies and can address them.
    c. Respond directly to the department leader with clear and specific questions to ensure the entire team is on the same page.
    d. Take no action and await further instruction from her supervisor because most of the misunderstanding will most likely be cleared up.

97. Tommy is reviewing the milestones of the HR department to determine if the new recruitment process is effective and provides departments with quicker turnaround to fill open positions. Which of the following metrics should Tommy review to assess the success of the new process?
    a. Percentage of open positions compared to total headcount, or attrition rate
    b. Direct feedback from supervisors on the quality of the candidate pools for open positions
    c. Comparison of the current number of days needed to fill positions with the former process
    d. Number of open positions per department across the organization prior to the new process

98. An organization with a commitment to diversity would like to conduct a gap analysis. What is this analysis likely to focus on?
    a. The pay gap between salaries for men and women in comparable positions
    b. How the organization has progressed in its hiring practices over the past decade
    c. The organization's current status of employee diversity in comparison to its stated diversity hiring goals
    d. How the organization's diversity statement and policies differ from those of other organizations in its field

99. What is the difference between a mission statement and a vision statement?
    a. A mission statement is what the company is currently doing, while a vision statement is what the company wants to accomplish in five to ten years.
    b. A mission statement should be very short, while a vision statement needs to be much longer.
    c. A mission statement and a vision statement are essentially the same thing.
    d. A mission statement is trying to encapsulate the big picture, while a vision statement is a how-to guide.

100. The statement "We value lightheartedness" is an example of a:
    a. Mission statement
    b. Value statement
    c. Vision statement
    d. Slogan

101. Which of the following statements is true regarding a vision and mission statement?
    a. A vision statement focuses on the future goals; a mission statement focuses on the values, standards, and organizing principles.
    b. A vision statement focuses on the values, standards, and organizing principles; a mission statement focuses on the future goals.
    c. A vision statement asks questions about what the organization wants to accomplish; a mission statement answers the questions about what the organization wants to accomplish.
    d. Vision and mission statements should be indirect, with high-level information.

102. A company with an open-door policy is trying to facilitate what type of communication?
    a. Downward communication
    b. Upward communication
    c. Diagonal communication
    d. Horizontal communication

103. Meeting, learning from, and socializing with colleagues within and outside of one's organization is known as which of the following practices?
    a. Networking
    b. Achieving work-life balance
    c. Formal education
    d. Fraternizing

104. Which of the following terms refers to the "mood" of an organization?
    a. Environment
    b. Values
    c. Climate
    d. Culture

105. While conducting job interviews, many hiring managers evaluate candidates based on whether they are a "good fit" with the company's culture. What is an appropriate policy to have regarding "good fit"?

a. Hiring managers should not consider it as a hiring a factor because candidates always lie about their personalities during interviews anyway.

b. Hiring managers should ensure that they are not relying on unconscious biases and determining fit based on shared age, race, socioeconomic status, or other demographics.

c. Hiring managers should make it a top priority because fitting in is the highest predictor of success.

d. Hiring managers should allow all applicants to work in the desired job for at least a day to test how well they fit into the work environment.

106. What are primary pros and cons of using large job board websites?

a. They reach many applicants, but they may end up being expensive in terms of price-per-click relative to click-to-hire ratios.

b. They take over all HR recruiting functions but leave HR professionals out of work.

c. They present a high-tech image to applicants but require too much training to implement.

d. They establish the organization's online presence, but they open it up to cybersecurity threats from hackers and viruses.

107. What role should social media play in HR?

a. HR can start an informational campaign warning employees that social media use is unprofessional.

b. HR can use social media to promote its organization's brand as an employer.

c. HR can create mandatory training sessions for all employees to incorporate social media communication into their job roles.

d. HR can bring all social media functions in-house for greater consistency.

108. Why is succession planning important for an organization?

a. It assigns a quantitative value to a company's future goals.

b. It takes a proactive approach to preserving continuity in the face of worker attrition.

c. It boosts morale by reducing interdepartmental competition.

d. It creates clear lines of responsibility for effective communication.

109. Kate has been given an assignment to prepare a trend analysis looking at multiple pieces of data, such as wages, medical costs, retirement costs, fringe benefit costs, and other employee-related costs. The analysis should take into account the organization's current position as well as industry standards and their primary competitor's current position. What is the first thing Kate should do before compiling the data?

a. Kate should determine if there is any data or published documents available.

b. Kate should gather all of the organization's current data and create her analysis.

c. Kate should create her analysis and then gather the data to support the analysis.

d. Kate should seek out third-party vendors who prepare this information.

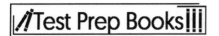
110. Elise is preparing the annual performance reviews for her team. Each team member submitted recommendations of initiatives they would like to individually focus on. Michelle submitted four items she would like to focus on in the next calendar year. Which of the following is NOT a standard initiative for the HR team to focus on and should therefore be replaced with a more appropriate initiative?
a. Review, update, and implement a robust and flexible recruitment process.
b. Audit the payroll processing to ensure that bills are being paid in a timely manner.
c. Establish a new exit interview process with specific questions based on the employee's tenure.
d. Conduct an annual salary survey to ensure salaries are aligned with the industry.

111. Onboarding is the process for new hires to learn about the knowledge, skills, and behaviors needed to become valued and productive contributors to the company. This process is also known as which of the following?
a. New-hire orientation
b. Organizational socialization
c. Preemployment screening
d. Organizational orientation

112. ADDIE is the most commonly used framework organizations use to enhance human resource development programs. What are the phases of the ADDIE model?
a. Analysis, Development, Distribution, Implementation, Engagement
b. Administration, Design, Delivery, Innovation, Evaluation
c. Analysis, Design, Development, Implementation, Evaluation
d. Administration, Development, Design, Instrumentation, Engagement

113. When a strategic plan calls for changes in employee skills, knowledge, behaviors, and/or work deliverables, what is the role of HR?
a. HR holds multiple meetings and initiates various types of communication to reach out to managers, ensuring they are on the same page and personally training their employees.
b. HR works with the legal team to ensure that the organization has the authority and management right to make the changes requested to the strategic plan.
c. HR prepares exit strategies and severance packages for employees who do not meet the new requirements necessary to accomplish the plan.
d. HR facilitates these changes by implementing updated policies, procedures, training, and other appropriate plans to ensure employees have the necessary skills to deliver the plan.

114. Tom is the engineering manager and has recently provided annual performance evaluations for his entire team. He noticed that the employees all seemed disengaged and unenthusiastic with the process. What can he do to improve employee engagement with the annual performance evaluations?
a. Focus on a self-evaluation tool versus a manager evaluation tool.
b. Focus on future goals and professional development.
c. Focus on a 360-evaluation tool for coworkers to evaluate each other.
d. Conduct evaluations on a Friday at the end of the day so they can head home right after the evaluation.

115. Employee business resource groups help to further promote which of the following efforts?
    a. Diversity and inclusion
    b. Professional growth and learning
    c. Relationships and communications
    d. Development and training

116. What is a lean way of communicating HR programs, policies, and practices, including real-time updates?
    a. An employee handbook that is reprinted and redistributed with each new version
    b. In-person conferences that regularly review protocols
    c. An online employee handbook that is accessible to every employee and is updated online
    d. Social media

117. Graham is the chief executive officer (CEO) of a reputable company that provides transportation services to local businesses. A customer service representative filed a complaint with the Equal Employment Opportunity Commission (EEOC) charging that she has been subjected to discrimination and harassment by a supervisor for a number of years. An attorney has taken the case, and a lawsuit has been filed. Graham has reviewed the claim and is weighing a settlement to close the claim so that the company can move forward. Which of the following factors is NOT an Influencer Graham should consider when deciding to settle?
    a. Damage to the company's reputation
    b. New systemic problems
    c. Financial cost of an investigation and trial
    d. Graham's personal financial concerns

118. Genevieve is interviewing a new candidate, Marcus, with whom she is very impressed. He has the perfect educational background, professional experience, and cultural fit for a position she is trying to fill. She has not met any comparable candidates during the hiring campaign for this position. However, when she runs a background check, she finds that he was arrested for a DUI approximately eight years prior but was not charged. Besides this event, his background check returns clear. What is the best course of action for Genevieve to take in this situation?
    a. Eliminate Marcus from the candidate pool and continue interviewing other candidates
    b. Assume there is an error on the background check
    c. Ignore the charge and offer Marcus the job
    d. Set up an appointment with Marcus to find out the context around the charge

119. Julia has recently extended an offer to a potential new hire. She is requesting feedback from past employers, coworkers, and individuals who know the new hire and can attest to the work ethic, past performance, and overall behavior exhibited. What is Julia conducting?
    a. Educational reference check
    b. Emotional intelligence test
    c. Performance review
    d. Employment reference check

120. Which of the following would be considered an inappropriate preemployment screening?
    a. Marital and parental history
    b. Criminal background check
    c. Medical and drug screenings
    d. Financial and credit history checks

121. How long should onboarding programs typically last?
    a. The employee's first week
    b. The employee's first day
    c. The employee's first year
    d. Ongoing throughout employment

122. Angel is working through an employee dispute that has resulted in an impasse between parties. Neither side is willing to consider compromise or accept anything other than their specific resolution. What should Angel consider next to attempt to work toward a resolution?
    a. Mediation process
    b. Compulsory arbitration
    c. Constructive confrontation
    d. Arbitration process

123. Which of the following statements is false regarding collective bargaining?
    a. All changes that management wants to implement, regardless of the subject, are required to be negotiated through the collective bargaining process.
    b. Collective bargaining is the act of negotiation between the employer and employees, with a union representing the employees' interests.
    c. The goal of collective bargaining is to develop a mutual agreement.
    d. There are several strategies that can be used during a collective bargaining process, including single-unit bargaining, coordinated bargaining, multi-employer bargaining, and parallel bargaining.

124. Julia has been working with her union representative regarding discipline for performance issues. Her supervisor has issued multiple disciplinary notices for her lack of attention to detail, which has resulted in errors and additional work to correct the mistakes, thus costing additional money. The latest discipline included an unpaid suspension for three days. Julia does not believe the discipline is warranted and has filed a grievance to have it removed from her record and the suspension reversed with pay. She claims she never received the appropriate training necessary to be able to perform at the level required; however, the grievance has been denied at the supervisor, management, and executive levels due to the documentation, which includes training records. A grievance arbitration ruled in favor of upholding the discipline. Does Julia have any additional options?
    a. Yes. Julia can appeal the grievance arbitration decision.
    b. Yes. Julia can resubmit her original grievance and go through the process again.
    c. No. Grievance arbitration is enforceable and cannot go to court to be changed.
    d. No. Julia needs to find another job with a new organization.

188

125. The HR department is starting to see an increase in employee complaints, specifically regarding inappropriate behavior, such as foul language, racist and sexist jokes, and inappropriate statements regarding personal and religious beliefs. Which of the following should the HR department immediately engage in to resolve these issues?
    a. Send out the code of conduct and applicable policies to all employees, requiring them to submit a notice of acknowledgment.
    b. Require employees to attend training related to workplace behavior.
    c. Investigate all complaints fully and take corrective action immediately.
    d. Communicate the current climate of the organization to leadership and request their support.

126. Which of the following should NOT be used to inform business decisions?
    a. Organizational metrics
    b. Key performance indicators
    c. Political trends
    d. Cost-benefit analysis

127. HR feels it is not being given the opportunity to operate to its full potential. How can HR professionals make a business case for their department to present to senior leaders?
    a. Compile a timeline demonstrating how HR has grown and developed over the years.
    b. Organize a group presentation in which members of HR explain the projects they are working on and their areas of expertise.
    c. Create an information session about industry best practices in HR and highlight places where the company is falling behind.
    d. Focus on issues that matter to executives, such as recruiting and retaining top employees and increasing operational efficiency.

128. During the evaluation stage, which of the following is vital information to seek from stakeholders?
    a. Documentation
    b. Feedback
    c. Questions
    d. Costs

129. An employer is closing a large facility with more than fifty employees and laying off all the employees that work there. What does the employer need to do before the job site closes?
    a. Give the employees a sixty-calendar-day notice in writings.
    b. No notice is required if they in an at-will state.
    c. Give the employees a two-week notice.
    d. Give the employees as long of a notice as possible as a good business practice, but there is no requirement.

130. The National Labor Relations Act (NLRA) protects the following EXCEPT:
    a. Allowing employees to talk about their wages
    b. Requiring employers to pay employees during the formation of a union
    c. Allowing employees to form or join a union
    d. Striking and picketing

131. When is an employer allowed to deny Consolidated Omnibus Budget Reconciliation Act (COBRA) to an employee?
    a. If the employee stopped showing up to work without putting in a resignation.
    b. If the employee passed away.
    c. If the employee went from full-time benefit eligible status to a part-time benefit ineligible status.
    d. If an employee was fired for gross misconduct.

132. The following are the federally protected classes of the Equal Employment Opportunity Commission EXCEPT?
    a. Pregnancy status
    b. Genetic information
    c. Disability
    d. Employees/applicants Between eighteen and twenty-six years old

133. What are the known benefits of showing concern for fellow employees at work?
    a. It correlates with higher pay over time.
    b. It builds employee morale and fosters positive working environments.
    c. It correlates with more frequent promotions.
    d. It leads to a self-reported sense of spiritual satisfaction.

134. Lisa is working with her team to address a talent surplus. She has identified multiple areas to focus on, such as a reduction in work hours, implementation of a hiring freeze, and creation of a voluntary separation program. By focusing on these items, what is Lisa working to avoid?
    a. Financial restructuring
    b. Workforce reduction
    c. Organizational restructuring
    d. Corporate restructuring

135. A company may decide to outsource which of the following functions to free up staff time, reduce costs, improve compliance, and avoid fines related to Internal Revenue Service (IRS) filings or incorrect payments?
    a. Payroll
    b. HR
    c. Information technology
    d. Marketing

136. To reduce operating costs, a company has decided to maintain its domestic headquarters but open an overseas manufacturing plant. What is the best word to describe this move?
    a. Outsourcing
    b. Downsizing
    c. Offshoring
    d. Globalizing

137. A small business owner has hired four staff members. The business owner considers herself a fair and ethical person. However, she has hired one relative, her best friend from college, and one person from a job posting site who was previously unknown to her. All three employees are highly qualified, care about the business, have exceptional work ethic, and will be cross-trained in the same functions. What is one way that the business owner can mitigate potential bias in her treatment of the employees?
    a. Go out of her way to be extra supportive and kind to the employee found from the job board.
    b. Pay each employee the exact same salary and give the same percentage of business tasks.
    c. Try to notice when she shows bias and stop the behavior whenever she catches herself.
    d. Go out to lunch daily as a group.

138. Which term refers to an organization's identity—including mission, values, and culture—as it is communicated to current and prospective employees?
    a. Transparency
    b. Social presence
    c. Employer brand
    d. Workplace statement

139. When using the empirical-rational strategy to initiate change, what is the best way to accomplish the change successfully?
    a. Provide an employee lunch when communicating the change.
    b. Educate employees with new information on the change.
    c. Incentivize the change to relay the benefit employees will experience.
    d. Have the leader of the organization communicate the change.

140. According to the 1961 text *The Planning of Change* which of the following is NOT a strategy for managing change?
    a. The normative-reductive strategy
    b. The power-coercive strategy
    c. The technology-innovation strategy
    d. The empirical-rational strategy

141. Which strategy assumes individuals are rational and will naturally follow a path that benefits their self-interest?
    a. The power-coercive strategy
    b. The empirical-rational strategy
    c. The technology-innovation strategy
    d. The normative-reductive strategy

142. Job ranking, paired comparison, and job classification are all forms of which type of job evaluation method?
    a. Quantitative job evaluation method
    b. Qualitative job evaluation method
    c. Nonquantitative job evaluation method
    d. Factor comparison evaluation method

143. Which of the following quantitative job evaluation methods is less complex and commonly used to evaluate the relative work of a job?
    a. Point factor method
    b. Factor comparison method
    c. Whole-job method
    d. Job classification method

144. Which of the following is an accurate statement about ambiguity?
    a. Ambiguity can cause conflict and distress for employees.
    b. Ambiguity is always preventable and should be avoided.
    c. Ambiguity will not affect business practices or processes.
    d. Ambiguity allows for creativity and innovation.

145. Emily and Chris have worked in the HR department for five years. They have wanted to launch a wellness program since they started working for the company and finally prepared a plan to roll out to the employees. After meeting one-on-one for months, they created all of the documents necessary to communicate the new program to employees. They created sign-up sheets, a summary sheet, a summary plan description that outlined the benefits of participating in a wellness program, and a lengthy frequently asked questions (FAQ) document. After emailing the documents to all employees, Emily and Chris were disappointed to see that very few employees were interested in the program. Which one of the following choices is best in describing what Emily and Chris could have done differently to get a better outcome?
    a. Made participation in the program mandatory.
    b. Conducted an employee survey to get direct feedback on employees' needs.
    c. Communicated program details to leadership to have them instruct employees to participate.
    d. Added a new line item of "wellness program participation" to employees' performance evaluations to ensure participation.

146. The employee value proposition (EVP) reflects employees' perceived valuing of the tangible and intangible rewards and benefits of working for an organization. What is an example of an intangible benefit?
    a. Holiday bonus
    b. Annual paid company retreat
    c. Flexible schedule options
    d. Retirement savings plan

147. When must an I-9 be completed by an employer?
    a. Within three business days of an employee's start date, either before or after
    b. On the employee's first day
    c. Before an employee starts employment
    d. Within the first forty-five days of employment

192

148. Miguel is working with the leadership team to reorganize the organization to ensure profitability based on the current economic situation. This action is a direct response to the company experiencing significant decreases in sales over a period of several quarters. What type of action is Miguel conducting?
    a. Financial restructuring
    b. Workforce reduction
    c. Organizational restructuring
    d. Corporate restructuring

149. An employer setting a policy that employees receive a verbal warning and then a written warning before being terminated is creating what type of policy?
    a. Termination policy
    b. Progressive discipline policy
    c. Offboarding
    d. Documentation process

150. Jenny is an introverted individual who works best alone and behind the scenes. She is hired by a small firm to do data analysis and scientific report writing, two tasks she loves and excels at. She enjoys her first week very much and receives a great deal of praise from her colleagues and manager. However, a staffing change causes the firm to give her additional responsibilities, including organizing large team-building and training events. Jenny struggles with these responsibilities and after her thirty-day probationary period, the firm lets her go. What is the probable reason for Jenny's termination?
    a. Jenny is not a team player.
    b. Jenny has poor work ethic.
    c. Jenny was not a good fit with her new responsibilities.
    d. Jenny is not smart enough to work at the firm.

151. Joseph is updating his organization's employee handbook. The handbook has not been reviewed or updated in years, and he finds that many policies are outdated and not in compliance with new state and federal regulations. Which of the following is NOT something Joseph should consider when updating the employee handbook?
    a. Update the policies regarding harassment, discipline, attendance, safety procedures, work hours, and compensation and benefits to include in the handbook.
    b. Create an acknowledgement of receipt and understanding for employees to sign saying they received, read, and understand the content of the updated handbook.
    c. Provide the updated handbook to current employees to ensure they are aware of the policies, procedures, and requirements.
    d. Include a disclaimer indicating that the handbook is intended to be the contractual agreement between the employer and employee.

152. What process deals with employee infractions, addressing each incident as a unique situation and developing consequences accordingly?
    a. Coaching and counseling
    b. Progressive discipline
    c. Consecutive discipline
    d. Employee reviews

193

153. When conducting a performance review, the company asks the supervisor, co-workers, customers, subordinates, and even suppliers for their input on working with the employee. What type of review would this be?
   a. 360-degree feedback
   b. Skill evaluation
   c. Leader assessment
   d. Team assessment

154. When conducting the IRS 20-Factor Test to determine if an individual is an employee or an independent contractor, which of the following factors is considered a "type of relationship" factor?
   a. Personal services
   b. Profit or loss
   c. Public availability
   d. Business integration

155. Which part of Medicare is hospital insurance, considered mandatory, and generally at no cost to qualifying individuals?
   a. Medicare Part A
   b. Medicare Part B
   c. Medicare Part C
   d. Medicare Part D

156. Which part of Medicare is prescription drug coverage, considered optional, and provided for a monthly fee to those enrolled?
   a. Medicare Part A
   b. Medicare Part B
   c. Medicare Part C
   d. Medicare Part D

157. Which part of Medicare is medical insurance that covers health care expenses such as outpatient care and physician's care, considered optional, and provided for a monthly fee for those enrolled?
   a. Medicare Part A
   b. Medicare Part B
   c. Medicare Part C
   d. Medicare Part D

Read the following scenario and answer questions 158-160.

Susan is responsible for administering the benefits program at her organization. Several employees have recently left the organization to take positions with other organizations or to retire. During their exit interview, she reviews the benefits coverage and ending date, retirement programs and options, and vacation leave payouts. Because the employees all indicated they would have health insurance with their new agencies or be covered under Medicare, Susan did not send out the applicable paperwork to select the option to continue the health care coverage at their own cost.

158. What ERISA amendment is Susan's organization in violation of by not sending out the paperwork for former employees with information on the options to continue the group health care coverage?
   a. Family Medical Leave Act
   b. Uniform Services Employment and Reemployment Rights Act
   c. Consolidated Omnibus Budget Reconciliation Act
   d. Health Insurance Portability and Accountability Act

159. If a former employee decides to select the option to continue the health care coverage, how is the premium paid?
   a. The organization pays the full cost of coverage.
   b. The organization and former employee both pay 50 percent.
   c. The organization pays 25 percent, and the former employee pays 7 percent.
   d. The former employee pays the full cost of coverage.

160. Because Susan's organization did not comply with the requirement of communicating with former employees their options to continue the group medical insurance coverage, what could the organization face?
   a. Civil and criminal penalties
   b. OSHA investigation and audit
   c. Civil penalties only
   d. FEHA investigation and audit

161. Monique has recently seen an increase in employee resignations within one particular department. Upon analyzing the demographics, she sees that a large majority of employees who left are minorities. Although the organization has established policies specific to diversity and inclusion, a barrier could still exist that is causing employees with a specific background to leave. What can Monique do to work with the leadership to identify and eliminate this barrier?
   a. Conduct internal interviews with employees to ask why others left.
   b. Audit the programs, practices, and policies regarding diversity and inclusion.
   c. Conduct mandatory diversity and inclusion training for all employees.
   d. Contact the employees who left and ask them to consider returning.

162. Rebecca is responsible for ensuring that the organization's recordkeeping processes and systems are in alignment with and meeting compliance requirements for the FLSA. Which of the following items is NOT a standard piece of information that Rebecca is responsible for monitoring?
   a. Performance evaluations and professional growth plan
   b. Personal information, such as address, date of birth, and position
   c. Work schedule, including day and time of the start of the work week
   d. Total wages paid during each pay period, including additions or deductions

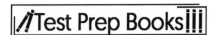
163. Soleil is working to implement a new payroll and time-tracking program that will be a large undertaking, involving numerous departments and costing a substantial amount of money. To ensure that all of the key stakeholders are on board and have their concerns addressed, she is conducting one-on-one and department meetings; sending status emails while soliciting feedback and documenting comments, ideas, and concerns raised; and compiling survey responses from employees. What practice is Soleil engaging in?
   a. Recordkeeping
   b. Project management
   c. Milestone tracking
   d. Strategic planning

164. How long does an employer need to retain an I-9?
   a. Three years after hire date
   b. One year after the employee terminates
   c. Three years after hire date or one year after the employee terminates, whichever is later
   d. Seven years after hire date or one year after the employee terminates, whichever is sooner

165. Which of the following laws establishes the minimum standards for benefits plans of private, for-profit employers?
   a. Pension Protection Act
   b. Employee Retirement Income Security Act
   c. Equal Pay Act
   d. Health Insurance Portability and Accountability Act

166. When a strategic plan calls for changes in employee skills, knowledge, behaviors, and/or work deliverables, what is the role of HR?
   a. HR holds multiple meetings and initiates various types of communication to reach out to managers, ensuring they are on the same page and personally training their employees.
   b. HR works with the legal team to ensure that the organization has the authority and management right to make the changes requested to the strategic plan.
   c. HR prepares exit strategies and severance packages for employees who do not meet the new requirements necessary to accomplish the plan.
   d. HR facilitates these changes by implementing updated policies, procedures, training, and other appropriate plans to ensure employees have the necessary skills to deliver the plan.

167. Which process administers, manages, and supports significant transitions related to resource allocation, operations, business processes, and other large-scale changes?
   a. Risk management
   b. Strategic planning
   c. Critical evaluation
   d. Change management

168. During the workday, a mechanical engineer at TLC Robotics was seriously injured onsite. The engineer's team called an ambulance, and the engineer was taken to the hospital for treatment. The manager of the team is filing a claim. What information should the manager include on the claim form?

    a. Witnesses, the employee's medical history, and details about how the injury occurred

    b. Witnesses, the employee's medical history, and the employee's social security number

    c. Witnesses, the employee's social security number, and details about how the injury occurred

    d. Witnesses, date and time of injury, and details about how the injury occurred

169. Which of the following terms refers to a planned and practiced protocol used during an emergency?

    a. Strategic plan

    b. Emergency response

    c. Evacuation plan

    d. Hazard communication

170. Tim has recently provided Human Resources with permanent restrictions due to a documented medical disability. He is an accountant, and the majority of his work relates to payroll processing, accounts receivable, and accounts payable. The restrictions address physical concerns as well as limit Tim's ability to work a full 8-hour shift. Tim has requested accommodations for each physical concern that includes installing better ergonomic-specific equipment, such as a keyboard tray, special chair with lumbar support, and a footrest. Additionally, he has requested an accommodation to limit his workday to no more than a 6-hour shift, resulting in a maximum 30-hour work week. How should HR respond to Tim regarding his accommodation requests?

    a. Automatically deny the accommodations because they were not received from his doctor.

    b. Automatically approve the accommodations to ensure compliance with the Americans with Disabilities Act (ADA).

    c. Review the accommodations and determine which are reasonable and which are not and then prepare a response to address each request.

    d. Lay off Tim and eliminate his position so that he will be eligible for severance and unemployment benefits.

Read the following scenario and answer questions 171–172.

    A fulfillment center recently opened to support the distribution needs of a growing city. The center hired more than a thousand employees quickly to ensure the staffing levels would be appropriate to handle the workload when the facility began operations. In addition to coordinating group orientations to navigate the hiring process, group meetings were also scheduled to familiarize employees with the benefits and programs offered by the company. Human Resources also wants to schedule group meetings to review the safety protocols and emergency response plans to ensure employees are aware and understand their role and responsibility if an emergency was to occur.

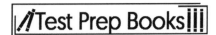

171. The plant manager does not support holding another set of group meetings to discuss the emergency response plans. He wants the staff to focus on the distribution operations for the first year and then would consider providing an hour or two to provide this training. How should HR respond to this situation?

a. Communicate to the plant manager that these plans protect lives and property, provide a level of security to employees, and ensure compliance with safety standards.

b. Schedule the group meetings to occur immediately, ensuring that employees receive this training and information promptly.

c. Create a formal memo that outlines the entire program and request that supervisors distribute the memo to each employee and post it in the break rooms.

d. Schedule the group meetings to occur exactly one year from the date of opening to align with the direction from the plant manager.

172. During the group meetings to train employees on the emergency response plan, HR also emphasizes the evacuation plan for the facility. Visual aids are provided with exit routes mapped out for the entire facility along with meeting places and procedures. In addition to providing this information to employees, what else can HR do to ensure employees effectively evacuate the facility in the case of an emergency?

a. Require employees to sign an acknowledgment statement at the end of the training.

b. Post special posters throughout the facility that showcase the exit routes.

c. Request that supervisors frequently quiz employees on the exit routes.

d. Coordinate a scheduled and unscheduled practice evacuation.

173. Leroy is working on an employee satisfaction survey. He wants to measure how satisfied employees are with the organization in areas such as salary and benefits, supervisory relationships, leadership, communications, and culture. Which of the following is the best method for collecting this type of information?

a. Sending out a survey

b. Establishing focus groups

c. Initiating observational data collection

d. Reviewing performance evaluations

174. An organization that has a lack of transparency will experience which of the following?

a. Innovation and higher satisfaction

b. Increased productivity and lower turnover

c. Decreased morale and higher turnover

d. Increased promotion rates and innovation

175. Which of the following focuses on creating opportunities for employees to learn about, engage in, and benefit from diverse ideas?

a. Group assessments

b. Mentoring program

c. Cross-cultural training

d. Diversity and inclusion

Answer Explanations for Practice Test #1

1. D: An organization should be diligent when ensuring they have clear and enforceable ethical standards. Asking an employee to "promise" they will behave in a certain way, however, will not ensure this is accomplished, nor will it protect the organization from liability. Additionally, each employee may define appropriate behavior differently, and therefore organizations should make sure all employees abide by the same guide of ethical standards.

2. B: The acronym in PEST stands for political, economic, social, and technological. This refers to categorized trends that influence the organization and can be used to anticipate potential opportunities and risks in a variety of areas.

3. D: A strong diversity and inclusion program will not only develop relationships with external stakeholders but will also build employee relations and satisfaction. Although it is important to ensure that any program, including diversity and inclusion, meets all federal and state regulations, Choice *C,* this should not be a primary focus of what the program will accomplish. Providing thorough investigations of complaints, Choice *A,* and ensuring a strong training and development program, Choice *B,* are important but may fall outside the scope of diversity and inclusion programs.

4. D: Employees from all levels of the organization should be included. Diversity and inclusion (D&I) should be part of an organization-wide policy that involves all employees. Choice *A* is not the best answer because key training messages may get lost in translation as they travel from leadership-level employees to their subordinates. Choice *B* is also not the best answer because it reacts to past problems rather than working to proactively create a workplace culture that avoids such conflict. Choice *C* is also not a good choice because long-standing employees also need training to adapt to changing workplace conditions.

5. D: Organize a week-long training class focused on desired skill development. Although building the skills, knowledge, and competencies of the workforce is an ongoing responsibility of the HR department, sometimes there are short-term skills gaps that need to be closed. In this case, organizing a class or workshop to directly target the missing skill is a practical and effective approach. For example, if many employees are struggling with adopting new workplace software, a few training courses can help them get up to speed. Choice *A* is not the best choice because interviewing and onboarding new employees is very time-consuming and not the best short-term strategy. Choice *B* is also not the best choice because a high-potential development program should carry employees throughout the time at an organization until they are positioned to become leaders; again, this is a long-term rather than short-term development strategy. Finally, Choice *C* is not the best choice because, while internal reassignment can help employees to find positions that best fit their competencies, this choice does not solve the problem because it removes underperforming employees without replacing them or building the skills of remaining workers.

6. B: Employee business resource groups are an excellent tool that can increase employee engagement by connecting employees to others outside of their usual working environment. These groups allow for new connections to be made between employees and opportunities for them to be more diverse and inclusive in their daily work and interactions.

7. D: Conducting stay interviews is a great way to get engagement information from your current staff in a targeted way. If you are unable to find the cause for the disengagement, it is crucial that you gather more information before trying to make a change. Without input from the department, you could lose great employees or not address the problem. Choices *B* and *C* try to recommend a solution without knowing the problem. Choice *A* could have you lose valuable staff before solving the problem.

8. C: Internal data can provide HR professionals with information about employees, specifically productivity trends, job satisfaction, and turnover rates. External data can provide the organization with information about consumer trends, customer preferences, client engagement, and advertising techniques, making Choices *A, B,* and *D* incorrect.

9. B: Stay interviews are conducted to stay in touch with employees to gauge how they feel about the organization, position, and culture. These interviews allow HR professionals to assess if there are changes that need to be made and to address any needs that are raised before issues arise that may be more complicated to correct. 360 feedback, Choice *A,* is a term that refers to employees rating their supervisors to provide insight into the supervisory and leadership skills. Exit interviews, Choice *C,* are conducted with exiting employees to understand why they are leaving the organization, and satisfaction surveys, Choice *D,* are conducted with all employees to gauge how they feel about certain topics, such as leadership, communication, salary, and benefits.

10. D: Margaret should immediately communicate with the department manager to identify if the manager wants to work to retain the employee. If the answer is yes, a discussion should occur to determine if there is an opportunity within the budget to provide a counteroffer. Although the other options could be acceptable, the best option is to work with the department manager first. If the employee cannot or should not be retained, an exit interview should be conducted and a new recruitment established.

11. B: You should pull employees in, preferably separately, if there was an altercation. It is very important that notes are taken and signed by both employees. That way you have the most accurate representation of events before you take any action. The signature on the notes ensures that you took notes correctly and that the employees have agreed to what was written down, in case there is litigation, or if notes need to be referenced in the future, so Choice *D is* incorrect. Choices *A* and *C* are incorrect, as documentation should always be kept for employment concerns, and so Human Resources can ask questions and clarify.

12. D: A crucial factor for the future generation of new employees to determine their job field is the social impact and engagement of the work they will do and the organization that will employ them. Although compensation and benefits, Choice *A,* retirement programs, Choice *B,* and flexible work options, Choice *C,* are important when joining an organization and picking a career, they are not the primary focus on the next generation coming into the workforce.

13. D: One of the strongest advantages of external sourcing for recruitment is that it supports building a diverse workforce and brings fresh perspectives to an organization. Although any recruitment should encourage connections with job seekers, external sourcing can be more costly than internal sourcing, making Choices *A* and *B* incorrect. Additionally, candidates who are sourced externally with no connection to an internal source will most likely not have familiarity with the organization and culture, making Choice *C* incorrect. This is a strength of internal sourcing.

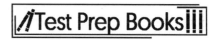

14. C: Walk-in applicants are considered a method of external recruiting. Employee referrals, Choice *A*, promotions and transfers, Choice *B,* and recruiter-sourced hires, Choice *D,* are all methods of internal sourcing. All methods have pros and cons regarding timeliness, cost, and quality of candidates.

15. B: Layla needs to focus her report on the requested subject matter—how the organization is making a difference in the diversity relative to the hiring activity across the organization. She should ensure that her report identifies the employee demographics compared to other organizations in the area. Additionally, she can discuss how the department is working toward meeting the hiring goal. This may be one key performance indicator that she can address, Choice *A*, but she should stay focused on the subject matter and not delve into all of the HR metrics. Discussing recruitment concerns, Choice *C,* and A campus recruitment initiative, Choice *D,* may be valid because they are related to the overall objective, and they will ensure transparency because they are part of the process to achieve the objective, but they should not be the main focus of the report.

16. B: Although the length of time an individual can be eligible for COBRA coverage will differ based on the circumstances, to comply, employers are required to provide an initial COBRA notice within ninety days of the individual's separation.

17. B: Jacobi should look for a vendor that learns about the organization's business goals so that the rewards program is tailored to the company's strategic initiatives. Choice *A* is incorrect because the right rewards program vendor may not be the least expensive. Choice *C* is incorrect because accommodating advance orders should be a given for any vendor, and it is more important to work with a vendor who can handle rush orders. Choice *D* is incorrect because the strength of the vendor's company culture does not necessarily indicate a good fit with the organization.

18. C: Non-discretionary benefits are benefits employers are legally mandated to provide such as social security, Medicare, workers' compensation, unemployment insurance, unpaid family medical leave, and continuation of healthcare coverage. Choice *A* is incorrect because non-discretionary benefits are not related to group discounts that save money for the organization. Choice *B* is incorrect because non-discretionary benefits are not optional for companies; rather, they are mandated by law. Choice *D* is incorrect because non-discretionary benefits are not pre-tax benefits.

19. B: Professional sabbaticals are not covered by the FMLA. Choice *A*, qualifying exigency leave, Choice *C,* leave for foster-care placement, and Choice *D*, military caregiver leave, are all covered by the FMLA.

20. B: Long-term disability insurance is a type of disability insurance that takes over when an employee cannot return to work after being out on short-term disability. It pays an employee a percentage of their salary until they can return to work or for the number of years listed in the employer's policy. Choice *A* and Choice *D* are both incorrect because the number of years an employer pays for long-term disability insurance is discretionary. Choice *C* is incorrect because it is short-term disability insurance that pays a portion of the employee's salary for shorter durations, typically between 10 and 26 weeks.

21. B: Front pay is money awarded to an individual that is generally equal to potential lost earnings and is usually required when a position is not available or an employer has not made any effort to address ongoing issues. Front pay could also be warranted if the employee would be forced to endure a hostile work environment if returned to the original position.

22. B: OSHA, the Occupational Safety and Health Act, is responsible for creating and enforcing workplace safety standards. OSHA sets minimum standards, provides job training in multiple languages to ensure understanding, and protects employees.

23. C: OSHA issues multiple types of violations, including the de minimus violation. This violation is issued when a condition is investigated to show that it is not directly and immediately related to an employee's health or safety and no fine or citation is required.

24. A: OSHA issues multiple types of violations, including the other-than-serious violation. This violation is issued when a condition is investigated to show that it could impact an employee's health or safety but probably would not result in death or serious harm.

25. B: OSHA is not responsible for providing fixed payments to employees who have suffered from an injury in the workplace. This function is provided by workers' compensation programs administered by organizations and their risk management departments.

26. A: Although all of the hazards listed can occur in a workplace and employers should have a plan to address each, the most common workplace safety risks employees are exposed to are bloodborne pathogens and tripping hazards.

27. B: Meet with local supervisors and managers to establish areas of shared goals and practices and focus on converging operations. Successful international operations are those that balance the parent company's culture with that of local operations. Especially when opening new stores, it is more productive to identify areas of similarities and overlapping objectives rather than only emphasizing differences. This enables the local employees to add value where their skills can contribute to the parent company's goals. Choice *A* is not the best choice because it defeats the purpose of buying an existing company—that is, to use their established practice and experience. Choice *C* is also not the most productive choice; again, if all employees require extensive, costly retraining, it does not make sense to retain experienced cosmetics salespeople. Finally, Choice *D* is not the best choice because, while it is definitely important to assess the capabilities of the new workforce, this choice does not fully explain how to integrate their skills into new ownership.

28. D: Arrange regular check-in meetings and agree on reporting times and methods. Constant coordination and communication with clearly defined objectives and performance measures is the best way to ensure that shared goals are being met. Choice *A* is not the best choice for addressing this particular issue because it doesn't mention how the leadership groups in each country will be communicating with each other. Choice *B* is also not the best choice; online messages (such as email and instant messenger) are important, but other forms of communication should be incorporated as well. Choice *C* is not a good choice because it doesn't consider possible time zone problems that could arise from simply putting local stores on American schedules; mutually agreed upon meeting times should be established instead.

29. C: Title VII of the Civil Rights Act of 1964 prohibits discrimination based on race, color, religion, sex, or national origin. The EEOC administers and oversees this law along with the Age Discrimination in Employment Act of 1967.

30. A: A bona fide occupational qualification, or BFOQ, is a qualification that has been determined to be justified by a business purpose. Minimum qualifications should be related to the job and established to reflect what experience would be needed to do the job being recruited for.

31. C: Liz should categorize the applications by age and use the same categories as FLSA to ensure accuracy and compliance when assigning work tasks and scheduling hours. These age categories are under 14, ages 14 and 15, ages 16 and 17, and age 18 and over.

32. D: Employees hired at the age of fifteen are not allowed to perform any work related to loading or unloading products to or from a conveyor line or a truck. Additionally, there are other limitations regarding the work employees aged fifteen can perform. They may not operate power-driven lawn mowers, work with any hazardous materials, work with freezers or meat coolers, or conduct any work with a power-driven machine.

33. B: Once youths reach eighteen years of age, the FLSA child labor laws no longer apply because they are now legal adults. Work, hours, and wages would now be regulated by the standard FLSA regulations, not the child labor law regulations.

34. D: When evaluating the program, if Liz sees that there is a higher number of candidates who are over eighteen, she should consider updating the applicant requirements to specifically indicate that only individuals under the age of eighteen will be considered. If an applicant is over the age of eighteen at the time of application, the application will not be considered.

35. B: It gives more timely and dynamic feedback to employees and helps solve performance problems as soon as they arise. One of the drawbacks of conducting annual performance evaluations is that they may take too long to address critical issues with performance; in other words, the damage has already been done or inefficient work practices have already been established. This app provides more opportunities for feedback from more perspectives. Choice *A* is not the best choice because encouraging phone use at work does not really contribute to productivity or engagement. Choice *B* could be a potential advantage to this new program, but technology for technology's sake is not the primary objective of any new processes in the workplace. Choice *D* is not the best choice, either, because the program should encourage better engagement, not allow supervisors to disengage from the workers they manage. In other words, it presents an opportunity for a different type of feedback rather than removing supervisors from the feedback process altogether.

36. D: The app will prove to be expensive and cost-prohibitive compared to traditional performance evaluations. Generally, most moves toward automation present opportunities to cut costs and operate more efficiently by removing hours of manual labor and paperwork, so this is least likely to be a major drawback of adopting an automated system. Choice *A* represents a major potential problem that HR should work to address: How can they prevent constant feedback from turning into an opportunity to bully or overly criticize some employees based on personal feelings? The same applies to Choice *B*. Choice *C* is also a potential hurdle HR should overcome because any new technology requires some time for users to learn how to operate and optimize the system's functionality.

37. B: Automation allows technology to take over manual tasks, while augmentation refers to ways that technology assists employees in their job function. Both automation and augmentation are terms related to incorporating new technology into existing work processes. However, whereas automation refers to instances in which digital processes can fully replace employee functions or actions, augmentation looks at areas where employees can continue to perform tasks with the help of new technologies. For people who fear that automation will lead to replacing entire groups of workers, augmentation is a more attractive way to approach bringing technology into the workplace.

203

38. A: Hold a demonstration of how the technology works in different situations, including information about user resources. With any new workplace technology, employees need to fully understand how to use the new system before they can engage with it. Holding a demonstration that addresses different scenarios can give employees ideas of how to integrate it into their work; offering user resources gives employees a way to find answers and solutions afterward. Choice *B* is not the best choice because it doesn't consider the needs of all stakeholders; for example, some supervisors may prefer to use both performance evaluation methods, or some employees may need longer than six months to adjust to a different management style. Choice *C* is also not the best choice because it isn't very practical and doesn't address engagement for employees who already have phones. Choice *D* is not a good choice because the videos are not likely to reach all employees who are using the app.

39. D: A human resources department might outsource the payroll function so employees can focus on the organization's other strategic initiatives. Choice *A*, eliminating human resources costs, would be impossible, even if the department chose to outsource payroll. Choice *B*, getting rid of direct deposit, is not a reason to outsource the payroll function because outsourcing typically adds or improves direct deposit services. Choice *C*, avoiding taxes associated with improper IRS filings, is incorrect because outsourcing payroll can only help companies avoid fines for improper filings, not taxes.

40. B: An employer is required to offer COBRA to all qualifying former employees, including their dependents and spouses, that were covered under the employer's medical, dental, vision, and specialty medical plans. Choice *A* and Choice *C* are incorrect, since you must have medical insurance through your employer before leaving to be eligible for COBRA. Choice *D* is incorrect since COBRA is for the continuation of benefits after employment, and would not impact current employees.

41. C: Identifying and setting goals relative to other organizations' performance. Benchmarking involves doing environmental scanning, locating leaders in the field, and determining what those organizations have done to achieve success. Through benchmarking, an organization can learn from others' success in setting and reaching performance goals.

42. C: HR staff members should help non-cooperating employees find common ground to work together toward an end goal, rather than separating or punishing employees, whenever possible. If there are too many failed attempts at resolution, it may be necessary to escalate tactics.

43. D: The statement that is accurate is that CSR has a positive impact on employee recruiting, retention, and overall satisfaction. CSR can be the defining factor for new and current employees to come to or stay with an organization. Although CSR involves and engages with local community representatives and leaders, CSR is guided and championed by internal leadership, making Choice *A* incorrect. Additionally, there may be federal statutes regarding specific environmental practices, and a CSR program is not regulated by federal or local statutes, making Choice *B* incorrect. Finally, even though environmental needs are a priority for the CSR program, they do not take priority over profitability and organizational success, making Choice *C* incorrect.

44. B: Collect, compile, and analyze data to demonstrate the quantitative and qualitative impacts of various CSR initiatives. HR can assist with communication and planning within CSR, and this involves analyzing metrics to understand how the CSR plan is functioning. This information is then communicated to various internal and external stakeholders and can influence CSR decision making moving forward. Choice *A* is not a good choice because CSR initiatives depend on the participation of all employees at every level. Choice *C* is also not the best choice because, while different business units may have different contributions to make to an organization's overall CSR efforts, they should be united by a common vision and interdepartmental communication should be facilitated. Choice *D* is also not the best choice. Incorporating CSR participation into evaluations is one way to emphasize its importance in the workplace. However, any such evaluation should include ways to recognize and reward employees for their contributions, rather than simply punishing them for not participating.

45. C: An organization's CSR can be evaluated on the three P's: people, planet, profit. Although the public, the organization's purpose and process, and overall proceeds will be important to the CSR, they are not the evaluation factors used to determine how effective an organization's CSR is.

46. B: The three factors that evaluate an organization's CSR—people, planet, profit—are known as the triple bottom line. The hat trick, Choice *A,* is a term used in hockey, the triple play, Choice *C,* is a term used in baseball, and the social responsibility scale, Choice *D,* is a made-up term.

47. A: Although all these actions may be appropriate at times to address the issue, the first thing Evelyn should do is to provide training to the managers and supervisors. This training should include information on the process, forms, and timeline as well as coaching on how to deliver an effective evaluation. Evelyn should respond to questions and provide real-life examples to situations that may arise during the process.

48. B: Susan should ensure that each objective includes the SMART aspects: specific, measurable, achievable, relevant, and time-based. Without these aspects, an objective may not be met, or the status could be unknown. By including the SMART aspects, there can be a clear understanding of performance expectations. Choice *A* is incorrect because all language should be well written, clear, concise, and specific, but without SMART aspects, there could still be misunderstandings as to what is to be accomplished. Choices *C* and *D* are inaccurate because professional development and recognition should be separate items contained within a performance review but separate from performance objectives. If a training opportunity is to be an objective for an employee, the item should be written as an objective, containing the SMART aspects.

49. A: Six Sigma is a specific technique that works to improve business processes by implementing various tools and concepts to reduce errors and eliminate waste. Gap analysis, root cause analysis, and cause-and-effect diagrams, Choices *B, C,* and *D,* are incorrect because they are all tools that would be used to determine why goals were not achieved or if there was a discrepancy between the expected results and actual results.

50. D: The most effective way to ensure that an evacuation plan will be implemented in the best way possible is to coordinate scheduled and unscheduled practice evacuations from the facility. Although acknowledge statements, special posters, and quizzes, Choices *A, B,* and *C,* will promote retention of the information, the best way to ensure that an evacuation plan will be effective is to practice the evacuation.

51. B: First aid and AED locations and procedures should be addressed during safety training and new-employee orientation. Although it may be prudent to review this information within the security plan training, it is vital to address specific items related to security measures during this training. These include emergency communication systems, Choice *A;* alarm locations, secure rooms, and security guard location, Choice *C;* and employee badges and facility security protocols, Choice *D.*

52. A: Employees should be trained annually to review the security plans, their importance, and the roles and responsibilities each employee has to the plan. Although it is a best practice to also provide this training during new-hire orientation, the best answer is annually.

53. D: Schedule mandatory in-person training with employee involvement, such as skits, role plays, and mock juries, to encourage engagement and focus on real-world implications. Workplace conduct is a topic that HR should emphasize for all employees with a high level of engagement. HR has made the right first step in deciding to proactively address workplace harassment and misconduct; however, establishing clear guidance and creating a culture of civility comes from true engagement with employees. For this reason, Choice *C* is not the best choice, because employees will be passive learners. Also, while Choice *A* might be a good supplementary resource, employees also need positive modeling and information about how they *should* behave in the workplace, rather than just negative information about how they *should not* behave. Finally, Choice *B* is not the best choice because abstract legal implications may not have a strong connection to employees. Instead, Choice *D* gives employees a chance to explore situations that affect their everyday workplace interactions.

54. B: Someone from the C-suite. An organization's culture of civility must be rooted in its leadership. If employees sense that rules about workplace conduct do not apply to an organization's executives, or are applied inconsistently, standards of civil behavior are less likely to take hold throughout the organization. It is important to engage leaders from the C-suite to lead by example. Choice *A* is not the best choice because some employees may prefer to keep their complaints confidential; experience with harassment may be personal and hurtful to share with a large audience. Choice *C* is not the best choice because, while guidance from the Department of Justice could be helpful, it is better to begin with leadership from inside the organization. Finally, while HR should be involved with all levels of this training, it is important to reach outside HR to leaders in other areas of the organization.

55. D: By engaging the team via meetings and recognition, providing information, and offering the ability to have a dialogue, the HR director is exhibiting characteristics of transparency and team-oriented culture. Employees who have this type of leadership often feel more valued, are more productive, and have greater satisfaction with their job and organization.

56. B: The HR director's recommendation to terminate Kyle is based on the violation of theft policy of the organization. Although Kyle has in fact committed a felony act, Choice *A,* this is for the police to investigate if the agency decides to press charges. The rationale for termination should be the policy violation. Choices *C* and *D* are incorrect.

57. D: A best practice organizations can implement to keep employees up-to-date regarding applicable laws and regulations is to display posters in common areas, such as breakrooms, meeting areas, or employee information boards. It is a best practice to provide employees the actual policies and procedures during new-hire orientation and show employees where to find this information, Choices *A, B,* and *C;* however, these answer choices are incorrect because they do not refer to keeping employees up-to-date but rather deal with employees being introduced to compliant behaviors.

58. A: Deauthorization is the official process to remove a union's security clause and negotiating authority. Deauthorization removes the requirement that employees must join the union; the process is identical to decertification. Arbitration, Choice *B,* is a form of mediation that is a formal process to settle disputes prior to going to court. Mediation, Choice *C,* is generally the precursor to arbitration through a less formal process to resolve concerns and issues. Confrontation, Choice *D*, is also a form of mediation that is used when a stalemate occurs and neither side is willing to consider resolving the matter.

59. B: Arbitration is a form of mediation but is the more formal process. Arbitration is a way to settle disputes using a third-party mediator without going to court. Deauthorization, Choice *A*, is the official process to remove a union's negotiating authority as well as the requirement that employees must join the union. Mediation, Choice *C*, is generally the precursor to arbitration through a less formal process to resolve concerns and issues. Confrontation, Choice *D*, is also a form of mediation that is used when a stalemate occurs and neither side is willing to consider resolving the matter.

60. B: The Fair Labor Standards Act (FLSA) is also known as the Wage and Hour Law. The FLSA established employee classification and regulated issues related to wages and child labor. The Family Medical Leave Act, Choice *A*, allows eligible employees in an organization unpaid leave time to care for themselves and family while protecting their jobs. The Davis Bacon Act, Choice *C*, *applies* to contractors working on federally funded contracts over $2,000. The Walsh-Healy Act, Choice *D*, applies to contractors working on federally funded contracts over $10,000.

61. A: Non-exempt positions fall directly under the regulations of the FLSA. Non-exempt positions do not involve the supervision of other employees, require specialized education or training, or use independent judgment for decision-making. Positions that are exempt, which include professional and administrative positions, do not fall under the regulations of the FLSA, so Choices *B*, *C*, and *D* are incorrect.

62. D: Exempt employees are not required to be paid overtime. To be exempt, an employee needs to meet criteria set by the Fair Labor Standards Act (FLSA). Choice *A*, FLSA, does not distinguish between different jobs; it defines the rule to be working for an employer more than forty hours a week. If an employee is working two different jobs, an employer still needs to track and pay overtime for their hours past forty. Overtime is calculated on a workweek; the employer can set what days that workweek starts and ends but is responsible for all hours past forty in a week regardless of the next week's hours, making Choice *B* incorrect. Lastly there is no form to waive overtime, making Choice *C* incorrect.

63. C: Employees that supervise other employees and have management as a significant part of their job are considered exempt. To classify as exempt, employees need to make over $23,600 per year and pass the duties test. The duties test needs to include either executive job duties, professional job duties, or exempt administrative job Duties. These two requirements eliminate Choices *A* and *B*, as Choice *A* does not meet the duties test and Choice *B* does not meet the salary level test. Choice *D* is incorrect, as an employer must justify why an employee is exempt.

64. B: Do you have any commitments that will conflict with your work? Employers are prohibited from asking applicants any questions that may lead to hiring discrimination based on things like age, gender, nationality, and religion. Questions about family, children, and marital status are particularly likely to target women. Interviewers must ensure that they are asking the same or similar questions to all applicants, and that the questions remain relevant to the job function. In this case, Choice *B* is the best because it approaches the important issue for the employer—how much availability does the applicant have? —without introducing needlessly personal or discriminatory factors. All the other choices include topics that would be inappropriate to ask about during an interview.

65. A: HR should evaluate the functionality of the new system from the perspective of stakeholders outside HR. Whenever HR is considering adopting new processes, such as selecting a new ATS, it must consider the needs of all stakeholders, including those outside HR. The purpose of ATS software is to help recruit the best employees to work throughout the organization, so HR needs to communicate with relevant stakeholders to determine which software functionalities will improve their experience. HR can also consider the ATS from the perspective of stakeholders outside the organization (i.e., applicants). Choice *B* is not the best choice because each organization may have unique needs for its ATS; serving the needs of the organization is more important than trying to outpace others. Choice *C* is also not a good choice because it will create confusion to maintain two systems at the same time. Choice *D* can also be eliminated because, while employees may have technical capabilities, they are not necessarily HR specialists, and this could detract from the overall goals of the organization.

66. D: Industry usage rates. Again, it is most important for HR to choose a product that fits their organization's and stakeholders' needs, rather than seeking a "one-size-fits-all" solution based on others in the industry. Choice *A* is important because any new software will have to integrate well with other systems already in use. Choice *B* is also important because any system is only as effective as the people who use it; if it is too difficult for stakeholders to use the ATS, it will not be effective. Vendors should also be able to devise a plan for user support after the software purchase. Finally, Choice *C* is also essential in selecting an ATS. The advantage of using a digital applicant management system is that it can easily generate reports and metrics to inform HR and organizational decision-making.

67. B: Determine essential qualifications for the job positions to categorize applications and help recruiters focus on a smaller pool of candidates. An ATS can help HR to sort and screen candidates' qualifications, which can be very useful when looking for highly specialized skills. Choices *A* and *D* can both be eliminated because they don't present solutions that increase the workforce; based on the scenario, the company is expanding, so hiring new employees is inevitable. Choice *C* is not a good choice either because, while all those functions may be possible through an ATS, it is not advisable to lump them all together for applicants. The application process should be easy to navigate and complete. Many job seekers report not completing their applications due to the length or complexity of some online job applications.

68. D: Although all these topics would be important for employees who are transferring to a new country, the most critical and essential would be the specific local labor laws, workplace etiquette, and cultural differences. Violating labor laws in other countries may result in fines, closure of the office, or even consequences specific to the individual. Many countries have severe penalties for violating cultural norms, and it is important for employees and their families to understand these to ensure compliance.

69. D: The Sarbanes-Oxley Act of 2002 is federal legislation designed to establish a higher level of accountability and standards for public institution boards and senior management. SOX was established to ensure high-level executives are held responsible for accounting misconduct, record manipulation, or inappropriate financial practices.

70. A: The ADA not only protects employees who have a physical medical condition but also applies protections to those with a mental medical condition. The ADA protections apply to every aspect of the job application procedure, employment, and promotions. The ADA also requires employers to provide reasonable accommodations to employees and is a federal law that prevents discrimination based on disability.

71. B: Veronica is utilizing the ergonomic evaluation test to ensure that Janine's workspace does not pose any physical risks, is an efficient space to work productively, and meets Janine's needs. Ergonomic evaluation tests protect employees and help to prevent serious injuries.

72. A: The NLRB can facilitate settlements of labor disputes between employers and employees. Although disputes can often be settled within an organization, some situational factors may require external assistance. (Factors like the level of the complaint, the number of people involved, the size of the liability, etc. can influence whether an organization chooses to seek external settlement or mediation.) Choice *B* is not correct because there are various forms of nonunion representation for employees. Choice *C* is also incorrect because, to be recognized as lawful, works councils must be elected by employees without employer interference. Choice *D* is incorrect because employees may choose different forms of representation for different situations. For example, union representation can aid with collective bargaining for employees across many different organizations with an industry. However, nonunion representation like a works council can help employees handle situations specific to their workplace. Unions sometimes help with the election of works council representatives.

73. C: Bill's next steps can be to request a right-to-sue letter and sue the employer in court. Although Bill does not have to proceed with these steps, he does have this option available to him. Choice *A* is inaccurate because he does have further options. Choice *B* is also inaccurate because filing a grievance should have been done prior to filing the complaint with the EEOC; however, Bill could have immediately filed with the EEOC and skipped filing a grievance. Choice *D* is also inaccurate because, based on Bill's claims and allegations, he is protected from retaliation from his employer or fellow employees.

74. B: An at-will employer can terminate an employee at any time, but still needs to follow all laws around discrimination and retaliation. An employee can also leave an employer at any time for any reason. Choice *A* is correct, but does not mention legal consequences, which are important even in an at-will state. Choices *C* and *D* both require the employer to provide a reason, which is not required in at-will employment.

75. A: Organizations that have a more diverse workplace experience higher rates of employee retention. Additionally, employees are generally more satisfied and perform at a higher level than employees in workplaces that lack diversity.

76. B: By expanding the list of campuses Rachel visits to outside of the area, she will be able to include candidates from different backgrounds and locations, ensuring a more diverse candidate pool for selecting recruits.

77. A: When conducting a salary survey to determine compensation, it is important to look at all components. This includes not only wages, overtime opportunities, car allowances, and other items specific to monies payable but also benefits costs, retirement costs, and vacation time. Benefits plans may be more expensive, with higher out-of-pocket costs for the employee. Retirement plans may not be funded at the same rates, also costing an employee more out of pocket. When conducting a salary survey, it is vital to consider all the items that affect an employee's compensation.

78. B: Benefits programs, such as alternate work schedules, flexible spending accounts, and wellness programs, are all excellent examples to highlight in job postings. Candidates should have a clear understanding of the programs available to employees.

79. A: Ling should indicate to the leadership team that she does not have this information. Ling should then let the team know that she will reach out to the vendor to get the information and send it to them for their consideration. She should ensure that she responds to any and all questions, even those she is unable to answer.

80. B: Melissa could suggest the manager direct the employee to the company's employee assistance program. An employee assistance program helps employees identify mental health, relationship, legal, or financial concerns and find short-term interventions. Choice *A*, defined contribution plan, refers to a retirement plan in which employees or employers can contribute a specific amount, so this wouldn't help a demoralized employee. Choice *C*, managed care plan, is a type of healthcare plan. While the employee's personal issues may have to do with healthcare, suggesting a managed care plan without first understanding the employee's situation would be unsupportive. Choice *D*, corporate wellness program, is a wellness program that encourages employees to maintain and improve their health. While the employee may benefit from participating in a corporate wellness program, they may need attention or assistance with an issue not addressed by the program.

81. D: This goal is ambiguous. It provides no baseline, no definition of what constitutes as a healthy employee, no definition of what constitutes as a successful initiative, and is very subjective in nature.

82. C: The list of goals and milestones was not specific and applicable to the new organization's goals and achievements. David should review the list and determine which items align with his new organization's strategic plan as well as the vision and mission statements. Each organization has specific goals that every employee should be working toward achieving at all levels. Although some of the items David was successful in implementing at his previous organization may be appropriate at his new organization, he should review how these items align with the overall strategic plan and goals and resubmit a list that is more appropriate.

83. A: Active listening engages all of the listener's senses to communicate with the speaker, and also asks for confirmation from the speaker to ensure communication is perceived correctly.

84. A: Soliciting feedback from senior leaders is a crucial component of program evaluation, guiding and sustaining initiatives, and providing valuable customer service. HR professionals serve all areas of the organization, including employees at all levels. Without this feedback, HR professionals are unable to fully gauge the success of initiatives and will not be able to provide the best programs, policies, and customer service for their employees.

85. B: Davina should conduct a PEST analysis to ensure she is aware of the Political, Economic, Social, and Technological trends that could influence or impact her product launch. The analysis can assist her with identifying anticipated opportunities as well as mitigate potential risks. Davina's product launch has a higher probability of success if these trends are identified during the planning process.

86. A: Commission pay is an example of a performance-based pay plan because it is used to motivate employees to perform at a higher level. Commissions incentivize sales by giving a percentage of each sale to the employee responsible for it. Choice *B*, base pay, is the basic pay the employee receives for performing their role. Choice *C*, shift pay, and Choice *D*, reporting pay, are both types of differential pay which reward employees for performing work that is less than desirable.

87. C: Avoiding controversial topics would render a salary and benefits survey ineffective because employees could not freely share their opinions. An effective salary and benefits survey should be

210

representative of the market and region, Choice *B,* inclusive of multiple positions at various levels, Choice *A,* low cost, convenient and easy to navigate, and precise and accurate, Choice *D.*

88. C: A W-4 form tells an employer how much to withhold from an employee's paycheck for federal income taxes. Choices *A, B,* and *D* are incorrect.

89. D: The Federal Insurance Contributions Act, known as FICA, includes Social Security, Medicare, and Additional Medicare taxes. Choice *A, B,* and *C* are incorrect because federal, state, and local taxes are designated as their own tax categories.

90. B: Analyze relevant performance metrics, such as sales per quarter. When it comes to total rewards design, ROI is determined by taking the value an employee adds to the organization and comparing it to the amount that is spent to retain that employee. In this case, metrics that can demonstrate this added value help HR and other stakeholders to develop a rewards package that fairly compensates employees. Choices *A* and *C* can both be eliminated because best practices and total remuneration surveys both consider standards for compensation throughout the industry, but they do not reflect rewards relative to the value that employees add to the company. Choice *D* is also not the best choice because HR should take the lead in determining and communicating employee value.

91. B: Recognition programs are programs used to promote a positive organizational culture by recognizing individual employees for the work they have done. Recognition programs can be formal or informal and can have a large impact on employees. Special event programs, Choice *A,* are designed to promote a positive culture; they generally do not reward employees for their work. Inclusion programs, Choice *C,* are incorporated into day-to-day operations to ensure that all employees' voices are heard. Incentive programs, Choice *D,* provide financial rewards to those employees who perform at a higher level than others and have a larger impact on the organization.

92. C: An open-door policy specifically encourages openness and transparency with employees. Managers and leadership often implement an open-door policy to ensure that employees know they are welcome to provide insights and feedback without fear of recourse. Choice *A* is incorrect because a communications policy is a broad policy that encompasses all areas of communication, which could include an open-door policy as well as a social media policy, which is Choice *B.* Choice *D* is incorrect because a code of conduct policy is written to ensure employees are aware of and understand ethical and appropriate behaviors in the workplace.

93. B: Large organizations that operate in several locations. In a decentralized HR structure, separate HR offices operate largely autonomously, based on separate business units such as different departments or locations. This is useful for organizations with regional or international operations, where HR professionals benefit from having local knowledge of business operations and employee needs. In fact, small businesses are the most likely to have a centralized HR structure. As organizations grow larger, they are more likely to outsource or decentralize certain HR functions.

94. C: A group created and led by employees who share common backgrounds or demographic factors. An ERG is often part of an organization's D&I plan. It allows employees to meet similar coworkers (in terms of things like age, race, gender, socioeconomic background, and other factors), build rapport, represent the needs of external stakeholders, and give feedback to the organization.

95. D: Newsletters do not allow for a formal two-way communication between the employer and employees. Newsletters are static and created by certain employees, conveying information deemed

211

appropriate at that time. Choices *A, B,* and *C* are all incorrect because they are accurate statements regarding newsletters. Newsletters are not the best method to relay urgent information to employees and can be labor-intensive and infrequent. Additionally, newsletters can provide information in an engaging and welcoming manner.

96. C: Amber should respond directly to the department leader, asking specific questions and requesting clarity regarding the discrepancies she noted. This will ensure the entire team is on the same page and the pilot program is implemented to address the actual issues. Choice *A* is incorrect; by moving forward with the role, she may end up needing to redo her work because there is ambiguity in the information provided. If she is unclear about any element, she should ensure this is cleared up before moving forward. Choice *B* is incorrect because this action could be seen as a passive-aggressive action and tattling on the department leader. Choice *D* is also incorrect because Amber assumes others will clarify the issues and provide her with direction later.

97. C: Tommy should review the current number of days needed to fill a position with the new process against the number of days needed to fill a position with the previous process. In doing so, he is comparing the metrics between the current and baseline data to show if there has been an improvement in filling positions faster with the new process. Choices *A* and *D* are important pieces of information but are specific pieces of data at a particular point in time. The attrition rate and number of openings do not show a trend or the effectiveness of a process. Choice *B* is an excellent source of information because it is always important to gauge the satisfaction of employees regarding specific processes and programs; however, this data would be subjective and could not be measured.

98. C: The organization's current status of employee diversity in comparison to its stated diversity hiring goals. A gap analysis is a method of studying a current state to determine how to move to a desired state. In this case, the organization is trying to meet its stated diversity goals, and it must first understand its current diversity status.

99. A: A mission statement is what the company is currently doing or trying to do right now; on the other hand, a vision statement is taking a five- to ten-year look at where the company wants to be. Both statements are dynamic and should change over time. When establishing a company identity, it is important to have both statements. Choice *B* is incorrect, as these statements don't have a required length. Choice *C* is incorrect based on the differences listed above and in Choice *D,* the correct answers are flipped.

100. B: This would be an example of a value statement. Value statements are a list of statements that the company holds itself to and creates policies around. Choice *A,* mission statement, is what the company does, while Choice *C,* vision statement, is what the company sees itself doing in the future. Choice *D,* slogan, would be used in a commercial for a company or used internally to build an employment culture.

101. A: A vision statement focuses on the organization's future goals and answers questions about accomplishments. A mission statement focuses on the values, standards, and organizing principles, with a focus on why the organization exists. Both statements should be clear and direct, and a vision statement should focus on specific future goals and steps that will be taken to accomplish these goals.

102. B: Upward communication is when employees communicate to their supervisors and the leadership within the company, and that is what this company is trying to promote. Choice *A,* downward communication, is when leadership is trying to communicate with their employees. Choice *C*, diagonal communication, is when employees communicate with a supervisor in another department. Lastly, Choice *D*, lateral communication, would be communication across company lines at the same level, such as line workers speaking to line workers in different departments, or supervisor to supervisor in different departments.

103. A: Networking refers to interacting with others who have knowledge and expertise that can provide personal and professional growth. This action does not relate to work-life balance and is not a type of formal education. It is also a positive experience, whereas fraternizing normally has a negative connotation.

104. C: An organization's "mood" refers to the organizational climate, which can be directly affected by the environment, policies, behaviors, and process. Choice *A* is incorrect because environment is a general term that refers to the actual surroundings or conditions in which employees work. Choice *B* is incorrect because values refer to the ideas that guide an organization's actions. Choice *D* is incorrect because an organization's culture refers to the overall working environment, employer standards, interactions, and how work is accomplished.

105. B: Hiring managers should ensure that they are not relying on unconscious biases and determining fit based on shared age, race, socioeconomic status, or other demographics. Although fit is always an important factor for ensuring a positive workplace dynamic, hiring managers should be conscious of how they determine fit, balancing it with an organization's D&I policies.

106. A: They reach many applicants, but they may end up costing more in terms of price-per-click relative to click-to-hire ratios. Large job sites like Monster, Indeed, Career Builder, and others help HR to reach a far larger applicant pool than other face-to-face recruiting strategies. However, the larger applicant pool also means that many more people click on job ads than will apply, and more will apply for jobs than will be hired. When devising a recruiting strategy, HR should consider the price of advertising on these sites (for example, some sites charge for job postings based on the number of visitors to the ad).

107. B: HR can use social media to promote its organization's brand as an employer. Today, there are countless ways organizations and HR can use social media. Branding is an important way to communicate to customers, applicants, and other stakeholders, and social media is an appropriate platform for reaching them. Choice *A* is not a good choice because social media is incredibly widespread already and there are appropriate, professional ways to use it, depending on each industry. Choice *C* is also not necessary because not all job functions require social media posting on behalf of the organization. Finally, Choice *D* depends on the needs of the organization and isn't a requirement of social media use.

108. B: It takes a proactive approach to preserving continuity in the face of worker attrition. Succession planning refers to the process of planning for future leadership in an organization to ensure that key knowledge, relationships, and other valuable assets are not lost when leaders resign or retire.

109. A: Kate should first determine if there is existing research or data available before embarking on the task of locating the necessary data. If this resource exists, she can then begin pulling in the organization's data and then create the analysis. If this resource does not exist, Kate can then pull the organization's data and create a plan to source the outside data as needed.

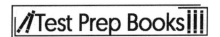

110. B: Appropriate HR initiatives generally focus on the recruitment process, Choice *A*, interview processes, Choice *C*, and annual salary surveys, Choice *D*. Although auditing the payroll processes to ensure timely payment is an ambitious initiative, it is not usually assigned to the HR function.

111. B: Onboarding, also known as organizational socialization, is the process for new hires to learn about the knowledge, skills, and behaviors needed to be valued and productive members of the team and organization. New-hire orientation, Choice *A*, refers to the administrative process of reviewing benefits, creating a security badge, and training on payroll processing, time-card management, and other important processes that all employees participate in. Preemployment screening, Choice *C*, is conducted prior to the actual hiring of a candidate, and organizational orientation, Choice *D*, is a term that combines several of these concepts.

112. C: The ADDIE model has five phases: Analysis, Design, Development, Implementation, Evaluation. It is vital to follow these steps in sequence. ADDIE is highly effective and can be applied to any project or program and is extremely flexible.

113. D: HR is responsible for facilitating the changes needed by implementing new training programs, updating policies and procedures, and ensuring the workforce has the needed knowledge, skills, and behaviors to accomplish the goals outlined in the new strategic plan. Additionally, HR may need to recruit new employees if the strategic plan calls for specific expertise or additional workload.

114. B: Tom should focus performance evaluations on future goals and professional development to engage employees with the process.

115. A: Employee business resource groups help to specifically promote the diversity and inclusion efforts of an organization. These groups help to connect employees and facilitate a positive working environment. Choices *B*, *C*, and *D* are incorrect because professional growth, better relationships, increased communication, and training opportunities are possible outcomes or products of employees engaging in a resource group.

116. C: This is a paperless method with an immediate notification system that minimizes waste yet keeps all employees informed.

117. D: When deciding whether to accept a settlement regarding a discrimination or harassment charge, the decision maker should consider damage to the company's reputation, Choice *A*, new systemic problems that could be uncovered, Choice *B*, and the financial cost of an investigation and trial, Choice *C*. Personal financial concerns should not be a consideration when reviewing and making a decision to move to settlement.

118. D: If Genevieve is truly impressed by Marcus and feels he could benefit the company, she should allow him the benefit of explaining any red flags, especially for events that occurred over five or more years prior.

119. D: Julia is conducting an employment reference check. This type of reference check gathers feedback from former employers, supervisors, coworkers, and other contacts regarding the performance, behaviors, and work ethic exhibited by the potential new hire. Educational reference checks, Choice *A*, are specific to degrees, certifications, diplomas, or other specific educational achievements. Emotional intelligence tests, Choice *B*, are preemployment screenings some organizations use to test leadership and interpersonal skills. Performance reviews, Choice *C*, are a formal process an organization conducts annually or as needed to communicate how employees are performing in their jobs.

120. A: Preemployment screenings generally include criminal background checks, medical and drug screenings, financial and credit history checks, and other background information reviews. An inappropriate screening would be checking the marital and parental history of a candidate, which would include asking questions regarding these subjects during the interview process.

121. C: Typical onboarding programs should last for the employee's first year to ensure there is ample time and opportunity for full orientation to the organization. Although there are some specific items, such as payroll processes or timekeeping management, that should be delivered on the first day or during the first week, the organization should make a concerted effort throughout the employee's first year of employment to ensure full orientation to the culture.

122. C: Angel should consider constructive confrontation as the next step in the process. Constructive confrontation is a form of mediation that is used in specific circumstances, such as the example provided. This process can break stalemates by working through secondary or tertiary issues instead of focusing on the primary issue.

123. A: Management does not have to collectively bargain all subjects and/or changes. Specific subjects are defined as mandatory and must be bargained, including working conditions and terms, hours, wages, benefits, and safety concerns. Many subjects are considered voluntary and can be discussed within the collective bargaining process but are not required.

124. C: No. Julia does not have additional options. Grievance arbitration decisions are enforceable and cannot be challenged or taken to court. She has exhausted all options through the grievance process, and the decision reached by the third-party arbitrator is final.

125. C: Although the HR department should take all of these actions, it is important to first investigate the complaints received and do whatever is necessary to resolve the issues. Once this has been done, the department should then engage in the other three actions quickly. When HR takes all of these actions, employees will be able to see that the organization is transparent in its work and policies and takes complaints seriously. These actions can increase morale and ultimately create a workplace environment that fosters increased efficiency and productivity among employees.

126. C: Although politics has been a subject that has infiltrated every aspect of life, it is important to make business decisions based on organizational metrics, Choice *A,* key performance indicators, Choice *B,* and cost-benefit analysis, Choice *D.*

127. D: Focus on issues that matter to executives such as recruiting and retaining top employees and increasing operational efficiency. In making a business case, it is important to target the things that matter to stakeholders and decision makers, not just to HR. By showing how HR can help the organization achieve its goals, HR professionals can make a better case for why senior leaders should value HR's contributions. Choice *A* is not a good choice because it focuses on past performance and not on the issue at hand (namely, that HR should be given increased scope of operations). Neither Choice *B* nor Choice *C* is an appropriate choice because they are based on HR-specific practices that may not be relevant to outside stakeholders. HR professionals need to remember to approach issues from the perspective of those who might be asking, "What does this have to do with me?"

215

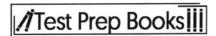
128. B: During the evaluation stage, it is vital to gain feedback from all stakeholders. This feedback will allow for a more aligned, cohesive, effective, and robust plan.

129. A: The Worker Adjustment and Retraining Notification Act (WARN) requires employers to provide a sixty-day calendar notice to works if a facility with fifty or more workers is closing. There are exceptions if it is due to natural disaster or an unforeseeable business circumstance, but it is required when possible. Choices B and D both imply it is optional, which is incorrect since it is a federal law. Choice C is incorrect because the law requires sixty days, rather than two weeks, to would give employees time to seek other employment.

130. B: An employer does not have to pay you for the time you are forming a union, but it does allow you to form a union on company property, such as break rooms and parking lots. The NLRA gives employees the right to discuss their wages, making Choice A incorrect. Choices C and D are rights also granted by the NLRA.

131. D: COBRA has a caveat that if there was willful misconduct by an employee, the employer does not have to offer COBRA. This is the only allowance for an employee who was covered and ended employment where the employer does not need to offer COBRA. Choice A and Choice C are both situations where an employee had coverage and lost it, so they would need to be offered coverage. Choice B is incorrect since that employee could have family members covered. COBRA should still be offered to those family members.

132. D: While you should not discriminate for any reason, the EEOC guideline on ageism protects those above the age of forty. Pregnancy status, genetic information, and disability are all protected under the Equal Employment Opportunity Commission, making Choices A, B, and C incorrect.

133. B: Employee morale and positive working environments are associated with compassionate and empathetic coworkers. This allows people to feel cared for and valued in the workplace.

134. B: Workforce reductions are the planned eliminations of a specific number of positions and therefore personnel to make a company more competitive. When a workforce reduction is being considered, HR can focus on several factors, such as reducing hours, implementing a hiring freeze, or creating a voluntary separation program, to avoid having to lay off personnel. As indicated earlier, financial restructuring, Choice A, is a form of corporate restructuring specific to addressing decreases in profits due to economic conditions. Organizational and corporate restructuring, Choices C and D, are terms that refer to realigning a company's departments and workflows to make processes more efficient and cost-effective.

135. A: Payroll functions are vital to the success of an organization and can be costly to maintain in-house. Organizations may make the decision to outsource this function to reduce costs and improve compliance and resource allocation.

136. C: Offshoring. Offshoring refers to the relocation of some or all of an organization's processes to an international location, either internally or through third-party vendors. Choice A is not correct because outsourcing refers to moving an organization's processes outside the company by contracting third-party vendors; outsourcing can take place either domestically or internationally. Outsourcing and offshoring may often coincide, but they are not necessarily the same thing. Choice B is also incorrect; an organization downsizes when it reduces its operations and eliminates previously staffed positions.

216

137. B: Standardizing pay and work tasks is one way to mitigate bias in situations where bias could arise.

138. C: Employer brand. Just as a company brands itself to customers—that is, it creates and presents an image encompassing its identity, quality, and personality—employers also brand themselves to employees. Employer brand is closely related to the EVP, which encompasses all the factors—tangible and intangible—that contribute to workers' perception of value gained from working for a particular employer. Employer brand is built on things like mission, values, and work culture.

139. C: To effectively manage change with the empirical-rational strategy, it is important to incentivize the change. If employees undergo a change but understand how it can positively impact them, they are more likely to accept it and agree with it.

140. C: The text *The Planning of Change* outlines three strategies for managing change. The technology-innovation strategy is not a strategy for managing change.

141. B: The empirical-rational strategy assumes that individuals are, in general, rational and will follow a path that benefits them. This strategy to affect change works well when individuals are presented with the benefits that will be experienced by embracing a specific change.

142. C: Non-quantitative job evaluation methods, also known as whole-job methods, include job ranking, paired comparison, and job classification.

143. A: The point factor method is a less complex and commonly used quantitative job evaluation method. This method uses specific, compensable factors, such as skill, responsibility, effort, working conditions, and supervision, to evaluate the worth of each job. The factor comparison method, Choice *B,* is more complex and used less frequently because it involves a much more complex process to determine pay rates using factors and values. Whole-job methods, Choice *C,* is another term for non-quantitative job evaluation methods, and the job classification method, Choice *D,* is one example of a non-quantitative job evaluation method.

144. A: Ambiguity should be avoided when possible because it can cause conflict, affect business processes, and create distress for employees. When it cannot be avoided, it is important to use clear communication methods and practices to ensure any ambiguity is resolved with clarity.

145. B: By conducting an employee survey to get direct feedback from employees, HR can focus efforts on what employees want, need, and ultimately, will use. Although the program may have been perfectly designed according to Emily and Chris's needs and wants, they failed to learn what other employees needed and wanted.

146. C: Rather than speaking about all his hard work and contributions, Ben chose to share his team's accomplishments without singling anyone out. This is a display of strong team-oriented culture in the workplace.

147. A: An I-9 must be completed within three days of an employee's start date. The start date is defined as their first day with paid hours, so it would not include the interview or a day an employee came in for pre-hire paperwork. Choice *B* is correct, and is when most employers complete the I-9, but fails to explain the time frame in which an employer could complete the I-9. Choices *C* and *D* are both incorrect and could lead to fines.

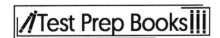

148. A: Financial restructuring is a form of corporate restructuring that is specific to when an organization has experienced significant decreases in profits primarily due to a poor economy. Workforce reductions, Choice *B*, are the planned eliminations of personnel to make an organization more competitive. Organizational and corporate restructuring, Choices *C* and *D*, are terms that refer to realigning a company's departments and workflows to make processes more efficient and cost-effective.

149. B: A progressive disciplinary policy is one with progressively higher discipline for repeated infractions. This type of policy helps create consistent employment practices, which can limit bias in termination, as well as help employees succeed by working with them to understand policies before termination. Choice *A*, termination policy, would vary by company, but would likely only involve the termination; any write-ups beforehand would not apply. Choice *C*, offboarding, is the term for all the processes and decisions after an employee resigns or is terminated, but this process doesn't take place beforehand. Lastly Choice *D*, documentation, should be taken and maintained for all performance conversations, but the question referred to discipline specifically.

150. C: Ensuring that employees are a good fit with their job duties is a critical component of job and employee success. When Jenny is hired for a job that was a good fit, she excels. When her responsibilities were no longer a match for her strengths and interests, she did not do well. However, this does not mean she has poor work ethic, low intelligence, or is not a team player.

151. D: Joseph should not consider including a disclaimer that indicates the employee handbook is intended to be the contractual agreement between the employer and employee. In fact, he should consider the exact opposite of this by including a disclaimer that the handbook is NOT intended to be an agreement between the employer and employee. Updating policies and including these in the handbook, Choice *A*, incorporating an acknowledgement form, Choice *B*, and providing this information to current employees, Choice *C*, are all considerations Joseph should incorporate with the new employee handbook.

152. B: Progressive discipline is the process by which employee infractions are responded to, with each incident identified as a unique situation with appropriate consequences delivered. Coaching and counseling, Choice *A*, may be used as a form of progressive discipline to address certain behaviors, if appropriate. Consecutive discipline, Choice *C*, is a made-up term, and employee reviews, Choice *D*, are typically scheduled evaluations of individual performance that may include training and other coaching opportunities to address behaviors.

153. A: 360-degree feedback is a type of review that evaluates the employee from all angles and directions, which is why so many people are contacted for the review. It is very informative, but takes significantly longer than many other types of reviews. Choice *B*, skill evaluation, is looking at the employees' knowledge, skills, and ability (KSA) to do the job. Choice *C*, leader assessment, is a broad category of assessment for leaders of an organization, and Choice *D*, team assessment, is looking at their contributions to a team and how they can improve.

154. C: Public availability is a factor under the "type of relationship" factors when determining if an individual is an employee or an independent contractor. Personal services and business integration, Choices *A* and *D*, are considered behavioral control factors, and profit or loss, Choice *B*, is considered a financial control.

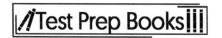

155. A: Medicare Part A is mandatory hospital insurance coverage that most individuals do not have to pay for once qualified.

156. D: Medicare Part D is voluntary prescription drug coverage that individuals pay a monthly fee for. Part D is available to those who are eligible for Part A and also enrolled in Part B.

157. B: Medicare Part B is voluntary medical insurance that covers health care expenses, such as outpatient care and physicians' services. Individuals pay a monthly fee for this coverage.

158. C: The Consolidated Omnibus Budget Reconciliation Act, commonly known as COBRA, is the amendment to the ERISA law that requires an organization employing twenty or more employees to allow for the continuation of health care coverage after separating from employment. Regardless of an individual communicating that they will not take advantage of the continuation of coverage option, this does not alleviate the organization from their responsibility to send out the paperwork to allow the individual to have the information to make this choice.

159. D: If a former employee decides to continue the group medical insurance coverage with their previous employer, the individual is responsible for paying the entire cost of the coverage. Organizations may also impose an administrative fee of 2 percent to cover the costs of keeping the former employee on the roster.

160. A: Because the organization did not comply with the COBRA requirements, they could face both civil and criminal penalties. Choice *C* is incorrect because the choice of criminal penalties is left out. Although there may be audits and investigations conducted to determine policy, procedure, and protocols, Choices *B* and *D*, these would most likely be conducted by the Department of Labor, not OSHA or FEHA.

161. B: Monique should audit the programs, practices, and policies regarding diversity and inclusion to ensure they are appropriate and being implemented. Choice *A* is incorrect because the remaining employees may be part of the issue or contain bias that an audit would otherwise uncover. Choice *C* is incorrect; diversity training could be part of the solution to this issue, but it does not identify the issue. Choice *D* is incorrect because it still does not identify the issue at hand.

162. A: Although it is important and necessary for HR professionals to track performance evaluations and growth plans, these items are not regulated under the FLSA to be included in the record-keeping system. Generally, they are tracked and monitored in a Human Resources Management System (HRMS) because there are no federal regulations that need to be maintained. FLSA record keeping pertains to personal information, Choice *B*, work schedules, Choice *C*, and total wages paid, Choice *D*.

163. A: Soleil is practicing recordkeeping to ensure there is documentation showing the involvement, discussions, and acceptance of items during the process. Recordkeeping can be instrumental in communicating why certain decisions were made during the process while also allowing multiple opportunities for stakeholders and leadership to be involved, regardless of their busy schedules.

164. C: When it comes to document retention, the answer is always whichever rule has the longest retention policy. Choices *A* and *B* are correct, but could lead to a violation if you do not follow both rules and use the one where you retain the document the longest. Choice *D* is incorrect, as I-9 retention lasts three years after start date.

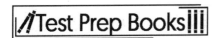

165. B: The Employee Retirement Income Security Act (ERISA) establishes the minimum standards for benefits plans of private, for-profit employers. ERISA also established the Pension Benefit Guaranty Corporation, which guarantees payment of vested benefits. The Pension Protection Act, Choice A, is an amendment to ERISA that strengthened the pension system by increasing minimum funding requirements. The Equal Pay Act, Choice C, is a law that requires employers to pay equal wages to both men and women who perform equal jobs in the same organization. The Health Insurance Portability and Accountability Act (HIPAA), Choice D, is an amendment to ERISA that improves the continuity and portability of health care coverage and addresses preexisting conditions.

166. D: HR is responsible for facilitating the changes needed by implementing new training programs, updating policies and procedures, and ensuring the workforce has the needed knowledge, skills, and behaviors to accomplish the goals outlined in the new strategic plan. Additionally, HR may need to recruit new employees if the strategic plan calls for specific expertise or additional workload.

167. D: Change management is the process that seeks to support significant transitions within an organization and could include large-scale changes, resource allocation, operations changes, and an updated business process. Effective change management can help an organization to be effective even while undergoing changes.

168. D: The manager should include the witnesses to the injury, the date and time of the injury, and details about the injury and how it occurred. The employee's medical history and social security number are not required to complete a claim form; therefore, Choices A, B, and C are incorrect.

169. B: An emergency response specifically refers to a planned and practiced protocol to be used in the event of an emergency. A strategic plan, Choice A, is an overall organizational plan specific to goals and objectives. An evacuation plan, Choice C, is a part of the emergency response and is a coordinated and planned exit from a specific location. A hazard communication, Choice D, also part of the emergency response, notifies employees when there is a physical danger regarding a hazardous chemical in the workplace.

170. C: The best course of action for HR to take is to review each individual accommodation and determine if it is reasonable or not. If the request will create an undue burden on the organization, it is appropriate to deny an accommodations request. In this case, requesting the position to be reduced to a 30-hour work week would most likely create an undue hardship based on the workload and importance of the job responsibilities. Although the ergonomic requests appear to be reasonable and appropriate, the reduced work schedule does not appear to be reasonable. It is perfectly appropriate to approve some accommodations and not approve others based on how reasonable they are.

171. A: HR should immediately communicate with the plant manager about the importance of an emergency response plan. By ensuring these plans are understood by all employees, the organization is protecting lives and property as well as providing a sense of security to employees. The organization will also be in compliance with safety standards.

172. D: The most effective way to ensure that an evacuation plan will be implemented in the best way possible is to coordinate scheduled and unscheduled practice evacuations from the facility. Although acknowledge statements, special posters, and quizzes, Choices A, B, and C, will promote retention of the information, the best way to ensure that an evacuation plan will be effective is to practice the evacuation.

173. A: Sending out surveys is the data collection method that gathers individual feedback from a wide group of employees. Surveys can be completed in numerous ways to ensure maximum participation, including entering answers online or completing a paper copy of the survey.

174. C: An organization that has a lack of transparency will experience decreased morale and higher turnover among employees. Choices *A, B,* and *D* are incorrect because they all align with a higher level of transparency. Organizations that are transparent with employees will experience higher levels of innovation, productivity, and promotion rates and lower turnover.

175. C: Cross-cultural training allows for employees to engage in opportunities that broaden their experience. This training allows for hearing about others' experiences so they can benefit from these ideas. Group assessments, Choice *A,* are a way to evaluate candidates in a group setting with exercises and sample issues to gauge how individuals respond to and resolve issues. Mentoring programs, Choice *B,* match two individuals for learning and growth opportunities. Cross-cultural training, Choice *D,* is a component of diversity and inclusion programs.

PHR Practice Test #2

1. What is the practice of benchmarking?
   a. Using statistics to make decisions
   b. Using chalk or other removable material to mark proposed specifications on a prototype
   c. Comparing an organization's initiatives and outcomes against industry standards
   d. Holding a back-up candidate for a position in case a primary candidate rejects a job offer

2. Which of the following is the keystone of HR's value to an organization?
   a. Talent acquisition
   b. Strategic planning
   c. Training and development
   d. Recruitment and retention

3. What is the purpose of a root cause analysis?
   a. To determine the foundation-level reason as to why an overarching issue is occurring
   b. To determine the exact employee that caused an error during a process
   c. To determine the best source of external funding
   d. To determine how to allocate fixed funds within an organization

4. Which of the following laws is also known as Obamacare, named after President Barack Obama?
   a. Americans with Disabilities Act
   b. Patient Protection and Affordable Care Act
   c. Mental Health Parity Act
   d. Family Medical Leave Act

5. Which of the following statements regarding the Family Medical Leave Act is accurate?
   a. Employers are required to maintain employees' group health insurance coverage while they are out on FMLA leave.
   b. Spouses who work for the same employer each receive twelve weeks of FMLA time for the birth of their child.
   c. Employers cannot require employees to take their paid leave, such as vacation or sick leave, when using FMLA.
   d. FMLA only covers leave for the birth or adoption of a child or a serious health condition of the employee or child.

6. Which of the following laws prohibits the discrimination against any individuals who are over the age of forty related to hiring, firing, promotions, changes in wages or benefits, or other employment-related decisions?
   a. Age Discrimination in Employment Act of 1967
   b. Fair Labor Standard Act
   c. Title VII of the Civil Rights Act of 1964
   d. Equal Employment Opportunity Commission

7. Which of the following situation(s) would be considered compensable time according to the Fair Labor Standards Act (FLSA)?
   a. An employee who is on-call, but is given a long lead time before they need to come back to work and is allowed to use the time as they want.
   b. An employee who is on-call but is required to remain on campus and be ready to work.
   c. The commute time from the employees' home to the normal work location
   d. Both A and B

8. The following are considered paid time according to Fair Labor Standards Act (FLSA) EXCEPT:
   a. Short rest periods during the workday
   b. Travel time during a workday commuting from job site to job site
   c. A voluntary lecture the employee attends that is outside normal working hours and is not job related
   d. Travel time to a special one-day location, much further than the normal job site, for the employee

9. Human Resources and Payroll will be implementing a new timekeeping and payroll system. This new system will require employees to enter their time worked and leave time directly into the system versus writing out a paper timesheet. Supervisors will therefore need to approve the timesheets of their direct reports within the system for Payroll to process paychecks. What can HR and Payroll do to encourage support and engagement with the new system?
   a. Provide in-person training complete with demonstrations on how to use the system, pointing out the efficiencies and available information.
   b. Create a train-the-trainer program and require these individuals to meet with employees and provide training as needed.
   c. Prepare an in-depth communication and training guide to send out to all employees and supervisors.
   d. Provide employees with the customer service contact information of the provider and direct them to the provider.

10. There is a new employee in Janelle's department. On the new employee's first day, Janelle sets up a team lunch at a nearby restaurant and asks the new employee to attend. During lunch, Janelle asks the new employee about his past work experiences and personal interests. She also lets him know that she can help him with any questions he might have during his first week. What skill is Janelle practicing?
    a. Relationship building
    b. Continuing education
    c. Empathy
    d. Critical thinking

Read the following scenario and answer questions 11 and 12.

> Adam is a benefits specialist for his organization and is preparing his annual objectives for the upcoming year. One of his objectives is to have healthier employees across the organization. This objective is the overarching goal, with specific tasks identified as a wellness fair, benefits expo, free flu shots, and a free smoking cessation program.

11. Adam's main objective to have healthier employees is a lofty goal to achieve. What could be problematic with this objective?
    a. It is vague, with no measurable data points to indicate achievable success.
    b. It is unachievable because employee health is not the business of an organization.
    c. It is too specific, and there are too many defined tasks that will most likely not occur.
    d. It should be a departmental objective, not an individual objective.

12. What can Adam do to correct this objective?
    a. Eliminate the objective and replace it with the defined tasks he identified.
    b. Rewrite the objective to reflect the SMART principles.
    c. Keep the objective as written because it is a philosophical objective.
    d. Keep the objective and add more defined tasks to accomplish the goal.

13. Why is networking outside of one's own organization a valuable professional experience?
    a. It can provide innovative insight that one can apply to their own organization
    b. It is nice to get out of the office once in a while
    c. It allows one to spy on the competition
    d. It allows one to learn more about their city

14. Ray and Nash report to team leader, Dan, who is regularly out of the office. Dan takes up to a week to respond to their emails and his phone usually goes straight to voicemail. Dan is always in the office on Tuesdays, when he checks in with Ray and Nash and answers any questions of theirs. What is a clear obstacle in this team dynamic?
    a. Ray and Nash have to share a single office
    b. Dan answers Ray's and Nash's questions together instead of individually
    c. Dan only has two reports
    d. Dan does not support a reliable communication channel

15. If an organization has a high turnover rate among employee groups that are already underrepresented, of what is this likely indicative?
    a. All employees at the organization are actually quite dissatisfied.
    b. The competition is poaching employees to make their own workforces more diverse.
    c. Underrepresented groups are actually not qualified to do the work they are hired for.
    d. A barrier exists within the workplace that makes underrepresented groups feel uncomfortable.

16. Stephanie has worked in the HR department for seven years. She has a full personal life and prefers to keep it private. She comes to work on time, takes her breaks, and leaves on time. She does her work with minimal direction or interaction with others and prefers to eat her lunch alone. Stephanie was recently assigned a project that requires her to interact with her team and engage with them to ensure that multiple opinions and expertise are considered; however, she has not received the most welcoming reception, and her peers do not seem to want to participate or engage with her on the project. What can Stephanie do to turn this situation around?

    a. Talk to her supervisor to let him know that the team is not working with her and ask that they be directed to do so.

    b. Do the project on her own to the best of her ability, without the team's input.

    c. Network with her colleagues and converse with them to gain trust and build interpersonal relationships.

    d. Continue to behave in the same manner, schedule more meetings, and hope the team will come around.

17. What exercise determines the knowledge, skills, abilities, and experience necessary to perform a job?

    a. Classification study

    b. Job analysis

    c. Skills gap assessment

    d. SWOT analysis

18. Cassandra is the new HR director at a small organization. She is reviewing her company's employee handbook when she realizes that large pieces of information have not been updated in four years. As she reviews further, she realizes much of the handbook is obsolete. What should Cassandra do?

    a. Inform the head of the company, and let the head deal with the situation.

    b. Speak to her superior and offer to develop a new online handbook that can be easily updated.

    c. Return to her old company, which was much more disciplined and high-tech.

    d. Say nothing, since she is a new employee.

19. Which of the following is NOT an element of navigating an organization to effectively implement HR initiatives?

    a. Facilitating communication and decision making

    b. Using an understanding of process, systems, and policies

    c. Using awareness and understanding of the political environment and culture

    d. Demonstrating an understanding of the formal HR work roles only

20. An organization's policies that govern employees' actions, describe acceptable and unacceptable behaviors, and guide employee behavior with specific details is referred to as which of the following?

    a. Code of conduct

    b. Values statement

    c. Ethical standards

    d. Employee handbook

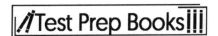

21. Patrick was involved in a lengthy and complex project to relocate office staff to a new building. At the end of the project, management reviewed the metrics and determined that not only was the project over budget, it took much longer than anticipated to complete and employees still had concerns, such as ergonomic issues and technology breaks. What should Patrick do?
    a. Communicate to the manager that the issues won't happen again and move to the next project.
    b. Conduct a gap analysis and a root cause analysis to determine why milestones were not met.
    c. Hold a team meeting to determine what the team members think should be done.
    d. Prepare an in-depth PowerPoint presentation of the items that were successful in the project.

22. Which of the following is the first necessary step in the risk management process?
    a. Mapping the full timeline and customer service processes
    b. Communicating with the team on the deliverables needed
    c. Identifying the potential risks
    d. Preparing a mitigation plan to eliminate any setbacks

23. Employees need to understand the options of an organization's benefits programs and choose their enrollment plan. What is the best way for HR to present this information to employees?
    a. Schedule a mandatory presentation with a detailed overview of all the benefits options so employees can make the most informed decision.
    b. Give employees the option of allowing HR to enroll on their behalf because HR has a more thorough understanding of the benefits programs.
    c. Employ a variety of communication strategies such as email, text message, postcard, and Q&A sessions.
    d. Display benefits program posters around the building so people in different departments can see the same information.

24. Olivia has a broad professional network she engages with frequently. She attends conferences and networking events and frequently assists other agencies with survey data and interview panels. She has met numerous individuals who have mentored her and assisted with her professional advancement. What is another benefit of networking and building relationships Olivia can specifically bring back to her organization?
    a. External networking should be solely about career advancement and personal growth.
    b. She can learn about successful HR initiatives with other agencies and implement them at hers.
    c. She can determine which specific HR area she wants to move into at her organization.
    d. She can obtain vendor recommendations to eliminate the need to request service proposals.

25. Josie is struggling with her workload. Numerous employees have retired, and a lot of the mandatory work has been given to her to handle while HR recruits new employees. She wants to be successful and help the team, but she is overwhelmed and not sure what to do. Josie reached out to HR to discuss her concerns and see what could be done. What should HR do to assist Josie with this situation?
    a. Approve the removal of the extra work and assure her that employees will be hired soon.
    b. Immediately bring in Josie's manager and instruct them to hire a contractor.
    c. Listen to Josie and work with her to find resolutions that would help with the situation.
    d. Expedite the recruitment process and hire a new employee by the end of the week.

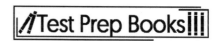
26. What term refers to employees becoming 100 percent vested in their retirement program after a specific number of years of service?
    a. Cliff vesting
    b. Graded vesting
    c. Immediate vesting
    d. Eligibility vesting

Read the following scenario and answer questions 27–29.

> Marisa is evaluating her organization's total rewards plan to ensure that employees are earning a fair and competitive salary against the competition. Additionally, Marisa is interested in learning if employees are satisfied with the benefits package and non-compensatory programs, such as the alternative work schedule.

27. Which of the following should Marisa implement to begin her review of how employees view the current benefits package and non-compensatory programs?
    a. Classification review
    b. Compensation study
    c. Remuneration survey
    d. Employee satisfaction survey

28. Once Marisa has collected the data internally, she needs to compare the data to external data and information to determine comparability, equitability, and competitiveness. Which of the following should Marisa consult to make this determination?
    a. Classification review
    b. Compensation study
    c. Remuneration survey
    d. Employee satisfaction survey

29. Once Marisa has concluded her study of the internal data collected from employees and communicated the results to leadership, what should she do next?
    a. Formally report the results to executive leadership to see what they would like to do next in the process.
    b. File the results and refer to them only to compare to any remuneration surveys available.
    c. Coordinate with the Bureau of Labor Statistics to upload the data received and report the information.
    d. Communicate with employees to ensure they know their input is valued and important to the process.

30. What is one way an organization can provide benefits that cater to a diverse talent pool?
    a. Provide higher salaries to underrepresented groups.
    b. Provide progressive options like benefits for same-sex partners or paternity leave.
    c. Provide different benefit options based on employee background and interests.
    d. Ignore benefits that deal with the employee's personal life, such as family benefits.

31. Which of the following would detract from work-life balance?
    a. Increased overtime
    b. Telecommuting options
    c. Onsite childcare
    d. Flexible schedules

32. Self-awareness, social awareness, relationship management, and self-management are components of which of the following?
    a. Emotional intelligence
    b. Intellectual quotient
    c. Company lunch-and-learn trainings
    d. New hire training

33. What term refers to the software, online systems, applications, or innovations that automate or simplify tasks within an organization?
    a. Information systems
    b. Business technology
    c. Workplace resources
    d. Reporting systems

34. OSHA requires that organizations adhere with specific regulations regarding hazardous chemicals, including providing training, labeling hazardous chemical containers, and providing access to MSDS information. What does MSDS stand for?
    a. Mandatory Substance Data Sheets
    b. Measurable Safety Detailed Slips
    c. Material Safety Data Sheets
    d. Menacing Safety Data Slips

35. Gabriel has heard that several employees are concerned for their safety in the working environment due to hazardous materials. Although he has not received an official report, he believes he has an obligation to look into the concerns. After Gabriel conducts an investigation, he provides his findings and recommendations to senior leadership. What should Gabriel's recommendation include?
    a. Counseling and potential discipline to the employees who began the rumors and caused other employees to be unnecessarily concerned
    b. Options to work with less hazardous materials that will address the employees' concerns and implementation of improved safety measures
    c. Requirement for all employees to purchase new personal protective equipment (PPE) to ensure their safety when working in the environment
    d. Ceasing operations immediately until OSHA can be contacted to address the issue and provide resolutions to implement

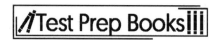

36. The Old Age, Survivor, and Disability Insurance Program was designed by the Social Security Act of 1935 to ensure a continuation of income for retirees, spouses and dependent children of employees who passed away, and those who qualify for Social Security disability. How long must an employee work to qualify for this program?
    a. 20 years, or 80 quarters
    b. 5 years, or 20 quarters
    c. 10 years, or 40 quarters
    d. 30 years, or 120 quarters

37. Under the Equal Pay Act, what are the four areas that must be equal to establish whether jobs are equivalent to each other?
    a. Qualifications, job duties, supervision, responsibility
    b. Skill, working conditions, effort, responsibility
    c. Qualifications, working conditions, teamwork, education
    d. Skill, education, qualifications, effort

38. Thiang and Sarah work in HR as specialists, supporting separate departments within the organization. Thiang recently distributed an employee survey to the finance department to gauge employee satisfaction in various areas, including work-life balance, leave procedures, communication, and resources. Thiang received an excellent response and was able to tailor new initiatives for the group to further increase satisfaction. He also received multiple new ideas for decreasing expenses and increasing efficiency, which yielded even further success. Sarah read about the success of the survey and departmental changes in the employee newsletter and wants to use the same technique in the IT department. How should Sarah begin this endeavor?
    a. Sarah should request that Thiang duplicate the process in the IT department and reply back with the final results, next steps, and recommendations.
    b. Sarah should work to re-create the survey for the IT department and initiate it immediately to capitalize on the momentum of the newsletter.
    c. Sarah should submit a proposal to her manager to hire an external vendor for the purpose of surveying the IT employees to gain the insight and information necessary for proposing new initiatives.
    d. Sarah should reach out to Thiang to discuss the survey, including the creation of the questions and finalizing the results as well as lessons learned, before implementing the survey in IT.

39. How can HR leadership best communicate appropriate and acceptable behaviors within the workplace?
    a. Specifically communicate this information to employees during orientation.
    b. Hang posters with federal and state regulations in break rooms and lunchrooms.
    c. Consistently display ethical, reliable, and acceptable behaviors.
    d. Communicate the required behaviors via email and newsletters on a regular basis.

40. Which of the following laws prohibits the discrimination against any individuals who are over the age of forty related to hiring, firing, promotions, changes in wages or benefits, or other employment-related decisions?
    a. Age Discrimination in Employment Act of 1967
    b. Fair Labor Standard Act
    c. Title VII of the Civil Rights Act of 1964
    d. Equal Employment Opportunity Commission

41. Masao is an entry-level HR employee in an advertising agency. He is working on a project that focuses on diversity trainings offered in the workplace and is conducting preliminary research to review best practices. Masao's manager asks for a compilation of key findings. Masao sends a zip file full of every evidence-based journal article relating to diversity trainings in the workplace that he could find using Google Scholar. Masao's manager responds that he is unable to review so many articles and doesn't say anything else. What would be a better approach for this task, moving forward?

    a. Masao asks his manager the total number of articles he should send at a given time.

    b. Masao works independently from now on and leaves his manager out of his planning work.

    c. Masao pulls specific information from recently published scholarly papers that pertain to the goals to share with his manager.

    d. Masao should be moved to a different team with different communication styles.

42. What is one of the primary benefits of an individual development plan (IDP)?

    a. It gives all the development responsibility to employees, freeing up HR professionals for other strategic work.

    b. It closely evaluates employees and documents mistakes to avoid wrongful termination complaints when employees are fired.

    c. It provides managers with greater control over workers' daily tasks.

    d. It helps workers become more invested in their professional development.

43. Which of the following is the most crucial component of fostering collaboration among a team?

    a. Maintaining a positive attitude

    b. Open communication

    c. Showing appreciation

    d. Building interpersonal skills

44. Tomas, an HR professional, is meeting with his direct manager, an entry-level employee in another department, and the vice-president of his organization to propose a system-wide HR initiative. What is the single most important thing Tomas can do during his proposal to promote buy-in?

    a. Wear his best suit and make sure his shoes are polished to give a solid first impression.

    b. Go to the conference room early and make sure all of his technological devices work properly for the presentation.

    c. Illustrate the value that the initiative will bring to the executive, managerial, and employee levels of the organization.

    d. Offer to pay for half of the required resources out of pocket.

45. HR has worked to expand its benefits package for employees, including new healthcare options. However, many employees failed to enroll before the deadline. How can HR best adjust its benefits policy for next year?

    a. Remove the new benefits options, because these rewards are not highly valued by employees and present an extra cost to the organization.

    b. Offer guided benefits counseling and advice leading up to the enrollment period.

    c. Give employees a lump sum payment so they can purchase their own healthcare coverage outside the organization.

    d. Move the deadline earlier so employees have less time to forget about completing their enrollment.

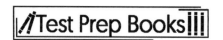

Read the following scenario and answer the questions 46 and 47.

The events planning department is having difficulty finding a capable assistant to handle their daily administrative workload. It is an entry-level, part-time job that has normally been staffed by students or recent graduates from local colleges. However, in the past five years, the position has had a high turnover rate, and the department director is perpetually dissatisfied with employee performance in this position.

46. How can HR help the department overcome this problem?
   a. Filling the position is taking too much time, so HR should eliminate the job and help department employees redistribute key tasks among themselves.
   b. Students and recent graduates lack the competency for this job, so HR should update the job qualifications to require an advanced degree and several years of experience.
   c. There is a clear disparity between the director's expectations and employees' performance ability, so HR should review the job description with the director and update it to reflect key skills and abilities.
   d. The department director is showing poor management skills, so HR should make sure this is reflected in their performance evaluation.

47. After helping the department overcome this problem, what can HR do next?
   a. Set up new employees with a mentor and proactively identify any skills gaps.
   b. Discontinue its participation in the local college fair and move to online-only recruiting.
   c. Enact a new policy to only hire temp employees for future administrative needs.
   d. Reduce director involvement in future hiring decisions.

48. Julian is working with the leadership team to ensure that the organization's employees have the skills and competencies needed to achieve the goals and objectives. He is conducting a skills gap analysis and discovers that many of the mid-level managers lack conflict resolution and team-building skills. What would be the best option for Julian to implement?
   a. Research training programs provided by external vendors and provide information to the employees.
   b. Require these employees' managers to indicate this lack of skill in the upcoming performance evaluation.
   c. Conduct a specific training program for these employees that provides an opportunity to learn these skills.
   d. Conduct a recruitment to hire new mid-level managers who specifically have this skill set.

49. It is a new fiscal year, and an HR department is unsure of which initiatives to implement during the upcoming year. What is the first step they can take to target some ideas?
   a. Search online for current trends in HR initiatives.
   b. Conduct a needs assessment for the interests of the employees.
   c. Ask their friends in the organization for ideas or personal interests.
   d. Select the ideas the HR department feels most passionate about.

50. What is a useful method to implement that can ensure HR staff and leadership have the same expectations of an initiative?
    a. Stakeholder mapping that avoids the initiative value
    b. A project proposal lacking financial analysis of the return on investment of the initiative
    c. The Myers-Briggs Type Indicator to predict leadership's expectations
    d. A written project proposal that outlines the timeline, milestones, needed resources, and dates for deliverables

51. Which of the following is the best definition of an organization's stakeholders?
    a. An organization's decision makers, including C-suite level leaders and other managers
    b. An organization's entire workforce
    c. An organization's workforce and its financial network, including customers and suppliers
    d. An organization's workforce and all those affected by its social, economic, and environmental impact

52. When working with multiple stakeholders who have varied interests, what is the best way to propose and develop a new initiative?
    a. Base the initiative around the interests of the stakeholder in the group who holds the highest position within the organization
    b. Place all interests into a random generator, and allow an initiative topic to be randomly selected
    c. Via email
    d. Select an overlapping interest that could have a feasible solution

53. Cynthia is initiating a new benefits program in the organization that will be deployed in the next calendar year. What can she do to best ensure that this program favors all employees equally and does not cater to one group of employees over another?
    a. Communicate the process used to choose the new program.
    b. Standardize the benefits program and make it equally accessible to all employees.
    c. Provide assurance to employees that the program is for everyone.
    d. Request the program be rolled out by executive management.

54. During a performance review, Jordan's manager shares some concerns that Jordan does not seem to have friends at work, show interest in others, or get along well with her team members. Jordan knows that she is a shy person but would like to use this opportunity for personal improvement. How can she proactively address this opportunity?
    a. Throw a weekend party for everyone at work and force herself to socialize
    b. Schedule a couple ten-minute intervals during her workday where she actively and positively engages with her coworkers
    c. Send a flowery apology email to her coworkers
    d. Ask her best friend to apply for a job at her company so that she can prove her manager wrong

55. Why do all employees need to build a wide range of intrapersonal skills?
    a. It correlates with higher pay overtime.
    b. It is the primary factor associated with cohesive teams.
    c. It leads to better relationships at home.
    d. It allows them to work well with other employees.

56. An organization's overall attitude towards dress code, working remotely, social retreats for employees, and designated break times can best be described as which of the following?
    a. Customer-centric
    b. Work-life balance
    c. Freebies
    d. Corporate culture

57. There are many quantitative and qualitative benefits from an efficient and productive corporate social responsibility program. Which of the following is a quantitative benefit of a robust CSR program?
    a. Improved employee engagement
    b. More positive workplace
    c. Reduction of legal liabilities
    d. Increased employee satisfaction

Read the following scenario and answer questions 58–60.

Leaders at a mid-size organization that specialize in producing car batteries are working on developing a strategic plan for the next ten years of the company. They are particularly interested in responding to the increased interest in hybrid and electric vehicles. Currently, the company's workforce is primarily concentrated in professionally licensed technicians working on the assembly floor.

58. Leadership has determined that more engineers with academic degrees will need to be added to the company. What is a first step that HR can take?
    a. Research and design meaningful job descriptions for desired new roles.
    b. Lay off enough factory technicians to offset the cost of new employees.
    c. Present a counter-strategy to maintain the current workforce as is.
    d. Canvas current employees who might be willing to change positions.

59. The factory technicians belong to a workers' union. Union negotiations have led to workers getting a 3 percent raise every year. However, to budget for the new strategic plan, company leaders cannot afford to continue this rate of salary increase; they would like to push for 2 percent or even 1 percent raises. What is an appropriate HR response?
    a. Survey employees to determine other rewards that might be valuable to workers but affordable for the company, such as flexible work scheduling.
    b. Devise a positive communication strategy for notifying employees of the new 1 percent raise policy.
    c. Transition to only hiring non-union factory technicians.
    d. Research annual raise policies at companies in other industries.

60. Part of the strategic plan involves building the company's battery research and development program capabilities. How can HR best assist with this part of the plan?
    a. Provide a budget plan for acquiring new research and development technologies.
    b. Organize a voluntary training session for employees who are interested in learning more about the projected research and development capabilities.
    c. Conduct a skills gap analysis to determine the capabilities of the current workforce and identify missing skills, and then develop a plan to fill the gap.
    d. Provide historical data about the battery research and development program's past performance.

233

61. What type of HR work is administrative and includes payroll and benefits administration?
    a. Tactical
    b. Personnel
    c. Transactional
    d. Strategic

62. Michael contacts HR to assist with a question regarding how to code a timecard. His employee, Jack, attended a training session for four hours outside of his normal workday. The training was conducted after hours and was provided to increase knowledge related to new tools and reports available in the payroll system. How should HR instruct Michael to report this time?
    a. Because the training was after hours and did not alter his usual work schedule, the timecard should reflect the training but with no pay.
    b. The training should be reported similar to stand-by pay and paid out at this same rate for the time he attended.
    c. The training was voluntary and not required as part of his job or assignment, so this time is not payable.
    d. The training should be reported per the standard process regarding payable hours and, if necessary, the overtime policy.

63. Which of the following is a fundamental component of an initiative's effectiveness?
    a. Fiscal responsibility
    b. Sustainability
    c. Environmental impact
    d. Employee satisfaction

64. Why is it important to collaborate with business partners who provide different strengths and experiences?
    a. Because these individuals can provide innovative solutions to problems that apply to other circumstances and situations an HR professional may not be aware of.
    b. Because the solutions should be provided by non-HR managers and HR should simply facilitate and manage the changes.
    c. Because HR professionals are in charge of writing overall policy, not developing solutions to address specific concerns.
    d. HR should not collaborate with professionals outside of HR.

Read the following scenario and answer questions 65 and 66.

Frederico Balzo began as a family-operated men's clothing store over fifty years ago. Fifteen years after the first store opened, the family decided to expand to a second location. Now Frederico Balzo operates over twenty stores and has expanded beyond suits to also sell shoes, watches, and other accessories. The company's latest plan is to open seven new stores within the next three years.

65. How can HR assist with the goal to open new stores?
a. HR can follow the steps laid out by C-suite leadership to handle workforce issues related to the expansion.
b. HR can participate in the strategic planning to offer input and highlight areas where workforce goals can be aligned with overall company goals.
c. HR can use the new stores as a testing ground to experiment with new workforce management techniques.
d. HR can assess and compare worker performance once all stores have opened.

66. Frederico Balzo's CEO wants an idea of the effort required to staff the new stores. Which of the following would be the most useful metric for HR to provide?
a. Time-to-hire
b. Annual attrition rate
c. Diversity ratio
d. Productivity rate

67. Which one of the following statements is true regarding developing jobs within an organization?
a. Jobs are developed based on an individual's particular skill set and background.
b. Jobs are developed based on goals and objectives established by leadership to ensure that qualified employees perform duties that contribute to the overall interests of the organization.
c. Jobs are developed based on the budget and what level of job responsibilities that budget can afford.
d. Jobs are developed based on the supervisor's discretion and the responsibilities that individual wants performed.

68. A company based in the United States is opening a new facility in Ireland. What will be a concern of HR professionals as the facility gets ready to launch?
a. US foreign policy relations
b. The assumption that the US site and the Irish site will not get along with one another
c. The weather in Ireland
d. Immigration laws and work visas for new employees at the site

69. An organization notices that its workforce is 78 percent females who are Caucasian. How can the organization make its workforce more diverse?
a. Actively recruit underrepresented employees by highlighting diversity as a priority in job postings and favoring it during hiring
b. Hire underrepresented workers even if they are not really qualified
c. Terminate current employees and hire underrepresented employees
d. The workforce is acceptable as is; clearly, candidates from other backgrounds are not available

Read the following scenario and answer questions 70 and 71.

Veronica is the HR manager for an accounting firm that employs individuals across the country. Each site maintains a separate operational structure and aligns their business practices to the customers they serve. Veronica has noticed that each site has specific needs and concerns, and she is working to align policies and procedures to establish a more consistent HR presence between sites.

235

70. What is Veronica addressing by establishing consistent policies and procedures?
    a. Behavioral concerns
    b. Workplace climate
    c. Resource allocation
    d. Mini-cultures

71. What should Veronica consider when establishing consistent policies and procedures?
    a. Employee demographics and turnover
    b. Specific state laws and regulations
    c. Supervisory complaints and concerns
    d. Customer demographics and sales

72. Which of the following is a way to ensure that diversity and inclusion practices are sustainable for an organization?
    a. Troubleshooting
    b. Recruiting
    c. Auditing
    d. Brainstorming

Read the following scenario and answer questions 73–75.

> Joseph is working on a recruitment for his marketing team. The team comprises employees who have been with the organization for at least five years, with the most tenured employee having more than twenty years of experience. The department manager has made it a priority to promote internally to ensure that employees are provided opportunities to grow and develop within the organization. The organization also has a robust employee referral program that many employees, including the marketing team, have taken advantage of. The open position is now vacant due to an employee retirement.

73. When proposing a recruitment plan to the department manager, which sourcing method should Joseph suggest as the most appropriate method for this position?
    a. Internal sourcing first and then external sourcing
    b. External sourcing first and then internal sourcing
    c. Internal sourcing only
    d. External sourcing only

74. After Joseph posts the position, he receives complaints from current employees that they should have been considered first for the position instead of external candidates. What should Joseph do to mediate this situation?
    a. Follow up with the individuals who complained and communicate the sourcing strategy for this position and the importance of sourcing externally to the entire team.
    b. Discuss the situation with the department manager and consider allowing internal candidates to be considered along with external candidates.
    c. Close the posting and initiate an internal promotion-only recruitment for the position to appease the current employees.
    d. There are no actions Joseph should take regarding this situation because the recruitment is appropriate for the organization and the manager should handle the complaints.

236

75. Joseph is concerned about the new team member fitting within the current workgroup dynamic. The team has been together several years and works extremely well together. What could Joseph add to the recruitment process to address the chemistry and fit of the potential new hires?
    a. Written exam and sample work assignment
    b. Myers-Briggs personality assessment
    c. Workgroup interview with the entire team
    d. One-on-one interview with the most senior team member

76. Creating candidate profiles, updating job postings, removing filled positions, and flagging resumes can all be accomplished by which tool?
    a. HRIS
    b. HIIT
    c. HIFT
    d. CHIT

77. Barbara, Cassandra, Debbie, and Enid have all worked in the same HR team for two years as generalists. Their supervisor currently left the organization to pursue another opportunity. All four employees are viable candidates for this position, and all have submitted applications. However, Barbara worked with the director of the group in another organization and has a close friendship with her. What is the fairest way to conduct interviews and selection for the supervisor position?
    a. Allow the director to have the final selection, as it is her department.
    b. Barbara should be given the position since she already has a close relationship with the director.
    c. A panel of interviewers from all parts of the company should make a selection based on merit.
    d. Allow the supervisor who resigned to provide feedback.

78. Elyse has experienced a high number of employees leaving the organization. The senior leadership would like a presentation given to provide current information and a plan to address the issue. What data piece should Elyse ensure is included in her presentation?
    a. Turnover rate
    b. Days to hire
    c. Number of openings
    d. Recruitment budget

79. What can an HR professional implement to gain insight into why employees resign from an organization?
    a. Classification review
    b. Exit interviews
    c. Employee surveys
    d. Compensation review

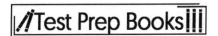

80. Louise is an HR director for a company that provides heating, ventilation, and air conditioning (HVAC) equipment and services to independent contractors. She routinely works with the executive leadership team to ensure the HR programs, policies, and practices are appropriate and necessary for the employees. Louise responds to every call, concern, and question, regardless of the level of the employee. She takes pride in her ability to communicate with all levels of the organization and in the relationships she has built with employees. During her performance review, the CEO admonishes her for not being available to him regarding a question he had because she was in a scheduled meeting with a line worker. How should she respond?
   a. Louise should apologize and offer to have her staff schedule meetings with employees to address concerns.
   b. Louise should offer to schedule daily check-in meetings with the CEO to ensure that he does not have any needs.
   c. Louise should take the feedback and not respond during the meeting.
   d. Louise should communicate to the CEO that all employees are her customers, and she provides the same level of customer service to a line worker as she does to the CEO.

81. Vera is an HR generalist that works for a medical devices company. She is in charge of recruiting and hiring engineers for the research and development team; however, she knows nothing about the product that the engineers will be building. Why could this be a major problem during the hiring process?
   I. Vera may hire engineers that do not have the correct skill set
   II. Vera may provide incorrect details about job responsibilities
   III. Vera may provide compensation packages that are too high or too low for the job
   a. I and II
   b. II and III
   c. I and III
   d. All of the above

82. A manager in a non-HR department is having difficultly scheduling leave for his team members in a new online scheduling system. How can an HR professional provide support in this situation?
   a. Offer to do all the scheduling for the manager
   b. Provide a training that walks through all of the steps of scheduling leave in the system
   c. Assume that the manager will eventually figure it out with time and practice
   d. Relay to the manager that the system has been easily adopted in other organizations

83. Which of the following is the process of securing personal information from identity theft or other corruptive activities?
   a. Workplace monitoring
   b. Surveillance techniques
   c. Internal monitoring
   d. Data protection

84. Which of the following is a policy employers implement that allows the organization to monitor a suspicious person and gather information that will be used to conduct an investigation?
   a. Workplace monitoring
   b. Surveillance techniques
   c. External monitoring
   d. Data protection

238

85. Why is technology management so important to the HR department?
    a. Technology management identifies and implements effective technology solutions that are most beneficial to the HR department.
    b. Technology management invests in project management software that increases productivity and maintains cost increases to a manageable level.
    c. Technology management implements and uses technology solutions that support, facilitate, and deliver effective HR services and critical employee data storage.
    d. Technology management analyzes the functionality of the organization's technology resources to ensure that the most effective systems are deployed.

86. An organization's HR leadership is considering switching to cloud database management. Which of the following is an important consideration in the contract with the software vendor?
    a. A plan for user training and software adoption
    b. An explanation of why cloud storage is a superior system
    c. Security standards for protecting sensitive employee data
    d. A written guarantee that the database cannot be breached by hackers

87. Which of the following is a way to learn more about the business operations, functions, products, and services of an organization?
    a. Read all of the job descriptions for every position within the organization.
    b. Review available internal documents, external literature, and customer service surveys.
    c. Send out an email to the department leaders asking them to respond to specific questions.
    d. Meet with employees to ask them questions about their goals, objectives, and work product.

88. Anna is responsible for tracking all of the HR information for the department. She uses multiple spreadsheets to keep track of merit increases, performance evaluations, addresses, emergency contacts, and other important information. Anna also uses a complex document to track job postings, recruitment, and hiring procedures. What tool would make her work easier to manage and allow for a more timely and accurate method of tracking employee information?
    a. Microsoft Access
    b. HR Information System (HRIS)
    c. Online business dashboard
    d. Document mapping system

Read the following scenario and answer questions 89 and 90.

Kevin is the HR director for a fulfillment center. He has recently undergone a complete review of the HRIS and determined that a new software program should be identified and implemented. Part of his review included speaking to employees to gain insight and feedback directly from the end users. He found that although many long-term employees were satisfied with the current system, newer employees struggled to work within the system and access information. He discovered that most employees spent inordinate amounts of time accessing information, entering information, and preparing reports. A new software package has been identified and is being tested to implement within the next quarter. This new package will address all of the concerns and deficiencies from the previous system.

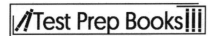
89. What should Kevin ensure is part of the transition plan with the vendor to guarantee a seamless and effective transition when implementing the new platform?
    a. A dual interface between the existing, legacy program and the new, updated software program to ease the transition
    b. A clean break with the legacy program ending effective at midnight and the new software beginning effective at 12:01 a.m.
    c. An opportunity for employees to provide feedback and look at other vendors and software platforms to provide this service
    d. Allowing both systems to be functional so that employees can choose which software they prefer to use

90. The new HRIS platform is a cloud database management system. Which of the following should Kevin ensure is provided in the new vendor's contract regarding employee data?
    a. Reporting metrics
    b. Written guarantee
    c. Security standards
    d. Password protocols

91. Sometimes there are many things that are out of a team's control, such as funding changes, new or updated regulations, and personnel changes. Which of the following concepts is important to understand when building milestones and objectives for a project?
    a. Rigidity
    b. Discipline
    c. Austerity
    d. Flexibility

92. Which of the following is NOT an accurate statement regarding the PEST analysis?
    a. A PEST analysis is an informal tool used to learn about trends that could influence an organization.
    b. A PEST analysis should be used by HR professionals to assist in guiding their work.
    c. A PEST analysis should include both internal and external resources.
    d. A PEST analysis often indicates process improvement needs to mitigate risks.

93. Which of the following functions is NOT performed through an HRIS?
    a. Initiate and run payroll functions, such as issuing paychecks and tax-related documents.
    b. Store data related to employee performance and job satisfaction.
    c. Manage and store employee documents and create reports.
    d. Manage, update, and store candidate profiles during a recruitment process.

94. Tools from which of the following approaches can be used to determine resources needed at each step of a project?
    a. Six Sigma
    b. Quality control
    c. Quality assurance
    d. Lean manufacturing

95. What can ambiguity, or being vague, cause when communicating with employees?
    a. Opportunities for employees to go above and beyond
    b. Innovation, productivity, and motivation
    c. Confusion, conflict, and distress
    d. Lower turnover and increased job satisfaction

96. Deidre is new to the HR field, and she has made it a priority to attend conferences and social events, participate in workplace events such as wellness walks, and engage in meaningful conversations with individuals and teams. She is committed to building valuable relationships that will allow her to receive and give support to others in the HR field. What activity is Deidre engaging in?
    a. Team building
    b. Networking
    c. Benchmarking
    d. Socializing

Read the scenario and answer questions 97–98.
    Until recently, a company has allowed different business units to operate and organize themselves fairly autonomously. However, new corporate leadership would like to increase collaboration between departments and has come in with a "silo-busting" objective. The new leaders are also looking to create more standardization in job functions and organizational structure between departments. HR has been called on to aid with this objective.

97. To standardize job functions between departments, HR is conducting job analyses. Which of the following is LEAST likely to be included in the scope of these analyses?
    a. The type and frequency of tasks performed
    b. The industry standard for required competencies in this position
    c. The supervisory chain of who reports and who is reported to for the position
    d. The personal and professional qualifications needed

98. As a result of the job analysis, HR has found that identical job titles in different departments in fact have different levels of responsibility. They would like to establish an added level of responsibility for those positions that have fallen behind. What is this process called?
    a. Job evaluation
    b. Job elaboration
    c. Job enrichment
    d. Job enlargement

99. Judy is reviewing several positions within a department to ensure that the pay structure is accurate and appropriate. She conducted a job analysis of each of the positions to determine the requirements and importance of each job duty. Once she completed the job analysis, she then reviewed the job descriptions to ensure that each one was an accurate listing of the general duties and responsibilities for each job. Judy is now creating a statement of the essential parts of these jobs that includes a summary of the duties performed, responsibilities, and qualifications necessary to complete the job. What did Judy create?
    a. Job specification
    b. Job evaluation
    c. Classification review
    d. Compensation study

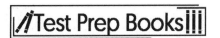

100. For several weeks after payroll is done, the payroll coordinator goes to HR to let them know an employee has been regularly using leave he has not yet accrued. What can HR do to address this concern?
    a. Contact the supervisor and allow for an in-person discussion to address the issue.
    b. Provide the employee with a formal, written reprimand.
    c. Monitor the situation and see if it occurs a few more times, and then address.
    d. Roll out mandatory training to all employees on proper leave usage and tracking.

101. Lars is collecting data relating to employee productivity. He notices that facility employees are more likely to take sick days in December, while the rest of the organization have sick days scattered throughout the year. Lars hypothesizes that facility employees call out sick to have extra holiday time. What is the issue with this reasoning?
    a. The program that generated this report has not been double-checked.
    b. Lars is clearly showing confirmation bias
    c. Facility employees often work outdoors, which could be a confounding variable.
    d. There are no issues with this reasoning.

102. Which of the following data collection method requires a skilled facilitator?
    a. Focus groups
    b. Paper and online surveys
    c. Customer satisfaction surveys
    d. Observational groups

103. Jose works for a small organization that employs approximately one hundred individuals. He wants to learn more about how the employees feel about their salary, benefits, and work. The organization does not have the budget to assist with this project. Additionally, his employees are skilled labor mechanics and do not have much experience with the computer. Which method of data collection should Jose use to gather this information?
    a. Paper survey
    b. Focus group
    c. Individual meetings
    d. Online survey

104. Why are interpersonal skills so important for all employees to develop?
    a. They allow employees to be ready for promotion opportunities.
    b. They allow employees to have a higher level of satisfaction with their work-life balance.
    c. They allow employees to work more effectively and productively with others.
    d. They directly correlate to a higher level of job satisfaction.

105. An organization is using a legacy HRIS because long-standing employees are comfortable with the software and feel it continues to meet their data management needs. However, several new employees are having difficulty using the outdated user interface and are pushing to adopt an entirely new platform. What is a good solution for this situation?
    a. Contract with a vendor that offers interface layer technology to develop a new user interface while maintaining the existing system.
    b. Get rid of the old system and invest in the latest HRIS before the current software becomes even more outdated than it already is.
    c. Reassign the new employees to positions that already have more cutting-edge software in place.
    d. Create an organization-wide site where employees can submit anonymous feedback about using the current HRIS.

106. When an HR professional shows and demonstrates an understanding of the importance of using data to make informed business decisions and propose solutions, which of the following is being exhibited?
    a. Service quality
    b. Customer service
    c. Data advocacy
    d. Critical thinking

107. Sophia is collecting data to complete a compensation analysis. This data will help the organization determine if salaries need to be increased or if they are appropriate and in alignment with the industry. Sophie has discovered a website that has information available on practically every job she needs to assess; however, she is hesitant to use the information. What factors should she rely on when determining whether to use this data?
    a. The data goes back several years.
    b. The data is recent and relevant.
    c. The data supports the recommendation of providing salary increases.
    d. The data supports the recommendation of not providing salary increases.

108. According to the Equal Pay Act, what aspects of a job must be equivalent to merit equal wages?
    a. Working conditions, responsibility, gender, seniority
    b. Effort, production quantity, responsibility, merit
    c. Skill, responsibility, production quantity, merit
    d. Skill, working conditions, effort, responsibility

109. Mina is conducting a professional development satisfaction survey. She needs to survey 75 percent of her organization, which has over 3,000 employees. What is the best way for her to collect detailed data from this many people?
    a. Online survey
    b. Paper survey
    c. A series of focus groups
    d. Face to face interviews

110. Which method of communication can spread information quickly but often becomes misinterpreted, misunderstood, and incorrect?
    a. Emails
    b. Newsletters
    c. Town hall meetings
    d. Word of mouth

111. Natalia, Lisa, Julian, and Louis are members of the HR team, and each has a different discipline they are responsible for. Natalia manages recruitment; Lisa manages employee benefits; Julian manages employee relations; and Louis manages risk management and workers' compensation. Their manager, Hannah, receives a call that Natalia was involved in a car accident and will be out of the office for at least two months recovering. She pulls together the team to discuss the plan for managing Natalia's workload during her absence and discovers that neither Lisa, nor Julian, nor Louis is familiar with the recruitment process or where Natalia keeps her recruitment documents. What should Hannah have done to ensure that this precarious situation did not occur?
    a. Familiarize herself with each discipline and serve as the secondary resource for all areas.
    b. There was nothing Hannah could have done to foresee an emergency such as this.
    c. Keep a consultant on retainer to come in and pick up the duties in situations like this.
    d. Ensure that each HR discipline has an assigned primary and secondary resource.

112. Which of the following is a vital component of communication that builds trust?
    a. Empowerment
    b. Courage
    c. Collaboration
    d. Transparency

113. Maryam writes a message to her team leader to ask a question about a project. The team leader answers back with one sentence that seems terse to Maryam. What should Maryam do in this situation?
    a. Assume the team leader is angry that Maryam asked a dumb question
    b. Feel angry that the team leader did not think to add a greeting, closure, or other kind words to set the tone for the email
    c. Assume nothing, and ask the team leader about the brevity of the message when possible
    d. Assume the team leader is busy and just answered as quickly as possible

114. What is one way to build credibility as an HR expert?
    I. Pursue a master's degree in Human Resources from an accredited university
    II. Take online personality surveys, such as Myers-Briggs, to determine your strengths
    III. Earn nationally recognized certifications in the field
    IV. Attend workshops and share key takeaways with your organization
    a. I, III, and IV
    b. I, II, and III
    c. I, II, and IV
    d. All of the above

115. Xiaoli is conducting a stakeholder meeting to review how a flu shot campaign conducted by the HR department is going. One of the stakeholders begins asking questions about the pharmacy that is providing the vaccines to the organization, and Xiaoli is unable to answer his questions. What is the best course of action for Xiaoli to take in this situation?
    a. Tell the stakeholder she doesn't know anything about the pharmacy, and move on to the next item on the agenda
    b. Tell the stakeholder information that she feels like is probably accurate, based on something she read the other day
    c. Provide the stakeholder with the pharmacy's contact information so that the stakeholder can call and get any information he needs
    d. Tell the stakeholder she doesn't know the answers to his questions, but will find out and follow-up with him within twenty-four hours

116. Which of the following data collection methods has a risk of low engagement or facilitator bias?
    a. Surveys
    b. Classroom training
    c. Focus groups
    d. Exit interviews

Read the following scenario and answer questions 117–119.

> Samantha's organization has made the decision to move forward with a workforce reduction due to costs and expenses exceeding sales and profits. Samantha has experienced being laid off with a previous organization and is bringing that experience to this circumstance. She wants to make certain that employees receive the necessary information to ensure a successful implementation of the workforce reduction.

117. What should Samantha focus on immediately?
    a. Communicate with employees about the decision, process, and timeline.
    b. Create separation agreements and general releases for employees to sign.
    c. Implement a hiring freeze across all departments.
    d. Attempt to change the decision of the executives by preparing a proposal.

118. Samantha is working on creating a benefits package for the employees who will be separated. One of these benefits will include resume writing, career counseling, and interview preparation. What benefit is Samantha offering with these services?
    a. Severance
    b. Separation agreement
    c. Employee assistance
    d. Outplacement services

119. Once the workforce reduction is complete, what should Samantha and the executive team focus on?
    a. Checking in frequently with the separated employees to ensure they gain employment
    b. Reporting out on the new profit and loss statements to show the new productivity rate
    c. Boosting the morale of the remaining employees to ensure productivity does not suffer
    d. Discussing potential future reductions in case more are needed

120. James is the new leader of an organization that employs many individuals in various disciplines and locations. He has initiated multiple methods to ensure that all employees receive communication that is relatable and appropriate. He sends out frequent email announcements and newsletters to discuss what is happening in the organization, hosts town hall meetings and informal brown bag lunches, and frequently walks around each location to engage with employees directly. What else can James do to make sure all employees have opportunities to engage with him directly and ensure open lines of communication?
- a. Host and pay for a Christmas party.
- b. Establish an open-door policy.
- c. There is nothing he can do.
- d. Take donuts to every location every Friday.

121. What benefit can be gained by serving as a team leader?
- a. Communicating with other team leaders and directors.
- b. Being able to supervise and direct the work of others.
- c. Reaching the endpoint of professional learning and growth.
- d. Gaining knowledge about the business and operations.

122. An organization eliminates its pension package for retirees, which causes a group of retirees to arrive in the HR department. The group is angry and yelling at the HR employees. One woman even bursts into tears at the thought of receiving less money in retirement. What is the best way for HR employees to respond to this outburst?
- a. Take it personally and feel defeated
- b. Close the doors to the HR department until the retirees leave; after all, the department is unable to change the outcome
- c. Provide the president of the company's direct line and tell the retirees to call
- d. Actively listen to the feelings of the retirees, show empathy, and try to communicate with logic and objectivity

123. Monica is interviewing interested vendors for services related to administering and managing the company's retirement program. Each vendor has submitted a cost proposal with specific details on the services provided along with a sample service agreement, which includes a cost breakdown. Which one of the following items should be discussed in the interviews to gauge which vendor will be the best selection?
- a. Retirement services and options available
- b. The company's retirement plans for their employees
- c. Communication and rollout plans
- d. Fixed and variable costs

124. Louise is meeting for the first time with a potential vendor to assist with her organization's annual wellness fair. What types of expectations should Louise discuss in person with the vendor?
- a. The vendor's role and communication timelines
- b. The vendor's work history and time in business
- c. The vendor's goods and services
- d. The vendor's personal health philosophy

125. Where is a location that informal, yet effective, communication takes place at work?
    a. The break room
    b. During webinars
    c. In a conference room
    d. In a company newsletter

126. Jennifer meets regularly with her team members, both as a group and individually, to ensure that each employee understands expectations and current projects and issues are handled timely and effectively. In each group meeting, she makes sure time is allocated for each individual to communicate concerns or ideas. During this time, she engages with the speaker, takes notes, responds with body language, and asks questions. What type of listening is Jennifer engaging in?
    a. Functional
    b. Operational
    c. Active
    d. Empathetic

127. Edward has been tasked with preparing a proposal for a new benefits program. The proposal will be presented to the leadership team for final approval before moving to implementation. He has reviewed the employee demographics, current trends and analysis from the marketplace, current benefits usage, best practices, costs, and benefits. Additionally, he assembled several employee panels to ask questions, receive input, and gain insight into what is important to employees. All this information has been put together to make a final recommendation for a new benefits program. What will the likely result be from the leadership team?
    a. The leadership team will most likely approve the new benefits program because a decision needs to be made quickly and to ensure implementation begins immediately.
    b. The leadership team will most likely deny the new benefits program because the current program meets the needs of the employees and there have been no complaints.
    c. The leadership team will most likely not make a decision because they will need more data and information along with additional options to consider versus one recommendation.
    d. The leadership team will most likely approve the new benefits program because Edward prepared the recommendation on relevant and current data as well as employee feedback.

128. Which of the following attributes is NOT an element of effective leadership?
    a. Managing time in a financially responsible manner
    b. Solving problems as they arise
    c. Strategic thinking
    d. Carrying out the requirements of the job

129. Jeremy wants to implement an HR initiative that allows department leads to swap employees for specified periods of time to facilitate cross-training. What sources could Jeremy share with leadership to support his case for trying this?
    a. A case study in the *New York Times* that features a Fortune500 company that did this successfully
    b. An online forum where this idea is casually referenced as something that could work
    c. Anecdotal evidence from a friend who tried it at his company of ten employees
    d. A college student's podcast that he listened to on the way to work

130. Laura has been hired to complete multiple human resources (HR) personnel tasks. These tasks can include which one of the following?
    a. Developing job postings
    b. Completing workplace investigations
    c. Establishing a benefits program
    d. Filing paperwork

131. Martin is hiring an entry-level accountant. This position is newly created due to the increasing workload. Martin would like to hire a seasoned individual who has earned a master's degree in the field of accounting and has ten years of experience. He reaches out to the HR analyst, Ally, to discuss his needs and ensure that he has a pool of candidates who are highly qualified and ready to take on this position. Which of the following responses would not be appropriate?
    a. Ally should schedule a meeting with Martin to discuss the position, qualifications, and needs of the department as well as the current positions, qualifications, and salaries.
    b. Ally should accept Martin as the subject matter expert on his needs for the position and proceed with the posting as Martin has described, including the qualifications.
    c. Ally should provide other options as to the position requirements, specifically the qualifications, to ensure that the best-fitting candidates will apply and interview.
    d. Ally should conduct market research to determine comparable positions with other agencies and provide a benchmark analysis to Martin to revise his position description and qualifications.

132. Which of the following is NOT an outcome of the performance management process?
    a. Salary increases and promotions
    b. Growth and development opportunities
    c. Employee satisfaction and morale rate
    d. Disciplinary actions and training needs

133. Karen is recruiting a new software engineer and is looking for a candidate that has experience as well as motivation and passion for the job. She has narrowed the candidate pool down to two candidates. Candidate A has ten years of progressive experience, has worked as a supervisor, and is highly recommended by references. Candidate B has four years of progressive experience, has not worked as a supervisor, and is highly recommended by references. Both candidates meet the required qualifications, and Karen must decide after her interviews. During the final interviews, she notices a fundamental difference between the candidates relative to their passion and motivation. Candidate A answers questions specifically and directly, with little passion or motivation to go above and beyond. Candidate B answers questions with passion and specific details as to going above and beyond the expectations as well as seeking out additional opportunities for growth. What should Karen decide to do?
    a. Create two positions and hire both candidates A and B because each individual brings necessary skills and experiences needed by the department.
    b. Delay deciding and request that the department director interview both candidates and make the decision on which candidate should be hired.
    c. Hire candidate A because the individual's experience is more extensive and includes supervision, and Karen can work to engage and motivate the individual later.
    d. Hire candidate B because the individual's passion, motivation, and experience align with what Karen is seeking for the department and this position.

134. Which of the following HR work is focused on multiple business units or the entire organization, with the main focus being the vision, mission, and goals of the company?
    a. Transformational
    b. Strategic
    c. Tactical
    d. Transactional

135. Which of the following is NOT an effective communication method when working with employee and management survey feedback?
    a. Allowing information to trickle down
    b. Engaging with employees at all levels
    c. Providing appropriate guidance as needed
    d. Implementing initiatives to address needs

136. Jessica recently received her performance review, and as part of her learning and development opportunities, a course in statistics and data analysis was recommended. Because Jessica has never been strong in this subject, she is hesitant to attend. Why is it important for her to have a working knowledge and understanding of statistics even though she works in HR?
    a. Jessica will be able to add this certification to her resume.
    b. Jessica will become more marketable as a candidate.
    c. Jessica will be able to promote to a higher-level position within the company with this higher skill set.
    d. Jessica will be able to identify flawed, misleading, or misrepresented data.

137. Elias sees a pie chart that shows about two-thirds of HR professionals hate their jobs, and only one-third find it satisfactory. What should he do before sharing this information with anyone?
    a. Ask his colleagues in the HR department how they feel about their jobs and see if it lines up with the chart.
    b. Source who conducted the research and the sample size of respondents.
    c. Review his own career choices so far.
    d. Nothing, he should feel free to share the graph because it looks professional and accurate.

138. Lisa is the chief negotiator for her organization and will be negotiating with four union groups that each represent a different group of employees—public safety, management, administrative and clerical, and skilled trades. Each group has a special and unique skill set, with employees each having their own needs specific to training, wages, specialty pay, time off, work schedules, and personal protective equipment. One of the memorandums of understanding (MOUs) is expiring soon, and therefore Lisa is working on her bargaining strategy and wants to ensure that her method is appropriate for the situation. Which strategy should she employ when working on her overall negotiations strategy for the upcoming discussions?
    a. Multi-employer bargaining
    b. Single-unit bargaining
    c. Parallel bargaining
    d. Coordinated bargaining

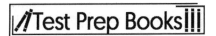

139. What type of bargaining occurs when groups negotiate terms for a contract while being mindful of the key issues to each side in the process?
    a. Distributive bargaining
    b. Principled bargaining
    c. Positional bargaining
    d. Coordinated bargaining

140. Stephanie is beginning her preparation for the upcoming negotiations with the bargaining unit. The previous three-year contract allowed for 4.5 percent cost-of-living increases annually for each year of the contract. In reviewing the financial forecasts for the next three years, Stephanie sees that the organization will be facing a budget deficit and unable to offer salary increases. What can Stephanie do as a proactive measure to address this concern in the preparation process?
    a. Identify several lower-level positions that, if eliminated, could fund a cost-of-living increase for the remaining employees
    b. Create an internal memo to send to all employees communicating the status of the financial forecast and budget deficits.
    c. Conduct a survey asking for feedback regarding rewards and benefits that are affordable to the company and valued by employees.
    d. Ask the bargaining unit to push negotiations to the next year until the budget deficits can be addressed and the organization is in a better financial position.

141. All except for which of the following terms refers to when a union successfully negotiates an agreement with a company and then uses these results to deal with another company?
    a. Whipsawing
    b. Multi-employer bargaining
    c. Leapfrogging
    d. Parallel bargaining

142. Amalia is a member of the negotiations team and is preparing for the upcoming round of bargaining. The union has a long history with the organization, and most negotiations end up extending way past the end of the current contract. Amalia personally does not believe unions are necessary due to the numerous and strict federal and state laws that protect employees. She decides to start speaking directly with employees to let them know what the organization would be able to do for the staff if there was no union. What practice is Amalia engaging in?
    a. Negotiating in bad faith
    b. Negotiating in good faith
    c. Collective bargaining
    d. Unfair labor practice

143. The local union and company representatives are beginning the negotiation process for the upcoming year. There are legitimate concerns on both sides, including wages, benefits, schedules, workload, and retirement costs, that must be addressed in the successor contract. Before presenting proposals, each side takes the floor to discuss their issues and relate their concerns. Both parties agree to negotiate in good faith and work together to find solutions for each item. Which bargaining practice are these groups engaging in?
    a. Parallel bargaining
    b. Principled bargaining
    c. Distributive bargaining
    d. Coordinated bargaining

144. Which of the following statements about strategic plans is inaccurate?
    a. Strategic plans involve objectives, analysis, looking at strengths and weaknesses, and implementation.
    b. Strategic plans are executed by employees and HR professionals to ensure these employees have the necessary skills to accomplish the plans.
    c. Strategic plans are a one-time activity that should always guide the organization toward the overall goals and objectives.
    d. Strategic plans should maximize the organization's strengths, take advantage of industry opportunities, and regularly be improved.

145. Which of the following is vital when operating in a global environment?
    a. Responding promptly to and fully addressing all stakeholders' needs
    b. Soliciting feedback from leadership concerning the HR functions
    c. Seeking further information to clarify any ambiguous issues
    d. Understanding and respecting differences in regulations and accepted business operations

146. Lucas is preparing to roll out several new HR programs that will change how employees receive their benefits. The organization has not updated these programs since their inception, and therefore has fallen behind the industry standards and seen substantial cost increases. Lucas is determining which strategic method to use to roll out these changes to ensure the best reception from employees. Which of the following should he consider when determining which strategy to deploy?
    a. Lucas should consider the overall employee makeup of the organization as well as the sensitivity of the changes being implemented.
    b. Lucas should consider having the CEO deliver the message and implement the power-coercive strategy, with the message being delivered by the highest level of leadership.
    c. Lucas should consider sending an email to all employees to avoid conflicts.
    d. Lucas should consider showing employees how expensive the programs were and implement the empirical-rational strategy, with employees having the information as to how costly this would continue to be.

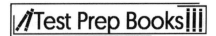

147. Karen is working on preparing a report that outlines how her organization will benefit from a new purchasing system. Within the report, she outlines the short-term and long-term benefits that will be realized. Additionally, she presents how these benefits compare to the costs of the new system. These costs include projected labor, equipment, materials, time, and other potential costs, such as a contingency budget to address unforeseen issues that arise. What type of analysis has Karen conducted?
    a. Key performance indicators analysis
    b. Needs assessment analysis
    c. Cost-benefit analysis
    d. SWOT analysis

148. Robert is working on a performance evaluation project with several managers from locations across the country. His primary goal is to roll out one comprehensive program to ensure alignment and consistency across the organization, regardless of the location. He is struggling with the information and feedback he is receiving from each manager because they are focusing on their individual location's needs versus the overarching organization's needs. What can Robert do to ensure agreement among the locations while achieving his goal of a comprehensive performance evaluation program that meets the organization's goals?
    a. Robert should continue on his structured path to roll out the program, with or without the managers' buy-in or participation.
    b. Robert should discuss the concerns with his supervisor and ask to get the location managers on board.
    c. Robert should clearly define the expectations of the project and establish aligned values.
    d. Robert should develop separate programs for each location to meet their specific needs.

149. Sylvia is working to establish a new policy related to parental leave. The organization has not historically practiced consistent procedures relative to maternity, paternity, and ongoing family leave. Although there are many federal and state laws, Sylvia needs to ensure the organization is not only in compliance with these laws but that consistent, fair, and equitable practices are put in place that align with an overall policy that addresses the process, time frames, exceptions, and other issues that could arise. Sylvia would like to survey employees to receive feedback as to what they would like to see in this new policy. Who should she survey?
    a. All employees
    b. Female employees
    c. Female employees who have used maternity leave
    d. Managers and supervisors

150. When preparing a workplace policy, which of the below statements is accurate?
    a. If there is a federal regulation regarding a program, a workplace policy is not needed.
    b. If there is a federal regulation regarding a program, the policy should mirror the regulation.
    c. Workplace policies should provide equal or greater benefits than the federal regulations.
    d. Workplace policies should provide equal or less benefits than the federal regulations.

151. Which of the following service models allows Human Resources (HR) to have a presence within different business units?
    a. Centralized
    b. Matrixed
    c. Outsourced
    d. Decentralized

152. Which of the following service models allows HR to have one corporate presence over the entire organization?
    a. Centralized
    b. Matrixed
    c. Outsourced
    d. Decentralized

153. Sarah has created an informational document for managers regarding all of the new state and federal regulations that impact the organization. She included the actual legislative language and what will change regarding day-to-day practices. Additionally, she added resources, such as external websites, for managers to have as much information as possible. Sarah sent the document to all managers along with an extensive email detailing the responsibilities of understanding this information. What should Sarah do to ensure that managers are fully aware of and have a complete understanding of the new regulations?
    a. Send out weekly emails with reminders to review the material.
    b. Conduct specialized trainings and reach out directly to managers to address questions.
    c. Require managers to respond to the email that they have received and understand the material.
    d. Print the document and place it in all of the managers' personnel files.

Read the following scenario and answer questions 154 and 155.

> Klaus is working on a compensation study for several departments within his organization. He has requested that employees respond to a position analysis so that he can review the accuracy of the current job descriptions and ensure that he takes into account all of the actual duties being performed when comparing salaries against the industry standard. He has located several data sources that provide information on various positions that he can use in his study.

154. What factors should Klaus confirm about the data sources before using the information?
    a. They are recent (within three years) and relevant to the positions being reviewed.
    b. They are from an online source that seems reputable.
    c. They are available online and at no cost to the organization.
    d. They support the current compensation levels set for the positions.

155. At the conclusion of the compensation study, Klaus makes recommendations for several positions to receive an increase to the compensation rate. One employee believes their position should also receive an increase and that the study was not accurate. What should Klaus do?
    a. Communicate to the employee that the decision is final and that when the next compensation study is conducted, the position will be reviewed again.
    b. Ask the employee's manager to discuss the study and provide the employee with the position analysis that was completed.
    c. Nothing; the study was finished, and the findings are complete, so there is no further action for Klaus to take.
    d. Schedule a meeting to discuss the study, including the position analysis the employee completed and the data used to make the determination.

156. What are an employer's responsibilities when an employee leaves for military duty under the Uniformed Services Employment and Reemployment Rights Act (USERRA)?

a. If the employee gets called to active duty, the employer is required to re-employ them upon their return.

b. When an employee is re-employed, they receive the full amount of employment benefits they would have received if they didn't leave for active duty.

c. The employee has indefinite job protection as long as the employee is actively serving in the military the whole time.

d. Both A and B.

157. What are an employer's responsibilities to an applicant that has past, present, or planned future military service under the Uniformed Services Employment and Reemployment Rights Act (USERRA)?

a. The employer is not allowed to discriminate against any military service and must work with applicants to understand comparable skills from previous service.

b. The employer can choose to not hire someone based on future military service if they know that person will be deployed soon.

c. The employer does have to consider any previous military experience towards job experience, since it is difficult to compare.

d. USERRA is focused only on current employees and does not have rules for job applicants.

158. The accounting manager recently retired, and several employees within the department are interested in applying for this position. The finance director will be making the hiring decision for this position, and it has been brought to HR's attention that he knows several of the employees on a personal basis. One employee is a member of the same church, one employee has children in the same school and grade, and one employee is a member of the same softball league. How can HR work to ensure an unbiased and fair recruitment and selection process?

a. Employees who have a personal relationship with the finance director should not be allowed to apply for the position because they will not be interviewed fairly.

b. Nothing; a finance director should be able to conduct himself in a professional, ethical, fair, and unbiased manner regardless of personal relationships outside of the workplace.

c. Establish an interview panel with stakeholders from across several departments who will interview all candidates and select the most qualified candidate.

d. Restructure the position to report to a different director to ensure there is no bias or unfairness in the recruitment and selection process.

159. Michelle is working with the sales department to initiate a recruitment for a new sales representative. She is new to the organization and industry and wants to ensure that she conducts an effective and successful recruitment. Michelle meets with the hiring manager and other employees in this position to gain insight and a full understanding of the position before initiating the recruitment. Why is it important for Michelle to have this information?

    a. It is not important to the recruitment because Michelle should proceed with the most recent job description for the recruitment process.

    b. It is important so that Michelle can provide correct details about the position in the recruitment brochure and hire a candidate with the right skill set.

    c. It is not important to the recruitment because Michelle should conduct the process with complete subjectivity, which will allow for an unbiased process.

    d. It is important so that Michelle can have a good working relationship with the hiring manager and employees beyond the recruitment for this position.

160. Which of the following strategies is the comparison of an organization's initiatives and outcomes against competitors, industry standards, or industry goals?

    a. Best practices

    b. Data collection

    c. SWOT analysis

    d. Benchmarking

161. Michael wants to update the organization's wellness policy, specifically the programs related to weight loss and smoking cessation. Who should he reach out to to gain insight and feedback regarding these programs?

    a. Female employees at all levels

    b. Male employees at the supervisory level

    c. All employees at all levels

    d. Female and male managers

Read the following scenario and answer questions 162–164.

> Amelia is conducting a recruitment for a new position within the organization. The new position requires a specific certification, undergraduate degree, and one year of experience. When Amelia reviews the applications submitted, she identifies those with these specific requirements and schedules an initial round of interviews. She prepares the questions to focus on the work the organization will need done to ensure the best candidates are selected to move to the second round of interviews with the hiring managers. At the conclusion of the initial interviews, she is disappointed in the results. Although most of the candidates provided answers to the questions, none of the answers were in-depth and lacked real-world experience.

162. What should Amelia do immediately following the initial interviews?

    a. Notify the candidates that the organization will not be proceeding with this recruitment.

    b. Prepare a new plan for the recruitment and present it to the HR team for feedback.

    c. Communicate the results and concerns regarding the candidates with the hiring manager.

    d. Repost the recruitment to engage a new group of candidates and conduct interviews.

163. What should Amelia consider changing in the required qualifications to ensure candidates with the right background and job experience apply?
    a. Nothing, as the qualifications are appropriate for the position.
    b. Eliminate the years of experience necessary and only require the degree and certification.
    c. Increase the years of experience and allow for experience to substitute for the degree.
    d. Add supervisory experience to the qualifications to attract candidates who have more experience.

164. If Amelia and the hiring manager decide to move forward with the highest-ranking applicants from the initial recruitment, which of the following would be an appropriate step to add to the recruitment process?
    a. No additional steps
    b. Written exercise similar to the work performed
    c. Additional interview with the entire team
    d. Longer interview with specific and difficult questions

165. If an organization strives to maintain competitiveness and maximize capabilities, which one of the following should management develop?
    a. Policies that streamline communications
    b. Free break room lunches
    c. Walking paths on site
    d. Update technology once a year

166. What can HR specifically do to alleviate employees' fears and concerns about reporting unethical behavior and possible retaliation?
    a. Provide annual training regarding the policies and expectations.
    b. Provide confidential and/or anonymous reporting methods.
    c. Provide all employees with the handbook to ensure knowledge of the policy.
    d. Provide frequent updates to the policies and procedures.

167. Jessie has recently joined a new organization as the HR manager responsible for labor relations and negotiations. One of the first items she wants to accomplish is understanding what each department does and what they need to ensure that future negotiations and day-to-day decisions are reflective of the departments' overall needs. How can Jessie best accomplish this in the most effective manner?
    a. Send out an introductory email with Jessie's background information and an invitation to visit any time to discuss concerns and needs.
    b. Review the current union contract and policies to establish a list of needed items that should be changed in upcoming negotiations.
    c. Survey current employees to determine satisfaction levels with compensation, benefits, leave programs, and retirement.
    d. Establish one-on-one and group meetings to engage in two-way dialogue that fosters information sharing.

168. What is one way to eliminate job applicants who may not be a good cultural fit for an organization?
    a. List aspects that are relevant to corporate culture on the job posting.
    b. Make assumptions based on looks and body language when candidates arrive for in-person interviews.
    c. Market all jobs at in-person job fairs only where HR staff can make decisions based on their first impressions.
    d. It is difficult to pinpoint a mismatch between the organization and applicants until they are on the job.

169. What federal institution measures and collates nationwide employment data, such as market activity, average salaries, and working conditions?
    a. Bureau of Labor Statistics
    b. Internal Revenue Service
    c. Department of Labor
    d. Equal Employment Opportunity Commission

170. Karen is recruiting a new software engineer and is looking for a candidate that has experience as well as motivation and passion for the job. She has narrowed the candidate pool down to two candidates. Candidate A has ten years of progressive experience, has worked as a supervisor, and is highly recommended by references. Candidate B has four years of progressive experience, has not worked as a supervisor, and is highly recommended by references. Both candidates meet the required qualifications, and Karen must make a decision after her interviews. During the final interviews, she notices a fundamental difference between the candidates relative to their passion and motivation. Candidate A answers questions specifically and directly, with little passion or motivation to go above and beyond. Candidate B answers questions with passion and specific details as to going above and beyond the expectations as well as seeking out additional opportunities for growth. What should Karen decide to do?
    a. Create two positions and hire both candidates A and B because each individual brings necessary skills and experiences needed by the department.
    b. Delay making a decision and request that the department director interview both candidates and make the decision on which candidate should be hired.
    c. Hire candidate A because the individual's experience is more extensive and includes supervision, and Karen can work to engage and motivate the individual later.
    d. Hire candidate B because the individual's passion, motivation, and experience align with what Karen is seeking for the department and this position.

171. When should an employee be introduced to an organization's ethical standards and policies?
    a. During the interview process with the hiring manager
    b. During the onboarding and new-hire orientation
    c. When reading the job posting to apply for the position
    d. When a complaint arises against them and HR begins the investigation

172. Lowry recently experienced the death of a loved one. While Lowry was once a stellar employee, he now begins to come to work late and is slow to finish his tasks. He appears disinterested in his work and eventually begins using up his sick days. Lowry's manager tries to support him by providing grievance resources, offering new job responsibilities, and providing the option of working from home; however, Lowry is not interested in any of these options. What lesson can Lowry's manager learn from this situation?

    a. Employees should be fired at the first sign of disengagement to avoid waste of time and resources
    b. Managers should not care too much about their employees, as it can cause emotional distress
    c. Managers should get to know their employees better outside of work, rather than only in the workplace
    d. Employee motivation is often influenced by factors that are outside of the manager's locus of control

173. Raphael has been asked by senior leadership to give a presentation at the next board meeting. He is to present information concerning the recent customer service survey that was sent out to new customers from the last year. Raphael is excited about the opportunity to present to the senior leadership, for both the experience and the exposure to the team. He spends a significant amount of time preparing the presentation, his talking points, and handouts. He delves into the history of the department, the current staff, issues they are dealing with, and compensation information. Raphael's information is very detailed, but he finds that after fifteen minutes, he is losing the team's attention. What could be the reason for this?

    a. The leadership team is simply not aware of this information, and Raphael needs to keep to his presentation.
    b. Raphael was not mindful of the leadership's time and did not address the specific item requested.
    c. The leadership team should have been offered the ability to ask questions throughout the presentation.
    d. Raphael's presentation is not clearly conveying the information that was compiled, and he should request a quick break.

174. Phoebe is working on a salary review an employee requested. The employee believes new work has been assigned that changes the job being done and therefore a higher pay rate should be applied. Phoebe wants to get this review completed today so that she can relay the results to the manager and come to a resolution for the employee. Halfway through her work, her director pulls her into a meeting and asks her to work on a special task that was requested by the vice president. How should Phoebe manage her workload?

    a. Phoebe should attend to the special task first and then finish the salary review.
    b. Phoebe should finish the salary review first and then attend to the special task.
    c. Phoebe should request that the special task be assigned to another team member.
    d. Phoebe should request that another team member finish the salary review.

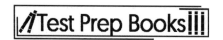

175. Edison is the chief financial officer (CFO) for a large accounting firm. He has recently been briefed on new legal regulations that require the company to change and update financial policies. If the organization does not comply with the new requirements and within the designed time frame, it could face substantial fines. Which of the following change management approaches would be the best option to use in this situation?

    a. Normative-reductive strategy

    b. Empirical-rational strategy

    c. Environmental-adaptive strategy

    d. Power-coercive strategy

Answer Explanations for Practice Test #2

1. C: Benchmarking compares an organization's initiatives or outcomes to those of competing organizations or industry standards to determine efficacy and added value to the organization. The other options listed do not apply.

2. A: Talent acquisition is the keystone of HR's value to an organization. HR is instrumental in strategic planning, Choice *B,* and in charge of training and development, Choice *C,* and recruitment and retention, Choice *D;* however, ensuring that the organization's needs are met with the human capital required to perform the job is a keystone to the HR function.

3. A: A root cause analysis is a systematic review of a larger issue that is broken down into smaller issues to determine the single "root cause" behind the larger issue. The aim of the root cause analysis is to resolve the root cause to have a positive domino effect on larger Issues.

4. B: The Patient Protection and Affordable Care Act is also known as Obamacare. This act made access to health care available to more Americans along with health care purchase options and subsidies to ensure affordability.

5. A: Employers are required to maintain group health insurance coverage for an employee who is out on FMLA leave. The coverage must be the same as prior to the FMLA leave. Spouses who work for the same employer receive a TOTAL of twelve weeks of FMLA time for the birth of their child, making Choice *B* incorrect. Employers can require employees to take their paid leave, such as vacation or sick leave, when using FMLA, and this requirement must be stated in the company policies, making Choice *C* incorrect. FMLA covers leave for the birth or adoption of a child; placement of a foster child; the serious health condition of the employee, spouse, child, or parent; and additional needs related to military servicemembers and caregivers, making Choice *D* incorrect.

6. A: The Age Discrimination in Employment Act of 1967 prohibits discrimination against anyone forty years of age or older regarding hiring, promotions, wages, benefits, termination, and other actions. The EEOC administers and oversees this law along with Title VII of the Civil Rights Act of 1964.

7. B: On-call time during which the employee cannot do any other activities is called "engaged to wait" and is compensable. Choice *A* is incorrect since the employee can use their time for their own purposes. This type of on-call status is called "waiting to be engaged" and is not compensable. Choice *C,* an employee traveling from their home to their normal worksite, is not required to be compensated.

8. C: If a lecture the employee attends is genuinely voluntary, outside of working hours, not job related, and no work activities take place, the employee does not need to be compensated for that time. Choice *A* is compensable since short rest periods, not including meal breaks, are typically paid. The time varies by state, but these are normally shorter than twenty minutes. Choice *B* and Choice *D* are both considered compensable working time, as they are traveling during normal working hours.

9. A: The best response to rolling out a new system, regardless of the function, is to provide in-person training that demonstrates the new system, uses, and functions. Additionally, pointing out the efficiencies and how the new system will positively impact the employee can increase engagement with the new system. Although a train-the-trainer program can be useful, Choice *B,* it is best to have one consistent training program to ensure the message and delivery are consistent. Additionally, an in-depth communication and training guide, Choice *C*, may work to ensure that all employees have information available to them in an easy-to-use guide, but it is not the best response out of the choices. This training guide could include the customer service contact information, Choice *D*, but if questions arise as to the functionality of the new system, an internal contact should be provided to employees. Choice *D* is not the best response to the new system.

10. A: Janelle is being friendly, providing support, showing kindness, and creating a positive work environment for the new employee. These are all aspects of building a relationship which promotes better teamwork and a positive work environment.

11. A: Adam's objective of having healthier employees is vague and ambiguous, with no measurable data points to successfully achieve this goal. Healthy employees are most definitely the business of an organization and can be achieved if done properly, making Choice *B* incorrect. The objective is not specific, and the defined tasks are all achievable, making Choice *C* incorrect. Finally, the objective should be defined further with specific measurements and data points before moving forward as either a departmental or individual objective, making Choice *D* incorrect.

12. B: To correct the objective, Adam should rewrite it using the SMART principles. The objective should be smart, measurable, achievable, relevant, and time-based. The SMART principles allow for measured success versus not knowing if an objective has been achieved. Choice *A* is incorrect because each of the tasks would still need to be written in a SMART manner; otherwise, the same issue exists. Choice *C* is incorrect because objectives should not be written as philosophical objectives but rather as tangible and achievable goals. Choice *D* is inaccurate because by keeping the original objective, the same problem of not being able to measure success exists regardless of how many tasks are identified to support the goal.

13. A: Networking outside of one's organization allows one to witness the successes of others, a learning experience that can benefit one's own workplace. The other options listed do not directly support professional growth.

14. D: As a leader, Dan should be more accessible to his employees, either through faster email responses or through a cellphone that is answered. A single weekly meeting is not sufficient to check in with a team, especially if an urgent issue arises.

15. D: This situation is likely to indicate that some barrier to inclusivity exists, and this is a cause for investigation, including follow-up with employees who may have resigned.

16. C: Stephanie needs to build rapport and relationships with her team before asking them for support and help with a project. She can maintain a private, personal life while interacting with others. Being kind, open, helpful, and engaging in small talk can assist in establishing relationships necessary to ensure a positive work environment.

17. B: A job analysis is an exercise used by HR professionals to determine the knowledge, skills, abilities, and experience required for a job to be performed successfully. A job analysis can also identify physical and environmental factors that could affect job performance. A classification study, Choice *A*, is an exercise used to determine if work currently being performed by an employee is appropriate based on the written job description. A skills gap assessment, Choice *C*, is an exercise to determine the skills and training needed by an employee to be successful in their current position or future positions. A SWOT

261

analysis, Choice *D*, is an exercise that reviews an organization's strengths, weaknesses, opportunities, and threats to assist with strategic planning and setting objectives.

18. B: This is a proactive, lean approach to find a solution for an existing problem. Cassandra also utilizes proven ways to communicate changes to her organization. The other options listed are not the actions of an engaged employee.

19. D: To navigate an organization to successfully implement HR initiatives, it is important to demonstrate an understanding of formal and informal work roles across the organization, not just limited to HR. Additionally, having an understanding of leadership goals and interests as well as employee relationships will assist in the successful implementation of initiatives.

20. A: An organization's policies that govern employees' actions, describe acceptable and unacceptable behaviors, and guide employee behavior with specific details is referred to as the code of conduct.

21. B: A gap analysis or root cause analysis can be used to determine when and why projects go off track. Understanding this is important to future tasks and projects so that issues can be managed before they become a problem. Although communicating issues, Choice *A*, holding a team meeting, Choice *C*, and *A* PowerPoint presentation of successful items, Choice *D*, are important, it is vital to understand what exactly will be done to correct the areas that were not completed successfully in the original project as well as to not repeat these in the future. Without knowing what needs to be done differently, these errors are likely to be repeated.

22. C: The risk management process begins with identifying the potential risks that may need to be mitigated in a process. Without establishing the risks, it is impossible for the team to map a timeline, communicate deliverables, or develop a plan to address them, making Choices *A, B,* and *D* incorrect.

23. C: Employ a variety of communication strategies such as email, text message, postcard, and Q&A sessions. Employee benefits such as health insurance and retirement planning are important but also complex and often difficult to understand, so it is HR's responsibility to present the essential facts that employees need to know to make decisions about their benefits. The best way to accomplish this is by using a variety of different methods than can appeal to employees' different communication styles. Some employees will learn better from face-to-face sessions, while others will appreciate being able to read the information in an email. Text messages and postcards can provide a small reminder that is enough to nudge employees to enroll without being overwhelming.

24. B: A major benefit of HR professionals networking outside of the organization is to learn about successful HR initiatives that have been implemented at other agencies and work to bring those initiatives into their own organization. External networking provides an excellent source of ideas from others who have wide and diverse experience. Choice *A* is incorrect because although career advancement and personal growth are benefits of external networking, there are numerous benefits for those who engage in networking. Choice *C* is incorrect because although networking may expose Olivia to new ideas and thoughts, which could in turn move her toward specific HR areas of work, this is not a specific benefit to the organization. Choice *D* is incorrect because although vendor recommendations may be provided by a professional network, this should not replace the formal process to review potential vendors.

25. C: The best thing for HR to do to assist Josie with this situation is to listen and work with her to find resolutions that may address the situation. This discussion may bring up new ideas and thoughts on how to move forward that HR can then discuss with Josie's manager to see if they are feasible. Choice *A* is incorrect because HR does not usually have the authority to remove work from another department's employees. Additionally, it is not appropriate to ensure when new employees will be hired with a current employee because if it doesn't occur, it could cause new problems. Choice *B* is not correct because although it may be a recommendation after speaking with Josie, HR should make recommendations and work to assist, not instruct, on specific actions for other departments. Choice *D* is incorrect because, based on the evaluation and background processes, it may not be possible to hire a new employee this quickly.

26. A: Cliff vesting refers to employees becoming 100 percent vested after a specific number of years of service. Cliff vesting has one eligibility point related to years of service, and once that is met, the employee is fully vested in the benefit. Graded vesting, Choice *B*, refers to a set schedule in which employees become vested at a certain percentage for each year of service. A typical graded vesting schedule would be 20 percent for each year, up to five years of service at which time the employee would be 100 percent vested. Immediate vesting, Choice *C*, refers to being automatically vested in 100 percent of the benefit—this would always apply to an employee's contributions regardless of a cliff vesting or graded vesting schedule. Eligibility vesting, Choice *D*, is also an incorrect answer choice.

27. D: An employee satisfaction survey is an excellent tool to establish how employees feel about internal programs, such as benefits and flexible work schedules.

28. C: To establish how the organization aligns with other agencies and competitors, a remuneration survey can be consulted to determine if the current salaries, benefits, and programs are in alignment with other agencies. Remuneration surveys are excellent sources to use as benchmarks.

29. D: It is vital to communicate with employees after requesting their participation in a survey. This ensures they know they are important to the process and that their feedback is vital to ensuring that proper programs are implemented.

30. B: Organizations that consistently rank high in diverse and inclusive business practices often base business decisions on personal needs of employees, such as offering spouse and dependent benefits to same-sex partners and offering paternity leave in addition to maternity leave.

31. A: Increased overtime would detract from work-life balance since it would take more time away from the employee's personal life. Choice *B*, telecommuting options, Choice *C*, onsite childcare, and Choice *D*, flexible schedules, are all ways a company can improve its employees' work-life balance.

32. A: Emotional intelligence refers to a person's capacity for positive human interaction and requires awareness of self, others, relationships, and surroundings. Higher emotional intelligence is associated with better communication and relationships.

33. B: Business technology is the formal term that refers to the software, online systems, applications, or innovations that automate or simplify tasks within an organization. Choices *A, C*, and *D* are incorrect because information systems, workplace resources, and reporting systems are all components of business technology and work together to further automate process.

34. C: The acronym MSDS stands for Material Safety Data Sheets. These sheets are required to include any potential hazards of the product and how to work with the product safely. Material Safety Data Sheets are vital to having a complete and effective health and safety program.

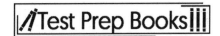

35. B: The best recommendation for Gabriel to include in his report is options to work with less hazardous materials and implement improved safety measures. It is unacceptable to counsel and discipline employees who are concerned about their safety and discuss these concerns with other employees, making Choice *A* incorrect. Additionally, even though new PPE may be required based on the new safety measurements, it would be the responsibility of the organization to purchase this equipment for employees, making Choice *C* incorrect. Although it may be prudent to notify OSHA depending on the safety concern, it will be the responsibility of the organization to propose and implement resolutions to address the concern, making Choice *D* incorrect.

36. C: To qualify for benefits under the Old Age, Survivor, and Disability Insurance Program, an employee must work at least 40 quarters, or 10 years.

37. B: The four areas the Equal Pay Act require to be equal when establishing if jobs are equivalent are skill, working conditions, effort, and responsibility. These factors allow for a clear comparison of positions to make a determination.

38. D: Sarah should reach out to Thiang to discuss the survey, specifically how the survey was created and how results were tallied to understand the data. It would also benefit Sarah to ask Thiang what didn't quite work or what should have been done differently to address these issues prior to initiating the survey. Choice *A* is incorrect because Sarah should not ask Thiang to do this same process with her department. Thiang may offer to assist, but Sarah should not expect another individual to conduct work that is within her scope of responsibilities. Choice *B* is incorrect because Sarah is working blindly and trying to figure out what was done so that she can attempt to re-create the process and products. Choice *C* is incorrect because it is highly unlikely that funding would be approved for a survey such as this, especially since one was just conducted in-house at a low, or even no, cost.

39. C: The best way for HR leadership to communicate appropriate and acceptable behaviors within the workplace is to consistently behave in an ethical, reliable, and acceptable manner. Choices *A, B,* and *D* are all acceptable best practices to ensure that the message of what is appropriate behavior is communicated frequently; however, the best way to communicate this is to model the behavior on a daily basis.

40. A: The Age Discrimination in Employment Act of 1967 prohibits discrimination against anyone forty years of age or older regarding hiring, promotions, wages, benefits, termination, and other actions. The EEOC administers and oversees this law along with Title VII of the Civil Rights Act of 1964.

41. C: As a less experienced employee, Masao should receive clear guidance from his manager on what he expects to receive as a result of Masao's research. Additionally, they should work together to review goals for the potential initiative so that Masao can better filter his results and key findings.

42. D: It helps workers become more invested in their professional development. Although many development programs may be extended throughout an organization or limited to specific business areas and departments, an IDP is tailored to an employee's specific needs and created with their input and objectives in mind. This makes workers more invested and involved in their own future success. Choice *A* is not correct because HR should still be involved with helping employees create and manage their IDPs. Choices *B* and *C* are not correct because the purpose of an IDP is to give employees a roadmap for their own development, not to create opportunities for punitive measures or micromanagement.

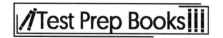
43. B: Open communication is the most crucial component of fostering collaboration among a team because it minimizes resistance, offers opportunities for individuals to lead, promotes an encouraging environment, and can eliminate a fear of retribution. Maintaining a positive attitude, Choice *A,* and showing appreciation, Choice *C,* are elements of open communication, and building interpersonal relationships, Choice *D,* is a by-product of having open communication.

44. C: Demonstrating how an initiative will bring value to each stakeholder is the best way to get buy-in for a new initiative. While looking professional and ensuring that all devices are working properly are important too, the question specifies *during the proposal* and not before. Finally, employees should not offer to pay out of pocket for company initiatives.

45. B: Offer guided benefits counseling and advice leading up to the enrollment period. While employees are attracted by an organization's benefits package, realistically, many employees get overwhelmed by the wealth of options and the decision-making factors that go into benefits enrollment. HR should offer accessible, plain-language information to employees, including offering personal guidance to walk employees through their benefits selection. Choice *A* is not the best choice because, while HR should constantly evaluate whether it is offering meaningful benefits to employees, HR should first consider whether poor communications rather than unpopularity of options is preventing people from enrolling. Choice *C* should also be eliminated because employees generally need more—not less—assistance when it comes to understanding their healthcare options; this choice removes all HR guidance from the process. Choice *D* is also not the best way of addressing the underlying problem.

46. C: There is a clear disparity between the director's expectations and employees' performance ability, so HR should review the job description with the director and update it to reflect key skills and abilities. HR needs to make sure that a capable candidate is selected for this position, and that begins with outlining the key responsibilities of the job. Job descriptions should be reviewed and updated regularly to ensure that they align with the actual skills and abilities needed to perform the essential job functions; since wrongly-qualified people keep getting placed in the job, it is likely that the job description is outdated and is attracting the wrong candidates.

Choice *A* is not the best answer because while it may save time on filling the position, it could also overburden other employees. Choice *B* is also not a good choice; the job is described as entry-level, part-time work, so experienced workers with advanced degrees would be overqualified. Choice *D* is also not the best answer because, while management may play a role in the assistant's success, it is impossible to determine without further review. Also, were that the case, HR should work to provide guidance to the manager rather than simply adding a negative note to their evaluation.

47. A: Set up new employees with a mentor and proactively identify any skills gaps. Mentoring can help aid employee satisfaction and retention, and it can help aid their integration into a new workplace. Also, by identifying skills gaps, HR can provide timely training opportunities for improved employee performance. Choice *B* is not a good choice because it cuts off an important external relationship for the organization. Choice *C,* hiring temporary workers, would only exacerbate the problem of high turnover. Finally, Choice *D* is not a good choice because clearly communicating with the director regarding department staffing needs is important for selecting the appropriate candidate.

48. C: The best option for Julian is to conduct a specific training program for the mid-level managers who lack the identified skills. He should ensure that the employees have an opportunity to learn these skills prior to taking any further actions. Julian may want to research external training programs, Choice

265

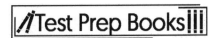

A; however, it is his responsibility to roll out this training to the employees, not to simply make them aware of the training. Although indicating the need for this skill in performance evaluations, Choice *B,* may be necessary in the future, it is important to ensure that employees have the opportunity to increase their knowledge and skills in these areas first. The same is true regarding recruiting new employees with this skill set, Choice *D.*

49. B: Accounting for the organization's needs and interests that represent a large majority of the employees in the organization is the best way to select initiatives that will be useful, welcomed, and supported.

50. D: A written project proposal that outlines the timeline, milestones, needed resources, and dates for deliverables is a useful method to make sure all stakeholders have the same expectations. Choice *A* is incorrect; stakeholder mapping should identify initiative value, not avoid it. Choice *B* is incorrect; a project proposal should include a financial analysis. Choice *C* is incorrect, as this would not be helpful in clear communication and getting everyone on the same page.

51. D: An organization's workforce and all those affected by its social, economic, and environmental impact. Stakeholders include everyone, both internal and external, influenced by an organization's operations. Choice *A* limits itself only to leadership, so it is incorrect. Choice *B* limits itself to the workforce, but stakeholders include people outside the workforce. Choice *C* is also incorrect because it considers only those influenced by the organization's economic impact.

52. D: When working with multiple stakeholders to develop a new initiative, one should select an interest that is held by the most stakeholders to provide value to as many people for the least amount of resources. HR professionals should be sure not to favor one particular stakeholder's interests, Choice *A,* not to select randomly, Choice *B,* and not to make initial inquiries solely via email, Choice *C,* because it can make the process seem impersonal and unimportant.

53. B: The best way for Cynthia to ensure that this new benefits program favors all employees equally and does not cater to any particular groups is to standardize the program and make it equally accessible to all employees. Although Choices *A, C,* and *D* are options that can be included in the rollout of the program, they do not actually ensure equality and accessibility of the benefit for all employees. Communication of a process used when making a decision, assurance of equity, and support from executive leadership are all best practices that could assist in the support and implementation of the program but would not ensure equity of the program itself.

54. B: Creating pockets of time during the day to cultivate positive interactions with colleagues is an effective way to work on intrapersonal skills. The other options listed would be inappropriate and socially unacceptable responses to a performance review.

55. D: Team members may be assigned by project rather than personally chosen; therefore, it is important to develop wide-ranging engagement skills that promote positive interactions. This is crucial to job satisfaction, since employees often spend full days with their team members. If they do not get along with their team, they will likely be miserable at work.

56. D: Corporate culture refers to the general attitude toward regular workday activities and how employees interact with one another. The categories listed have nothing to do with customers, life outside of work, or freebies, making Choices *A, B,* and *C* incorrect.

57. C: A reduction of legal liabilities is considered a quantitative benefit of a robust CSR program because it is a metric that can be measured, or quantified. Qualitative benefits include improved employee engagement, Choice *A*, a more positive workplace, Choice *B,* and an increase in employee satisfaction, Choice *D.* These benefits, although critical and important, are not measured in the same manner and are considered qualitative.

58. A: Research and design meaningful job descriptions for desired new roles. Whenever new job positions are added to an organization, HR is responsible for creating the job descriptions for them. The job descriptions serve as a blueprint for hiring and organizing the expanded workforce. Particularly because these positions play an innovative and cutting-edge role in the organization, HR may need to conduct research by looking at similar jobs in other organizations to determine what to include in the scope of the job description. Choice *B* is not a good choice because laying off experienced employees to make way for unfilled positions is premature and will lead to staffing instability. Choice *C* is also not a good choice because HR should present workable solutions to help achieve future goals, and changing management is part of that. Finally, Choice *D* is not the best answer because, while some internal transfers may be possible, there is a difference between technical and academic skills. And again, the job descriptions must be in place before filling any roles.

59. A: Survey employees to determine other rewards that might be valuable to workers but affordable to the company, such as flexible work scheduling. HR is responsible for designing fair and competitive total rewards packages; however, not all rewards are monetary or tangible. HR should work to determine what rewards are most valuable to employees and may find that some of these come at a lower cost to the organization. Choice *B* is not the best answer because HR should be more proactive about advocating for fair employee compensation. Choice *C* is also incorrect because it would take too long to carry out this transition and might also make it hard to hire qualified workers in the future. Also, while Choice *D* might be a good step in designing employee rewards, it does not present an overall solution to the current situation.

60. C: Conduct a skills gap analysis to determine the capabilities of the current workforce, identify missing skills, and develop a plan to fill the gap. Strategic planning involves determining where an organization currently stands, where it wants to be, and the steps it needs to take to move from the present to the future. The same is also true of its workforce—HR needs to know the current capabilities of employees and plan how to fill any gaps that impede future performance. Choice *A* is something that would be handled by staff in the new department, not by HR. Choice *B* might be a good idea, letting employees know about the future of the organization, but it does not present actionable solutions for achieving the strategic plan. Finally, Choice *D* is not the best answer because it focuses on past trends rather than future goals.

61. C: Transactional HR work is administrative in nature and includes services such as payroll and benefits administration. Transactional work can include preparing and processing new-hire paperwork, employee benefits enrollment or updating benefits selections, and entering performance evaluations into a tracking system.

62. D: The training should be reported as time worked because this is considered a postliminary task per the Portal-to-Portal Act, which is an amendment to the FLSA. Because the training is job related and was recommended by the supervisor, this time should be paid at the employee's normal rate of pay and, if necessary, the overtime rate.

63. B: Sustainability of a new initiative is a fundamental component to determine its effectiveness. Positive results that are immediate are always fantastic; however, these positive results should be sustained over a period of time to determine the overall effectiveness of an initiative, program, or solution.

64. A: When HR professionals collaborate with business partners outside of HR, they are bringing to the table different strengths and experiences that can provide diverse and innovative solutions to concerns HR may not be aware of or understand. HR professionals do not typically work in the same environments as other employees and may not have an understanding of the daily operations and issues employees face. By bringing individuals who have this experience to the table, a more holistic solution can be considered because multiple perspectives and expertise are being taken into account.

65. B: HR can participate in the strategic planning to offer input and highlight areas where workforce goals can be aligned with overall company goals. HR participation is essential from the earliest stages of the strategic planning process to provide insight and predict challenges and solutions related to HR. Choice *A* is not the best choice because HR should contribute to the planning process; senior-level leaders might not be able to anticipate all the workforce challenges involved with the expansion. Choice *C* is also not the best choice. HR should always work to improve and innovate its processes. However, when opening new stores, the company first wants to establish a consistent brand and culture with existing stores. It would not make sense to introduce too many uncertainties to the new project. Finally, while Choice *D* might be a good step for HR to take in reviewing and evaluating the strategic plan, it is not the best choice because there are many other proactive measures that HR should take first.

66. A: Time-to-hire. This is the KPI most closely related to filling the positions at the expanded locations. Knowing the current time-to-hire helps the company budget for how long it will take to recruit and onboard new employees based on the number of vacancies and available HR staff. The other choices do not refer to KPI that measure things related to hiring.

67. B: Jobs within an organization are developed based on goals and objectives established by leadership to ensure that qualified employees perform duties that contribute to the overall interests of the organization. Establishing jobs with this criterion helps to establish a robust candidate selection pool as well as ensuring that the selected individual is performing tasks and duties that align with the organizational, departmental, and divisional goals.

68. D: Depending on the candidates that apply for jobs at this new site, immigration and work visas will need to be considered based on what is required by Irish law.

69. A: To make workforces more diverse, organizations sometimes need to focus on actively recruiting underrepresented candidates that have qualifying credentials and experiences for the position. Workplaces that are more diverse are associated with better financial gains and higher rates of employee retention, reported satisfaction, and performance. However, qualified candidates sometimes are unaware of job opportunities or may not feel comfortable being the minority in an organization.

70. D: Veronica is specifically addressing the "mini-cultures" that have been created within each site. By establishing consistent policies and practices, she can work to align the sites in how operations are conducted. Choice *A* is incorrect because individual concerns regarding behavior should be addressed separately and specifically in alignment with policy. Choice *B* is incorrect because workplace climate

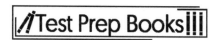
refers to the mood and pulse of the employees within an organization. Choice *C* is incorrect because resource allocation refers to the personnel who are conducting the work needed.

71. B: Veronica should ensure that she is fully aware of and understands all applicable state laws and regulations when establishing new policies and procedures. State laws could provide additional benefits or require additional levels of compliance, and the policies and procedures should reflect this to ensure alignment. Choices *A, C,* and *D* are all pieces of information that may prove to be helpful when reviewing which policies to update or specifically address, but policy should not be created specific to employee demographics, supervisory complaints, or customer sales.

72. C: Auditing diversity and inclusion practices provide an organization the ability to ensure they are sustainable. Choice *A,* troubleshooting, is a term that refers to solving an issue or discovering the reason behind a problem. Choice *B,* recruiting, is a term that refers to the hiring process of new employees. Choice *D,* brainstorming, refers to the process in which ideas are discussed among a team to deliver new options to accomplish a task.

73. D: Based on the current demographics of the team, the most appropriate sourcing method would be external sourcing. By sourcing candidates externally, the team will be provided with a new employee who will bring new experiences and ideas to the group, which could produce better team and individual results, including new perspectives and ways to work. Although it may be prudent to also include an internal sourcing method at some point in the process, an external sourcing method would be the best approach.

74. B: The best course of action is for Joseph to discuss the complaints with the department manager and consider allowing internal candidates to apply for the position along with the external candidates. Although Joseph could follow up with employees to communicate the sourcing strategy and its importance, Choice *A,* the complaints were specific to not being allowed to apply for the position, and therefore this action will not address the main issues. Joseph should work with the department manager, and HR should own any communications to employees regarding a recruitment strategy, Choices *C* and *D.*

75. B: A Myers-Briggs personality assessment or an equivalent personality test may be a great option for Joseph to add to the process. This test will show personality differences as well as communication styles, leadership styles, and other important pieces of information that could help Joseph and the department manager make the best candidate selection. Although written exams, sample work assignments, and additional interviews could provide important information, they generally will not allow for specific personality traits to be displayed.

76. A: HRIS, or HR information systems, are a component of business technology that automates a great deal of HR-related paperwork and other tedious tasks.

77. C: In this case, it seems as though Barbara might be favored even though all four candidates are equally qualified. Utilizing a panel of interviewers can reduce or eliminate any unconscious or conscious biases that a single leader may have during the hiring process.

78. A: Although all of the data options are excellent pieces of information, one of the most important pieces of data is the turnover rate. The turnover rate is the percentage of employees leaving the workforce during a specific period of time. Turnover rates should be calculated at an organizational,

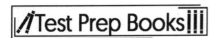

departmental, and divisional level to determine specific pockets of the organization that may be experiencing a higher turnover than others.

79. B: An HR professional can incorporate exit interviews to the process when individuals resign from an organization to gain insight into why they are leaving. Exit interviews can include questions specific to compensation, job benefits, retirement, leave benefits, training, supervisory relationships, and other items that can help HR determine if there is a root cause that needs to be addressed. Choices *A, C,* and *D* are incorrect because they are all tools that can be used to provide other important information separate from when an employee resigns.

80. D: HR professionals have numerous customers, including everyone who works within the organization. They should strive to communicate with and assist all employees, regardless of their position and level. Respecting and making a commitment to all employees is vital to ensuring robust relationships and establishing a positive work environment.

81. D: HR responsibilities have a major influence on other departments within the organization. HR professionals' determination of what talent the organization needs, who is hired to fill these needs, how employees are compensated, how to mitigate personnel liabilities, and so forth should be based off internal demands of the organization. If Vera does not know this information, she cannot make appropriate hiring decisions.

82. B: Taking the time to teach the manager how to use a new system is the best way to show support without taking over the manager's responsibilities or ignoring expressed concerns.

83. D: Data protection is the process of securing personal information from identity theft or other corruptive activities. This process involves storing important materials, such as employment data that includes social security numbers, dates of birth, dependent information, and other highly sensitive data. The principal purpose of data protection is to maintain the integrity and proper storage of information. Workplace monitoring, Choice *A,* refers to a policy employers use to monitor suspicious activity within the organization and gather information to investigate. Surveillance techniques, Choice *B,* refer to particular methods, such as wiretapping or Global Positioning System (GPS) tracking, to monitor an employee's actions. Internal monitoring, Choice *C,* is a different term that could be used to describe workplace monitoring.

84. A: Workplace monitoring is a specific policy employers use to monitor a suspicious person within the organization and gather information to investigate the activity. Surveillance techniques, Choice *B,* refer to particular methods, such as wiretapping or GPS tracking, to monitor an employee's actions. External monitoring, Choice *C,* is not a correct answer. Data protection, Choice *D,* is the process of securing personal information from identity theft or other corruptive activities.

85. C: Technology management is important to the HR function because it implements and employs technology-focused solutions that support, facilitate, and deliver effective services. Additionally, technology management stores critical employee data. Technology management does identify and implement technology solutions that benefit HR as well as invests in software that increases productivity; however, these are standard functions of technology management and not specific to the HR function, and therefore Choices *A* and *B* are incorrect. Choice *D* is incorrect because HR professionals are responsible for analyzing the functionality of the resources to ensure effectiveness and then work with the IT professionals to prepare a technology management plan to address.

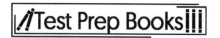

86. C: Security standards for protecting sensitive employee data. HR must ensure that industry-standard security practices are in place when it comes to protecting sensitive employee records. Choice *A* is something that HR professionals should develop within their organization, and it does not need to be provided by the vendor. Choice *B* is also part of the organization's due diligence to fully understand the platform it is adopting. Choice *D* is not a good choice because it is impossible to fully guarantee that any storage system is completely invulnerable; it is more important to ensure that the vendor is complying with the latest security standards and is equipped to deal with security threats.

87. B: The most appropriate method for learning about the business operations of an organization is to review available internal documents, external literature, and customer service surveys.

88. B: Anna and the organization would greatly benefit from implementing a robust HRIS that can manage, track, update, and report on employee information. It is critical that organizations embrace technology and new ways of being productive, efficient, and accurate.

89. A: The best way for Kevin to ensure a seamless transition is to work with the vendor to guarantee that a dual interface between the current and new programs is offered. This will allow employees to gain a better understanding of the new system and how it relates to the legacy system. A clean break of turning off the legacy program will eventually need to occur; however, it is best to not do this immediately, making Choice *B* incorrect. Additionally, although it is important to continue to receive employee feedback on the new system, it should not be used to look at other vendors and software platforms, making Choice *C* incorrect. The feedback could, however, be used to improve the new platform. It is not in the best interest of employees or employers to have two functional systems. This can create confusion, errors, and overall, an unproductive and inefficient working environment, making Choice *D* incorrect.

90. C: Kevin should ensure that the new vendor's contract addresses security standards for protecting and safeguarding employee data. Reporting metrics and written guarantees, Choices *A* and *B*, are usually standard items within a contract, but these items do not specifically address employee data security. Password protocols, Choice *D,* are typically not part of a vendor contract but may be required as part of the operating procedures for the software.

91. D: When establishing a project's milestones and objectives, flexibility is important to understand. Conditions may change outside of the team's control that need to be accounted for, which could result in making updates and changes to the project's status. Additional resources could be needed, team members could need more training, or the budget may have been constricted due to financial changes. All of these issues could result in the need to allow flexibility in the project, milestones, and achievements.

92. A: Choice *A* is the inaccurate statement because a PEST analysis is a formal, structured tool used to determine trends that could influence an organization. Choices *B, C,* and *D* are not correct because they are all accurate statements regarding a PEST analysis. A PEST analysis should be used by HR to guide work, should include internal and external resources, and often indicates process changes to mitigate risks.

93. A: Payroll functions are typically managed through a separate information system. Although there will most likely be connectivity between the HRIS and payroll system, they are separate systems that manage technology specific to the function. HRIS manages historical data, Choice *B,* employee

271

documents, Choice *C,* and candidate and employee profiles, Choice *D,* among other important information.

94. A: Six Sigma is the approach that has many tools available to determine the resources a project may need. From process mapping to value stream mapping, these tools can be instrumental in the success of a project.

95. C: Ambiguity, or being vague, when communicating with employees can cause confusion, conflict, and distress. When employees do not have a clear direction, they will not be motivated or engaged to do their best work, and therefore, Choices *A, B,* and *D* are incorrect. When an organization's leader is ambiguous in their communications, results will not include employees going above and beyond, innovative and productive work, or lower turnover and higher satisfaction.

96. B: Deidre is engaging in networking by interacting with others in both formal and informal settings. Networking is a means to build valuable relationships and create support systems among peers and colleagues.

97. B: The industry standard for required competencies in this position. Because this effort is intended to standardize positions within different departments of the same organization, HR is less likely to consider outside evaluation criteria. Looking at industry standards for job positions is relevant when crafting new job descriptions, which is not the objective in this case. All the other choices refer to important criteria about the qualifications, type of work, and organizational structure essential to the function of the position.

98. C: Job enrichment. Job enrichment refers to increasing a job's depth by adding new responsibilities to an existing job title. Choice *D,* job enlargement, refers to broadening the scope of a job by adding new tasks. Job evaluation and job elaboration are not established HR terms.

99. A: Judy completed a job specification. A job specification is a detailed statement of the essential parts of a particular class of jobs. It includes a summary of the duties to be performed and responsibilities and qualifications necessary to do the job.

100. A: HR should first reach out to the supervisor. The issue could easily be remedied with an in-person discussion to be sure the supervisor is aware of the situation and has an understanding of how to ensure the employee is not using leave that has not yet been accrued.

101. C: Since facility employees often work outdoors, they could truly be sicker in December, which is a colder month. Lars cannot jump to conclusions from a single data collection without investigating all potential variables. There are no indicators in the case as described that he is showing confirmation bias or that there are issues with his data software.

102. A: Focus groups use a skilled facilitator to organize, administer, and manage the sessions. These facilitators solicit feedback and opinions about specific topics and questions identified by the organization prior to the sessions.

103. A: The best data collection method for Jose to use to gather employee satisfaction information would be a paper survey. Because there are no resources available, he could prepare a paper survey and send it out to employees to complete and submit. Choice *B* is incorrect because focus groups are targeted discussions, usually conducted by a facilitator, to discuss specific issues and gain insight about a process. Choice *C* is not the best option because meeting with individuals would take an extreme amount of time and not allow for any level of confidentiality and may not produce the best results. Choice *D* is also incorrect because without resources, Jose may not be able to produce the tools necessary to initiate a survey and employees may not be receptive to taking an online survey.

104. C: Employees are encouraged to develop interpersonal skills because these skills allow for a more effective and productive working relationship with others. Choices *A, B,* and *D* are incorrect because these circumstances rely on multiple factors, not just an employee's interpersonal skills, that would need to be considered relative to an employee's readiness for a promotion and their satisfaction with work-life balance and the job.

105. A: Contract with a vendor that offers interface layer technology to develop a new user interface while maintaining the existing system. Because the main issue is the user interface—that is, the part of the software that employees use to access and manage the data—interface layer technology can help to extend the usefulness of the system. Although it is important to stay on top of technology developments, it is impractical and costly to make major system changes that may not be necessary.

106. C: Being a data advocate allows for the use of data to make informed business decisions and propose appropriate recommendations. It also allows for a number of benefits and additional credibility to the HR professional proposing the changes.

107. B: Data should be recent and relevant while answering questions the organization may have regarding the analysis. If the data cannot be confirmed as to when it was collected or how it was collected, it should not be used, making Choice *A* incorrect. Furthermore, data should not be used simply because it supports or does not support a particular recommendation because this creates bias, making Choices *C* and *D* incorrect.

108. D: According to the Equal Pay Act, equivalent jobs are required to have equal skill, working conditions, effort, and responsibility. Choices *A, B,* and *C* are incorrect because the act does allow for pay differentials for seniority, merit, production quantity or quality, and geographic work differentials.

109. A: Online surveys can be quickly distributed to a large group of people, can collect any type of information the researcher needs, and do not have paper waste. However, since surveys can have low completion rates, Mina may need to send regular follow up reminders or ask leadership to make the survey required to reach her completion goal.

110. D: The word-of-mouth communication can spread information quickly; however, individuals may inaccurately represent the information, which can lead to misinformation and misunderstandings. The individual who initiated the information can quickly lose control over the message, its accuracy, and its effectiveness.

111. D: To ensure that all disciplines have appropriate resources and work could continue when a team member must be out of the office unexpectedly, Hannah should have identified not only a primary team member to be responsible for the discipline but also a secondary team member. Having this backup allows the knowledge to be transferred and shared with more than one team member and alleviates situations that could arise and jeopardize getting the work done.

112. D: Transparency is a vital component of communication that builds trust within an organization and between employees.

113. C: HR professionals should not make any assumptions behind communications. They can make educated guesses to provide context, but if they truly cannot be objective in their reasoning, they should solicit more information from the person with whom they are communicating.

114. A: Taking online personality surveys, such as Myers-Briggs, to determine one's personal strengths is not a way to build professional credibility. Such inventories can be helpful, in certain circumstances, if administered to job candidates to determine the most appropriate fit given the job responsibilities.

115. D: Stakeholders are extremely valuable to initiatives, and their questions should be answered thoroughly, accurately, and promptly. Although Xiaoli did not know the answers to her stakeholder's questions, she offered to find out and provided a specific timeframe in which she would provide them.

116. C: Focus groups work to solicit feedback and opinions about certain topics while engaging the group through a facilitator. Unfortunately, focus groups run the risk of low participation or engagement and could have an issue with facilitator bias.

117. A: Once the decision to implement a workforce reduction has been made, it is critical to immediately communicate with employees. This communication should include information such as the specific decision, process moving forward, and timeline. Although it will be important to create separation agreements, Choice *B*, this is not an immediate need and can be addressed further along in the process. Additionally, a hiring freeze, Choice *C,* may be necessary across all departments, but communicating first to current employees to ensure productivity continues during the process is crucial. Attempting to change the decision, Choice *D,* at this point in the process is usually not worthwhile because by this stage, all other avenues have been reviewed and there are no other options to resolve the matter.

118. D: Outplacement services provide career counseling, resume writing, and interview preparation to assist separated employees with future employment.

119. C: Samantha and the executive team should immediately focus on boosting the morale of the remaining employees to ensure that productivity does not suffer as a result of the reductions. Samantha may want to implement a new best practice by checking in with the separated employees to see if they have been employed, Choice *A;* however, this is not mandatory and should only be done when all other checkpoints have been completed. Although new reports, Choice *B,* will eventually be created to show the new profit and loss information, it should not be the initial focus of leadership. Although future reductions may be necessary, Choice *D,* it should not be an immediate concern to address but only looked into after a new, thorough review of the organization's productivity and profitability.

120. B: James is doing a great job in establishing various methods of communication to ensure that all employees are engaged and have an opportunity to connect. Establishing an open-door policy gives employees the opportunity to meet with James one-on-one outside of their normal work environment. Employees may not feel comfortable bringing up issues in front of other coworkers or even a supervisor, and therefore this gives them another venue to communicate freely.

121. D: Gaining knowledge about the business and operations, such as financial information, is a benefit of being able to serve as a team leader. This can be rewarding—both personally and professionally. Choices *A* and *B* are incorrect because communicating with others, supervising, and directing work are specific job duties a team leader would engage in and not examples of a benefit gained by serving in this role. Choice *C* is incorrect because an HR professional should never reach the endpoint of their professional development but should always strive to continue learning and growing.

122. D: In all HR-related matters, staff members should welcome competing points of view, remain objective, and not take attacks personally. HR professionals often have to deal with emotional topics, so they should prepare to remain calm and professional in such events.

123. C: During the interview process, Monica should ask questions about the communication and rollout plans should she be selected as the retirement administrator. Retirement services and options, Choice *A,* retirement plans for employees, Choice *B,* and fixed costs, Choice *D,* should have been included in the cost proposal provided.

124. A: These topics cover the relationship that Louise expects to have with the vendor leading up to the fair and during the event. The vendor's business history, work history, and services are items that should have been reviewed (such as online or over the phone) before taking the time to meet with the vendor. The vendor's personal health philosophy is not relevant.

125. A: Break rooms are not places where formal work matters take place, such as the other options listed. However, it is an area where employees convene, relax, and often discuss work in an informal way that can often generate new and creative ideas.

126. C: Active listening is when the participants are engaged in the discussion and using senses beyond just hearing, such as body language. Active listeners engage in the discussion but allow the speaker to fully communicate their thoughts and concerns without interruption.

127. D: The leadership team will most likely approve the new benefits program being recommended. Edward has based his recommendation on current data, both internally and externally, as well as input from current employees, and therefore the leadership team can have confidence in the analysis. The first step that should be taken when a decision needs to be made is to examine relevant data and research. Edward has done this and gone further in his analysis by conducting the sessions with employees.

128. D: Although it is necessary for all employees to carry out the requirements of the job, it is not a component of being an effective leader. Effective leadership skills include managing time in the most financially responsible manner, Choice *A,* solving problems as they arise, Choice *B,* and strategic thinking, Choice *C.*

129. A: The *New York Times* is a reputable publication, and the case study is an in-depth investigation at a large business. The other sources are not very credible, as they either have not successfully tried testing this initiative or utilized a very small sample size (which cannot be statistically significant).

130. A: Common HR personnel tasks include developing job postings. Although workplace investigations, Choice *B,* benefits programs , Choice *C,* and paperwork, Choice *D,* are all responsibilities performed within the HR function, usually these tasks are performed at a higher level.

131. B: An inappropriate response to this situation would be to simply accept Martin's recommendations and proceed forward with his excessively high qualifications for an entry-level position. Martin is setting up unrealistic qualifications that do not match an entry-level position. He may not realize that he is establishing an artificial recruitment barrier and potential discriminatory hiring

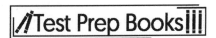

practice. Additionally, with such high qualifications for an entry-level position, Martin may not get many candidates, which is a much lesser concern than having a discriminatory hiring practice. Ally should meet with Martin to discuss equitable positions within the organization, Choice A, and comparable positions to benchmark against outside the organization, Choice D, as well as to provide options for him to establish qualifications that better align with the position, Choice C.

132. C: Employee satisfaction and morale rate, Choice C, is not an outcome of the performance management process. This rate is determined by an employee survey to establish what the organization does well and what needs to be improved. Standard outcomes of the performance management process are salary increases and promotions, growth and development opportunities, and disciplinary actions and training needs, Choices A, B, and D.

133. D: The best decision for Karen to make is to hire candidate B based on the passion, motivation, and experience aligning with the needs of the department and position. Choice A is not a feasible option because budgets and staffing are determined well in advance of recruitments. Choice B is not an appropriate option because Karen is the hiring manager and therefore tasked with making this decision. She should not push this decision up to the next level in the organization; this is part of her responsibilities. Choice C is not the best option because if an employee is not motivated and passionate prior to starting with a new organization, these qualities probably cannot be instilled later.

134. B: Strategic HR work focuses on multiple departments, or even the entire organization, with an emphasis on the company's vision, mission, and goals. Although this work may be transformational, Choice A, it is primarily defined as strategic in nature. Tactical HR work, Choice C, focuses on workplace solutions for the day-to-day operations, whereas transactional HR work, Choice D, focuses on the administrative tasks.

135. A: The LEAST effective communication method listed is allowing information to trickle down. This method places the burden on each level of the organization to not only communicate the information but to do so in a manner that is consistent each and every time. HR should own the message by engaging with employees at all levels, providing guidance as needed, and implementing initiatives to address the needs identified within the survey feedback.

136. D: HR professionals regularly review, analyze, and interpret data. Being able to understand when the data does not make sense is vital to ensuring that appropriate recommendations are made based on the data. If one cannot recognize when there is an issue with a data set, improper results and decisions could be made, having far-reaching negative impacts. Although having this knowledge does mean Jessica can add it to her resume, Choice A, be more marketable as a candidate for future jobs, Choice B, and potentially be considered for a promotion opportunity, Choice C, this should not be the sole motivation for adding this skill set to her resume.

137. B: Sources should always be checked for any data report. Also, visual representations of data are more susceptible to misconstrue the true meaning and should always be examined further. Elias may find out that the study only surveyed six people, or that it was conducted at a career fair, which would contribute a level of bias.

138. B: Lisa should employ the single-unit bargaining strategy when negotiating with each union group. This will allow each group to bargain on behalf of the unique needs of the group of employees represented. It should be noted, however, that the union representatives for each group could be parallel bargaining at the same time. Union representatives could strategically use what each group bargains separately to promote their requests and wants. Although parallel bargaining is usually used by one union group with each organization they have agreements with, it can also be used between union groups within one organization.

139. B: Principled bargaining occurs when groups negotiate a contract while being aware and mindful of the key issues to each side. Principled bargaining is a process of finding solutions so that both sides gain from the agreement. Choices A and C, distributive bargaining and positional bargaining, both refer to bargaining that takes place to achieve a specific objective. Choice D, coordinated bargaining, refers to bargaining that occurs when multiple unions within one organization meet to negotiate as one group to benefit all employees.

140. C: During the preparation process prior to bargaining, Stephanie should focus on data and information that can be used to prepare offers and ideas to propose to the bargaining unit. Based on the financial status of the organization, an excellent tool Stephanie can deploy is a survey for employees. This survey can ask employees how they value different rewards and benefits so that the organization can come up with unique, valued rewards that are cost-effective and affordable to propose to the bargaining unit for the next contract. These rewards could help offset a salary expectation if they are valued by employees.

141. B: Multi-employer bargaining specifically refers to bargaining that occurs when a union with employees at multiple companies meets with all of the companies in one negotiation. Choices A, C, and D, whipsawing, leapfrogging, and parallel bargaining, all refer to when a union successfully negotiates an agreement with a company and then uses these results to deal with another company.

142. A: Amalia is engaging in the practice of negotiating in bad faith. Regardless of her own feelings about unions or how long it takes to negotiate a successor contract, she is putting the organization at risk by attempting to negotiate directly with employees. Amalia should work within the guidelines of negotiating in good faith and discuss any actions she believes are necessary with her negotiations team before taking action.

143. B: Principled bargaining occurs when both sides that are negotiating understand each other's concerns and agree to search for solutions together to reach an agreement.

144. C: Strategic plans are an ongoing and continuous process. Plans should be evaluated to determine effectiveness and whether new strategies or resources should be considered to accomplish the identified goals. Strategic plans should be regularly reviewed and updated as necessary to ensure the mission and vision of the organization are met.

145. D: When HR professionals are operating in a global environment, it is vital to conduct business with an understanding of and respect for differences in rules, laws, regulations, and accepted business operations and practices. Operating with this global mindset allows HR professionals to adhere to legal requirements as well as creating and fostering a healthy and productive workplace for employees.

146. A: When rolling out changes, especially ones that are sensitive or important, it is vital to ensure an understanding of the employees within the organization and the culture. Understanding these factors will assist in selecting the best strategy to use when rolling out changes, especially substantial changes. Small changes should be considered in the same light as substantial changes because the subject matter, although seemingly small in the scope of the larger business, may be a substantial change to an individual employee.

147. C: A cost-benefit analysis works to outline in specific detail costs related to a project regarding labor, equipment, materials, time, and other costs. This analysis shows how both short-term and long-term benefits will outweigh the costs and can be instrumental in gaining support from key stakeholders in agreeing to proceed with a new program or project where there are financial requirements.

148. C: HR professionals often have to manage contradictory practices or needs to ensure alignment within a project. Robert should communicate the overall objective with the location managers while working to understand their individual, specific needs. He may be able to work within the planning process to address these needs or discuss how they can be addressed in other ways.

149. A: Sylvia should survey all employees because anyone could have a need for parental leave, not just female employees who have used maternity leave. Additionally, although some employees may not need parental leave, they may have ideas that could be useful to consider when developing the policy.

150. C: Workplace policies should strictly follow federal laws to legally secure a workplace that satisfies minimum standards regarding health, safety, security, privacy, and benefits. The policy should provide equal or greater benefits than the federal regulations to be in compliance. Benefits can never be less than what the federal regulations mandate. Additionally, organizations must create policies that align with federal as well as state regulations, so mirroring federal laws may not align with the state laws.

151. D: When the HR department has a presence within different business units, the service model being used is a decentralized model. A decentralized model focuses on having HR individuals assigned to specific areas and working within that specific department, unit, or location.

152. A: When the HR department has one corporate presence over the entire organization, the service model being used is a centralized model. A centralized model focuses on having HR employees from a main office oversee management functions in a separate unit.

153. B: HR professionals can provide specific and specialized training to make sure managers understand any new regulations, laws, or policies. It is especially important for managers to understand how these changes will impact them on a daily basis. Offering an opportunity to ask questions and discuss specific situations can also ensure that managers fully understand the changes. HR professionals should also be available on an as-needed basis to answer questions and offer advice on situations that arise.

154. A: Klaus should confirm that the data sources are recent (within three years) and relevant to the positions he is reviewing within his own organization. Choices *B, C,* and *D* are incorrect because they do not support the actual validity or relevancy of the data, and Klaus should not be seeking data that supports a predetermined conclusion.

155. D: Klaus should schedule a meeting to discuss the study, including the position analysis the employee completed and the data used to make the determination. By providing the employee with this information, there may be an understanding of why the decision was made. Additionally, if there was information that Klaus missed or misunderstood, he may want to take this into account and revise the recommendations. Choice *A* is not correct because this is not the best way to communicate this type of decision and could create a negative working environment for the employee and coworkers. Choice *B* is not correct; this message should be owned by Klaus because this was his survey. By passing the

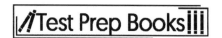

responsibility to the manager, there is an increased opportunity for misinformation that could cause further issues. Choice *C* is not correct; Klaus should follow up with the employee because this is the professional thing to do. Although there may not be an opportunity for Klaus to revise his study and recommendations, follow-up is important to ensure good working relationships and customer service.

156. D: An employer is required to bring the veteran back to their position or equivalent position if they leave for active military service. The employer is also required to provide all length of service benefits that employee would have received if they were actively working for the employer the time they left to serve. Choice *C* is incorrect as the employer is responsible to maintain the position for five years or less.

157. A: An employer cannot discriminate against employees that have or plan to serve in the military. There also is an obligation to review candidates and use comparable skills from their military experience to the job that they are applying for. USERRA rules are for applicants and current employees. Choice *B* is incorrect because not hiring based on future service would be discrimination. Choice *C* is incorrect since previous military experience should be considered. Choice *D* is incorrect since USERRA has rules for applicants as well as current employees.

158. C: HR can work to ensure an unbiased and fair recruitment and selection process by establishing an interview panel with stakeholders from other departments who interact with this position. This panel can interview all candidates and make a selection based on the qualities of the individuals. Although the finance director may be a part of this panel or have the final decision of who will be selected, incorporating this step in the process will help to ensure an unbiased process. Choice *A* is incorrect because all employees should have the ability to apply for any position within an organization regardless of relationships outside of the workplace. Choice *B* is incorrect because although it should be expected that a director will always act with the best intentions, employees may not have this same understanding and think there is bias. Any actions that can be taken to eliminate even the perception of bias will help to ensure all parties are happy with the process. Choice *D* is incorrect because restructuring the reporting relationship or a position due to external relationships is not a realistic option.

159. B: It is important for Michelle to have this insight and information prior to the recruitment so that she can provide accurate information about the position in the recruitment flyer. This will also help to ensure that the best candidate is hired with the right skill set to accomplish the objectives of the position. Choice *A* is not the best choice because without gaining the insight from the department manager, Michelle may be working with an outdated job description that does not fully describe the work or reflect new work. Choice *C* is incorrect because although subjectivity can be important to a recruitment process, it should align with the importance of understanding the needs of the department and position. Choice *D* is incorrect because although having a good working relationship with the hiring manager beyond the recruitment is important, it should not be the primary reason for discussing the current recruitment needs.

160. D: Benchmarking is one way for HR professionals to determine the effectiveness and values of programs by comparing the initiatives and results against competition, industry standards, and other outside standards.

161. C: Michael should reach out to all employees for information related to wellness programs, such as weight loss and smoking cessation. Employees at all levels of the organization could be considered a

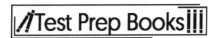
stakeholder in these programs, and each individual may have different insights or experiences that could greatly maximize the effectiveness of a program.

162. C: Amelia should immediately meet with the hiring manager and discuss the results from the interviews. This meeting should include ideas for a new plan for the recruitment, options for moving forward with the current applicant pool, and other ideas to ensure the best candidate is identified and selected for the position.

163. C: Amelia should consider increasing the years of experience with an allowance for experience to substitute for the degree. Many organizations will substitute two years of additional experience for a degree so that candidates with different backgrounds and career paths still qualify for the position. Eliminating the experience, Choice *B*, would most likely not yield more qualified candidates and may result in fewer candidates with the ability to perform the job functions. Similarly, adding supervisory experience, Choice *D*, may not yield more qualified candidates but could deter qualified candidates. Some positions prioritize work experience over a degree, and Amelia should consider this when preparing job descriptions and minimum requirements.

164. B: Amelia and the hiring manger should consider adding a step to the process that involves a written exercise that is similar in nature to the work that would be performed. Many organizations conduct typing tests, report writing, presentation delivery, or other methods to determine the most qualified candidate. Although adding another interview to the process, Choice *C*, with the entire team may provide more information, it may not provide the most appropriate and applicable information necessary to select the best candidate. The same could be said about adding more questions that are difficult to answer, Choice *D*.

165. A: The best way for an organization to maintain competitiveness and maximize capabilities is to develop and implement policies that streamline communications. These policies may specifically delve into areas of electronic media, social media, and the internet; however, it is vital for each policy to tie back to an overall communications policy to ensure each is streamlined and they all work together. It is also vital to ensure each method of communication is properly addressed within one primary communications policy to ensure that they are each streamlined and working together.

166. B: HR can specifically alleviate employees' fears and concerns about reporting unethical behavior and possible retaliation by providing them with a confidential and/or anonymous reporting method. This will protect their identity while still allowing for a proper and thorough investigation to occur. Although Choices *A*, *C*, and *D* are all appropriate actions to take to ensure a robust policy that is compliant with the law and is understood by employees, these actions may not specifically address employees' concerns about making a report.

167. D: The best way for Jessie to fully understand the organization's needs as well as individual departmental needs is to establish one-on-one and group meetings. These meetings will assist in facilitating a two-way dialogue that fosters the sharing of information that will yield more successful contract negotiations. Although Choices *A*, *B*, and *C* are all best practices that would be beneficial to include in the overall process when preparing for negotiations, they do not provide specific departmental needs and wants. Choice *A* does not specifically provide a set meeting to discuss issues, and it places the burden of initiating the communication on the managers. Choice *B* does not provide insight into departmental knowledge and needs. This task may be necessary after meeting with the departments to gain knowledge and insight into how the contract can be changed. Choice *C* would provide insight as to how employees are satisfied with the total rewards package but would not provide the information needed to address department needs.

168. A: The job posting should highlight aspects of corporate culture that are likely to attract the ideal applicant fit and may seem unattractive to those who are not good fits.

169. A: The Bureau of Labor Statistics is a division of the Department of Labor that measures and collates nationwide employment data. These data include market activity, average salaries, job duties, and working conditions. The BLS also provides state-specific data, with each state having its own department.

170. D: The best decision for Karen to make is to hire candidate B based on the passion, motivation, and experience aligning with the needs of the department and position. Choice *A* is not a feasible option because budgets are set and staffing determined well in advance of recruitments. Choice *B* is not an appropriate option because Karen is the hiring manager and therefore tasked with making this decision. She should not push this decision up to the next level in the organization; this is part of her responsibilities. Choice *C* is not the best option because if an employee is not motivated and passionate prior to starting with a new organization, these qualities probably cannot be instilled later on.

171. C: Employees should be introduced to the organization's ethical standards and policies prior to being employed. This information should be included in the job description and available to all candidates prior to submitting an application. In doing so, the recruitment process is working to identify the most suitable and best-fit candidate, beginning with the first interaction as an applicant.

172. D: Managers can try a number of different avenues to help disengaged employees; however, they may not always be able to help with personal issues and should not be expected to always cater to employees outside of the workplace. Managers should try to come to a resolution before terminating an employee for major life-events.

173. B: In this situation, it does not seem as if Raphael is being mindful of the senior leadership's time. At fifteen minutes, he should have concluded his presentation and allowed for discussion time. Additionally, although his presentation may have been fantastic with the data he put together, he was specifically asked for the recent customer service survey data. Raphael should have focused only on the requested item instead of adding unnecessary data and information, regardless of how good it is.

174. A: Phoebe should attend to the special task first and then finish the salary review. Specific tasks and individuals within an organization may need a higher and faster level of customer service. If Phoebe believes the special task will not allow her to complete the salary review within a reasonable amount of time, she should contact the employee and let them know the status and that she is working to finalize her review.

175. D: In the case presented, the best change management approach would be the power-coercive strategy to implement these changes. This strategy would be appropriate because the CFO will give the instruction as to what is expected and what could occur if these changes do not happen. Employees will need to be compliant in making these changes to ensure the organization is not placed in a position of risk. Choice *A,* normative-reductive strategy, is the change management technique used when a change is related to cultural norms and social values. Choice *B,* empirical-rational strategy, is the technique used to educate individuals with the alternative options that will incentivize them to move to the new

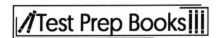

change. Choice *C*, environmental-adaptive strategy, is the technique used when there is an organizational change such as layoffs or retirements and the remaining employees need to adapt.

PHR Practice Test #3

1. In regard to corporate social responsibility, the most common ways for a corporation to assimilate into a community includes all of the following EXCEPT?

    a. Establish alliances with respected members of the community and outside organizations

    b. Deliver inexpensive goods and services for the community

    c. Hiring as many locals as possible

    d. Maximizing their profits despite any consequences to the surrounding environment

2. What's the primary purpose of organizational branding?

    I. The intent of organizational branding is letting customers know when they walk into a store.

    II. One purpose of organizational branding is to establish a distinctive image for consumers to automatically recognize.

    III. Organizational branding allows entities to create a perception of the values and ethics for which it stands.

    IV. Organizational branding focuses on promoting the benefits of the company to appeal to a target audience.

    a. I, II, and IV only

    b. I, III, and IV only

    c. II and III only

    d. I, II and III only

3. What are business metrics?

    a. Business metrics are quantifiable measures that describe the productive capacity of a policy, program, or product.

    b. Business metrics are informal activities that management occasionally conducts to discover the feasibility of a policy, program, or product.

    c. Business metrics are typically utilized to weed out underperforming employees.

    d. Business metrics are meetings with representatives from each department to voice concerns and establish harmonious, firm-wide standards and practices.

4. The best guidelines for employee handbooks include which of the following?

    a. A disclaimer that states the handbook is not intended to be any type of contractual agreement between the company and employee.

    b. Requiring employees to sign off on revised versions of the handbook.

    c. Inclusion of policies that prevents the employee from leaving the company.

    d. Distributing printed copies of the handbook to new staff members during new employee orientation.

5. On January 1, 2015, an employer had 1,000 employees, and on December 31, 2015, the same employer had 1,200 employees. During the year, the employer had 125 employees exit from the organization. What is the employer's turnover rate for 2015?

    a. 10.42%

    b. 11.36%

    c. 12.5%

    d. 62.5%

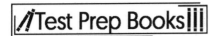

6. Which of the following communication strategies is used to establish a relationship where employees feel comfortable speaking directly with management about problems and suggestions?
a. Town hall meetings
b. Management by Walking Around (MBWA)
c. Open-door policy
d. Department meetings

7. Which of the following involvement strategies allows staff to work together in a temporary fashion to focus on a specific problem?
a. Task force
b. Committee
c. Employee participation group
d. Employee-management committee

8. Which of the following best represents 360-degree feedback?
a. A method by which employees receive anonymous feedback from their managers, peers, direct reports, and customers.
b. A method by which employees perform a self-appraisal regarding their own performance at several different points over the course of a year.
c. 360-degree feedback features reviews only by fellow employees. This is most effective because learning how employees interact with each other is indicative of their attitudes and efforts.
d. 360-degree feedback uses reviews only by management. Only management can assess an employee's suitability in an organization by evaluating productivity levels.

9. In performance management, what is a principel function of rating?
a. Rating allows management to identify their most productive workers and provide them incentives to retain them.
b. Because of its narrow statistical application, rating is generally an infrequent practice by management.
c. To provide a way for management to designate their most favored employees.
d. By employees rating management, they can more accurately decide for whom and under which conditions they wish to work.

10. Peter Senge postulated that there are five disciplines that complete a learning organization. When appropriately used in an organization, what is the purpose of these disciplines?
a. The purpose of Peter Senge's five disciplines is to permit an organization to function more comprehensively by augmenting communication and establishing common goals.
b. The purpose of Peter Senge's five disciplines is to articulate management's exact expectations to employees.
c. The purpose of Peter Senge's five disciplines is for employees to compete for the best ideas and to incorporate them into a productive strategy.
d. The purpose of Peter Senge's five disciplines is discovering different modes of innovation and to force employees to conform to them without engaging in dialogue.

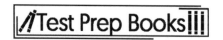

11. All of the following are part of the core meaning of competitive advantage EXCEPT?
    a. Competitive advantage is the practice of constantly attempting to increase market share by exploiting advantages.
    b. By constantly developing a labor force and technology, competitive advantage is pursued by all corporations to edge out competitors in the market.
    c. It's mandatory that organizations pursue policies of competitive advantage because they all want to maximize output and increase market share.
    d. Competitive advantage is a type of benefit that customers believe they could not get anywhere else.

12. Which of the following statements LEAST describes corporate governance?
    a. Corporate governance is the established policies, rules, and standards that organizations follow to fulfill its vision and goal as a for-profit entity and a stakeholder in the broader community.
    b. Public policy influences corporate governance, i.e. the Sarbanes-Oxley Act.
    c. Corporate governance addresses rules, practices, and institutions that protect and manage ecosystems in relation to the environment.
    d. Corporate governance is necessary to establish an organization's self-image and can be used as an instrument to restore institutional trust.

13. Which of the following is true about corporate restructuring?
    a. Corporate restructuring is intended to make a firm more competitive.
    b. Corporate restructuring is a change in operations, legal code, or ownership inside of a firm.
    c. Corporate restructuring is only a euphemism for cutting labor and lowering wages.
    d. The principal purpose of corporate restructuring is to increase profits for senior executives.

14. Which of the following best describes enterprise risk management (ERM)?
    a. Enterprise risk management is when each department crafts its own policies and procedures for handling issues of risk and loss.
    b. Enterprise risk management policies are crafted only by senior executives and then handed down to all departments to follow.
    c. Enterprise risk management is the process of establishing a broad but comprehensive protocol for handling issues of risk and loss.
    d. Enterprise risk management is when a company participates in a high-risk situation to maximize profits for the good of the company.

15. Which of the following is a guideline that focuses on organizational actions?
    a. Policy
    b. Rule
    c. Procedure
    d. Standard Operating Procedure (SOP)

16. Which of the following is more specific to the situation and is used to regulate and/or restrict an individual's behavior?
    a. Policy
    b. Rule
    c. Procedure
    d. Standard Operating Procedure (SOP)

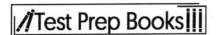

17. In an organization with a progressive discipline policy, an employee has received a verbal warning for a performance issue. The same employee is later found to be in violation of a different company policy. How should this infraction be handled?
    a. The employee should be immediately terminated.
    b. The employee should receive coaching from their manager.
    c. The employee should receive a second warning, followed by a formal written warning.
    d. The employee should receive another verbal warning, since this is for a different violation.

18. After a staff member violates a work rule that is a dischargeable offense, an HR professional should follow through with which of the following actions?
    a. Terminate the staff member on the spot.
    b. Coach the staff member immediately.
    c. Give the staff member a final written warning.
    d. Conduct an investigation after placing the staff member on administrative leave.

19. Which of the following activities is an example of downsizing?
    a. Implementing a hiring freeze.
    b. Reducing the number of hierarchical levels.
    c. Utilizing contingent workers to fill in.
    d. Outsourcing work to an external service provider.

20. A detailed list of broad skills or traits needed for a position is known as which of the following?
    a. Job analysis
    b. Job description
    c. Job competency
    d. Job specification

21. Tasks and responsibilities that are fundamental to a specific position are known as which of the following?
    a. Job competencies
    b. Marginal job functions
    c. Job specifications
    d. Essential job functions

22. Which type of interview utilizes questions that are developed from an applicant's answers to previous questions?
    a. Unstructured
    b. Nondirective
    c. Semi-structured
    d. Structured

23. Which of the following items is inferred from an employer's actions or conduct?
    a. Express contract
    b. Employment-at-will
    c. Golden parachute clause
    d. Implied contract

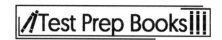
24. Which of the following is an example of a wrongful discharge?
   a. An employee who shared company information with a competitor
   b. An employee who takes home office supplies to help with an in-home consulting business
   c. An employee who accepts a gift in excess of $50 from a single client
   d. An employee who took time off from work to serve on a jury

25. Which of the following is true regarding severance pay?
   a. Severance pay is not required by law.
   b. Receipt of severance pay guarantees a former employee will not file a lawsuit against the employer.
   c. Severance pay increases an employer's contributions to unemployment tax.
   d. Severance pay guarantees that an employee will receive other benefits such as the continuation of health care coverage or outplacement services.

26. An HR professional uncovers during an exit interview that an employee is leaving the organization because she was bullied by two of her co-workers. The employee chose not to file any type of complaint or talk with HR during the course of her employment. She simply wants to leave the company and move on. Now that the HR professional is aware of the bullying and has details of the employee's experiences, what should the next move be?
   a. Terminate the identified co-workers who were performing the bullying.
   b. Conduct a full investigation and take the matter seriously.
   c. Comply with the exiting employee's wishes and ignore the matter.
   d. Let the matter go, since the affected employee is exiting the organization.

27. Which of the following statements is true under the Americans with Disabilities Act?
   a. An employer does not need to make an accommodation for a disabled employee if doing so will result in an undue hardship.
   b. Employers are required to establish affirmative action plans for the disabled.
   c. Drug users who are rehabilitated are excluded by this law.
   d. Pre-employment medical exams may be required before extending a job offer.

28. The Americans with Disabilities Act does not provide protection for which of the following employees?
   a. An employee who is diagnosed with AIDS
   b. An employee who is found using illegal drugs
   c. An employee who suffers from epilepsy
   d. An employee who has serious psychological problems

29. Under the Pregnancy Discrimination Act of 1978, which of the following statements is TRUE?
   a. An employer can refuse to provide a pregnant woman with reasonable accommodation if she is unable to do her job and approaches her manager to that effect.
   b. An employer can ask a pregnant interview candidate when she is due and how much time she will plan to be off of work after the baby arrives.
   c. An employer must give a woman a comparable position to the one that she held prior to her maternity leave (if the company does so with employees on short-term disability).
   d. An employer can discriminate against a female employee who has undergone an abortion if this act is against their personal, religious convictions.

287

30. A company must set a placement goal when which of the following situations occurs?
a. Minorities and women are assigned to jobs that are not challenging at the company.
b. The company experiences adverse impact in its hiring practices.
c. The company is unable to determine its applicants' ethnicity.
d. The company is found to employ a smaller number of minorities and women than is indicated by their availability.

31. Under the Uniform Services Employment and Reemployment Rights Act (USERRA), which of the following actions are employers prohibited from taking?
a. Halting an employee's vacation accrual while they are out on military leave
b. Continuing health care coverage at their expense for an employee who is out on military leave for six months
c. Continuing to pay an exempt employee who is out on military their full salary, minus their earning for serving in the military
d. Making reasonable efforts to accommodate a disabled veteran returning from military leave

32. Lisa is an HR generalist that is posting a job online. She is proud of her company's benefits system and wants to highlight some of them in the posting. What types of benefits could she include in the job posting?
a. Company-sponsored worksite wellness program, 401(k) matching up to 5%, and an annual sponsored mindfulness retreat
b. Job tasks, including the amount of time spent sitting each day
c. Number of direct reports for the position
d. An exact salary number

33. During new hire orientation, Joe wants to illustrate the company culture to new employees. What are some things he could share with them to show the organization's culture?
a. Share that employees can choose to work remotely one day per week, that leadership sits with employees in an open workspace, and the last Friday of each month is used to celebrate an employee's personal heritage
b. Share that new equipment will be delivered at the end of the month, and that he will follow up with each employee on assignment
c. Share his personal career story, beginning from choosing a major in college
d. Enroll employees in a required CPR/AED course

34. An organization is trying to improve its parental leave policy. Who in the organization could be considered key stakeholders for this initiative?
a. Pregnant female employees
b. Male employees
c. Managers of both sexes
d. All of the above

35. Which of the following is an example of an employee recognition program?
a. An end of year bonus
b. A plaque given for fifteen years of service to the organization
c. A thank you note and a gift card for a job well done
d. A merit given during annual review time

36. A company is laying off 20 percent of its workforce. Which of the following must be afforded to the individuals whose positions are being eliminated and are presented with documents known as a separation agreement and general release?
    a. They must sign and return the agreement during the meeting where they are presented with it.
    b. They must be given severance pay in return for signing the agreement.
    c. They must be given a period of forty-five days to sign and return the agreement, with a seven-day revocation period.
    d. They must be given the advantage of having a lawyer review the agreement for which they will be reimbursed by the company.

37. An employee files a grievance. After the employee discusses the grievance with the union steward and the supervisor (who are both in agreement), what is typically the next step in the formal grievance process?
    a. A committee of union officers will discuss the grievance with the appropriate managers in the company.
    b. The national union representative will discuss the grievance with designated company executives.
    c. The grievance will go to arbitration.
    d. The union steward will discuss the grievance with the supervisor's manager and/or the HR manager.

38. An employee must file a complaint charge of discrimination with the Equal Employment Opportunity Commission (EEOC) within a period of how many days of the alleged incident?
    a. 180 days
    b. 90 days
    c. 120 days
    d. There is no time limit associated with filing a complaint charge of discrimination with the EEOC.

39. Which of the following employers is required to have an affirmative action plan in place?
    a. An employer who has sixty employees and $55,000 in federal contracts
    b. An employer with $40,000 in federal contracts
    c. An employer with fifty-five employees
    d. An employer who is part of the Department of Transportation

40. Which of the following is the major element of an affirmative action plan that examines the internal and external population of women and minorities to determine their theoretical opportunity for employment?
    a. Utilization analysis
    b. Availability analysis
    c. Job group analysis
    d. Organizational profile

41. Which of the following is the major element of an affirmative action plan that compares the availability of women and minorities to their current representation within each job group at the company?
    a. Availability analysis
    b. Job group analysis
    c. Utilization analysis
    d. Organizational profile

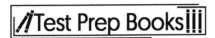
42. Under federal guidelines, under what length of time is an employer required to keep employment applications and resumes?
    a. Three years
    b. One year
    c. Three years after creation or following the hire/no hire decision (whichever date is later)
    d. One year after creation or following the hire/no hire decision (whichever date is later)

43. Which of the following statements is true regarding a learner analysis in the needs assessment process?
    a. Data is gathered from both mid-level and senior level managers.
    b. It will ensure the company is on board with the training.
    c. It can be completed in conjunction with the task analysis.
    d. Data is gathered from individuals who have direct knowledge of the work.

44. Which of the following accurately represents the Fishbone Diagram?
    a. The Fishbone Diagram is centered on the analysis of management and does not consult the entire organization.
    b. The Fishbone Diagram identifies the effects and works to determine causes.
    c. The Fishbone Diagram investigates the causes of problems. It is crafted after comprehensive brainstorming, determines positive and negative consequences, and isolates various components.
    d. The Fishbone Diagram is a way to provide a visual representation of a distribution of data.

45. Which of the following best represents the purpose of Six Sigma?
    a. Six Sigma is a rationally motivated and methodological process that seeks to eliminate ineffective and wasteful techniques that diminish productivity.
    b. Six Sigma is a process that seeks to terminate wasteful programs through organizing management and employee councils.
    c. The major purpose of Six Sigma is to use brainstorming techniques to gain valuable feedback from employees to determine the most ineffective use of company resources.
    d. To increase productive capacities, organizations employ Six Sigma. Six Sigma recruits employees with the most experience, not necessarily the most highly trained in Six Sigma methodology or statistics.

46. Which of the following communication types, while making it easy to distribute information to a large group of individuals very quickly, may also lead to "information overload"?
    a. Intranet
    b. Email
    c. Newsletter
    d. Word-of-mouth

47. In which of the following elements of alternative dispute resolution are the parties required by law to follow the decision reached as a result of the arbitration process?
    a. Compulsory arbitration
    b. Binding decision
    c. Voluntary arbitration
    d. Constructive confrontation

48. Which of the following types of picketing is done by employees for the purpose of letting the public know that they are not represented by any one authority and thus plan to organize?
    a. Recognitional picketing
    b. Organizational picketing
    c. Consumer picketing
    d. Informational picketing

49. What percent of eligible employees are required to sign authorization cards by the National Labor Relations Board before it will order an election where employees can vote on whether to be represented by a union?
    a. At least 30%
    b. At least 50%
    c. 51%
    d. A majority of the employees who are eligible to vote

50. If employees win the vote to decertify their union on August 31 in a given calendar year, what is the next earliest date that a new election can be held?
    a. After January 1 of the following year
    b. After one year has passed
    c. After thirty days
    d. After ninety days

51. If a manager is questioning a union employee and it may ultimately lead to a disciplinary action via the Weingarten rights, the employee is entitled to have which of the following present?
    a. A relative or close friend
    b. An attorney
    c. A representative from the union
    d. Another manager

52. Which of the following is considered to be an illegal subject that cannot be discussed during a collective bargaining negotiation?
    a. Voluntary subjects
    b. Worker safety conditions
    c. Working conditions and terms
    d. Security clauses

53. Which definition most accurately explains a whistle-blower?
    a. A whistle-blower is a person who reports any unethical information about an organization.
    b. A whistle-blower is a person hired by an organization to cover up illicit or unethical activity.
    c. A whistle-blower is a person who reports or publicizes any illegal or unethical information about the institution. Whistle-blower status is only granted when the organization is private.
    d. A whistle-blower reports or publicizes any illegal or unethical information about the institution. Whistle-blower status is only granted when the organization is public.

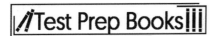

54. Which of the following is NOT a key component of a business plan?
    a. Annual goals
    b. Projected growth targets
    c. Net income expectations
    d. Bonuses for executives

55. A stakeholder is any actor that affects or can be affected by a business but doesn't own property of the business. Which of following groups of people are NOT stakeholders?
    a. Employees
    b. Surrounding businesses
    c. Shareholders
    d. The local community

56. Which of the following types of strategies that are commonly employed by unions during a collective bargaining negotiation occurs when a union successfully negotiates an agreement with a company, then uses the result of that negotiation as an example while dealing with a different company?
    a. Parallel bargaining
    b. Coordinated bargaining
    c. Multi-employer bargaining
    d. Single-unit bargaining

57. Which of the following is an exception to the concept of employment-at-will?
    a. An employee who decides to willingly sever the employment relationship
    b. An employee who is terminated for whistleblowing or for reporting unlawful conduct by the employer
    c. An employer who lets an employee go who does not have an employment contract
    d. An employee who is fired for willful misconduct

58. A truck driver kills a family's small child in an accident, and it is later uncovered that the truck driver lied on his employment application, had a history of unsafe driving, and had his license revoked twice. The employer was ultimately held responsible by the family's attorney for which of the following?
    a. Negligent retention
    b. Constructive discharge
    c. Negligent hiring
    d. Defamation

59. Which of the following activities is considered to be a fair labor practice?
    a. Hot cargo agreement
    b. Jurisdictional strike
    c. Secondary boycott
    d. Sympathy strike

60. Which of the following employees would not be eligible to vote in an upcoming union election?
    a. An employee who is temporarily laid off
    b. An employee who is out sick with the flu
    c. An employee who is out on military leave right before the election
    d. A staff member who is out of the office on a medical leave of absence and who will not be returning to work

61. Under the Taft-Hartley Act, which of the following is illegal?
    a. Creating a company-sponsored labor union
    b. An employee deciding to contribute to a charity instead of paying union dues, due to their religious objection
    c. An employer filing an unfair labor practice charge against a union
    d. A union representing nonunion employees in the bargaining unit

62. Under federal guidelines, under what length of time is an employer required to keep employee records associated with employment benefits?
    a. Six years
    b. Three years
    c. Five years
    d. One year

63. Under federal guidelines, under what length of time is an employer required to keep employee records associated with family medical leave?
    a. One year
    b. Three years
    c. Five years
    d. Two years

64. Which of the following would MOST likely be considered an essential job function?
    a. An employee participates in an ongoing employee committee assignment as time permits.
    b. An employee devotes approximately 8 percent of her time to making cold calls to obtain new business.
    c. An employee delegates preparation of a template to their administrative support.
    d. An employee regularly reviews engineering design documents.

65. Which of the following situations would more than likely warrant a written employment contract?
    a. An employee who is a salesperson
    b. A full-time telecommuting employee
    c. An employee who is a department manager
    d. An employee who is a graphic artist

66. Before extending a contingent offer of employment, an employer should obtain which of the following?
    a. Medical records and completion of a physical examination
    b. Signed consent from the candidate to check work references
    c. Verbal consent from the candidate to check work references
    d. Polygraph test

67. Which of the following is an exception to Title VII of the Civil Rights Act of 1964?
    a. An employer with only twenty employees
    b. A new seniority system that is being implemented at a workplace
    c. A bona fide occupational qualification
    d. A work-related requirement that is not truly legitimate

68. When performing a cost-benefit analysis of a proposed project, what is a project worker's salary an example of?
    a. A stakeholder
    b. A cost
    c. A benefit
    d. A dependent variable

69. When making project proposals to leadership, HR professionals should have a written outline containing everything EXCEPT:
    a. A timeline
    b. Milestones
    c. The fiscal year
    d. Resources needed

70. Myra and Angela are two HR professionals who work in the same organization. Recently, Myra successfully implemented a sustainability initiative with the marketing department, where she helped them reduce the amount of paper they use. This led to saved paper, printing, and labor costs as well as reduced physical waste. Angela would like to try this initiative with the finance department, which is welcome to this idea. How can Angela begin to allocate resources for this project?
    a. Copy Myra's initiative as closely as possible, right down to the budget and timeline
    b. Use her best guess to document what she believes the finance department will need to reduce their paper waste, and provide a written copy to the manager
    c. Set up a meeting with Myra to discuss how she allocated resources and what went successfully, as well as what did not go successfully, and use this data to plan
    d. Ask the HR intern to devote all of his time to her initiative

71. Michael leads an HR department at a federal agency. He is in the planning stage for the new fiscal year and is thrilled that he has created initiatives that are highly detailed and comprehensive and use the resources of contracts his agency currently has in place. He is very attached to the outcomes of these initiatives. However, a presidential election is taking place in one month that will likely affect the contracts that are awarded to his agency. What can Michael do to protect his new fiscal year plans?
    a. Ensure that there is leftover money from the previous fiscal year to serve as a cushion should he not receive expected contracts
    b. Create backup plans for all of the contracts that may be affected, while calmly accepting that some changes may be unanticipated and out of his control
    c. Nothing, he has already distributed them to employees and archived them on the organization's servers
    d. Find a new job

294

72. Larry manages three HR employees. Jane is in charge of compensation and benefit tasks, Ira is in charge of risk management tasks, and Samir is in charge of recruitment and hiring. Samir has an illness that takes him out of the office for six weeks, and during this time, all recruitment and hiring processes freeze. This majorly impacts two other departments that were waiting on new employees to begin. How could this situation have best been prevented?

    a. Larry should have cross-trained his three employees to fill in for each other should emergencies come up.

    b. Samir should have worked remotely to handle the candidates needed by the other two departments.

    c. Larry should have filled in for Samir's role for the entire duration of his absence.

    d. Ira should have analyzed Samir's workday operations to see if anything at work caused his illness.

73. Which of the following is a true statement regarding a modified duty assignment?

    a. A modified duty assignment is a temporary reassignment that seeks to accommodate employees who are recovering from illness or injury.

    b. A modified duty assignment is a permanent arrangement of work to accommodate employees who are injured.

    c. To make more money, a modified duty assignment is more work given to employees who ask for it.

    d. Injured employees must accept a modified duty assignment and be examined by a licensed physician to be cleared for the assignment.

74. Which of the following most accurately describes a procurement policy?

    a. A procurement policy is a strategy that employers use to find the most qualified employees.

    b. A procurement policy is an organization's strategy to obtain and secure goods and services in an orderly and beneficial way to minimize cost and maximize savings.

    c. A procurement policy is an analysis of an organization's inventory to determine what supplies are needed.

    d. A procurement policy is any action that an organization takes to find a new location.

75. What is a hazard communication program, and is it legally binding?

    a. A hazard communication program is a guideline that gives employers the option to inform employees when they are working with hazardous materials and is not legally binding.

    b. A hazard communication program is a mandate from OSHA that requires employers to inform employees when they are working with hazardous materials and the nature of each material and is legally binding.

    c. A hazard communication program is an evacuation procedure that is intended for emergencies and is legally binding.

    d. A hazard communication program is an educational training program that OSHA offers to employers regarding dangerous chemicals and is not legally binding.

76. What is the primary goal of a business continuity plan?
   a. A business continuity plan is a strategy that is implemented in a time of an organization's prosperity to sustain growth.
   b. A business continuity plan is a portion of the hiring process where employers ask job candidates how they specifically plan to contribute to the organization.
   c. A business continuity plan is the maintenance of productivity during and after a disruption.
   d. A business continuity plan is when an organization uses a disruption to fire workers to increase productivity.

77. In what ways can a social engineer impact an organization?
   a. A social engineer can impact an organization by implementing policies that promote a healthier and more enjoyable working environment.
   b. A social engineer can impact an organization if they are tasked with the responsibility of administering sanctions and punishments
   c. A social engineer can impact an organization by implementing policies that promote equality and prohibit discriminatory behavior.
   d. A social engineer can impact an organization by manipulating members to extract sensitive or classified information.

78. What does a plateau learning curve indicate?
   a. A plateau learning curve represents initially slow learning but then a rapid acceleration.
   b. A plateau learning curve indicates quick initial learning followed by a stoppage.
   c. A plateau learning curve indicates sluggish learning, acceleration in learning activity, and then a deceleration.
   d. A plateau learning curve represents quick initial learning followed by a slowdown.

79. What are the three types of organization development interventions?
   a. Human process intervention, sociotechnical intervention, techno-structural intervention
   b. Human process intervention, managerial intervention, techno-structural intervention
   c. Managerial intervention, human process intervention, techno-structural intervention
   d. Employer intervention, sociotechnical intervention, techno-structural intervention

80. Which statement is most reflective of the Pareto analysis system?
   a. 20 percent of output is generated by 80 percent of input.
   b. 80 percent of output is generated by 20 percent of input.
   c. Decisions should be made democratically rather than statistically.
   d. Resources need to be allocated according to need rather than according to productivity.

81. Public domain is a copyright provision that posits which of the following?
   a. Under no circumstances can a previously copyrighted work be used without authorization.
   b. Any work published by the federal government can be used freely without authorization.
   c. Items that are considered to be works-made-for-hire never fall into the public domain.
   d. Works protected by a copyright can be used without consent if they are used for a public purpose.

82. Which of the following pieces of legislation dictates what are known as unfair labor practices?
    a. The Wagner Act
    b. The Norris-LaGuardia Act
    c. The Taft-Hartley Act
    d. The Railway Labor Act

83. Which of the following is prohibited by the Taft-Hartley Act?
    a. The formation of monopolies
    b. Forcing employees to join a union
    c. Refusing to allow for a closed shop exception for construction trades
    d. Union members' inability to sue their union

84. Under the WARN Act, which of the following employers are required to provide a minimum of sixty days' notice to their employees in advance of a plant closing or mass layoff?
    a. An employer shuts down a plant facility that employs fifty total employees, twenty-five of which are working part-time. The company employs over one hundred full-time employees.
    b. Thirty full-time employees are laid off by a company at a single site that employs 120 full-time individuals for a three-month period.
    c. A company lays off 250 full-time employees at a single site that employs 650 full-time individuals for more than a six-month period.
    d. An employer shuts down a plant facility that has already been partially idled for quite some time. Only forty employees remain working at the site. The company employs over one hundred full-time employees.

85. What is the best way for HR leaders to communicate acceptable and ethical behaviors in the workplace?
    a. Provide written protocols about what constitutes as ethical and unethical behavior
    b. Relay that employees are continuously monitored with in-house cameras, so they should be especially mindful of their work behavior
    c. Model acceptable and ethical behavior themselves, as much as possible
    d. Tell employees at their new hire orientation

86. The CEO of a company holds bi-weekly meetings with his entire organization to relay new information about company performance, trends, and personal opinions relating to the industry. What is this an example of?
    a. Transparency
    b. Overshare
    c. Validation
    d. Process control

87. Where should an employee first encounter an organization's ethical standards and policies?
    a. At the new hire orientation
    b. During the first interview
    c. In the job posting for their role
    d. By reading a company press release

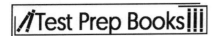

88. The vice-president of an organization has noticed that a particular employee, Ben, has been working extremely hard and has made a positive impression on a large majority of the organization's leadership. The vice-president meets with Ben and asks him about his work. Ben shares all of the accomplishments that his team has achieved in the last quarter. What is Ben displaying during this meeting?
    a. Ego
    b. Individualistic behavior
    c. Team-oriented culture
    d. Humility

89. Soliciting feedback from stakeholders is an important part of which of the following process stages?
    a. Evaluation
    b. Control
    c. Testing
    d. Documentation

Read the following scenario and answer questions 90–91.

The manager of the IT department currently conducts biannual employee evaluations. The evaluation is filled out on a single sheet of paper. On the front of the paper, employees are scored as "meets/does not meet expectations" on fifteen core skills and competencies. On the back of the paper, the manager writes more detailed feedback about areas in need of improvement. The paper is returned to employees within two weeks of the evaluation period.

90. The IT manager would like HR's feedback about how to improve this evaluation. What would be the most helpful recommendation?
    a. IT employees are used to working with cutting-edge technology, so the paper form should be replaced by an electronic one.
    b. Biannual evaluations are not frequent enough; employees should get official managerial feedback every 1–2 months.
    c. There should be additional evaluation standards beyond "meets expectations" to recognize and encourage employee achievement.
    d. The front page of the evaluation is too formulaic and should be eliminated; the manager can just relay the back page of feedback.

91. The IT manager has also noticed that employees seem to have negative feelings about the evaluations. What could be done to improve employees' attitudes?
    a. Replace manager-led evaluations with employee-led self-evaluations.
    b. Focus feedback on future goals rather than past mistakes.
    c. Create a competition and post evaluation results to reward top performers and motivate lower-performing employees.
    d. Schedule evaluations for the end of the day so employees can go home afterward.

92. What is an example of the qualitative impact of a well-managed corporate social responsibility (CSR) program?
    a. It improves feelings of employee satisfaction.
    b. It generates revenue by developing new customers and contacts.
    c. It reduces an organization's legal liabilities.
    d. It involves many activities that are tax-deductible.

298

93. Which of the following is not a law or regulation that is administered by the Equal Employment Opportunity Commission (EEOC)?
    a. EPA
    b. ADEA
    c. Title VII of the Civil Rights Act
    d. FMLA

94. All of the following is true about offshoring EXCEPT?
    a. Offshoring is typically done to reduce the costs of business.
    b. Offshoring involves shifting business operations to a country where business can be conducted at lower costs.
    c. The only beneficiary of offshoring is the company itself.
    d. Offshoring is one aspect of corporate restructuring that permits a company to remain competitive.

95. All of the following is necessary for an organization to pay attention to the legislative and regulatory environment EXCEPT?
    a. To anticipate changes and craft corporate governance policies that address new regulations and legislation.
    b. To engage in lobbying efforts to fight proposed changes that could be damaging to the corporation.
    c. To modify and make new legislative and regulatory changes more palatable.
    d. To examine competitors and match their own legislation to that of other corporations.

96. Which of the following best describes mergers and acquisitions (M&A)?
    a. Mergers occur temporarily to consolidate resources and beat out a competitor; acquisitions occur permanently.
    b. Mergers occur when one company purchases another without a new company being formed. Acquisitions occur when two companies combine to form a new one.
    c. Mergers occur when two companies combine to form a new one. Acquisitions occur when one company purchases another without a new company being formed.
    d. Mergers and acquisitions often occur temporarily to consolidate resources and beat out a competitor; then the actions are rescinded, and the entities disband.

97. What is the most crucial aspect of successfully implementing organizational change?
    a. Work ethic
    b. Leadership buy-in
    c. Highly compensated employees
    d. Terminating employees who do not agree

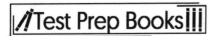

98. An employee sees a close colleague change numbers in an accounting spreadsheet to reflect incorrect values. The employee feels uncomfortable reporting the colleague, due to their friendship and close working relationship. However, the employee feels very concerned about the situation. What is one feasible resource that could help this employee in a situation like this?
    a. An anonymous and confidential HR hotline
    b. A close relationship with a superior
    c. An in-house coffee shop where the employee can go with the colleague to discuss their feelings about the situation
    d. Regular communication training sessions

99. What was the principal intent of the Sarbanes-Oxley Act of 2002 (SOX)?
    a. The SOX Act deregulated accounting standards for senior executives of accounting firms.
    b. The SOX Act established high levels of transparency and accountability for senior executives in accounting and recordkeeping.
    c. The SOX Act encouraged companies to increase transparency for shareholders by offering subsidies for compliance.
    d. The SOX Act decreased protections for shareholders that were defrauded by institutions.

100. Which is a true statement about the Americans with Disabilities Act (ADA)?
    a. The ADA is a federal law that prevents discrimination based on disability and requires employers to provide reasonable accommodations to disabled employees.
    b. The ADA applies only to full-time employees, but not part-time or temporary employees.
    c. The ADA exempts private employers and only applies to municipal, state, and federal organizations.
    d. The ADA was included in the Civil Rights Act of 1964.

101. What is a true statement about alternative work locations?
    a. No companies have experimented with alternative work locations, so their benefits cannot yet be evaluated.
    b. Alternative work locations are generally discouraged since it is difficult to trust employees to work outside of the office.
    c. Alternative work locations have been proven to reduce employee productivity.
    d. Because alternative work locations help decentralize operations, the organization is better protected from the destructive efforts of a single person.

102. Why should employers train employees to use social media effectively?
    a. Employers generally do not like to train employees to use social media because it can be a distraction from their work.
    b. An employee with social media skills provides an organization with an advantage in the fields of marketing and advertising.
    c. Employees using social media are friendlier in the work environment.
    d. If employees can use social media, they are more likely to be up to date on current news.

103. What is a needs analysis?
    a. A needs analysis is a data-gathering activity where all members of an organization are surveyed about specific needs and requests. This information is assessed and then employed in ways to improve the functionality of the organization.
    b. A needs analysis is a data-gathering activity where only senior management is surveyed about their specific needs and requests. This information is assessed and then employed in ways to improve the functionality of the organization.
    c. A needs analysis is a data-gathering activity where all members of an organization are surveyed about specific needs and requests. However, the surveys must be completed in secret because employees can be fired for expressing critical views of management.
    d. A needs analysis is a data-gathering activity only performed at a company after a major safety or security incident.

104. Considering they have met all of the necessary requirements, which of the following individuals is eligible to take unpaid, protected leave from work under the Family Medical Leave Act (FMLA)?
    a. An employee who is non-weight bearing, recovering from ankle surgery, and who will have multiple follow-up appointments with his surgeon and numerous physical therapy visits to attend.
    b. An employee who is out of the office for three days sick with the flu.
    c. An employee who wants to take care of her aunt who is suffering from end-stage lung cancer.
    d. An employee who wishes to travel to China to support her sister who is in the process of adopting a child in that country.

105. Which of the following benefits is considered to be discretionary?
    a. Unpaid family medical leave
    b. Life insurance
    c. Continuation of healthcare coverage
    d. Worker's compensation

106. Which of the following is considered to be indirect compensation?
    a. Bonus
    b. Incentive pay
    c. Pension plan
    d. Hourly wage

107. Which of the following is used to describe the knowledge, skills, abilities, education, and experience that are essential to performing a specific job?
    a. Job analysis
    b. Job description
    c. Job specification
    d. Job evaluation

108. Which of the following is a quantitative method of job evaluation?
    a. Job ranking
    b. Paired comparison
    c. Factor comparison method
    d. Job classification

301

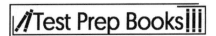

109. Once a salary survey is completed, what is the term used for weighting the data for jobs included on the survey that are similar, but not identical, to positions with the organization? This process is done to create a more accurate match.
    a. Aging
    b. Benchmarking
    c. Leveling
    d. Wage compression

110. Which of the following is a direct result of broadbanding?
    a. Green-circle rates
    b. Taller organizational structures
    c. Red-circle rates
    d. Flatter organizational structures

111. Which of the following types of compensation is given to employees when they work during holidays or vacation days?
    a. Reporting pay
    b. Shift pay
    c. Premium pay
    d. Emergency shift pay

112. What is an example of a factor that influences workforce supply?
    a. Worker attrition
    b. Number of customers
    c. Seasonal workload
    d. Economic downturn

113. What is the relationship between diversity and inclusion in the workplace?
    a. Diversity reflects legally-mandated equal opportunity hiring practices, while inclusion reflects company culture.
    b. Diversity refers to only hiring employees from underrepresented groups, while inclusion refers to hiring employees from all demographics.
    c. Diversity involves hiring employees with a variety of backgrounds, personalities, and working styles, while inclusion involves making sure those differences are heard and represented in the workplace.
    d. Diversity means respecting and encouraging workers to retain their individuality in the workplace, while inclusion means integrating all workers into one shared corporate culture.

114. Which of the following is true of workplace accommodations?
    a. Employers must take the lead in offering accommodations to employees.
    b. Employees need to complete legal paperwork before requesting an accommodation.
    c. Accommodations only cover conditions under the Americans with Disabilities Act (ADA).
    d. Accommodations must not place an undue burden on the employer.

Read the following scenario and answer questions 115–116.

Several employees at a battery factory are concerned about their level of exposure to chemicals used on the assembly floor. One employee has read an article about how certain chemical fumes have been linked with eye disease and even blindness. This employee has been circulating the information to other workers.

115. Which agency or department is responsible for the standards that guide HR's response in this type of situation?
   a. NLRB
   b. EEOC
   c. OSHA
   d. EBSA

116. What is an appropriate HR response?
   a. HR should caution the employee about spreading rumors without first talking to their supervisor.
   b. As a preventative measure, all employees should be required to buy stronger, more advanced safety goggles if they are assigned to positions on the assembly floor.
   c. HR should combat the rumors by circulating a more detailed scientific analysis of the batteries' chemical properties.
   d. After investigating the validity of the report, HR should determine whether it is possible to work with less hazardous materials or develop improved safety measures in collaboration with factory managers.

117. The federal minimum wage is currently set at $7.25/hour. However, in the state of Maryland, where Rachel's ice cream parlor resides, the minimum wage is currently set higher at $12.50/hour. Which statement below accurately reflects the rate of pay at which Rachel's new employees starting out at the minimum wage would receive?
   a. The new employees will receive $7.25/hour. When the federal minimum wage is set lower than a state's minimum wage, an employer can go with the lower rate of pay as its standard.
   b. The new employees will receive $12.50/hour. When a state's minimum wage is higher than the federal minimum wage, an employer must use the higher state minimum wage as its standard.
   c. The new employees will receive $9.88/hour, which is an average of the federal minimum wage and the state's minimum wage.
   d. Rachel's ice cream parlor does not have enough employees to fall under the guidelines of the Fair Labor Standards Act (FLSA), which governs minimum wage.

118. Which piece of legislation requires employers to pay employees for preliminary and postliminary tasks, such as job-related travel time that is outside of an employee's regular work commute and time spent in job-related training?
   a. Equal Pay Act
   b. Portal-to-Portal Act
   c. Fair Labor Standards Act (FLSA)
   d. Davis Bacon Act

119. Which of the following statements is true regarding differential pay?
    a. Differential pay is required by the Fair Labor Standards Act (FLSA).
    b. Differential pay programs are used to reward employees for performing work that is viewed as less than desirable.
    c. Pay practices regarding differential pay are standardized among employers.
    d. Differential pay programs are used to motivate employees to perform their work at a higher level.

120. What is the compa-ratio for a salary range of $10 – $22 and an entry-level employee salary of $12.50?
    a. The compa-ratio is 70 percent.
    b. The compa-ratio is 78 percent.
    c. The compa-ratio is 1.04 percent.
    d. The compa-ratio is .96 percent.

121. Based on the compa-ratio determined for the previous question, which of the following can be deduced about the employee and/or the company's pay strategy?
    a. The employee is new to the job and/or the organization, is a low performer, or is working for a company that has adopted a lag behind the market pay strategy.
    b. The employee is new to the job and/or the organization, is a high performer, or is working for a company that has adopted a lag behind the market pay strategy.
    c. The employee is long-tenured, a high performer, or is working for a company that has adopted a lead ahead of the market pay strategy.
    d. The employee is long-tenured, a low performer, or is working for a company that has adopted a lead ahead of the market pay strategy.

122. An employee has passed away on the job. For what length of time is his surviving wife eligible for continuation of healthcare coverage under the Consolidated Omnibus Budget Reconciliation Act (COBRA)?
    a. Three months
    b. Eighteen months
    c. Thirty-six months
    d. Twenty-nine months

123. A Material Safety Data Sheet (MSDS) contains which of the following elements:
    a. Lockout and tagout signs
    b. Directions regarding emergency exit procedures
    c. Information about confined space entry
    d. Information about how to handle contact with a hazardous chemical

124. The CEO wants to cut costs by eliminating a popular employee program that subsidizes public transportation commutes. HR is concerned about the effect this proposal will have on workers. What is an appropriate response?

a. HR does not have the authority to overrule the CEO and should avoid giving negative feedback unless it is specifically solicited by the CEO.

b. HR should engage in environmental scanning and research ways that other companies have enacted cost-cutting measures.

c. HR should eliminate the program and create a feedback survey where employees can share their feelings if they don't like the CEO's decision.

d. HR should inform the CEO of the value of the program by presenting metrics related to the ROI of the current plan, such as the ability to reach more productive and qualified workers thanks to the transportation program.

125. A large public relations firm is evaluating its HR functions to determine which tasks should be kept in house and which tasks should be outsourced. Which task are they most likely to outsource?

a. Payroll administration

b. Performance evaluations

c. Recruitment

d. High-potential development program management

126. Which of the following is a tool from the Six Sigma approach?

a. Value stream mapping

b. HRIS

c. SMART

d. Flow state diagram

127. Mila is in the planning stages of an HR initiative that focuses on providing a catered healthy lunch to all employees each Monday. What is something she should focus on during the planning stage?

I. Developing a SMART goal to determine why she wants to pursue this initiative and how she will know if it is successful

II. Identifying stakeholders and gathering their opinions on meal types and the value of this initiative

III. Surveying employees who attended about how they enjoyed the food served

IV. Creating a budget proposal

a. I and II

b. I, II, and III

c. I, II, and IV

d. All of the above

128. An HR team is developing a budget for a hiring campaign. The associated costs include marketing materials; a venue rental for a hiring fair; and the time, labor, and salaries of the staff who will work at the fair. What types of cost are these?

a. Indirect costs

b. Regulatory costs

c. Direct costs

d. Training costs

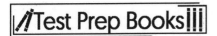
129. Quinn is an HR recruiter who has a quarterly goal of hiring 35 percent of all employees that reach the interview process. He normally meets this goal. However, one quarter found him at a rate of 10 percent. What tool can Quinn use to learn more about this poor performance?
    a. Lean
    b. Oracle
    c. Gap analysis
    d. Value stream map

130. Fiona is mapping out a process for a new initiative. She compiles the full timeline and processes of customer solutions, then brainstorms with her team about potential failures, obstacles, or setbacks that could occur at each stage. In what practice is Fiona engaging?
    a. Process mapping
    b. Negative facilitation
    c. Value stream mapping
    d. Risk identification

131. Each fiscal quarter within a fiscal year is an example of which of the following?
    a. Benchmarking
    b. A milestone
    c. Calendar divides
    d. Bonus assessment period

132. Ashley is conducting a workflow analysis in a patient clinic to identify sources of waste. Each day for two weeks, she sits in different areas of the clinic and examines the daily activities of each staff member. She records each task that the staff member completes, the amount of time it takes to complete the task, any obstacles that arise during the task, and anything that Ashley feels makes the task easier for the staff member she is observing. What is this type of data collection called?
    a. Focus group
    b. Work in progress
    c. Observational
    d. Transactional

133. Nate is an HR employee who works with his organization's operations departments. He is in the middle of resolving a short-term disability claim for an employee who is not present in the office. As he is working, the CFO of his organization visits his desk and asks for assistance with an urgent task that affects all employee data. This task is expected to take a full workday to complete. What should Nate do?
    a. Tell the CFO he is finishing a task for an employee, but will come help as soon as he is finished.
    b. Pause work on the short-term disability claim till the next day to help the CFO, but communicate a status update to the employee it affects.
    c. Immediately stop working on the short-term disability claim and help the CFO.
    d. Tell the CFO he is not available and refer him to another HR staff member.

Read the following scenario and then answer questions 134–136.

Over the past decade, an advertising agency has steadily grown its client list in a particular foreign country, and it has decided to open a satellite office in that country to more easily handle day-to-day operation of its accounts there. Although several employees have made international business

306

trips before, it will be the first time the organization has had a full-time presence in a foreign country. As such, the HR department is devising a strategy to prepare for expatriate employees.

134. The HR manager's first goal is to establish a clear duty-of-care policy. Which of the following best describes duty of care?

a. The moral and legal obligations of an employer to care for employees' safety, security, and wellbeing when assigned to a foreign country

b. International law mandating a minimum level of health insurance for expatriate workers and their families

c. Identifying available services such as police officers, healthcare workers, and other first responders responsible for emergency response in a given country

d. A system of compensation when employees incur health, safety, housing, and other expenses when on an international assignment

135. HR is trying to set up some learning sessions for employees who will be posted in the new satellite office. Which of the following classes would be most essential to provide for workers?

a. An intensive language course in becoming fluent in the native language

b. A culture class on local food, music, and famous landmarks

c. A reminder of the company's mission, vision, and values

d. An overview of applicable local labor laws and workplace etiquette

136. Some employees have never lived in a foreign country before and are concerned about their safety in case of an emergency. How should HR address these concerns?

a. Prepare a presentation comparing crime statistics between the United States and other countries to reassure employees that expatriate life is safe.

b. Monitor and share information regarding potential safety concerns in the foreign post and establish a system for employees to check in regularly.

c. Provide employees with the numbers of local emergency response services.

d. Only offer international assignment to employees who are confident about taking care of themselves in a foreign country.

137. An organization's executives require that all HR policy recommendations be evidence-based. In this context, what is the best definition of "evidence-based"?

a. Based on information from research studies by prominent academics outside the organization, to avoid conflict of interest

b. Based on data from internal and external sources that is collected and analyzed in a standardized way to drive decision-making

c. Based on conclusions made from careful observation of everyday working conditions in the organization

d. Based on conceptual frameworks for understanding complex business trends

138. What are the results of a total remuneration survey?

a. A comparison of workers' actual and desired salaries

b. A list of pay gaps within an organization

c. A report of market data on compensation and benefits plans

d. A group of employees who qualify for pay increases

139. What is it called when HR decides to transition manual tasks (such as completing and filing paperwork, tracking benefits eligibility) to a digital management system that completes these tasks?
    a. Restructuring
    b. Outsourcing
    c. Automation
    d. Integration

140. Which of the following is NOT a good example of useful information HR can supply during the strategic planning process?
    a. Number and type of ongoing projects
    b. Budget for total rewards plans
    c. Number of employees
    d. Education and development initiatives

141. Eric is a team leader in the HR department and supervises HR professionals at various levels, including analysts, administrators, and supervisors. He is struggling with the team's motivation to go above and beyond in providing customer service. Although the team answers questions and handles situations appropriately, Eric wants to elevate the team's performance to deliver even better results. What should he do to effect this change in the team?
    a. Eric should work to display these characteristics in his daily work, verbally communicate expectations to the team, and recognize when an employee goes above the standard.
    b. Eric should immediately deliver performance reviews to the entire team to formally communicate the new level of service expected.
    c. Eric should work with finance to budget a new position and hire an energetic individual who goes above and beyond in their work to motivate the team.
    d. Eric should email the team to communicate the new expectations for customer service.

142. How can a site's geographic location affect business operations?
    a. All locations should be managed the same to ensure equity and that one location does not receive more attention and resources than another.
    b. Each location will have a separate management team that will run the operations differently based on their own unique experience and background.
    c. Some locations may require additional resources or plans to address specific needs, such as climate change, harsh weather conditions, and coastlines.
    d. The home-base location should allocate resources equally, with management distributing them as appropriate.

143. Mark is concerned with the number of employees leaving the organization. He believes they are resigning due to the company not paying a competitive salary. What can Mark analyze to determine if his belief is accurate?
    a. Exit interview data
    b. Job descriptions
    c. Cost-of-living index
    d. External salary data

144. Jake prepared a cost-benefit analysis as part of a presentation to pitch a new HR training program that would provide all employees an opportunity to enhance their interpersonal and communication skills. He focused on equipment, materials, time, and the corresponding benefits related to training employees. Management was impressed but concerned that this proposal was not holistic and complete. What did Jake forget?
   a. Legal fees
   b. Labor costs
   c. Marketing costs
   d. Nothing. Jake provided a complete analysis with no missing information.

145. Which skill helps to recognize the feelings and communication styles of both one's self and others, resulting in being able to build better relationships?
   a. Intelligence quotient
   b. Athletic abilities
   c. Cognitive dissonance
   d. Emotional Intelligence skills

146. Which of the following is an inaccurate statement regarding grievances?
   a. Grievances allow management to respond appropriately through proper methods.
   b. Grievances follow a specific process that is identified by the organization's contract.
   c. Grievances are informal and should be resolved verbally by the supervisor.
   d. Grievances are complaints made formally and in writing.

147. Stephanie is conducting research into employee satisfaction surveys. She has been tasked with researching industry standards, samples, and communication plans. Which of the following should guide the type of research design and data Stephanie collects for this project?
   a. Customer service complaints
   b. Benchmarks and HR metrics
   c. Exit interview information
   d. Strategic goals and objectives

148. Rebecca is working to develop metrics and key performance indicators that measure how effective the new marketing programs are in driving new business to purchases. She is researching how other organizations measure this data to show how the marketing initiatives compare with the competition. Which of the following practices is Rebecca engaging in?
   a. Comparable review
   b. Statistical analysis
   c. Six Sigma
   d. Benchmarking

149. Which of the following are the two primary methods to examine HR programs, practices, and policies objectively for effectiveness and sustainability?
   a. Risk analysis and evaluation
   b. Risk analysis and process evaluation
   c. Program and process evaluation
   d. Program and risk analysis

150. When a process is tightly controlled and the results produced are the same each time the process is duplicated, which of the following can be said about the process?
    a. The process has no confirmation bias.
    b. The process is statistically valid.
    c. The process is validated and consistent.
    d. The process has been approved by management.

151. What does a total remuneration survey provide a report on?
    a. Salary ranges, including the minimum and maximum, for all positions in an organization
    b. Annual financial report showing personnel costs, including total budget versus expenditures
    c. Total rewards data, including compensation and benefits, for the market
    d. Satisfaction levels of employees regarding wages, benefits, programs, and culture

152. Sharon is working on the department's new objectives. She was successful in meeting all of the established objectives for the previous two years, and therefore wants to branch out and identify some new, creative, and different objectives to take the department in a new direction. What should Sharon do first to identify some new ideas?
    a. Work with leadership and employees to conduct a needs assessment.
    b. Discuss the idea with her LinkedIn network of colleagues to get their thoughts.
    c. Revamp the previous years' objectives with new results and time frames.
    d. Conduct an industry analysis to see what competitors are doing.

Read the following scenario and answer questions 153–154.

Monica's distribution company recently expanded operations into a new international country. To ensure the company's standards are established with the new workforce, senior leadership selected high-performing managers across the organization to be transferred to the new location. These managers are tasked with hiring the workforce from the local talent pool and working to train potential managers for future installation. After six months, Monica has received numerous complaints from employees regarding inappropriate behavior from several of the managers who were placed to lead the new location. Several of the complaints are similar in that they focus on managers disciplining employees for tardiness, taking excessive breaks, and frequently extending lunch breaks.

153. What should Monica do first to address these complaints?
    a. Provide a template for disciplinary memos to be placed in each of the employee's files.
    b. Terminate the employees who have been violating the attendance policy.
    c. Schedule a meeting with the managers to discuss the specific concerns and details.
    d. Coordinate a transfer of several employees for training purposes.

154. Once Monica has a clear understanding of the issues, she realizes the root cause is a difference of understanding related to expectations. Additionally, after researching culture norms and labor laws of the country, she realizes the managers do not have a clear understanding of these elements. What should Monica do next?

a. Work with senior leadership to replace the managers and course-correct the entire location's workforce.

b. Conduct a training session for the managers and then hold a group staff meeting to discuss expectations and attendance policies.

c. Continue with the course of action the managers have initiated and proceed with progressive discipline.

d. Close out the complaints with responses that indicate the management has the right to discipline employees for policy violations.

155. Hector has seen a recent increase in employee complaints that specifically relate to behavior that is inappropriate for the workplace. Although not a violation of the harassment or bullying policy, Hector believes the behavior is not contributing to a positive work environment. What program should Hector consider implementing to provide some opportunities and benefits to his employees, such as counseling and conflict resolution?

a. Life insurance plan

b. Employee Assistance Program

c. Education assistance

d. Smoking cessation program

156. Sandra is working on getting her information technology (IT) department to select a new Human Resources Information System (HRIS). The HR department needs an updated system that will allow for managing employee data, administering benefits, tracking leave time, and initiating recruitments. Which of the following is NOT something Sandra should consider?

a. The types of information that are currently being collected and stored

b. A one-size-fits-all system that provides general resources across the HR spectrum

c. The information that will need to be collected and stored in the future

d. How data can be integrated for easier access, reporting, and analysis

157. What is the primary benefit of a well-designed and well-managed HRIS?

a. The ability to run generalized reports

b. The ability to use data to develop evidence-based solutions

c. The ability to provide subjective perspectives

d. The ability to meet goals and objectives specific to hiring

158. Which of the following tools is used to identify an initiative's value to a stakeholder along with the investment and influence specific stakeholders have in promoting and supporting the initiative?

a. Stakeholder mapping

b. Stakeholder analysis

c. Stakeholder diagramming

d. Stakeholder review

311

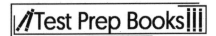

159. Blair has recently joined a new organization that maintains a policy regarding customer service. The policy requires that all requests and inquiries be responded to within 24 hours. Blair has always prided himself on his customer service skills and used a personal guideline of 48 hours to allow for time to research and educate himself on the issue. How should Blair proceed when responding to customers?
   a. Institute a new personal guideline of a 12-hour response time to exceed expectations.
   b. Abide by the organization's policy requiring a 24-hour response time.
   c. Continue working within his own personal guideline of a 48-hour response time.
   d. Institute a new personal guideline of a 36-hour response time.

160. When a project goes over budget and exceeds the proposed time frame, what analysis should be conducted?
   a. SWOT analysis
   b. Gap analysis and root cause analysis
   c. PEST analysis
   d. Outcome and needs analysis

161. Why is it important for HR professionals to have an understanding of and ability to work with statistics?
   a. This skill is not important for HR professionals to have because the finance department typically employs individuals who are experts in this field.
   b. This skill allows HR professionals to promote to higher levels of responsibility more quickly than those who do not have this skill.
   c. This skill is not important for HR professionals to have because their sole responsibility is policy, process, and protocols.
   d. This skill allows HR professionals to identify trends and use the data to support initiatives while also seeing errors or flaws in the data.

162. Which of the following statements is an inaccurate representation of the importance of evidence-based decision making?
   a. It provides credibility and logical support for initiatives.
   b. It allows the process to be contained to one or two individuals.
   c. It provides transparency as to why certain decisions are made.
   d. It can be easily communicated and shared with others.

163. Which of the following is the process of establishing a relevant, unbiased system of data collection?
   a. Benchmarking
   b. Validation
   c. Quality assurance
   d. Quality control

164. Which of the following is the most effective, streamlined, and lean method to communicate policies, programs, procedures, forms, and information?
   a. A secure online portal where employees can find updated information
   b. A printed manual distributed to each employee annually
   c. An in-person employee orientation delivered annually
   d. An electronic newsletter delivered via email to all employees monthly

165. When gaining buy-in for large-scale projects that impact the entire organization, which of the following terms describes the concept of finding values or interests across multiple departments that would encourage support?
    a. Leadership support
    b. Work-life balance
    c. Employee morale
    d. Umbrella goals

166. Which of the following is a direct benefit of analyzing labor markets during workforce planning?
    a. Recruiting top talent for open positions
    b. Identifying where employers are competing for labor
    c. Gaining insight as to why employees are leaving
    d. Benchmarking with other competitors

167. When an organization identifies, targets, and strives to minimize unacceptable dangers or threats, what process are they engaging in?
    a. SMART goals
    b. Myers-Briggs Type Indicator
    c. Risk management
    d. Corporate social responsibility

168. Lucy is the HR director for an organization that employs individuals across the country. A majority of the employees are located in the corporate headquarters; however, many work in service centers located in large metropolitan areas. Although the majority of her HR team supports and works at the corporate headquarters, she also has team members stationed at each of the service centers to allow all employees to have access to HR support. Which service model is Lucy using?
    a. Centralized
    b. Matrixed
    c. Outsourced
    d. Decentralized

169. Which of the following statements is true regarding outsourcing of HR work?
    a. HR work that is dependent on having knowledge of workplace relationships, organizational culture, or team dynamics is not appropriate to outsource.
    b. Performance management, strategic planning, and employee communications are all appropriate examples of HR work that should be outsourced.
    c. A general rule of thumb is to always perform HR work in-house through a centralized, decentralized, or matrixed service model.
    d. A general rule of thumb is to outsource HR work as much as possible to free up valuable time and resources to train and problem solve.

170. Why should a company create a mission statement and a vision statement?
    a. To establish an intentional culture across a large company and many employees. To help influence all actions employees and leaders in the company take.
    b. To generate external support for the company by creating good will from customers.
    c. They are required when you register a business.
    d. Both A and B

313

171. What is an advantage of hiring from external sources rather than internal sources?
    a. It is more time- and cost-effective.
    b. It adds to workforce diversity.
    c. It has a lower interview-to-hire ratio.
    d. It leads to more rapid promotions.

172. In addition to improving training for employees, HR would also like to update its own policies to better address issues of workplace misconduct. Which of the following would be a useful measure to enact?
    a. Developing the HR workforce to handle all aspects of reporting, investigating, and addressing complaints internally.
    b. Contracting with a telecommunications group to set up a 24/7 harassment reporting phone hotline.
    c. Prioritizing diversity when hiring new HR employees.
    d. Maintaining close communication with senior-level leaders to streamline efforts.

173. Carol was tasked with researching, initiating, and implementing a new online training module for employees. The module would allow all employees, regardless of level and position, to complete mandatory training related to compliance, ethics, and regulatory topics. Unfortunately, the project did not meet the established goals regarding training offerings, budget, and timing. Certain regulatory trainings were not included, the final costs were over budget, and the rollout was more than three months late. Which of the following methods should Carol apply to this situation to determine why the objectives were not met?
    a. Process mapping
    b. Cause-and-effect diagram
    c. Value stream mapping
    d. SMART objectives

174. What tasks are associated with offboarding an employee?
    a. Returning any company equipment and keys
    b. An exit interview
    c. A tour of the job site and new hire orientation
    d. Both A and B

175. What is an employer with more than fifty employees required to do for a nursing mother employee under the Fair Labor Standards Act (FLSA)?
    a. Provide a private bathroom for a mother when it is their normal break time.
    b. Provide a private non-bathroom space for the mother during their normal break time.
    c. Provide a private non-bathroom space for the mother as frequently as needed.
    d. There is no space requirement for accommodation if the mother has a car in the parking lot and breaks are provided when necessary.

Answer Explanations for Practice Test #3

1. D: Maximizing profits despite any consequences to the surrounding environment is not part of social responsibility. When practicing corporate social responsibility, there are several ways an organization can engage the community. First, a firm can establish alliances with influential members of the community or a respected local organization. Secondly, a firm can deliver on its promise of delivering low-cost goods and services to the community. Lastly, as one tenet of corporate responsibility is improving the quality of life in a community, it should hire as many locals as possible.

2. D: Organizational branding can serve multiple purposes. One is creating a distinctive logo that is easily identifiable to consumers. Furthermore, organizational branding represents an opportunity to establish a perception of values and ethics that consumers understand when they see the logo. The famous logo for the Michelin Corporation is a jovial tire man, which articulates friendly service and exactly what the firm sells. The numeral IV is not part of branding, but more of a characteristic of marketing.

3. A: Business metrics are quantifiable ways to assess and measure the efficacy of specific policies, programs, or products. Similar to cost-benefit analysis, these metrics are objective and inform the firm whether an action should proceed. Metrics should be used when speaking to consumers and investors to establish trust and confidence.

4. A: To guarantee that employment-at-will remains in effect, one of the best guidelines for employee handbooks is to include a disclaimer that states the handbook is not intended to be any type of contractual agreement between the company and employee.

5. B: The turnover rate is calculated by taking the number of employees that exited the company during the year, dividing it by the average number of employees during the year, and then multiplying that amount by 100. In this example, this equates to $\frac{125}{1100} \times 100$, which is 11.36%.

6. C: An open-door policy is used to establish a relationship where employees feel comfortable speaking directly with management about problems and suggestions. Town hall meetings, Choice *A*, formal gatherings for the entire company that are commonly referred to as "all-hands meetings," tend to focus on sharing information "from the top down" concerning the overall organization. These meetings are not usually designed to allow feedback from employees about smaller detail issues. Management by Walking Around (MBWA), Choice *B*, as the name suggests, involves having managers and supervisors physically get out of their offices and interact with employees in person. MBWA allows management to check on employee progress, inquire about potential issues, and gain other feedback without relying on employees to "make the first move." Finally, department meetings, Choice *D*, are formal gatherings of employees and management in a given department that typically take place on a set day and time, allow everyone involved to share ideas, and offer solutions to company challenges.

7. A: A task force is an involvement strategy that allows staff to work together in a temporary fashion to focus on a specific problem. Employees can also work together in a formal capacity as part of a committee to address company concerns, Choice *B*. Committees may be temporary or ongoing, and employees' service on a committee may also be for a specific term or a permanent appointment. Moreover, an employee-management committee, Choice *D*, is a specific kind of committee where employees work alongside management to address company concerns. Sometimes known as employee

315

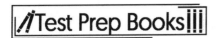

participation groups, Choice *C,* these committees also can be temporary or ongoing, depending on the needs of the organization.

8. A: 360-degree feedback is a method by which employees receive anonymous feedback from their managers, peers, direct reports, and customers. Choice *B* is incorrect since 360-degree feedback involves much more than employee self-appraisals. Choice *C* is incorrect since 360-degree feedback involves much more than reviews by only fellow employees. Choice *D* is also incorrect since 360-degree feedback involves much more than reviews only by management.

9. A: There are multiple functions for rating in performance management. The first purpose of rating is to give management the opportunity to identify the best performing employees. Once this is done, these employees can be rewarded in various ways. Conversely, rating is a technique used by management to distinguish poorly performing employees. Underperforming employees can be dealt with in many ways: they can receive a decrease in pay, be forced to attend additional training programs, or ultimately have their employment terminated.

10. A: The intended purpose of the five disciplines outlined by Peter Senge is to enable organizational apparatuses to remain adaptable and capable of change. Essential to the five disciplines are communication, dialogue, team learning, and establishing common goals. Individuals must develop personal skills and mastery, but there remains an equal focus on the organization itself. It must be able to adapt to extemporaneous circumstances, adopt innovative tactics, and embrace participatory approaches that permit the fluidity of ideas. By compelling members of an organization to communicate and work cooperatively, the concept of systems thinking is critical to Senge's five principles.

11. D: A type of benefit that customers believe they could not obtain anywhere else is an example of differential advantage, not competitive advantage. Competitive advantage is the strategy of maintaining maximum competitiveness by pursuing policies and programs that increase one's advantage. Examples of competitive advantage are implementing new technology, offshoring to lower business costs, and shedding underperforming or unnecessary laborers.

12. C: Rules, practices, and institutions that address ecosystems in relation to the environment are known as environmental governance. Corporate governance refers to the policies and institutional code that a firm establishes to fulfill its role as a for-profit entity and an integral stakeholder in the community. Of course, firms are not the only actors that shape its governance laws—public policy has a salient role. The Sarbanes-Oxley Act mandated new protocol that senior executives must follow to increase transparency and accountability. Moreover, corporate governance can serve as a valuable tool for cultivating a firm's self-image.

13. B: Corporate restructuring is a broad term to describe a change in a firm's operations, legal code, or ownership to make it more competitive by increasing productive potential and lowering costs. One aspect of corporate restructuring is offshoring. Offshoring—moving the physical operations of a firm to a different country—is done to lower business costs while maintaining maximum competitiveness.

14. C: Enterprise risk management (ERM) are comprehensive policies and procedures that dictate how an organization handles risk and loss. The purpose of ERM is to coordinate and create a harmony of responses to problems facing an organization. ERMs lead to greater levels of stability and structure.

15. A: A policy is a guideline that focuses on organizational actions. A rule, Choice *B,* is more specific to the situation and is used to regulate and/or restrict an individual's behavior. A procedure, Choice *C,* is a detailed description that answers when, what, who, and where. Finally, a Standard Operating Procedure (SOP), Choice *D*, is a written set of instructions that documents how to perform a routine activity.

16. B: A rule is more specific to the situation and is used to regulate and/or restrict an individual's behavior. A policy, Choice *A*, is a guideline that focuses on organizational actions. A procedure, Choice *C*, is a detailed description that answers when, what, who, and where. Finally, a Standard Operating Procedure (SOP), Choice *D*, is a written set of instructions that documents how to perform a routine activity.

17. C: In a progressive discipline policy, a verbal warning is typically followed with a second warning that is paired with a formal written warning (even if the warning is for a different type of employee violation).

18. D: A staff member who violates a work rule that is a dischargeable offense does not need to go through all of the steps in the progressive discipline process before they are terminated. However, instead of terminating the staff member on the spot, it is best for an HR professional to place the staff member on administrative leave while conducting an investigation. This ensures that all parties are interviewed, and all of the necessary facts are gathered to protect the company against any possible future claims of wrongful termination.

19. A: Implementing a hiring freeze is an activity that is an example of downsizing. Reducing the number of hierarchical levels, Choice *B*, is an example of corporate restructuring. Utilizing contingent workers to fill in, Choice *C*, and outsourcing work to an external service provider, Choice *D*, are examples of workforce expansion.

20. C: Job competency is a detailed list of broad skills or traits needed for a position. Job analysis, Choice *A*, is a way of gathering and analyzing information systemically about the context, content, and human resource requirements of jobs within an organization. Job description, Choice *B*, is a detailed breakdown of specific tasks, skills and knowledge required for a position. Finally, job specification, Choice *D*, is a detailed description of specific qualifications, experience, or education that is needed to perform tasks.

21. D: Essential job functions are tasks and responsibilities that are fundamental to a specific position. Job competencies, Choice *A*, are detailed lists of broad skills or traits needed for positions. Marginal job functions, Choice *B*, are duties that are ancillary or incidental to the nature or purpose of a job. Finally, job specifications, Choice *C*, are detailed descriptions of specific qualifications, experience, or education that is needed to perform tasks.

22. B: A non-directive interview utilizes questions that are developed from an applicant's answers to previous questions. An unstructured interview, Choice *A*, takes place when an interviewer improvises and asks applicants questions that were not prepared prior to the start of the interview. A semi-structured interview, Choice *C*, occurs when an interviewer has guided conversations with applicants that involve broad questions and new questions that come about from the discussions that take place. Finally, a structured interview, Choice *D*, is controlled by the interviewer, who has a list of specific, job-related questions prepared prior to the start of the interview. The same questions are asked of all applicants.

23. D: An implied contract is inferred from an employer's actions or conduct. An express contract, Choice *A*, is based on an employer's written or oral words. Employment-at-will, Choice *B*, is a common-law doctrine that states employers have the right to hire, promote, demote, or fire whomever they choose, provided there is not a law or contract in place to the contrary. Under this doctrine, employees are also free to leave an employer whenever they choose to seek other employment. Finally, a golden parachute clause, Choice *C*, is an agreement between an employer and an executive that guarantees the executive the right to certain benefits if their employment is terminated.

24. D: Wrongful discharge can occur when an employee is terminated after they refuse to do something unsafe, unethical, or illegal, such as a pharmacist refusing to sign off on a prescription to be dispensed that does not have a date. This type of termination is wrongful because it violates public policy. Additionally, a charge of wrongful discharge can also occur when an employee is terminated after an employer promised them job security, thus violating an implied employment agreement. In this example, an employee should not be fired for taking time off work to serve on a jury, which falls under the category of violating public policy.

25. A: Severance pay is not required by law. Receipt of severance pay does not guarantee that a former employee will not file a lawsuit against the employer, Choice *B*. Severance pay does not increase an employer's contributions to unemployment tax, Choice *C*. Finally, severance pay does not guarantee that an employee will receive other benefits such as the continuation of health care coverage or outplacement services, Choice *D*.

26. B: Although the employee who was bullied is leaving the organization and did not file a complaint regarding the bullying during the course of her employment, the HR professional is still obligated to treat this matter seriously and should conduct a full investigation.

27. A: Under the Americans with Disabilities Act, an employer does not need to make an accommodation for a disabled employee if doing so will result in an undue hardship. Employers are not required to establish affirmative action plans for the disabled (but may choose to do so). This law does not exclude rehabilitated drug users. Pre-employment medical exams cannot be required before extending a job offer.

28. B: The Americans with Disabilities Act does not provide protection for an employee who is found to be using illegal drugs. Employees who are diagnosed with AIDS, those who suffer from epilepsy, and those with serious psychological problems are protected under this act.

29. C: Under the Pregnancy Discrimination Act of 1978, an employer must give a woman a comparable position to the one that she held prior to her maternity leave (if the company does so with employees on short-term disability).

30. D: A company must set a placement goal when it is found to employ fewer minorities and women than is indicated by their availability. This is known as underutilization.

31. A: Under USERRA, employees who are out on military leave are expected to receive the same seniority-based benefits that they would have received had they not been out of work on leave, such as vacation time and 401(k) contributions. After the first month of military leave, employers are not required to continue group healthcare coverage at their expense. An employer is expected to continue to pay exempt employees who are out on military leave their full salary, less any compensation that they receive for serving in the military. Additionally, employers are encouraged to make reasonable efforts to accommodate disabled veterans returning from military leave.

32. A: These are all unique benefits that would seem attractive to most employees. While job tasks and reports could be listed on the job posting, they do not fall under benefits. Salary is considered compensation and not an exact benefit; in addition, an exact salary is not usually posted in a job description.

33. A: These behaviors describe the attitudes, beliefs, and values that dictate the company's work days. The other options are relevant to job duties or could be ways to connect with the employees but do not reflect the overall company culture.

34. D: All of these could be key stakeholders for a parental leave initiative. Pregnant mothers, male employees who have, are expecting, or want children, and managers who have to manage operations with decreased staff are all affected by decisions made to parental leave policies.

35. C: A thank you note and a gift card for a job well done is an example of an employee recognition program. An end of year bonus, Choice *A,* is an example of additional compensation an employee receives as a one-time payment that does not become part of their base pay. A plaque given for fifteen years of service to the organization, Choice *B,* is an example of a service award. Finally, a merit given during annual review time, Choice *D,* is an example of incentive pay given to employees for good performance.

36. C: During a larger group RIF, the affected employees who are being laid off and given a document to sign, known as a separation agreement and general release, must be given forty-five days to sign and return the agreement, along with a seven-day revocation period. This allows them time to consider the terms of the agreement and to review the agreement with a lawyer, if they choose to do so.

37. D: The next step in the grievance process would involve the union steward discussing the grievance with the supervisor's manager and/or the HR manager. Then, a committee of union officers should discuss the grievance with the appropriate managers in the company. The national union representative would then discuss the grievance with designated company executives. If, after this process, the grievance is still not settled, it would then go to arbitration.

38. A: An employee must file a complaint charge of discrimination with the EEOC within a period of 180 days of the alleged incident.

39. A: Employers with fifty or more employees and $50,000 in federal contracts are required to have affirmative action plans in place, as well as employers who are a member of the federal banking system and employers who issue, sell, or redeem U.S. Savings Bonds.

40. B: An availability analysis is the major element of an affirmative action plan that examines the internal and external population of women and minorities to determine their theoretical opportunity for employment. A utilization analysis, Choice *A,* compares the availability of women and minorities to their current representation within each job group at the company. A job group analysis, Choice *C,* is a list of all titles that comprise each job group. Jobs are grouped according to whether they have similar content, responsibilities, compensation, and opportunities for advancement. Choice *D,* an organizational profile, is a snapshot of an organization and organizes the key components and competitions within that organization.

41. C: A utilization analysis is the major element of an affirmative action plan that compares the availability of women and minorities to their current representation within each job group at the company. An availability analysis, Choice *A*, examines the internal and external population of women and minorities to determine their theoretical opportunity for employment. A job group analysis, Choice *B*, is a list of all titles that comprise each job group. Jobs are grouped according to whether they have similar content, responsibilities, wage rates, and opportunities for advancement. Finally, an organizational profile, Choice *D*, depicts the organization's staffing patterns to determine if any barriers exist to equal opportunity employment.

42. D: Under federal guidelines, an employer is required to keep employment applications and resumes for one year after creation or following the hire/no hire decision (whichever date is later).

43. C: A learner analysis can be completed in conjunction with a task analysis during the needs assessment process. Data is gathered from both mid-level and senior level managers during an organizational analysis, and the point of performing this type of analysis is to ensure that the company is on board with the training. Data is gathered from individuals who have direct knowledge of the work during a task analysis.

44. C: The Fishbone Diagram is a tool that seeks to analyze the primary causes of an effect of a problem. Ultimately, the diagram engages problems and investigates remedial efforts for improvement. In a group formation, a consensus is gathered to identify possible causes, which could range from employee performance or outdated technology to inefficient methods of production or environmental implications. By isolating each factor, the diagram details organizational procedure to scientifically diagnose potential inefficiencies.

45. A: Six Sigma is a method used by organizations to reduce inefficiencies and other cumbersome techniques that diminish profitability. It is a rationally organized process that is enlisted to constantly increase productive capacities by eliminating antiquated or outdated machinery and technology. Furthermore, Six Sigma may scrutinize opaque bureaucratic structures or wasteful practices that obstruct maximum profitability. Grounded in statistical analysis, this methodology exhibits a scientific and technical approach to solving critical problems facing an organization.

46. B: Email makes it easy to get information to a lot of people very quickly. However, this communication method can result in employees suffering from "information overload" from too many emails. The intranet, Choice *A*, has the benefit of no risk of important information being accessed by someone outside the organization. Intranets can be effective at communicating important ongoing information about the company, such as policies and procedures. Newsletters, Choice *C*, can provide a variety of information and have the potential to do so in an engaging and welcoming manner. However, newsletters can be labor-intensive. Finally, word-of-mouth, Choice *D*, can quickly spread information throughout a group of people. However, information can become muddled, misinterpreted, and unrecognizable as it is passed from person to person.

47. B: In a binding decision, the disputing parties are required by law to follow the decision reached as a result of the arbitration process. In compulsory arbitration, Choice *A*, the disputing parties are required by law to go through the arbitration process. In voluntary arbitration, Choice *C*, the disputing parties choose to undergo the arbitration process. Finally, constructive confrontation, Choice *D*, is a type of mediation used in some extremely complicated or contentious disputes, particularly ones where neither party is able to agree to a compromise.

48. D: Informational picketing is done by employees for the purpose of letting the public know that they are not represented by any one authority and thus plan to organize. Recognitional picketing, Choice *A*, is done by employees for the purpose of encouraging their employer to recognize their union as their representative. Organizational picketing, Choice *B*, is done by employees for the purpose of convincing other employees to join their union. Finally, consumer picketing, Choice *C*, takes place when employees picket to discourage the public from doing business with the employer in question.

49. A: At least 30% of eligible employees are required to sign authorization cards by the National Labor Relations Board before it will order an election where employees can vote on whether to be represented by a union.

50. B: If employees win the vote to decertify their union on August 31 in a given calendar year, a new election cannot be held until after one year has passed.

51. C: Via the Weingarten rights, a union employee is entitled to have a union representative present if they are being questioned by a manager in a discussion that may ultimately lead to a disciplinary action.

52. D: Security clauses are considered to be an illegal subject that cannot be discussed during a collective bargaining negotiation. Voluntary subjects, worker safety conditions, and working conditions and terms are all legal subjects that can be discussed during a collective bargaining negotiation.

53. A: A whistle-blower reports or publicizes any illegal or unethical information about an organization or industry. An example of a whistle-blower is former tobacco industry official Jeffrey Wigand, who confessed in a televised interview that the tobacco industry was intentionally packing cigarettes with addictive levels of nicotine. Whistle-blowers are generally perceived as villains to institutions, while others believe they risk their livelihood for a just cause. Whistleblowers can operate in public or private institutions.

54. D: A business plan has a variety of different projections. Some of these projections are annual goals, projected growth targets, and net income expectations. However, bonuses for executives aren't calculated in a business plan, which are intended to increase the firm's profitability and productivity.

55. C: Although shareholders can be affected by a business, they are not stakeholders because they have stock ownership. Stakeholders have other interests in a business besides profitability. Employees, surrounding businesses, and the local community all have a stake in the financial state of a business, but their concerns transcend the appreciation of its stock.

56. A: Parallel bargaining is a strategy that is used during a collective bargaining negotiation when a union successfully negotiates an agreement with a company, then uses the result of that negotiation as an example while dealing with a different company. Coordinated bargaining, Choice *B*, takes place when several unions within an organization meet with the employer to negotiate beneficial results for all the different groups they represent (also called multi-unit bargaining). Multi-employer bargaining, Choice *C*, occurs when a union with employees in multiple companies meets with all of those companies as a single negotiation. Finally, single-unit bargaining, Choice *D*, occurs when union representatives meet with one employer at a time, concerned only with that particular agreement, and not attempting to use the process as a springboard or advantage in separate negotiations.

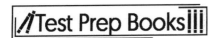

57. B: An employee who is terminated for whistleblowing or for reporting unlawful conduct by the employer is an exception to the concept of employment-at-will, since these activities are protected under the law.

58. C: The employer was ultimately held responsible for negligent hiring. In this example, the employer should have known that the employee posed a risk to other employees or to customers. If the employer had completed a thorough background check, they would have checked the employee's past driving record (since it was relevant to his position).

59. D: A sympathy strike is considered to be a fair labor practice. Choice A, hot cargo agreements, Choice B, jurisdictional strikes, and Choice C, secondary boycotts, are all considered to be unfair labor practices.

60. D: An employee who is out of the office on a medical leave of absence and who will not be returning to work would not be eligible to vote in an upcoming union election. An employee who is temporarily laid off, an employee who is out sick with the flu, and an employee who is out on military leave right before the election would all be eligible to vote in an upcoming union election.

61. A: Under the Taft-Hartley Act, creating a company-sponsored labor union is illegal.

62. A: Under federal guidelines, an employer is required to keep records associated with employment benefits for a period of six years.

63. B: Under federal guidelines, an employer is required to keep records associated with family medical leave for a period of three years.

64. D: When an employee regularly reviews engineering design documents, this would most likely be considered an essential job function.

65. A: An employee who is a salesperson would more than likely warrant a written employment contract to outline information, such as salary (including guaranteed or discretionary bonuses), commission structure and payment processes, and clauses referencing non-compete agreements.

66. B: An employer should obtain signed consent from the candidate to check work references before extending a contingent offer of employment. This is due to the fact that many companies have been sued by job applicants who have discovered that they have been given poor references. Physical examinations cannot be required by an employer until after a job offer has been made. Finally, polygraph tests cannot be required by the majority of employers.

67. C: A bona fide occupational qualification is an exception to Title VII of the Civil Rights Act of 1964. This act applies to most employers with fifteen or more employees. A new seniority system implemented in the workplace and work-related requirements that are not truly legitimate are not exceptions to Title VII of the Civil Rights Act of 1964.

68. B: The worker's compensation is calculated as one of the costs needed to get the project done. Without paying the worker, he or she cannot be used as a resource on the project. The worker is not necessarily a stakeholder. The worker's salary is a benefit to the worker directly in return for their work, but it is not considered a benefit for the purpose of a cost-benefit analysis. The worker's pay is also fixed as a salary and is not considered a dependent variable for the purpose of the analysis.

69. C: Bringing up a company's fiscal year is not necessary to make a proposal to management. Fiscal periods are only relevant to accountants for tax purposes.

70. C: When implementing a new initiative, HR professionals can examine internal data from similar projects to help make their planning stage as useful and accurate as possible before beginning implementation. However, Angela should not copy Myra's initiative directly, as she is working with a different team that has different needs.

71. B: Even with the most diligent planning, HR leaders should expect the unexpected and never be too emotionally attached to outcomes. Michael should realize that all baseline plans are fluid and manage his expectations accordingly, while also preparing contingency plans for his operations. Most federal funds cannot roll over from fiscal years, and simply communicating information does not set them in stone.

72. A: Larry should have cross-trained his employees to fill in for one another in the case of emergencies. This allows normal business operations to continue, rather than halt, if an employee is absent. Samir should not have to work remotely when ill, and as a team leader, Larry should not be expected step in and fulfill Samir's entire full-time job. Analyzing Samir's workday for causes of the illness is unnecessary unless Samir requests it.

73. A: A modified duty assignment is a temporary arrangement that offers injured or sick employees the option to work through their condition at a reduced capacity. These assignments are also dubbed "light work." Under many circumstances, modified duty is beneficial to both employers and employees, but employees do have the right to deny an employer's request if they are unable to perform the task.

74. B: Procurement policies are regulations that allow an organization to obtain and secure goods and services in an orderly and beneficial way to minimize cost and maximize savings. The size of an organization needs to be carefully considered when crafting a procurement policy, but the intent is to maximize productivity and minimize expenses. Typically, large organizations command greater bargaining power than smaller organizations.

75. B: A hazard communication program is a federal law mandated by OSHA that requires employers to inform employees when they are working with hazardous materials and the nature of such materials. It stipulates that dangerous health and noxious physical effects must be communicated to employees before they begin a specific job. The provision of OSHA that deals with hazard communication is the Hazard Communication Standard (HCS). In addition to the HCS, all organizations containing hazardous chemicals must provide hazardous material training to employees, access to material safety data sheets (MSDS), and proper labeling of containers. Hazard communication is legally binding.

76. C: Business continuity plans are tools used to identify potential threats and their associated impacts. These plans establish procedures to handle interruptions, disruptions, and/or loss of business functions. Business continuity plans respond to a variety of crisis scenarios, such as loss of administrative capacities, a hack into the operating system, and threat of workplace violence. These plans must be observed by all staff to ensure the plan's effectiveness. If an employee does not comply, disciplinary measures should be enforced by the organization.

77. D: A social engineer can impact an organization by manipulating members to extract sensitive or classified information. Typically, an attacker will employ deceptive tactics to convince the target to provide information such as bank numbers, passwords, and Social Security numbers. Organizations

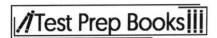

should educate employees on security and the identification of untrustworthy individuals. Employees should be able to assess suspicious situations and clearly recognize red flags.

78. B: A learning curve is a graphical representation of a person's learning progress. A plateau learning curve indicates that learning takes place at an accelerated rate and then comes to a halt. Out of the four types of learning curves discussed, the plateau learning curve is unique. It is the only learning curve that indicates a stoppage in learning. A positively accelerating learning curve represents slow initial learning, but then a rapid increase. A negatively accelerating learning curve depicts an accelerated beginning followed by a slowdown. Lastly, an S-shaped learning curve denotes initial sluggishness, heightened learning activity, followed by a return to lethargy.

79. A: The three types of organization development interventions are human process interventions, sociotechnical interventions, and techno-structural interventions. Human process interventions are coordinated efforts to correct inefficiencies through human contact. Specific types of human process interventions are coaching, mentoring, training, or using a third party to mediate disputes. Sociotechnical interventions attempt to integrate new machinery and technology into pre-existing organizational models. Lastly, the goal of techno-structural interventions is to use technology to its most productive capacities.

80. B: The Pareto analysis system is a statistical model that postulates that 80 percent of output is generated by 20 percent of input. Management can use this rule to identify where to invest scarce resources. Other names for this rule are the "80-20 rule" and "law of the vital few." Remembering these other names can be helpful because they highlight the essential functionality of the rule. By constantly searching for the most productive members of an organization or the resources that yield the most revenue, management personnel are able to prioritize employees or investments over others. This analysis can be useful when restructuring an organization, rating employee performance, capital investment, and much more.

81. B: Public domain is a provision in federal copyright law stating that work that meets designated criterion can be used without authorization. There are two possibilities where one can use material without obtaining consent. First, if the federal government publishes a work, then it is considered to be public, thus falling into the public domain. Second, copyrights can expire. Material that is created on or after January 1, 1978 is protected for the remainder of the author's life plus seventy years after death. Anonymous material, works made for hire, and articles are protected for ninety-five years from the date of creation or 120 years after being published.

82. A: The Wagner Act dictates what are known as unfair labor practices. The Norris-LaGuardia Act, Choice *B,* outlawed yellow-dog contracts. The Taft-Hartley Act, Choice *C,* established the Federal Mediation and Conciliation Service. The Railway Labor Act, Choice *D,* resolves labor disputes by substituting bargaining, arbitration, and mediation for strikes.

83. B: Forcing employees to join a union is prohibited by the Taft-Hartley Act. The Sherman Antitrust Act prevents individuals and organizations from forming monopolies, Choice *A.* The Landrum-Griffith Act allowed for a closed shop exception for construction trades and gave union members the right to sue their union, Choices *C* and *D.*

84. C: In Choice *C*, the employer has one hundred or more full-time employees. The mass layoff is expected to last for at least six months, and at least 33 percent of the workforce at the employment site is being laid off.

Under the WARN Act, an employer is required to provide a minimum of sixty days' notice to their employees in advance of a mass layoff if the following criteria are met.

The employer has one hundred or more full-time employees (or a total of full-time and part-time employees working 4,000 hours per week, not counting overtime, at all of their employment sites combined)

The layoff will result in an employment loss at a single site for either fifty or more full-time employees, if they make up at least 33 percent of the workforce at the employment site, or 500 or more full-time employees, and the layoff is for more than six months.

The WARN act also requires that an employer provide a minimum of sixty days' notice to their employees in advance of a plant closing if the following criteria are met.

The employer has one hundred or more full-time employees (or a total of full-time and part-time employees working 4,000 hours per week, not counting overtime, at all of their employment sites combined)

The plant closing will result in the temporary or permanent shutdown of an entire site or one or more facilities or operating units within a single site that results in an employment loss during any thirty-day period of fifty or more full-time employees.

85. C: Modeling ethical behavior is the most effective way to show employees what is acceptable in the workplace. The other methods listed can help, but they may not be very effective on their own.

86. A: Transparency allows employees to know what is going on in most, if not all, aspects of the organization as it relates to their job. High transparency is associated with employees who feel valued, validated, and report high morale.

87. C: The job posting is the first place to share the company's mission, vision, and ethical standards. This attracts candidates with similar values to apply. Ethical standards should be reviewed again during the interview process and new hire orientation to ensure good fit and promote the values.

88. C: Rather than speaking about all of his hard work and contributions, Ben chose to share his team's accomplishments without singling anyone out. This is a display of strong team-oriented culture in the workplace.

89. A: Feedback is an important part of the evaluation stage, which examines if processes were implemented smoothly, effectively, and provided value.

90. C: There should be additional evaluation standards beyond "meets expectations" to recognize and encourage employee achievement. The purpose of an employee evaluation is to give meaningful feedback that leads employees to set and achieve new goals. If employees are simply scored on whether they meet expectations, they may not be given the impetus they need to set and achieve high performance objectives. Choice *A* is not the best answer because, while HR should work to incorporate new technologies where appropriate, this is not the most meaningful change that the process needs.

325

Choice *B* is not the best answer because evaluations that are too frequent can be just as harmful as evaluations that are too infrequent; they might increase employee stress, feelings of micromanagement, or feelings that evaluations are not very meaningful. Finally, Choice *D* is not the best answer because the back page of the evaluation only focuses on areas of improvement and doesn't recognize any positive areas of performance.

91. B: Focus feedback on future goals rather than past mistakes. Evaluations should be presented as a chance for employees to focus on their achievements. If they didn't achieve their goals to their full potential, how can they reach their goals next time? Future-focused evaluations give employees a concrete action plan moving forward. Choice *A* is not the best answer because, while self-evaluations are a useful tool, they should be used alongside evaluations from someone in a supervisory role. Choice *C* is also not a good choice. Rewards for performance may work well in some organizations; however, publicly posting the results of employees' evaluations would violate their privacy, and many employees react negatively to competition. Finally, Choice *D* is not the best way to make a meaningful change.

92. A: It improves feelings of employee satisfaction. Employee satisfaction is closely linked to feelings of contributing to meaningful work. Particularly for the younger generation of workers, employees want to feel that they are making a positive impact on society. CSR is one way that an organization can allow employees to feel that they are helping others, the environment, and/or their community. The other choices refer to things with a monetary benefit, which would be quantitative rather than qualitative.

93. D: FMLA. This acronym stands for the Family Medical Leave Act, which outlines standards by which employees are granted unpaid time off for family or medical leave without being terminated from their jobs. All the other choices refer to things covered by the EEOC: EPA (Equal Pay Act, which prohibits salary discrimination based on sex), ADEA (Age Discrimination in Employment Act, which prohibits age discrimination for workers who are forty and older), and Title VII of the Civil Rights Act (which prohibits discrimination based on race, color, sex, religion, or national origin).

94. C: Offshoring can have many positive effects that transcend the corporation. Offshoring reduces the costs of business, which leads to lower prices for consumers. Lowering business costs doesn't just lead to lower prices—it also frees up revenue to participate in philanthropic activity.

95. D: Choice *D* mimics the wording of the question, but the explanation is irrelevant. It's imperative that firms anticipate potential changes in public policy because they must adjust. The success of this adjustment will depend upon institutional preparedness. Furthermore, if anticipated changes are expected to be damaging, a firm will want to engage in lobbying efforts to modify and amend the policies.

96. C: Mergers occur when two companies combine to form a new one. Acquisitions occur when one company purchases another without forming a new company. One notable merger occurred in 1999, when Exxon and Mobile merged to form ExxonMobil. It can be helpful to think of mergers as consolidations.

97. B: Leadership buy-in promotes top-down change; without leaders in the company supporting new initiatives, it is highly unlikely that subordinate employees will embrace change. They are more likely to resist if they feel those in leadership positions do not find the change valuable.

98. A: An anonymous and confidential hotline can help employees report potentially unethical behaviors and feel less discomfort than if they had to do so publicly.

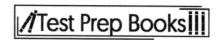

99. B: The Sarbanes-Oxley Act (SOX) established high levels of transparency and accountability for senior executives in accounting and recordkeeping. Passed in the wake of global corporate accounting scandals, SOX provides greater protection to shareholders and investors by emphasizing transparency and accountability. The legislation mandates that senior executives report financial information to shareholders and the Securities and Exchange Committee (SEC). Furthermore, SOX imposes harsher penalties for white-collar crime and requires detailed reporting to the SEC whenever there is a significant fluctuation in a company's finances.

100. A: The Americans with Disabilities Act (ADA) is a federal law that prevents discrimination based on disability and requires employers to provide reasonable accommodations to disabled employees. Additionally, the ADA stipulates that public entities be accessible for disabled persons. The law applies to all types of work (part-time, full-time, or work during a temporary period) in organizations with fifteen or more employees. The ADA became a law in 1990.

101. D: Alternative work locations permit organizations to decentralize operations, thus minimizing the possibility for a person to cause significant destruction.

102. B: Employees who possess an aptitude for social media skills provide an additional asset to the company in the areas of marketing and advertising.

103. A: A needs analysis is the process in which an organization gathers information about the principal needs and requests of its members. This analysis studies the expectations and requirements of subjects who are affected by workplace programs or regulations. Surveys and questionnaires are the primary means of procuring information about specific needs and requests. After the needs analysis is conducted, the information is assessed and incorporated into plans to improve the functionality of the organization.

104. A: FMLA only covers unpaid, protected leave for the following reasons: the birth of a child, adoption or foster-care placement; the serious health condition of a spouse, child, or parent; the serious health condition of the employee—one requiring inpatient care or continuing treatment by a healthcare provider, qualifying exigency leave, or leave to address the most common issues that arise when an employee's spouse, child, or parent is on active duty or call to active duty status—e.g., making financial and legal arrangements and arranging for alternative childcare; and military caregiver leave or leave to care for a covered service member—employee's spouse, child, parent, or next of kin—with a serious injury or illness. Employees are to be granted up to twenty-six weeks of job-protected, unpaid leave during a twelve-month period to care for a covered service member.

105. B: Life insurance is a discretionary or voluntary benefit that is provided by employers. Choice *A*, unpaid family leave (based on FMLA), Choice *C*, continuation of healthcare coverage (based on COBRA), and Choice *D*, worker's compensation, are all non-discretionary benefits, since employers are mandated to provide them based on certain statutes.

106. C: Pension plan. Indirect compensation, most commonly referred to as employee benefits, includes such elements as healthcare coverage, retirement/pension plans, paid time off from work, and short-term and long-term disability.

107. C: Job specification is the knowledge, skills, abilities, education, and experience that are essential to performing a specific job. Choice *A*, job analysis, is the process used to identify the particular job requirements and duties and their relative importance. Choice *B*, job description, is a general written

327

statement for a specific position based on a job analysis. Choice *D,* job evaluation, determines the relative worth of each job position by creating a hierarchy.

108. C: Factor comparison method. Quantitative job evaluation methods use a scaling system and provide a score that indicates how valuable one job is when compared to another job. The two specific examples noted are the point factor method and the factor comparison method. Choice *A,* job ranking, is when an organization defines the value of a specific job compared to other jobs in the organization. Choice *B,* paired comparison, is when an individual and their position is compared to another individual and their position. Choice *D,* job classification, is a system designed to evaluate the duties and authority levels of a job.

109. C: Leveling can be used if a job included on a salary survey is similar, but not identical, to a position within the organization. The data for that job can be weighted or leveled to create a better match. Choice *B,* benchmarking, is used to evaluate something by using a comparison. Choice *D,* wage compression, is when a new employee is paid at a higher wage than an individual who is currently employed in a similar position and with similar skills.

110. D: Broadbanding leads to flatter organization structures. Broadbanding occurs when employers decide to combine multiple pay levels into one, which results in only a handful of salary grades with much wider ranges. This type of pay structure is easier to administer and eliminates green and red circle rates. Broadbanding also leads to a flatter organizational structure, which encourages employees' horizontal movement through skill acquisition versus the traditional vertical movement through promotions to new pay grades.

111. C: Premium pay can be given to compensate employees as a higher rate of overtime pay for working on holidays or vacation days. Some employees receive shift pay, Choice *B,* for working second or third shifts or for being called into work during an emergency, also known as emergency shift pay, Choice *D.* Reporting pay, Choice *A,* can be paid to employees who arrive at their place of employment and find that there is no available work for them to perform.

112. A: Worker attrition. Workforce supply may refer to the number of workers available for a specific position or for the industry as a whole. Worker attrition, or the number of workers who leave due to things like retirement or resignation, affects the workforce supply. The other choices all refer to factors that influence workforce demand, or the number of workers needed by an organization at a given time.

113. C: Diversity involves hiring employees with a variety of backgrounds, personalities, and working styles, while inclusion involves making sure those differences are heard and represented in the workplace. Choice *A* is not the best answer because, while some aspects of an organization's diversity program may be guided by EEOC regulations, it does not include other diversity considerations like a variety of personality types, working styles, and backgrounds. Choice *B* is also incorrect because inclusion refers to integrating the contributions of diverse employees into the workplace. Finally, Choice *D* is not the best answer because diversity and inclusion are complementary rather than competing ideals.

114. D: Accommodations must not place an undue burden on the employer. Employers are required to provide reasonable accommodations to employees as long as these do not place an undue burden on the employer. There is room for interpretation in the meaning of "undue burden," however; generally, it refers to anything that would be cost-prohibitive or would go against the nature of the organization's work. The other choices are incorrect because employers are not required to offer any accommodation that employees do not ask for themselves; however, employees are allowed to ask in plain language without necessarily using the legal or technical terminology. Also, accommodations cover more than just the ADA; employees can also request accommodations on religious grounds, for example.

115. C: OSHA. OSHA refers to the Occupational Health and Safety Administration, which administers workplace safety standards. The other choices are incorrect: NLRB stands for the National Labor Relations Board, which provides standards for unions and other employee relations. EEOC stands for Equal Employment Opportunity Commission, which oversees cases of workplace discrimination. EBSA stands for Employee Benefits Security Administration, which administers and enforces standards for employee benefits like retirement and health plans.

116. D: After investigating the validity of the report, HR should determine whether it is possible to work with less hazardous materials or develop improved safety measures in collaboration with factory managers. HR should conduct due diligence into any employee's claims of workplace hazards. If the concerns are valid, OSHA guidance indicates that employers should look for ways to eliminate hazards completely before enacting other measures like improved safety practices or protective equipment. Choice A is not the best answer because employees should not feel punished or silenced for raising safety concerns. Choice B is also not a good choice because OSHA standards prohibit employers from requiring employees to buy necessary safety equipment; this should be provided by the employer. Finally, Choice C is not the best choice because health and safety information should be presented in a way that can be easily understood by employees. Not all factory workers can be expected to understand a highly technical report about chemicals.

117. B: The new employees at Rachel's ice cream parlor will receive $12.50/hr. When a state's minimum wage is set at a higher rate than the federal minimum wage, such as Maryland's minimum wage, an employer must use the higher state minimum wage as its standard when paying employees.

118. B: The Portal-to-Portal Act deals with the preliminary and postliminary tasks of employees. The act requires employers to pay employees who are covered under the FLSA for time spent traveling to perform job-related tasks, if that travel is outside of the employees' regular work commute. Additionally, employees are to be paid for hours spent in job-related training that is outside of their normal workday.

119. B: Differential pay programs are used to reward employees for performing work that is viewed as less than desirable, and these programs vary greatly among employers. Differential pay is not required by the FLSA.

120. B: The compa-ratio is computed by finding the mid-point of the salary range, which is $16 in this example. Then, the pay level of the employee ($12.50) is divided by the midpoint of the salary range ($16) to receive a compa-ratio of .78 or 78 percent.

121. A: Since the compa-ratio in the previous question is 78 percent and, thus, below 100 percent, the employee is paid less than the midpoint of the salary range. This can be attributed to the fact that the employee is new to the job and/or the organization, is a low performer, or is working for a company that has adopted a lag behind the market pay strategy.

122. C: Thirty-six months is the period of eligibility under COBRA for a divorce/legal separation or death of an employed spouse, as well as for a dependent child who loses eligibility status under the plan rules.

Eighteen months is the period of eligibility under COBRA for an employee's reduction in hours or an employee's termination. Twenty-nine months is the period of eligibility under COBRA for the disablement of an employee.

123. D: A Material Safety Data Sheet (MSDS) identifies all hazardous substances in the workplace and describes procedures for handling these substances. These sheets state what should be done if someone has inappropriate contact with a hazardous substance.

124. D: HR should inform the CEO of the value of the program by presenting metrics related to the ROI of the current plan, such as the ability to reach more productive and qualified workers thanks to the transportation program. HR wants to demonstrate the importance of the program; however, the CEO is mostly interested in its cost. In this case, HR should translate the program's value into monetary terms by analyzing its ROI. Choice *A* is not a good choice because HR has a responsibility to provide input regarding changes that affect workers. Choice *B* is also not the best choice because, while it can be part of an overall fact-finding strategy, it does not present actionable results for decision making now. Also, Choice *C* is not a good strategy because it seeks worker feedback after the decision has already been made.

125. A: Payroll administration. There are many factors that determine which, if any, HR functions an organization chooses to outsource. Overall, though, it is easier to outsource transactional tasks that are largely administrative in nature, such as payroll administration. HR functions that are more likely to be kept in house are those that require working knowledge of the organization's culture or relationships between employees (things like Choice *B*, performance evaluations, or Choice *D*, high-potential development program management).

126. A: Value stream mapping is a tool from the Six Sigma approach that shows the value added by each step within a process. HRIS, Choice *B*, refers to information systems. SMART, Choice *C*, is an acronym to guide goal setting. Flow state diagrams, Choice *D*, are not a business tool.

127. C: These are all tasks that should occur during the planning stage of this initiative. Surveying employees who attended to inquire about how they enjoyed the food would be part of the evaluation stage, not the planning stage.

128. C: Direct costs refer to costs that are associated with a single project, its processes, and its outcomes.

129. C: A gap analysis views a process when there is a discrepancy between expected performance and actual performance, especially when milestones, goals, or benchmarks are not met.

130. D: Risk identification is a way for HR professionals to mitigate or eliminate all potential setbacks, especially when delivering a solution to a valued customer. By identifying risks, they are able to develop contingency plans that allow the delivery of solutions to continue uninterrupted.

131. B: Milestones are progressive periods by which certain business activities are expected to be completed.

132. C: This is an example of observational data collection that is recording both quantitative (time spent) and qualitative (type of task, obstacles) sources of data.

133. B: Nate should prioritize the leadership issue that will impact a large number of employees, especially since the employee with the disability claim is not physically in the office. While Nate cannot share that he is prioritizing a leadership matter over an employee matter, he can inform the employee with the short-term disability claim that he is still working on the issue and will have a resolution the following day.

134. A: Duty of care refers to the moral and legal obligations of an employer to care for employees' safety, security, and wellbeing when assigned to a foreign country. It is important to note that duty of care encompasses both legal *and* moral obligations, so organizations should not limit themselves to only providing the minimum legal protections for expatriate workers. Choice B is not correct because no such law exists and, as mentioned, not all duty-of-care concerns are legal mandates. Choice C is not correct because, while organizations should provide employees with this essential information, it only covers an emergency response, whereas duty of care should also address day-to-day living concerns. Finally, Choice D is not the best answer because duty of care refers to all kinds of support offered to expatriate workers, not simply monetary compensation. Also, duty-of-care policy should be proactive, not reactive (in this case, only coming into play after employees incur an expense).

135. D: Before an organization begins operating in a foreign country, it is important to understand that laws and customs are not the same in every country. Violating local labor laws could result in excessive legal fees, fines, or even the closure of the organization's foreign office; ignorance of local workplace etiquette could create misunderstandings that lower morale and make it difficult for collaboration to occur. Choice A is not the best answer because, while foreign language skills can be an asset, it is unlikely that employees will become fluent in a short time; if native-level fluency is essential for the job, it would be more efficient to identify employees who already possess this qualification. Cultural understanding is another important part of adapting to a foreign assignment, but it does not eclipse the need for legal compliance in the workplace, so Choice B is not the best answer. Finally, Choice C is not the best answer, either. Although the organization may want to ensure consistency between their domestic and foreign operations, this option does not address the changes and differences that employees will inevitably encounter in their new office.

136. B: Monitor and share information regarding potential safety concerns in the foreign post, and establish a system for employees to check in regularly. As part of duty of care, HR's role is to stay informed about situations in the foreign country that may affect employees and to communicate relevant information to employees. Also, because of emergencies such as terrorist attacks or natural disasters when it is necessary to account for employees quickly, employers should establish a system for employees to check in regularly. Choice A is not the best answer because it downplays employees' concerns rather than addressing them. Choice C is too reactive; employers and employees should have a plan in place ahead of time, rather than simply waiting until after an emergency occurs to seek help. Choice D is also not a good choice because it causes HR to discount otherwise qualified employees. Indeed, it is HR's responsibility to provide employees with the resources they need to succeed in various roles in the organization, including international assignments.

137. B: Based on data from internal and external sources that is collected and analyzed in a standardized way to drive decision-making. Rather than simply basing decisions on current practice or "the way it's always been done," evidence-based decision making requires factual data collection and analysis to support key decisions. Choice A is not the best answer because, while this could be one source of evidence, it is also possible to gather evidence from within the organization. Choice C is also not the best answer because it only focuses on qualitative data rather than incorporating quantitative analysis as well. Choice *D* is also incorrect because it doesn't reference data.

138. C: A report of market data on compensation and benefits plans. A total remuneration survey helps HR to design total rewards plans for their organization that are fair and competitive based on available market data about rewards for similar jobs, industries, companies, etc.

139. C: Automation. Automation helps HR reduce time-consuming busywork, paperwork shuffling, and redundant tasks by transitioning manual tasks to automatic digital functions.

140. A: Number and type of ongoing projects. All the other choices indicate relevant metrics from HR that can influence and inform the strategic planning process. However, Choice *A* refers to information that should be supplied from many different areas of the organization, not just from HR.

141. A: Eric should work to display these characteristics in his daily work, recognize when an employee goes above the standard level of service and award this behavior, and clearly communicate expectations to the team. Although he can indicate these performance levels in future reviews, Choice *B*, he first needs to ensure that his behavior models the characteristics he wants from his team and that the team is aware of these expectations. Hiring a new individual to motivate the team, Choice *C*, is not the best answer, as Eric can work to motivate his own team members without stretching the budget. Eric can communicate these expectations in an email, Choice *D*, but it would be better to verbally communicate the expectations first to allow for a dialogue and questions.

142. C: Geographic locations can impact business operations, requiring different resources from each other. Circumstances such as climate (extreme heat or cold weather) or naturally occurring disasters (hurricanes or tornados) can require a location to tailor a specific disaster plan and identify resources to provide. Some locations may require additional financial resources or extensive plans to address location-specific needs.

143. D: External salary data is the best source of data to review and analyze when determining if a company is paying their employees a salary that is competitive against the industry standard.

144. B: Jake failed to add in the costs of labor, such as the costs of the employees delivering the training as well as the employees taking the training and being backfilled with overtime by other employees. When preparing a cost-benefit analysis, it is vital that all costs are included to ensure the entire cost is accounted for.

145. D: Emotional Intelligence (EI) skills allow one to recognize the feelings and communication styles of others as well as one's self. EI includes being socially aware, managing relationships, managing one's self, and being self-aware. The components of EI all allow for building and maintaining better relationships.

146. C: Grievances are not informal and are handled in a prescribed and methodical manner. Once a grievance is filed, all communications and remedies should be made in writing, not verbally.

147. B: Benchmarks and HR metrics should always guide the types of research design and data collection that are being used. Using the benchmarks and HR metrics will ensure that the most appropriate and applicable data is collected for the assessment.

148. D: Benchmarking involves developing metrics for key items that can be used to determine the effectiveness of a program as well as how the initiatives compare to the competition and the industry.

149. C: Program evaluation and process evaluation are the two primary methods HR professionals should use to determine if programs, practices, and policies are effective and sustainable.

150. C: A process is considered validated and consistent when, after a tightly controlled process is completed multiple times, the same results and output are produced each time.

151. C: A total remuneration survey provides an analysis of total rewards information, including compensation and benefits plans, for an entire market. These data can be used to determine competitiveness and equity against competitors and other agencies to ensure that employees are paid appropriately.

152. A: Conducting a needs assessment with leadership and individual employees will help Sharon identify the organization's needs—either new or ongoing. These needs can then assist her in tailoring initiatives to support them. Although it is a great idea to solicit ideas from peers outside of the organization, it is critical to first understand the organization's overall objective and goals. This will ensure that any objectives identified, including new and innovative ideas, support the overall mission of the organization.

153. C: Monica should first schedule a meeting with the managers to discuss the concerns and complaints filed. She should ask specific questions to get as much information and details regarding the situation as possible.

154. B: The best course of action is for Monica to first train the managers regarding cultural norms and local labor laws and how the company's policies align with these. She should then conduct a group staff meeting to ensure that the entire workforce, including management, is on the same page regarding expectations and attendance policies.

155. B: Hector should consider implementing an Employee Assistance Program, which provides various resources to employees to handle situations, such as mental health, work-life balance, difficult situations, conflict resolutions, personal concerns, financial issues, and many other issues an individual may deal with. An Employee Assistance Program is considered a flexible benefit program and should be a part of an organization's offerings to employees.

156. B: When Sandra is considering a new HRIS with her IT department, she should consider the information that is currently being collected and stored as well as the information that will need to be collected and stored in the future, Choices *A* and *C*. Additionally, she should consider how the data stored within the system can be integrated with other systems for easier access, reporting, and analysis, Choice *D*. Sandra should not consider a one-size-fits-all system because no two agencies are alike and each has its own unique methods, processes, and pieces of information that need to be collected.

157. B: The primary benefit of a well-designed and well-managed HRIS is the ability to use data to develop evidence-based solutions. Choice *A* is incorrect; a benefit of HRIS is that it can run unique and specialized reports. An effective HRIS provides objective, not subjective, perspectives by removing the human factor from the information, making Choice *C* incorrect. Additionally, although the system will provide insight and data, it will not meet goals and objectives by itself but will provide the data in order for the HR team and departments to achieve success, making Choice *D* incorrect.

158. A: Stakeholder mapping is the official term that refers to a tool used to identify the value an initiative would have for a stakeholder as well as the investment and influence the stakeholder would have in promoting the initiative. Choices *B, C,* and *D* are incorrect; although they are other terms similar to mapping, they are not the actual defined term.

159. B: Blair should abide by his new organization's policy of requiring a 24-hour response time for customer service inquiries. Although he may not be able to answer all the issues at this time, he can let the customer know he is aware of the issue and working toward resolution. Choice *A* is incorrect because although it is commendable that Blair wants to exceed expectations, he may be putting himself in an unrealistic and unachievable position. Choices *C* and *D* are incorrect because both time frames, 36 hours and 48 hours, are outside of the policy and Blair would be in violation of the required 24-hour response time.

160. B: When a project goes over budget and exceeds the proposed time frame, the team leader should conduct a gap analysis and root cause analysis to determine the reasons the milestones and objectives were not met and how to address these in the future. Choice *A*, a SWOT analysis, is not correct because this analysis determines the strengths, weaknesses, opportunities, and threats of an organization. Choice *C*, a PEST analysis, is not correct because this analysis determines factors associated with political, economic, social, and technological trends that influence an organization. Choice *D*, an outcome and needs analysis, is incorrect because it is not an actual analysis.

161. D: It is important to have an understanding of and ability to work with statistics because this skill allows HR professionals to identify trends and use the data to support initiatives while also seeing errors or flaws in the data. Choices *A* and *C* are incorrect because this skill is vital to ensuring that data is incorporated into effective and productive HR initiatives. Choice *B* is incorrect because although this skill may make an HR professional more marketable in their career goals, it does not specifically equate to a faster career progression.

162. B: Evidence-based decision making allows the process to be collaborative, involving leadership, employees, stakeholders, and others who may be impacted by a decision. This process provides credibility and logical support for initiatives, provides transparency as to why certain decisions are made, and can be easily communicated and shared with others, making Choices *A, C,* and *D* incorrect.

163. C: Quality assurance is the process of establishing a relevant, unbiased system of data collection. Quality assurance ensures that the data collected is applicable and appropriate to the outcome. Without quality assurance, an HR professional may be looking at data that is not relevant to the subject matter and, as a result, making decisions based on inaccurate conclusions.

164. A: A secure online portal where employees can find updated information is by far the most efficient, streamlined, and lean way to communicate information. Employee handbooks, benefits forms, direct deposit forms, safety policies and forms, and other important information can be made available and updated as needed. Although it would be great to provide all employees a manual, Choice *B*, in-person training, Choice *C*, or a newsletter, Choice *D*, with this information, these options could be costly. Updates are sometimes needed frequently, and employees can be in a classroom for lengthy periods of time versus doing the job.

165. D: Umbrella goals, or interest overlaps, can be extremely helpful when presenting a large-scale project to leadership for their buy-in and support. Identifying goals that will extend beyond and reach into other departments will increase the likelihood that the project will be supported.

166. B: Identifying where employers are competing for labor is a benefit of analyzing labor markets during the workforce planning process. Additionally, other benefits include gaining an understanding of the unemployment rate, researching salaries paid for certain positions, and identifying employment trends. The remaining choices may be indirect benefits from this analysis but are not direct benefits.

167. C: Risk management is the process an organization engages in when identifying, targeting, and striving to minimize unacceptable dangers, threats, or risks. Choice A, SMART goals, are steps used in future planning and goal setting. Choice B, the Myers-Briggs Type Indicator, is an assessment that shows the differences in how people make decisions based on their personality. Choice D, corporate social responsibility, is when a corporation aims to contribute to charitable, activist, or philanthropic practices involving the community.

168. B: A matrixed service model is one that uses both a centralized and decentralized service model. Matrixed service models can be instrumental in ensuring that an organization employing individuals in various locations gives all its employees access to HR support while also ensuring one HR message, or vision, is implemented.

169. A: The best type of HR work to outsource is work that does not depend on knowledge specific to workplace relationships, organizational culture, or team dynamics. This knowledge, which typically only individuals within the organization have, should be used as much as possible to ensure the best results. The best rule of thumb is to outsource work that does not require in-depth knowledge of the organization or internal dynamics.

170. D: A mission statement and vision statement help create a culture and reference for all employees and decision makers within the company. They can refer to what we do, and what we are trying to do to create a shared purpose across different positions or locations. This also can influence customers, as they are looking at which companies share their values. It is not a required part of filing for a business license, making Choice C incorrect.

171. B: It adds to workforce diversity. Internally sourced hires such as internal transfers can lead to employees who are already familiar and comfortable with workplace culture, but external hires are more likely to add diversity in terms of demographics, backgrounds, personalities, and working styles. Choice A is not correct because far less time and money are needed to recruit internally sourced hires. Also, internal hires have a lower interview-to-hire ratio (that is, far more interviews are needed to lead to a hire from an external source compared to an internal source), so Choice C is also incorrect. Choice D is also not an advantage of external hires.

172. C: Prioritizing diversity when hiring new HR employees. Particularly in cases of workplace harassment based on sex, race, religion, or other factors, employees need to know that their concerns are taken seriously by HR and that their needs are reflected in the makeup of the HR department. Ensuring that HR follows the same D&I hiring standards as the rest of the organization can set the stage for building rapport with employees and helping them feel represented. Choice A is not the best choice because there are situations in which HR should seek external help, especially in cases of a conflict of interest or high legal liability. Choice B is not the best choice, either, because many employees are

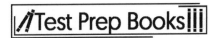

unaware of hotline numbers, and the reporting may go through outside channels before returning to HR. Moreover, there could be significant lag time between the incident, the reporting, and the HR response. As for Choice *D,* while it is important for HR to keep an organization's leaders on the same page with regards to workplace conduct, it is also important that HR maintain a level of objectivity in case complaints are lodged against senior leaders themselves.

173. B: Carol should initiate a cause-and-effect diagram to determine why her project did not meet the established objectives. She can also use a gap analysis or root cause analysis to pinpoint where the process deviated from the plan.

174. D: Offboarding an employee is an important part of Human Resources' duties to ensure that the employee leaves with a good perception of the company. The offboarding process can include an exit interview, turning in equipment, changing of login information for computer systems, and even the temporary transference of job duties. Choice *C* is describing two processes that would be associated with new employee, not one that is leaving.

175. C: Under the Patient Protection and Affordable Care Act (PPACA) in the FLSA, employers that have fifty or more employees are required to take extra precautions for their employees. This requirement is that employers provide a non-bathroom private location for expressing milk and provide breaks as much as needed. Compensation for breaks occurs the same as it would for other employees, but the breaks must be provided when needed. Choices *A, B,* and *D* fail to meet this criterion.

Index

Dear PHR Test Taker,

We would like to start by thanking you for purchasing this study guide for your PHR exam. We hope that we exceeded your expectations.

Our goal in creating this study guide was to cover all of the topics that you will see on the test. We also strove to make our practice questions as similar as possible to what you will encounter on test day. With that being said, if you found something that you feel was not up to your standards, please send us an email and let us know.

We would also like to let you know about another book in our catalog that may interest you.

SHRM CP

This can be found on Amazon: amazon.com/dp/1637758820

We have study guides in a wide variety of fields. If the one you are looking for isn't listed above, then try searching for it on Amazon or send us an email.

Thanks Again and Happy Testing!
Product Development Team
info@studyguideteam.com

FREE Test Taking Tips Video/DVD Offer

To better serve you, we created videos covering test taking tips that we want to give you for FREE. These videos cover world-class tips that will help you succeed on your test.

We just ask that you send us feedback about this product. Please let us know what you thought about it—whether good, bad, or indifferent.

To get your FREE videos, you can use the QR code below or email freevideos@studyguideteam.com with "Free Videos" in the subject line and the following information in the body of the email:

    a. The title of your product

    b. Your product rating on a scale of 1-5, with 5 being the highest

    c. Your feedback about the product

If you have any questions or concerns, please don't hesitate to contact us at info@studyguideteam.com.

Thank you!

Made in the USA
Columbia, SC
18 October 2022

69680086R00193